W9-BFP-285

SIMÓN BOLÍVAR'S QUEST FOR GLORY

Joseph G. Dawson III, General Editor

Simón Bolívar's Quest for Glory

Richard W. Slatta

& Jane Lucas De Grummond

TEXAS A&M UNIVERSITY PRESS   COLLEGE STATION

The paper used in this book meets the minimum requirements
of the American National Standard for Permanence
of Paper for Printed Library Materials, z39.48-1984.
Binding materials have been chosen for durability.

Unless otherwise noted, illustrations are from Vincente
Lecuña's *Selected Writings of Bolívar*.

Library of Congress Cataloging-in-Publication Data

Slatta, Richard W., 1947–
    Simón Bolívar's quest for glory / Richard W. Slatta and Jane Lucas
De Grummond.—1st ed.
        p. cm.—(Texas A&M University military history series ;
no. 86)
    Includes bibliographical references and index.
    ISBN 1-58544-239-9 (cloth : alk. paper)
    1. Bolívar, Simón, 1783–1830. 2. South America—History—
Wars of Indepencence, 1806–1830. 3. Heads of state—South
America—Biography. I. De Grummond, Jane Lucas, 1905–
II. Title. III. Series. Texas A&M University military history
series ; 86.
F2235.3.S66   2003
980'.02'092—dc21   2002015717

In memory of my brother
Lauren Eugene Slatta (1935–68),
teacher, coach, fun-loving father.
His tragic death left his three children,
Connie, Neal, and Kirk, with little chance
to know their wonderful father.
—Richard W. Slatta

To my students—Jane Lucas De Grummond

CONTENTS

Part V. Political Failure to Postmortem Glory

ILLUSTRATIONS

MAPS

PREFACE

Born on December 30, 1906, in central Pennsylvania, Jane Lucas De Grummond grew up in a family of the "laborin' class," as her father used to say. She worked her way through college and taught for twelve years at Tryone High School in Pennsylvania. She began graduate work in history at Louisiana State University in 1942 and completed her doctoral studies four years later. The first woman to receive a doctorate in history at LSU, De Grummond also became the first woman to teach history there. Over the next three decades, she taught thousands of students before her retirement in 1976.

Professor De Grummond specialized in Latin American history. Many of her graduate students came from Central and South America. The ideas and information that they shared with her and the theses they wrote added to our knowledge of the Western Hemisphere.

De Grummond took her first research trip to Venezuela in 1947, the year of Richard W. Slatta's birth. She intended to write a biography of the *llanero caudillo* José Antonio Páez. The Venezuelan scholar Vicente Lecuna, however, advised: "Don't write about him. Write about Bolívar." De Grummond continued gathering material on Bolívar during several subsequent research trips to South America.

Completing five books in all, De Grummond wrote about ambassadors, generals, revolutionaries, buccaneers, and rebels. Over a period of three decades, she wrote *Envoy to Caracas* (1951), *The Baratarians and the Battle of New Orleans* (1961), and *Renate Beluche: Smuggler, Privateer, and Patriot* (1983). She also edited *Caracas Diary* (1954) and coauthored, with Beulah de Vieré Smith Watts, *Solitude: Life on a Louisiana Plantation, 1788–1968* (1970), an account of the plantation home of her husband, Ernest De Grummond.

De Grummond had the ability, tenacity, and durability to interpret the dusty old manuscripts, proclamations, treaties, diaries, and letters that she uncovered in a variety of collections. Venezuela recognized her efforts by inscribing her name in its National Pantheon of Heroes in Caracas. She completed the essential narrative of Bolívar's life during the 1980s. At the time of her death in 1991, the manuscript remained unpublished. Half the royalties from the book go to scholarship and professorship funds established at LSU in De Grummond's name.

THE COLLABORATION

De Grummond's brother, the late George B. Lucas, professor emeritus of plant pathology at North Carolina State University, asked Richard W. Slatta to revise and update her manuscript. From reading *Cowboys of the Americas* (1990), Lucas knew of Slatta's research on *llaneros* in Venezuela and the important role played by these fierce horsemen in South American independence.

De Grummond provided the essential structure and narrative of events that serve as the book's backbone. She also did all the newspaper research, which included many newspapers from the Caribbean. Slatta added most primary source quotations, all interpretive and historiographical commentary, and extensive biographical and geographical information. He also reorganized and rewrote the entire text, so that the final manuscript is approximately 60 percent Slatta and 40 percent De Grummond.

—Richard W. Slatta

ACKNOWLEDGMENTS

Many people and institutions helped me along the way. I am especially in-debted to Alfredo Boulton, president of the Junta Directiva of Fundación John Boulton, Caracas, and Manuel Pérez Vila, secretary of the Fundación John Boulton; Enrique Ortega Ricaurte, director of the Archivo Nacional de Colombia; Enid L. Roberts, secretary to the Principal Education Office in the Ministry of Education, Kingston; Tom Cambridge, secretary of the Ministry of Public Utilities in Port of Spain; my nephew Guy Boyd Lucas, Patricia O'Brien Smylie, and Margaret Fisher Dalrymple, who read and criti-cized my manuscripts; Sociedad Bolivariana de Venezuela, and Louisiana State University.

—Jane Lucas De Grummond

Thanks to Jane Lucas De Grummond's brother, the late Professor G. B. Lucas, for asking me to complete this enjoyable project. Thanks also to North Carolina State University for providing release time for manuscript revi-sions. History graduate students Corinne Frist Glover, Louise (Wesie) Liggett, and Mark Mayer provided valuable research assistance. Thanks also to Pam Murray for insights on Manuela Sáenz, to Rebecca A. Earle for her exem-plary work on Colombia's independence, and to my friends and colleagues Steven Middleton and John David Smith for their comments and sugges-tions. Lara Alcantara, Dr. Susan Berglund, Ralph Blessing, Daniel Buck, Liza Rivera, and the Banco de Venezuela generously helped locate or provided illustrations.

—Richard W. Slatta

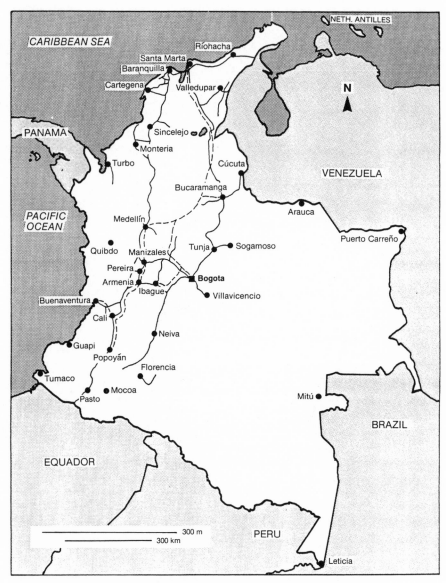

Map of Colombia. Courtesy *Maps on File*

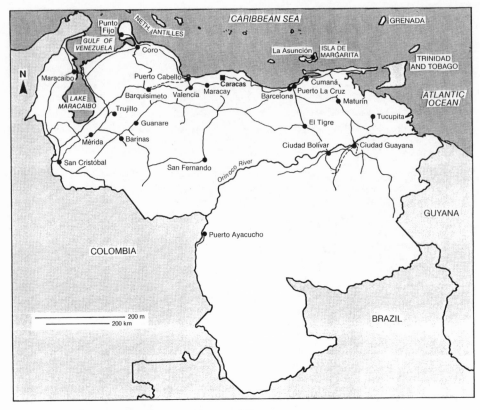

Map of Venezuela. Courtesy *Maps on File*

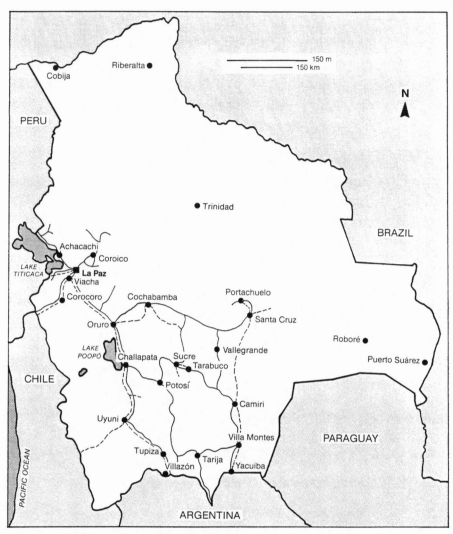

Map of Bolivia. Courtesy *Maps on File*

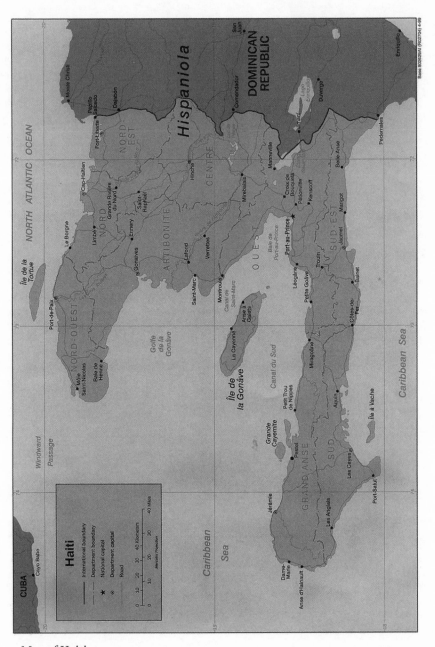

Map of Haiti

Map of Latin America. Courtesy *the Conference on Latin American History*

PART I

The Education

of a Liberator

CHAPTER 1

Introduction

Bolívar and Washington

George Washington (1732–99) and Simón Bolívar (1783–1830) stand out as two great leaders of anticolonial struggles in the New World. Washington's fight to free the United States from British colonial rule is well known. Unfortunately, hardly known in the United States is Simón Bolívar's struggle to free half of South America from Spanish domination. Both men came from the landed elites of their respective nations, and both lost their fathers at an early age. As young soldiers, both men suffered discrimination serving in the armies of their colonial masters, and neither benefited from much formal military training. Despite Washington's distinguished service commanding the Virginia Regiment against French and Indian forces in the 1750s, the British army refused him a regular commission. The two keenly enjoyed the exhilaration of combat. As Washington put it, "I heard bullets whistle and believe me there is something charming in the sound." Bolívar said, "My glory has been in the leading of these brave soldiers. Neither vanity nor lust for power inspired me in this enterprise." As a commander, Washington inspired soldiers to persevere and win against long odds, as did Bolívar. The armies of both men included among their ranks Irish and other European volunteers. Both lost major battles and suffered other reversals, yet they fought to victory. In their twenties both faced serious defeat, Washington at Fort Necessity and Bolívar at Puerto Cabello. Neither fathered any children.

Both held important military and political roles as commanders, writers of constitutions, and presidents. Washington commanded the victorious Continental army, presided over the Constitutional Convention in Philadelphia, and served as the new nation's first president. Grateful countrymen urged both men to accept royal crowns that they refused. Both faced powerful centrifugal political forces and divisive partisanship that threatened to destroy their new nations. As president, Washington faced down the so-called Whiskey Rebellion of 1794, asserting federal over local control. Angered by federal taxes, farmers in four counties of western Pennsylvania attacked federal officials. Washington mobilized nearly thirteen thousand troops and crushed the rebellion. Bolívar would be much less successful in holding together his beloved "Gran Colombia" (modern Colombia, Venezuela, and Ecuador). These men of the Enlightenment championed anticolonialism and fervently worked on behalf of republicanism, progress, reason, and freedom.

Despite the overall parallels in their careers, however, the two men also exhibited fundamental differences of personality and legacy. Washington's fellow Virginian Thomas Jefferson clearly described his character and personality: "His mind was great and powerful . . . as far as he saw, no judgment was ever sounder. It was slow in operation, being little aided by invention or imagination, but sure in conclusion. . . . Perhaps the strongest feature in his character was prudence, never acting until every circumstance, every consideration, was maturely weighed; refraining if he saw a doubt, but, when once decided, going through with his purpose, whatever obstacles opposed." Although enemies accused him of imperial ambitions, the modest, almost self-effacing Washington clearly did not pursue his own personal fame. Upon taking command of the Continental army in 1775, he said, "I beg it may be remembered by every gentleman in the room, that I this day declare with the utmost sincerity, I do not think myself equal to the command I am honored with." Later, as president, he exercised power carefully, with an obvious concern, even anxiety, that his every action created a precedent.

In sharp contrast, Bolívar exhibited a rash, impulsive, mercurial nature that often thrust him into peril but at times lifted him to great victories. In fact, we suggest that he may have suffered from bipolar disorder, given the extreme swings in temperament and actions that characterized his life. Unlike the methodical, rational Washington, he seemed almost mystical and fatalistic in his worldview, trusting in his destiny and given to visions, such as his delirium at Chimborazo, the great mountain peak in Ecuador (see chapter 12). Vain and proud, "the Liberator," as he came to be called, relent-lessly pursued his own dreams of personal glory with an almost messianic zeal. Bolívar himself recognized clearly how his path diverged from that of Washington. Addressing the Senate of Colombia on February 6, 1827, he sadly observed that "zealous republicans regard me with a secret fear, for history teaches them that men in my position have always been ambitious. In vain does Washington's example rise in my defense, for, in truth, an oc-casional exception cannot stand up against the long history of a world that has always been oppressed by the powerful."

While they share the halo of military glory, the political legacies of Wash-ington and Bolívar diverge sharply. Washington served his country ably, prudently, and wisely as its first president. Refusing to run for a third term as president, he incarnated the principle of a nation of strong institutions, not strong men. "Steer clear of permanent Alliances, with any portion of the foreign world"—his warning to avoid foreign entanglements—set the tone for several generations of American foreign-policy makers.

Physically, the two men stood poles apart. Washington, pale and strong, towered beyond six feet in height. Bolívar stood at five and a half feet, com-pact, slight, often depicted as swarthy, with the quickness and demeanor of a bullfighter. His faithful aide-de-camp and confidant Daniel Florencio O'Leary described the mature Bolívar:

> [His] forehead was very high but not unusually broad. It had many wrinkles. His eyebrows were thick, but well shaped; his eyes were dark and keen; his nose rather long and handsome. . . . His cheek bones were salient, his cheeks sunken ever since I first knew him. His mouth was ugly, his lips being thick, the upper one long. His teeth were regular, white and beautiful. He took particular care of them. His jaw bones and chin were long. His ears were large. His hair, which he wore long, was extremely black and curly. His whiskers and mustachios [were] light colored. . . . His chest was narrow and his whole figure thin, his legs particularly so. His skin was dark and rough, his hands and feet remarkably small and pretty. His countenance at times was pleasing, when in good humor. When irritated, it was ferocious. The change was incredible.

Intellectually, Bolívar seemed to recognize the danger of accumulating excessive political power. Writing on October 21, 1825, he acknowledged that "the Liberator of North America [Washington] was not in office that long—nor should I continue in office any longer, lest some should say that I am more ambitious than he." However, his seemingly visceral need to seek his own glory often sacrificed institutional growth for *personalismo,* a continuing problem in Latin American political culture. As he wrote on October 28, 1828, "As for me, I think that glory is a thousand times preferable to happiness." His mania for power provoked assassination attempts, mutinies, and vile attacks on his character and policies. Washington exhibited an impeccable honesty and morality still admired, whereas Bolívar ordered heinous war crimes and lived his life as a profligate womanizer, even by the lax standards of his time.

Bolívar recognized the long strands of history that connected him to America's first president. Writing to Lafayette on March 20, 1826, he expressed gratitude for a medallion of Washington that symbolized the connection between the two great freedom fighters.

> From the public papers, I have learned, with inexpressible pleasure, that Your Excellency has been so kind as to honor me with a treasure from Mount Vernon: The image of Washington, some of his mementos, and one of the monuments to his glory are to be bestowed upon me by Your Excellency in memory of that great man, the New World's foremost son. Words cannot express how greatly my heart cherishes so glorious an assembly of thoughts and objects. Washington's family honors me in a manner far exceeding my remotest hopes, as a reward from Washington, given by the hand of Lafayette, is the ultimate in human compensations. He was the outstanding *citizen-hero,* the champion of freedom, who on the one hand has served America and on the other the Old World of Europe. What mortal then is deserving of the high honors which Your Excellency and Mount Vernon propose to confer upon me? My embarrassment is equaled only by the infinite sense of gratitude with which I tender Your excellency the respect and veneration due the Nestor of human freedom.

Henry "Light Horse Harry" Lee, one of Washington's officers, aptly summed up the general's esteemed position: "First in war, first in peace, and first in the hearts of his countrymen." Washington died a national hero, and, thanks to the hagiography of Parson (Mason L.) Weems, gained legendary status. People honored him as early as 1776 by giving the name Washington to their sons (as did Lafayette), towns, and ships. Paintings and statues that once depicted George III now featured George Washington, who lived well into his sixties.

Bolívar died at age forty-seven in political disgrace and poverty while awaiting a ship to carry him to European exile. He had sacrificed his family fortune of perhaps 200,000 pesos for the cause of freedom. Toward the end of his life, in dinner conversation with a young French officer named Louis Peru de Lacroix, Bolívar aptly summarized the forces that led him on his path to glory: "circumstances, my talent, my character, my passions are what put me on my way; my ambition, my constancy, and the ardor of my imagination made me continue and have sustained me." Seeing Napoleon in his splendor made him "think of the slavery of my country and the glory that would befit the one who would liberate it." At his death he had little more than charity, borrowed clothing, and a largely unworked copper mine as assets.

After his death, however, Latin Americans gradually began to realize the significance of Bolívar's contributions and sacrifices. He is revered in the countries that he liberated: his native Venezuela, Colombia, Ecuador, Peru, and Bolivia. The latter country was named for him, and he drafted its constitution. Eventually Venezuela reburied him in a "Pantheon of Heroes" and named a city, province, and its national currency in his honor. He now has near godlike status as "the Liberator," honored throughout Latin America.

In reality, the tarnished idol of Bolívar, Napoleon Bonaparte, perhaps offers a better basis of comparison than does Washington. The youthful Venezuelan first admired the courage and accomplishments of the ambitious Frenchman. However, disillusionment set in when Bonaparte abandoned his republican principles and crowned himself emperor. Bolívar would also face the temptations of absolute power and the allure of pursuing unfettered personal glory. Both men shared a warrior's temperament that reveled in combat, conquest, and adoration that ultimately led them to political disgrace.

As then-president of Venezuela, Rafael Caldera wrote in 1993, Bolívar still remains the "highest expression" of Venezuelan national values, the inspiration for its constitution. Yet despite his great historical importance as an independence hero, Bolívar remains little known outside Latin America. This narrative biography brings his entire life and influence to the general reader, with special attention to his military career.

Bolívar proved equally adept at wielding the pen and the sword; however, he earned his glory on the fields of battle. Thus, much of our attention focuses on his military struggles to liberate South America from Spanish rule. His repeated comebacks from defeat, flashes of military genius, tremendous mood swings, persistence, near manic quest for glory, and fall from political grace give his life an epic, tragic quality. Like the Spanish conquistadors before him, he looms larger than life. His political legacy remains hotly debated. He committed acts of almost unspeakable brutality, but no one would deny his historical significance.

We have tried to make Bolívar's life and times accessible and intelligible to general readers and students. Our goal is to transport the reader back to the places and times where the Liberator met triumph and defeat. Readers will encounter his supporters and enemies and cheer and cry along with Bolívar. The Liberator did not win Spanish American independence all by himself, so we have taken pains to introduce lesser-known people who also valiantly waged the battle against colonialism. We have kept scholarly accouterments to a minimum. Instead of a plethora of footnotes, there is a brief bibliographical essay that features other important sources in English and Spanish. The concluding bibliography lists all major works consulted as well as suggestions for further reading. A chronology of the Liberator's life and times, along with a glossary of Spanish terms, follows the main body of the text.

Bolívar, his allies, and his enemies left an immense corpus of writings, so we have quoted often from those primary sources. The historiography on Bolívar is likewise immense but also badly flawed. Specialists have explored virtually every facet of his life. Much of the writing about Bolívar is hagiography. It treats him as a godlike figure rather than as a human being. One example is the 1921 biography penned by Guillermo Antonio Sherwell (1878–1926). While we find much to admire in his courage, leadership, and vision, we try to represent his actions and character fully and accurately, blemishes and all.

Bolívar's compelling, eventful life reminds us powerfully that individuals make a difference in history. Bolívar recognized that "to understand revolutions and their participants, we must observe them at close range and judge them at great distance." We hope that this narrative of his life and times brings Bolívar into close range, the better to judge the long-term impact of his words, inspiration, and actions.

CHAPTER 2

A Young Man Seeks His Destiny,

1783–1806

Simón Bolívar (1783–1830) led a long, bloody fight to free northern South America from Spanish colonial rule. He labored from the early declarations of independence in 1810 through final victory over Spanish forces in 1824. Bolívar and his Argentine counterpart Gen. José Francisco de San Martín (1778–1850) share the honor of liberating much of the continent. Bolívar led a life of passion and extremes. Defeat plunged him repeatedly into abject depression, but he struggled back each time to new military triumph. On the heels of his military victories, however, came political defeats. Ideological and personalistic battles turned friends into foes as the new Spanish American nations endeavored to create viable republics. Flawed by his tremendous ego and distrust of popular democracy, Bolívar nevertheless stands as a champion of free peoples. He remains a venerated hero in Latin America, just as George Washington is honored in the United States.

Bolívar had a complicated lineage. Biographer Salvador de Madariaga explained part of the complexity: "An examination of his family tree shows that in twelve generations, including only one hundred and thirty known ancestors, no less than sixty different names occur, any one of which, but for our habit of calling persons by the name of the paternal line, could have been his name." Included among those many ancestors is probably a mixture of Spanish, Indian, and African slave blood. The repetition of names over the generations reminds one of the familial labyrinth created by Colombian writer Gabriel García Márquez in his powerful novel, *One Hundred Years of Solitude.*

We begin our look at family history with Simón de Bolívar e Ibargüen (1532–1612), a twenty-seven-year-old lesser noble who sailed from the Basque area of Spain in 1559 to serve his king in the New World. On the island of Santo Domingo, his wife conceived Simón the Younger. When their kinsman Don Diego de Osorio won appointment as captain general of Venezuela, he chose the two Bolívars to serve with him. In 1589 they took up residence in the infant city of Santiago de León de Caracas, founded in mid-1567. The trio found themselves in the center of Venezuelan politics, Caracas having been the capital since 1578. The city lies in a narrow mountain valley, some fifteen miles from east to west, ringed by peaks rising 7,000–9,000 feet. A bumpy ride of some ten to twelve miles up over the northern slopes brought one to the important harbor at La Guaira, from which merchants shipped cacao, corn, wheat, cattle, and mules. The region also raised sugar, beans, fruit, and other foodstuffs for local consumption.

Venezuela's complicated topography naturally pointed Caracas outward toward the Caribbean Sea and Europe. Directly west lies the Maracaibo Basin, surrounding South America's largest lake, covering 5,217 square miles. To the southwest rises the mighty Merida Range of the Andean Highlands, reaching beyond 16,000 feet in elevation. The Central Highlands lie to the southeast, with its fertile valleys bounded by two mountain ranges running parallel along the Caribbean coast, and beyond that the Northeastern Highlands, consisting of low mountains and rolling hills. Inland to the south of Caracas, the *llanos,* later described in much greater detail, create a swampy barrier to travel between the Andean Highlands to the northwest and the Guiana Highlands to the south. Myriad rivers, including the Orinoco (1,284 miles long), crisscross these tropical plains, which hosted many key battles for independence. Beyond the llanos to the south, the Guiana Highlands rise up to cover nearly half of Venezuela. Here one finds Angel Falls, the world's highest waterfall at 3,212 feet, and lush, almost impenetrable tropical forests.

Young Simón followed in his father's footsteps and became auditor of the royal treasury. He served his king well and in 1593 received an *encomienda,* a grant giving him the labor of Quiriquire Indians in the valley of San Mateo. He married the daughter of another *encomendero.* Following customs of the time, their son Antonio married into another *encomendero* family. Antonio's son, Juan de Bolívar de Villegas (grandfather of the Liberator) married María Petronila de Ponte y Marín. With this union, his second, Juan became one of the richest men in Venezuela.

Juan and Petronila had a son, Juan Vicente de Bolívar y Ponte (the Liberator's father), born on October 15, 1726. Twenty years later the Caracas *cabildo* elected Juan Vicente *procurador general* (attorney) for the city. What did the young Creole aristocrat know of the law? His first important duty seems to have been to proclaim Ferdinand VI as the new king of Spain.

This distinguished family shone brightly as part of the white elite *matuano* society of Caracas. The Liberator would inherit his father's considerable wealth, which eventually grew to a sizable family fortune. He would also share with his father an extreme fondness for the company of women. In 1765 Juan Vicente lived as an unmarried student at the Academy of Santa Rosa in San Mateo. His name came up repeatedly in the bishop's confessional. During one pastoral visit, at least five women confessed to "sinning" with Juan Vicente. María Jacinta Fernández allowed that "I am a weak woman and I do not know if I can resist temptation. I am pressed by an infernal wolf who is bent on the Devil taking both of us. This wolf is Don Juan Vicente de Bolívar. He has sent my husband to the llanos to his herds to fetch cattle. For God's sake help me, for I am on the brink of falling." Indeed, she had "fallen" repeatedly during the past three years.

The bishop offered the amorous, young aristocrat some straightforward advice punctuated with a threat: "Avoid all commerce with women, especially married women. Do not call to your house church-school girls nor enter into theirs. If you wish to show charity to them do so through the priest. Spare me the regret I would feel in being bound to believe what I now refuse to believe, and to have to correct you by force of law."

Juan Vicente married María de la Concepción Palacios y Blanco on December 1, 1773. Eight days later, they celebrated her fifteenth birthday. Juan Vicente, forty-six years old, enjoyed considerable possessions at the time of his marriage. He held 258,000 in pesos, owned two cacao plantations, four houses in Caracas and nine in La Guaira, a riverfront villa, sugarcane lands in San Mateo, three cattle ranches in the llanos, an indigo plantation, a cooper mine, thousands of slaves, and other properties.

Nearly four years passed before the birth of their first child, María Antonia, on November 1, 1777. They had a second daughter less than two years later and a son, Juan Vicente, in 1781. The future liberator was born on July 24, 1783. His parents christened him Simón José Antonio de la Santísima Trinidad.

Concepción could not nurse the baby, so her best friend nursed Simón until she could find a wet nurse among the slaves, as was the custom among aristocrats. When Concepción could travel, the family went to San Mateo.

There they found Hipólita, a strong, intelligent, thirty-year-old black woman. She loved Simón and cared for him like a second mother. Simón recalled his wet nurse in a letter written much later (in 1825) to his sister María Antonia. "I am sending you a letter from my mother, Hipólita, so that you will give her everything she wishes, and so that you will treat her as though she were your own mother. She nourished my life. I know no other parent but her."

Tragedy struck the Bolívar family in January 1786, when Simón was two years old. His father became violently ill, and on the thirteenth of the month, Juan Vicente gave his wife and father-in-law, Feliciano Palacios y Sojo, power to draft his will. He also named them executors of the will. One of his notes said that because of his great love for his wife, he wanted her to have more than the property she had acquired during their marriage. He gave her the best diamond in his collection as well as other valuable items. He divided the rest of his possessions among his five children, including the one Concepción was carrying. Juan Vicente died on January 19. His third daughter, María del Carmen, born on June 16, died in infancy.

Twenty-eight-year-old Concepción had little time to grieve the loss of her husband and infant daughter. She had four children, aged two through eight, to raise and a huge estate to administer. Her status-conscious father advised her to negotiate for the title of Marqués de San Luis for her eldest son Juan Vicente. His grandfather (Juan de Bolívar y Villegas) had purchased the title in 1722 for 22,000 ducats, but he died before he could assume it. His son made no effort to claim it. Concepción petitioned the king for a royal order to confer the title on her son. Receiving no answer, she dispatched her brother Esteban (1767–1830) to Madrid to inquire. He sailed in April 1792. Three months later, on July 6, Concepción died of hemorrhage induced by tuberculosis. As young Simón approached age nine, he faced life as an orphan.

The so-called Bourbon reforms, instituted by the Spanish Crown in its American colonies, created myriad problems. Creoles found themselves discriminated against for public office as nepotism and favoritism brought a stream of Spanish bureaucrats from across the Atlantic. Even so-called free trade, not instituted in Venezuela until a decade after the original act of 1778, was not what it might appear to be. The powerful Caracas Company (Compañia Guipuzcoana, 1728–85) long enjoyed a monopoly over cacao exports and successfully lobbied against expanded trade and lowered tariffs. Thanks to its power, Latin Americans paid higher prices for goods, and small farmers as well as larger plantation owners saw their profits suffer. Instead of open exchanges of goods and services, as envisioned by Adam Smith's economic liberalism, Bourbon "free trade" meant an expansion of colonial commerce in order to tax and control it. Spain, not its colonies and certainly not Creoles, would be the beneficiaries. In 1797 Venezuela's Creole merchants would complain directly to the king that commerce existed "solely for the benefit of the metropolis." Like liberalism, free trade, as defined in Spain, meant something far different from what it meant elsewhere in Europe—and in the New World.

Concepción's father served as guardian to the children and administrator of their properties. Don Feliciano moved the children and servants, including Hipólita, to his home. His three sons and three daughters still lived at home. The aunts, especially Josefa, became surrogate mothers to the children. Hipólita, however, remained Simón's "best" mother. Simón's grandfather became ill soon after the children arrived. In mid-August he empowered his eldest son, Carlos, to write his will. Don Feliciano then arranged the marriages of his two granddaughters. María Antonia, almost fifteen, married Pablo Clemente y Francia in October. Juana María, not yet fourteen, married her mother's cousin Dionisio Palacios Blanco in December.

With husbands to administer their estates, the girls did not require guardians. Don Feliciano asked his grandsons which of their relatives they wanted to serve as guardians. Juan Vicente chose his Uncle Juan Félix Palacios Blanco. Simón chose his beloved godfather, Uncle Esteban, who was still in Spain in quest of the royal title. Don Feliciano, however, named his son Carlos as Simón's guardian. His will stipulated that the orphaned boys should remain with their aunts and uncles. Simón's grandfather died on December 5, 1793.

The Bolívar children received educations befitting their upper-class status. They had early learned to read and write. Bolívar remained an avid reader all his life, even reading French philosophy in the heat of military campaigns. Bolívar studied and absorbed the lessons of the Enlightenment. As historian John Lynch noted, "he read deeply in the works of Hobbes and Spinoza, Holbach and Hume; and the thought of Montesquieu and Rousseau left its imprint firmly on him and gave him a life-long devotion to reason, freedom and progress." Voracious reading and wide travels stimulated his powerful native intelligence and shaped him into the quintessential Enlightenment man who deftly combined contemplation and action.

Much later, in 1822, Bolívar nicely summed up his educational philosophy as he made suggestions to his nephew Fernando (1810–98).

The education of children should always be in keeping with their age,
   inclinations, ability, and temperament.
As my nephew is now past twelve years of age, he should be introduced
   to modern languages, without neglecting his own. The dead languages should be studied only after one has learned the living.
Geography and cosmography are among the first subjects a young man
   should learn.
History, like languages, should begin with a study of the present day,
   going back by degrees to the remote ages of the fable.
It is never too early to make the acquaintance of the exact sciences, for
   they teach us how to analyze all things; passing from the known to
   the unknown, they thus train us to think and to reason logically.
Further, the pupil's aptitude for ciphering must be kept in mind, for not
   all are equally apt in mathematics.
In general, all may learn geometry and understand it; but the same is
   not true of algebra or of differential and integral calculus.

Bolívar also included in his diverse curriculum "the art and science of
civil engineering, but not against his will," music, dancing, "draftsmanship,
astronomy, chemistry, and botany," "instruction in good breeding and social behavior," Roman law, and "the love of cultivated society." "Morality in
the form of religious maxims and of practices conducive to the preservation of health and life is a subject no master can neglect." Bolívar also put
his finger on a key weakness in Latin American education and cultural values, the disparagement of manual labor. "If he is inclined to learn some
skill or trade, I should welcome it, for doctors and lawyers abound among
us, but we lack good mechanics and husbandmen upon whom the country
must depend to advance its prosperity and well-being."

Young Simón soon showed the independent, rebellious nature of his own
temperament. In 1795, at the tender age of twelve, he ran away from his
uncle's house. He fled to his sister and absolutely refused to accept his uncle's
authority over him. The *audiencia* decreed that he should return to Carlos,
but he still refused. In a compromise, the family sent the child to live with
his tutor, Simón Carreño Rodríguez (1771–1854), for two months.

Of his many teachers, Rodríguez most influenced Bolívar. A foundling,
Rodríguez gained a strong education, largely through dint of his own
efforts. He dropped the family name Carreño after a dispute with his
brother. Beginning in 1794, he worked to expand popular education in
Caracas. However, Rodríguez and others plotted to make Venezuela a re-

Young Bolívar with his tutor, Simón Rodríguez.

public, but betrayal frustrated them. Spanish officials hanged some of the prisoners, severed their heads, arms, and legs from their bodies, and displayed the parts as an object lesson to one and all. Released for lack of evidence, he changed his name to Samuel Robinson, thus honoring the hero of Daniel Defoe's novel, and fled Caracas about 1796. During his absence from his native land, he traveled to the United States, working as a printer in Baltimore, and then to France. Teacher and pupil would meet up again in Paris in 1803.

Rodríguez imparted to Bolívar his understanding of and deep devotion to the ideas of Jean Jacques Rousseau. Bolívar would gratefully write to his mentor, "I have traveled the road you have shown me. You have molded my heart for liberty and justice, for the great and the beautiful." Bolívar recalled the value and scope of his education in a letter written in 1825. He was responding, as would often be the case, to criticisms directed at him.

> It is not true that my education was badly neglected, since my mother and father made every possible effort in order that I might have proper instruction. They secured for me the foremost teachers in my country. Robinson [Rodríguez], whom you know, taught me reading and writing. Our celebrated [Andrés] Bello taught me the art of composition and geography: Father Andujar, of whom the Baron von Humboldt had a high opinion, created an academy of mathematics especially for me. I was sent to Europe to continue my study of mathematics at the Academy of San Fernando. I studied foreign languages with selected teachers in Madrid— all under the direction of the learned Marquis de Uztaris, in whose home I lived. While I was still very young, perhaps too young for such arts, I took lessons in fencing, dancing, and horsemanship.

Andrés Bello López (1781–1865), another of Venezuela's leading intellectuals, would also influence Bolívar. Born in Caracas, Bello's genius and writings extended to law, philosophy, poetry, grammar, science, and statesmanship. His nationalism resonated well with that of his fiery countryman, just two years his junior. In his many writings Bello reflected a new spirit of independence from European influences. He edited Caracas's first newspaper beginning in October 1808 and two years later published the first book in Venezuela. In 1810 he accompanied Bolívar as secretary for a failed diplomatic mission to London. The collapse of the First Venezuelan Republic left him penniless and stranded, so there he turned to teaching and writing. Later in life, he relocated to Santiago, where in 1843 he founded and became the first rector of the University of Chile. A true man of letters, he authored poems, textbooks, and a code of civil law for Chile.

The winds of change that swept the Western world in the late eighteenth century also shaped Bolívar's thought. He was but six years of age when reports of the French Revolution reached Venezuela in mid-1789. The leaven of "liberty, property, security, and resistance against oppression" began to rise in Spain and in her American colonies. Young Simón had heard his elders complain of Spanish policies that goaded Creoles into rebellion. His family enjoyed high status as one of the most aristocratic in America and among the richest in land. As far as Spain was concerned, however, the members of that family merited little status and few rights. Galling restrictions forced Creoles to grow only crops not cultivated in Spain. Creoles could trade only with Spain, and, to a lesser degree, with Mexico. Venezuelans could manufacture only items that did not compete with Spanish monopolies.

Simón tended to his business and social affairs, as befitted his status. In July 1798 the king granted him the title of *subteniente* of the Sixth Company of the Aragua White Militia. His title and uniform gave evidence that he was a nobleman, not a professional soldier. He received no appreciable training and remained largely ignorant of the science of warfare, a circumstance often criticized by European professional officers who fought for him. Fortuitous circumstances in Spain, however, soon brought him better military training and knowledge.

Soon after Bolívar received the military title, his uncle Esteban invited him and Pedro Palacios Blanco to Spain. The ascendancy of Manuel Mallo and Francisco de Saavedra, two of Esteban's friends, made it a favorable moment. Born in Popayán, Mallo had grown up in Caracas with the Palacios Blanco brothers, Esteban, Carlos, and Pedro. He had displaced Manuel de Godoy (1767–1851) as Queen María Luisa's court favorite. His official position of weekly steward gave him access to the royal family. Saavedra, a Spaniard, and the Palacios Blancos had become friends during his term as finance minister in Caracas (1783–88).

To many critics, weak King Carlos IV seemed almost a slave to his lascivious consort María Luisa. The ambitious and incompetent Godoy had dominated them both. His sudden rise to political power rested more on his sexual relationship with the queen than with his abilities in statecraft. Two of her children resembled Godoy. His influence inspired such indignation in Spain that an opposition party formed against him. At the same time, French authorities, suspicious of Godoy's relations with England, sent an agent to the Spanish king. His political enemies and the agent persuaded Carlos to dump Godoy in favor of Saavedra. In March 1798 he supplanted Godoy as minister of state, a post held by the latter since 1792. With his friends Mallo and Saavedra wielding influence in court, Esteban expected good things for his family and for Bolívar. Godoy remained a power behind the throne, however, because of his continued influence over the queen.

Bolívar sailed on the warship *San Ildefonso* from the Venezuelan port of La Guaira on January 19, 1799. In Veracruz, Mexico, the ship loaded specie worth several million pesos and prepared to depart. An English squadron, however, blockaded the ship's next port, Havana. The blockade delayed the ship's departure for another seven weeks, which gave Bolívar ample time to visit Mexico City. The *San Ildefonso* finally sailed to Havana, stopped briefly, and then headed for the north coast of Spain. It dropped anchor at Santoño, Spain, on May 31, 1800.

Bolívar traveled overland another ten days to Madrid. He lived with Esteban at Mallo's house until Esteban's brother Pedro arrived. The Palacios Blanco brothers and Bolívar then moved to another house. Esteban hired tutors to teach Bolívar mathematics, Spanish, French, dancing, and fencing. Appearance at court frequently interrupted these studies because Mallo was the patron of the young Venezuelans.

One night, the queen appeared at Mallo's house disguised as a monk. Bolívar later escorted her back to the palace. Several times he saw the queen pay Mallo's bills or give him money. Bolívar heard a story told by the French ambassador about the night the king, queen, and Godoy stood on the balcony at the royal residence at Aranjuez. The king asked Godoy: "Manuel, who is this Mallo? Every day I see him with a new coach and new horses. Where does he get his money?" "Your Majesty," answered Godoy, "Mallo does not have an ochavo; but it is said that he is supported by an ugly old woman who robs her husband to enrich her lover." The king, bursting with laughter, said to his queen, "What do you say to this, Luisa?" "Carlos," responded the queen, "You know that Manuel is always joking." The degeneracy of court life—the promiscuity of the queen, the weakness of the king, and the naked ambition of Godoy—surely did nothing to elevate the Spanish monarchy in impressionable, young Simón's eyes.

Despite their ties to Mallo and Saavedra, not all went well for the young Venezuelans. When Esteban was arrested for some obscure reason, Bolívar sought asylum at the home of the marquis of Ustaris. The Caracas native, a brilliant scholar, enjoyed great prestige in Spain. He had served the king very well as governor of Estremadura, intendant of Badajoz, and in other important offices. In his presence Bolívar became acutely aware that the literary side of his education had been neglected. Under the direction of the marquis, he read and studied widely. As he noted later, Bolívar read "the classicists of antiquity, whether they be philosophers, historians, orators, or poets, as well as the modern classics of Spain, France, and Italy, and not a few of the English."

At the home of the marquis, he met María Teresa Rodríguez del Toro y Alayza and her widowed father, Bernardo Rodríguez del Toro y Ascanio, a

Caracas native. They enjoyed two homes, one in Madrid and one in Bilbao to the north. Simón and María Teresa (twenty months his senior) quickly fell in love and wished to marry. Don Bernardo and the marquis agreed to permit the marriage after Bolívar was a little older. Bolívar wrote on September 30, 1800, to his Uncle Pedro in Cádiz: "I have told the Marquis de Ustaris, the only guardian I have here, that I am going to marry María Teresa; and I am telling you because you are the closest relative I have here, and Don Manuel Mallo because his is our friend and patron."

Court intrigues continued to shape Bolívar's life. Apparently tiring of Mallo, Queen María Luisa brought back Godoy in 1801. Early that same year the queen or Godoy probably orchestrated an unfortunate incident that forced Bolívar to flee Madrid. A squadron of police stopped him as he rode through the Toledo Gate. A police officer pointed to diamonds in his cuff links and handed him an order from the finance minister. The law declared that no one could make an excessive display of diamonds without a special permit. When the police tried to search him, Bolívar drew his sword. The encounter earned him banishment from court.

The young Venezuelan requested a passport to leave Madrid. On March 20, 1801, he received permission from the king and Mallo to leave. He joined María Teresa and her father at their house in Bilbao. Five months later, when father and daughter returned to Madrid, Bolívar could not join them because of his banishment. He traveled instead to Paris, where enthusiasm for First Consul Napoleon and the Republic engulfed him. Napoleon had ended the first coalition against him and made France the dominant power in Europe. In March 1802 England recognized that dominance at Amiens with a peace treaty. Viewing the ratification, Bolívar sensed the wide admiration for Napoleon. He concluded that only republican government could ensure the happiness of its citizens. But love, not politics, absorbed his energies.

After the peace celebration, he returned to Bilbao and impatiently awaited permission to return to Madrid. He and María Teresa married in Madrid on May 26, 1802. "My head," he confided, "was only filled with the mists of the most ardent love, and not with political ideas." They left Spain immediately and sailed for La Guaira. They made their home in Caracas at the house known as Vínculo de la Concepción, on the corner of Las Gradillas. Tragedy quickly struck the honeymooning couple. María Teresa died of a fever on January 22, 1803. Bolívar had her buried at the cathedral in Caracas the following day. He never remarried.

The distraught young widower resolved to leave his homeland forever. He would indeed return, however, and play a mighty role in the nation's history. Toward the end of his life, Bolívar shared with Louis Peru de Lacroix, a young French officer, the impact of María's death on his life. "I loved my wife very much, and her death made me swear not to marry again; I have kept my word. Notice how things go; if I had not been widowed, perhaps my life would have been different: I would neither be General Bolívar nor the Liberator, although I agree that my genius was not intended to be mayor of San Mateo." "The death of my wife," he continued, "put me on the road to politics very early; it made me follow the chariot of Mars instead of following the plow of Ceres."

He sold some of his properties and gave power of attorney to his brother. He then chartered a ship, loaded it with produce from his plantations, and sailed for Spain. He debarked at Cádiz near the end of the year. Nearly 90 percent of American commerce passed through that prosperous Spanish port, as did all American transfers of funds. The trade enriched the city's merchants and whetted their interest in policies toward the American colonies. For the coming decades, the city's capitalists would successfully promote their own economic interests at the expense of American merchants and producers. After selling his cargo, he returned to Madrid to visit his father-in-law. In a tender reunion they shed tears of sorrow together. A friend, Tomás Cipriano de Mosquera (1798–1878), later recorded that "Bolívar never forgot this scene; and I record it now because he was always influenced by sentiments which came from his heart." Mosquera would go on to a checkered military and political career, eventually serving several terms as Colombia's president.

A new municipal ordinance published a few days later forced Bolívar to leave Madrid. Because of a food shortage, the law ordered all foreigners who were not permanent residents to leave. The volatile young Bolívar had planned to leave anyhow, but the forced departure rankled. For two centuries his family had returned part of its wealth as tribute to Spain. Spaniards ruled Bolívar's native land, and Spain now considered him a foreigner and expelled him from the capital.

Fernando Rodríguez del Toro, María Teresa's cousin, was another unhappy son of Caracas. He and Bolívar had been friends since childhood. May 1804 found them back in Paris, where Napoleon still enjoyed the adulation of the crowd. He had given laws a new, healthy direction, reformed the tax system, and invited émigrés to return home. His concordat with the pope had restored a working relationship between the French government and the Vatican. The concordat recognized the Roman Catholic faith as the religion of most of the French people but not as the state religion.

First Consul Napoleon ruled France, the Netherlands, the Rhineland, and much of Italy. Crowned heads ruled the rest of Europe. The once republican Napoleon also wanted a crown, but a mere kingly crown was not enough. On May 18 his servile senate proclaimed that "the government of the Republic is to be entrusted to an emperor. Napoleon Bonaparte is Emperor of the French." The sudden death of the French Republic shocked Bolívar. No longer the symbol of liberty, Napoleon had become a tyrant. Despite his disenchantment with the First Consul, Bolívar would exhibit similar characteristics later in his own career. The two seemingly shared many attributes. An extreme egotism, an inability to abide rivals, a profound desire for personal glory, and a thirst for power also marked Bolívar's trajectory.

Despite his disenchantment, Bolívar did not leave Paris. He and Fernando found living quarters on the Rue Vivienne, and, in 1804, Bolívar's teacher Simón Rodríguez joined them. For a while, Bolívar's life revolved around the dark-haired, charming Fanny du Villars (her maiden name was Fanny Louise Trobiand Aristeguieta). Juan Félix Jeres Aristeguieta y Bolívar, the priest who had christened Bolívar, was also his uncle. Because of the name common to both families, Fanny and young Bolívar decided that they were cousins. He took an apartment in her house. They became fast friends and probably lovers.

Fanny, aged twenty-eight, had married a man twice her age—Col. Dervieu de Villars, an army contractor and diligent military administrator. Great sums of money passed through his hands, and his work took him away from home frequently. Fanny, however, did not grow lonely during his long absences. An excellent hostess, she invited varied and interesting people to her receptions. The young Venezuelan had a fine life, enjoying grand company and leaving more than a little money at the gambling tables of Paris.

Bolívar met Napoleon's stepson, Eugéne de Beauharnais. Only two years younger than Bolívar, Eugéne was already a general. Fanny teased them both. One day she asked Eugéne what animals Simón resembled. He answered *moineau* (sparrow). The always sensitive Bolívar mistook the French word for the Spanish term *mono* (monkey). The "little sparrow" flared, called Eugéne a raven, and challenged him. Fanny the peacemaker prevented the foolish duel by persuading Simón that Eugéne had not called him a monkey.

In September 1804, Bolívar met two famous naturalists, probably at Fanny's salon. Friedrich Wilhelm Heinrich Alexander von Humboldt (1769–1859) and Aimé Jacques Goujaud Bonpland (1773–1858) had recently returned from a five-year survey of Cuba, Venezuela, New Granada (Colombia and

Ecuador), Peru, and Mexico. Bolívar's tutor, Andrés Bello, accompanied the two naturalists for part of their journey. The German and French natural scientists had spent more than a year in Venezuela studying the Caracas valley. They then turned south from Calabozo to the Apure River and east on the Orinoco to return to the sea. They sailed to Cartagena, Colombia and ascended the Magdalena River, a route that would play a major role in Bolívar's life, navigable for most of its 956 miles. The mighty river flows northward between Colombia's Central and Eastern Cordilleras (mountain ranges) and empties into the Caribbean Sea near Barranquilla. The Cauca River is one of its major tributaries. From the founding of Bogotá in 1539, the great river offered the only practical means of transporting goods between that venerable city and the Caribbean. The explorers then worked their way south through the Andes Mountains of New Granada (Colombia) to Quito. They investigated neighboring volcanic peaks, including Chimborazo, an Ecuadorian mountain with a summit of 20,561 feet that later would figure strongly in Bolívar's life. Indeed, Humboldt ascended the mighty peak to an elevation of 19,280 feet, suffering the debilitating *soroche*. The energetic scientists moved south across head streams of the mighty Amazon and crossed the Andes five times before reaching Lima, Peru.

Humboldt's glowing descriptions of the wealth, richness, and vastness of South America likely inspired pride and a nascent nationalism in the young Venezuelan. Their meeting also had concrete future ramifications. Bolívar later studied all of Humboldt's maps and vast reconnaissance as he planned his military maneuvers for the independence wars. For example, Bolívar would make use of Venezuela's many excellent ports. "The coasts of Venezuela," wrote Humboldt, "from their extent, their stretching toward the east, the number of their ports, and the safety of their anchorage at different seasons, possess all the advantages of the interior Caribbean Sea. The communications with the greater islands, and even with those that are to windward, can no where be more frequent than from the ports of Cumana, Barcelona, La Guayra, Porto Cabello, Coro, and Maracaybo; and no where has it been found more difficult to restrain an illicit commerce with strangers." Bolívar shrewdly put Humboldt's natural science at the service of military science.

Although he greatly admired South America, the liberal Humboldt had little use for despotic Spain. The naturalist told Bolívar that the great potential of Spain's colonies could be developed only if they were freed from Spain. Bolívar readily agreed. "In truth, what a brilliant fate—that of the

New World, if only its people were freed of their yoke." Bolívar asked the scientists whether the time had come for revolution. Humboldt answered in the negative. "I believe that your country is ready for its independence. But I can not see the man who is to achieve it." Bonpland disagreed, prophesying that revolution would produce sons worthy of it. Time would prove Bonpland the more correct of the two.

Growing excitement in Paris briefly deflected Bolívar's groping journey toward his destiny. Preparations for the coronation of Napoleon and Josephine had the French capital abuzz. Notre Dame Cathedral had been repaired, the interior carpeted, walls adorned with tapestries and pillars with fragrant flowers. Legions of workers tore down old buildings on the south side of Notre Dame and swept and sanded streets and quays along the Seine. The 140 Spanish horses for the grand procession cost 1,300 francs each; the imperial coach, 114,000 francs. Josephine's robe cost only 75,000 francs, but her 2,000 diamonds cost nearly one million francs.

On December 2, 1804, a vast throng of dignitaries filled Notre Dame to overflowing. Napoleon took a crown from the hands of Pope Pius VII and crowned himself emperor of France. Then all eyes focused on the beautiful Josephine. Like Bolívar, she was a Creole. Robed in heavy magnificence, she played her role with superb style. (Josephine so impressed Jacques Louis David that he made her the central figure in his famous painting of the coronation.) Napoleon held up a crown, radiant with diamonds, placed it on the head of the kneeling Josephine, and proclaimed her empress of France.

Bolívar had mixed feelings about the momentous events in France. Napoleon's betrayal of the republic galled Bolívar: "Since that day I regard him as a dishonest tyrant." On the other hand, the emperor's glory and the adulation accorded him clearly thrilled the ambitious, young Bolívar. "I saw the coronation of Napoleon in the last month of 1804," Bolívar told an acquaintance:

> That august and magnificent act filled me with enthusiasm but less for its pomp than for the joy and love which an immense populace showed for its hero. That exaltation of all hearts for the one who received the ovation seemed to me the supreme goal of human ambition, the ultimate desire and aspiration of man. The crown which Napoleon placed upon his head was a thing of no importance, a miserable relic of the past. That which seemed great to me was the universal acclaim and the interest which the person of Napoleon inspired. I confess this made me think of my country's enslavement, and of the glory that would cover the man who liberated her.

The multitude of distinguished foreigners that witnessed the coronation began to depart Paris in March 1805. Many headed to Milan when Napoleon crowned himself king of Italy. Bolívar, Fernando del Toro, and Rodríguez left Paris by stagecoach in April 1805. Their leisurely journey took them via Lyon, Chambéry, and Turin. On May 26, they saw Napoleon crown himself king of Italy with the iron cross of the Lombards. Soon after the ceremony, Bolívar and his two friends departed. They continued down the Po Valley to the Adriatic Sea, turned north to Venice, and then headed southwest to Padua, Ferrara, Bologna, and Florence. The grandeur that was Rome began to fill and overwhelm the three young Venezuelans as they approached the Eternal City.

On a sweltering afternoon in mid-August, the trio climbed historic Monte Sacro. In 494 B.C. exasperated plebeians had fled up the hill from Rome. The demands, injustices, arrogance, and violence of their patrician rulers had infuriated them. The plebeians built a fortified camp and threatened to secede from Rome. The patricians panicked. What would happen if foreigners invaded the divided city? The rulers agreed to negotiations on Monte Sacro. They granted the plebeians tribunes, special magistrates above the law who could veto harmful legislation. The protesters on the mount chose the first two tribunes.

Throughout Bolívar's life, mountaintops seemed to inspire him and make him philosophical. Atop Monte Sacro his thoughts turned to his native land. Suddenly he cried out: "I will break the chains that bind Venezuela to Spain!" Twenty years later, having accomplished his dream, he asked Rodríguez to recall that inspired day above Rome. "Surely you have not forgotten this day of immortal glory. It was the day when my prophetic soul anticipated the hope, which we dared not yet voice." The young Venezuelan's impetuous, emotional, even mystical nature would show itself many times over the course of his life.

Even some Spanish officials recognized growing cracks in the nation's colonial system. In 1781 José de Abalos, the Spanish intendant in Venezuela, warned of a "vehement desire for independence" in the colonies, fanned by the model of the United States. In 1803 Pedro de Mendinueta, the viceroy of New Granada, warned of possible unrest owing to peasant grievances. "I understand that the same wages are paid now as were paid fifty or more years ago, despite the fact that prices of all essential goods have risen. . . . I am convinced that the day will come when the laborers will dictate to the landowners and these will be obliged to admit to a share in the profits those who have helped to produce them." The viceroy also cautioned that mounting Bourbon taxes "are almost never received without irritation, resistance, and even unrest among the people." Longstanding social, political, and economic grievances among all social classes provided a fertile, receptive environment for calls to separate from Spain.

A few days after this mountaintop experience, Bolívar accompanied the Spanish ambassador to the Vatican. The proud, headstrong youth refused to show traditional respect by kneeling and kissing the cross on the pope's sandal. Observing the ambassador's acute embarrassment, Pope Pius VII said, "Let the young Indian do as he pleases." The pope then extended his hand, and Bolívar kissed his ring in a most respectful manner. The ambassador reprimanded the young Venezuelan as they departed. "The Pope must have little respect for the symbol of Christianity," Bolívar replied righteously, "if he wears it on his shoes while the proudest sovereigns of Christendom wear it in their crowns."

Bolívar may have visited Naples and climbed Mountain Vesuvius before returning to France. He remained stranded in Paris for months, however, because of Adm. Horatio Nelson's smashing victory over the combined French and Spanish fleets at Trafalgar on October 21, 1805. The British lost not a single ship, but they did lose their brilliant Admiral Nelson. In May 1806 Great Britain declared the French coast blockaded from Brest to the Elbe River.

No money from Venezuela could penetrate the blockade, but Bolívar found another way to get home. In late summer he borrowed twenty-four hundred francs from a friend and journeyed to the German free port of Hamburg on the Elbe. In October 1806 he secured passage on an American ship bound for Charleston. Bolívar fell ill with fever on the long, stormy North Atlantic voyage. He reached South Carolina sick and penniless, unhappy conditions that would plague him repeatedly. Fortunately, a shipboard acquaintance, Mr. M. Cormic of Charleston, befriended and assisted him.

Because ships sailing from Venezuela's port at La Guaira did not call at Charleston, Bolívar did not stay long. He recovered and traveled north to Philadelphia to await money from Caracas. He then visited Washington, New York, and Boston before sailing home to Caracas, where he arrived June 1807. Reminiscing later with a friend, he said, "During my short visit to the United States, I saw rational liberty." Although he carried that inspiring vision of liberty with him to the end of his life, he found it impossible to realize in his native land.

CHAPTER 3

Stirrings of Independence, 1807–10

In mid-1807 the gilded youth of Caracas, now boasting a population of some forty-two thousand persons, began holding literary meetings in Bolívar's home. Throughout Spanish America, such literary gatherings actually represented political discussions favoring independence from Spain. Members included Bolívar's brother, Juan Vicente, Andrés Bello (already famous for his poetry and other literary works), Tomás and Mariano Montilla (close boyhood friends), and José Félix Ribas (1775–1815). The latter, only nine years older than Bolívar, had married the Liberator's aunt. Ribas would play key roles in maneuvering for independence and in commanding Patriot troops. Francisco Rodríguez de Toro, the marques del Toro and older brother of Fernando (still in Europe) also joined the group.

These self-confident elite youths believed themselves capable of ruling Venezuela and conspired toward that end. In September some of the conspirators accompanied Bolívar to his cacao plantation about thirty-seven miles southeast of Caracas in the Yare Valley. Bolívar had become entangled in litigation with a neighbor over a right-of-way. The charges and counter-charges, as well as business at his other estates, required that Bolívar visit Caracas often. The news and gossip-rich city kept him well abreast of political events in America and Europe.

By the spring of 1808 Bolívar and his friends knew that a French army had entered Spain the previous October. The ambitious, deceitful Godoy had collaborated with Napoleon in the occupation. Napoleon's forces marched across Spain and occupied Portugal. Prince João, along with his royal retinue and army, hastily fled Lisbon and boarded British ships. Escorted by a small British fleet, they sailed away to Río de Janeiro on November 29, 1807, just as the French army appeared on the crest of the hills above Lisbon.

Meanwhile, in Spain riots at Aranjuez near Madrid in March 1808 forced the unpopular Godoy from office, and a frightened King Charles IV abdicated in favor of his son Ferdinand (1784–1833). The youngster had hardly been a court favorite; he had already been threatened with disinheritance, but enemies of his father made him their symbol. A French army under Gen. Joachim Murat occupied Madrid on March 23. When Ferdinand VII entered his capital the next day, the French ambassador refused to recognize him as king. General Murat then informed Ferdinand that the young king should travel to meet Napoleon en route from France. Leaving a French-dominated junta to rule in Madrid, Ferdinand's plotting French escort lured him across the Spanish-French border to Bayonne. Charles IV, Queen María Luisa, and Godoy arrived a few days later. Napoleon bribed his royal prisoners with rich French estates in exchange for their abdications. The monarchs abdicated in early May and remained in their royal cages while Napoleon placed his brother Joseph on the Spanish throne. Ferdinand's weakness of character and insistence on an archaic absolutism would bring grief to Spain and Spanish America for the next fifteen years.

By the last week of May 1808, all of Spain had learned of Ferdinand's abdication at Bayonne. Some Spaniards, the so-called *afrancesados,* urged cooperation with the occupiers. These members of the Spanish aristocracy and bourgeoisie admired and emulated French thought, fashion, and politics; however, the term took on a strongly pejorative meaning after the French invasion of 1808. Being labeled *afrancesado* became tantamount to an order of exile or worse. Many other Spaniards, however, rose to fight against the French pretender. With British help, they fought a guerrilla campaign to restore Ferdinand to his throne. Nobles and aristocrats formed juntas in nearly every region of Spain to lead the popular uprisings. Asturias, on the north coast, formed the first junta. It met in Oviedo and declared war on Napoleon. On May 30 the Asturians sent envoys to London requesting aid. A representative from Galicia arrived in London, followed by envoys from Seville's junta, which styled itself the "Supreme Junta of Spain and the Indies."

The British government responded promptly, but Iberia's gain would be the New World's loss. The British had massed an army ready to sail with Francisco de Miranda to free Venezuela or Mexico. However, Napoleon's occupation of the Iberian Peninsula forced the British to divert those forces to Portugal. Miranda supporter Edmund Burke (1729–97) fired off an angry criticism of the change. "I should be exceedingly sorry to find we thus risked certain and important advantages, for what are extremely dubious gains." Burke, born in Dublin, served as a Whig member of Parliament from 1765 until 1794 and spoke forcefully on behalf of freeing the Spanish American colonies. He had earlier urged conciliation between Great Britain and its colonies and believed that colonists should enjoy all the rights of British citizens.

Who was this Miranda who had nearly gained direct British aid in the fight against Spanish colonialism? Sebastián Francisco de Miranda (1750–1816) had been born to a wealthy Caracas merchant family, immigrants from the Canary Islands. Bolívar's father and Miranda's father had crossed paths many times in the realms of politics and business. The latter shared the view of Creoles as inferior, a prejudice common among Canary Islanders and peninsular Spaniards. In 1772, at the age of twenty-two, young Miranda had purchased a post as captain of infantry in the Princess Regiment of the Spanish army. The honor cost his family eight thousand pesos (forty thousand pesetas). The fiery, young Creole often ran afoul of his Spanish superiors and landed in jail briefly in 1777 for "neglect of military duty." He served under Bernardo de Gálvez when Spanish forces attacked Pensacola in 1781, Spain having allied itself with the rebels in the American Revolution. He suffered further intrigues against him while serving in the Caribbean in the early 1780s. The discrimination he suffered during his military career intensified his dislike of Spaniards and his desire to liberate his homeland. His early, long-term efforts on behalf of independence would earn him the title "the Precursor."

In late 1783 the Spanish government leveled at him further charges of misuse of funds. He had already fled to the United States, carrying useful letters of introduction, including one to George Washington. He visited Philadelphia and Boston, meeting with George Washington, Alexander Hamilton, and other notables over the course of the next two years. The inglorious end of Miranda's career in the Spanish military marked the beginning of his efforts on behalf of Latin American independence. The cloud of disgrace, the charge of conspiracy, and Spanish agents dogged him for years. Miranda protested his innocence, and sixteen years after the fact, the Spanish Supreme Court agreed, pronouncing him innocent.

For nearly a decade, Miranda traveled and studied in the United States, Europe, and Russia. Thanks to letters of introduction and his great charm, Miranda often lived and traveled at the expense of other people. He became a well-known world citizen. Highly energetic, intelligent, imaginative, and curious, Miranda quickly made favorable impressions wherever he went. Tall, strong, and handsome, the young Venezuelan attracted many friends and lovers, although his rumored affair with Russia's Catherine the Great probably never happened. Had it been so, the immodest Miranda would assuredly have informed someone. He conversed comfortably in Spanish, English, and French and read several more languages.

Unfortunately, Miranda could also be vain, opinionated, and totally blind to the realities around him. He exhibited a seemingly boundless capacity for self-delusion. Miranda had gone to France in the early 1790s and enlisted in the army. Robespierre disliked Miranda and imprisoned him. As the Terror subsided, Miranda regained his freedom in January 1795. In December 1797 Miranda and several other South Americans signed a declaration demanding freedom from Spain. He also publicized the anti-Spanish thoughts of Juan Pablo Viscardo, a Creole born in Guayaquil. Miranda received Viscardo's papers from American ambassador to London Rufus King and published "A Letter Directed to American Spaniards." Despite a ban by the Inquisition in Mexico, the letter circulated in the New World, trumpeting a call for independence, in language reminiscent of Tom Paine. Of course, the Inquisition itself, dating back to 1478 in Spain, seemed to many Creoles yet another example of the long-term peninsular repression of rights and thoughts in the New World.

About the same time, on November 28, 1796, the city council of Caracas revealed in a letter to the king the depth of Creole alienation from Bourbon abuses. "European Spaniards consider it vital to occupy all the public offices, and they spend their time pressing their claims, regardless of their qualifications. The American Spaniards devote themselves to the cultivation of the land, enduring the toils and tasks of this arduous occupation." Owing to this discrimination, the council warned, with considerable prescience, that "the grim day will arrive when Spain will be served by mulattos, zambos, and blacks, whose service will be exacted by force and whose doubtful loyalty will be the cause of violent upheavals; then there will be no one, for the sake of self-interest, honor, purity of blood, and reputation, who will risk his life in calling on sons, friends, relatives, and countrymen to control the lower orders and defend the common cause and their own."

Concerned more with its own economic self-interest than hemispheric solidarity, the United States turned a mostly deaf ear to calls that it should support Latin American independence. Thanks to the war between Spain and England, the United States authorized neutral ships to trade with its colonies. Ships carried food and other supplies from the United States to many Spanish American cities, including Cartagena and Venezuelan ports. American merchants had no desire to disturb this profitable flow, but in Spanish America, it only whetted Creole appetites for more expanded trade with other nations. Miranda returned to London in January 1798 to continue lobbying for British support of Latin American independence. Prime Minister William Pitt welcomed him. Miranda submitted his liberation plan to Pitt, asking for ships, supplies, and troops in exchange for trade concessions from the newly liberated nations. Miranda would spend the next decade cajoling and lobbying the British.

The Precursor returned to the United States in 1805. Again, he failed to secure government assistance, but he did collect a force of two hundred volunteers. Social prejudice against things Spanish and, by extension, Spanish-American hurt the Precursor's efforts. Many North Americans maintained a fervent belief in the "Black Legend" of Spanish cruelty and atrocities against their New World subjects. However, many Protestants distrusted or even hated all Roman Catholics, including those of Spanish America. John Adams remarked disparagingly that one might as well attempt to establish democracies among birds, beasts, and fishes as among Spanish Americans. New England Federalist and secretary of state to Washington Timothy Pickering dismissed Spanish Americans as "corrupt and effeminate beyond example." Prejudice, cautiousness about international entanglements, and enlightened economic self-interest would temper U.S. support for Spanish American independence until it became a fait accompli.

Despite the lack of fervor in North America, in February 1806 Miranda sailed from New York on the *Leander*, red-yellow-blue tricolor of Colombia flying. Alas, Spanish forces had full knowledge of Miranda's arrival near Puerto Cabello. The invaders lost two ships and sixty men captured. Royalists promptly hanged ten of the traitors, then decapitated and quartered them. Expedition member James Biggs, in his book *The History of Don Francisco de Miranda's Attempt to Effect a Revolution in South America* (1810), described the disaster, which included fifty residents of the United States captured and eight put to death. Others loyal to Spain burned Miranda in effigy and trumpeted the thirty-thousand-peso reward for his capture, dead or alive.

Six months later, in August, Miranda tried again, this time with a larger force. In Barbados, Miranda had the good luck to meet Adm. Sir Alexander Cochrane, uncle of the future admiral of the Chilean navy, Thomas, Lord Cochrane (1775–1860). In 1820 Cochrane, the nephew, would play a key role in moving Argentina's José de San Martín and his invasion force by sea from Chile to Peru. Alexander Cochrane, seeing great trade potential between Great Britain and new Spanish republics, wrote to London requesting five thousand troops. Those troops did not materialize, but through Cochrane's efforts, Miranda did add another five hundred men locally to his force. The independence forces landed at Coro and occupied the town, but militia forces soon expelled them. In the minds of many Venezuelan Peninsulars and Creoles, Miranda represented the excesses and radicalism of the French Revolution. While local Creole planters and merchants had complaints about Spanish policy, they did not embrace wild-eyed revolutionaries like Miranda. In later engagements Miranda would again demonstrate that his talents lay in the salon, not on the battlefield.

In late 1807 Miranda and his staff embarked on the *Alexandria* and returned to London. He continued to agitate for Latin American independence until Bolívar arrived in 1810 and convinced him that Venezuela needed him. The persistent, patient Miranda finally seemed on the verge of success in 1808. Sir Arthur Wellesley (1769–1852, the future duke of Wellington), commander of the army promised to Miranda, instead brought him ill tidings. As had happened repeatedly over the past thirty years, the English again put Miranda on hold. Sir Arthur knew that "hope deferred maketh the heart weary," but he feared not Miranda's weariness but his wrath. Hoping the volatile and outspoken Miranda would control his temper in public, the British officer explained, "I thought it best to walk out in the streets with him and tell him there, to prevent his bursting out. But even there he was so loud and angry, that I told him I would walk on first a little that we might not attract the notice of everybody passing. When I joined him again he was cooler."

On July 4, a few weeks after Miranda's angry outburst, King George III announced a major change in British policy. Because of the popular uprising in Spain, that nation would no longer be considered an enemy of Great Britain. This announcement seemingly ended three centuries of implacable British-Spanish hostilities. It also dampened Miranda's hopes for British intervention on behalf of the independence (Patriot) forces in Latin America.

British-French conflict continued, however, and the effects soon spilled over to the New World. On July 15, 1808, a French corvette anchored in Venezuela's La Guaira harbor. Two officers debarked and rode up over the mountains to Caracas. A few hours later a British frigate anchored at La Guaira. The English captain debarked and rode to Caracas. The French officers had the ear of Don Juan de Casas, the captain general, who received them cordially at the Government House. The French assured the Spanish officials that they would retain their offices and special privileges if they recognized Napoleon's brother Joseph as "King of Spain and the Indies."

The Frenchmen had barely departed when the English captain arrived. Don Juan received him coldly. Meanwhile, the French officers spread news of the abdication of Charles and Ferdinand at a popular Caracas coffeehouse. They proclaimed Joseph Bonaparte to be king of Spain and the Indies, news that spread quickly through the city. The English captain, who dined at another inn, told a very different story. He informed those present that Ferdinand and his parents were prisoners of Napoleon and that the Spanish people had risen up against their French occupiers.

Those who heard this news also spread it far and wide. The streets soon filled with people denouncing the French and hailing the English captain as their savior. The Englishman returned to the captain general and demanded permission to take possession of the French corvette. "I have given orders for her immediate sailing," replied Don Juan frostily. "My second-in-command has orders to seize her if she sails," replied the English captain calmly. Both men could hear a screaming mob drawing nearer. When the mob reached the Government House, they demanded that Don Juan proclaim Ferdinand VII as king of Spain and the Indies. The quailing Spaniard, fearing the throng, joined in an oath of obedience and loyalty to Ferdinand. As in many internecine conflicts, switching loyalties back and forth became a common survival mechanism during the hectic years of independence struggles.

The mob tried to capture the French officers, who barely escaped their fury by hiding in a prominent citizen's house. Troops escorted them to La Guaira that night and they boarded their ship. The British second in command had the pleasure of seizing the French ship in the morning. The actions of mid-July 1808 served as prelude to months of extraordinary agitation. Creoles and Spaniards wavered from option to option. Should they submit to the Francophile junta in Spain or create an autonomous junta? Should they proclaim independence and put government into the hands of Creoles?

Don Juan de Casas appointed a junta on July 16. He selected members from the *audiencia, cabildo,* army, clergy, and other important corporate bodies. The junta advised Don Juan to uphold the throne of Ferdinand, as the people had demanded. A member of the cabildo criticized the governor general for appointing the junta without consulting the people. The vacillating Don Juan dismissed the junta and muddled through the next ten days. Then, with no evidence except a simple accusation, he arrested Manuel Matos and two friends for allegedly proclaiming "We must kill the Spaniards!" He ordered the prisoners to Puerto Rico, where they were jailed in a fortress. Matos had indeed met with other conspirators at Bolívar's house. Don Juan sent his son to warn Bolívar not to host any more seditious meetings. Bolívar and his friends left Caracas for his estate on the Río Guaira.

Changing fortunes in Europe kept Venezuelan politics in flux and turmoil. As Napoleon's troops advanced on Madrid, the junta at Aranjuez (near Madrid) fled to Seville. They joined with the Seville junta to create the Junta Central. On August 5 commissioners from the Junta arrived in Caracas. They informed the captain general that he and his officials had to recognize the Seville junta in order to retain their offices.

Don Juan consulted the audiencia and then recognized the junta. When Antonio Fernández de León heard of this submission, he protested to his followers that neither the captain general nor the audiencia had the right to recognize the Seville junta. Only the people had that right. Soon thereafter, Bolívar, Fernández de León, and other pro-independence leaders returned to Caracas. Simón and Juan Vicente Bolívar argued that Venezuela was already independent. They insisted that the conspirators immediately establish a republican form of government. Most other Creoles and Spaniards did not agree with the Bolívar brothers. Losing the argument, they left the ferment in Caracas and retired to San Mateo.

On October 24 the marques del Toro delivered a letter from Miranda to the captain general in which he urged the city council to take the government into its own hands. He wanted Toro to send agents to London for discussions with English ministers. After much wrangling, the marques del Toro, José Félix Ribas, Mariano Montilla, and other conspirators wrote and signed a petition. The petition, with forty-five signatures, stated that neither the captain general nor the audiencia had the authority to recognize the Seville junta, to declare war on France, or to make peace with England. Only the people had the right to take such actions. The Seville junta had no jurisdiction in Venezuela or elsewhere in America. The petition asked for the creation of a junta in Caracas "to exercise authority on behalf of our august sovereign and lord Ferdinand VII, whom God preserve."

Bolívar disagreed with the wording of the petition, and his goals extended much further. He wanted immediate independence and a new republic. On his initial visit to Spain, Simón had witnessed firsthand the weakness and corruption of the royal family. He had heard the many rumors of the illicit affairs of Queen María Luisa. One day at Aranjuez, fifteen-year-old Ferdinand had invited sixteen-year-old Simón to play a game of battledore (an early form of badminton). When the shuttlecock hit Ferdinand on the head, he lost his temper and demanded an apology. Simón refused to apologize, and the queen reprimanded Ferdinand for not controlling his temper. We might speculate that the queen, hobbled with a weak husband and a weak son, perhaps recognized and admired the young Venezuelan's strength and spirit.

Six years later Bolívar now vowed on Rome's Monte Sacro to break the chains that bound Venezuela to the king of Spain. When Ferdinand and his father and brothers abdicated their rights to the throne, they broke those chains. Bolívar would not recognize Ferdinand as his sovereign and thereby restore Venezuela's chains. Ferdinand would become a weak, inept, corrupt king, and his manifold, multiple shortcomings, not Bolívar's actions, would precipitate much of the horror and bloodshed that Spanish America suffered.

Don Juan presided over and consulted with the audiencia on how to respond to the petition. The high court decreed on November 24 that the petitioners were under arrest. Officials confined most of the signers to their country estates for three months. They dispatched Antonio Fernández de León, the ringleader, under guard to the junta in Seville.

Newspapers and broadsides played an important propaganda role during the independence struggles. However, the one-month-old *Gazeta de Caracas*, Venezuela's first newspaper, mentioned nothing about the conspiracy or the arrests. Two Britons, Matthew Gallagher and James Lamb, had purchased a printing press abandoned by Miranda in Trinidad after his failed invasion. They took the press to Caracas and shrewdly persuaded Capt. Gen. Don Juan and Intendant Juan Vicente de Arce that a newspaper, circulating in all the provinces, would help them maintain control in Venezuela. Their newspaper focused mostly on European news. Clearly recognizing local political realities, however, it included flattering remarks about Don Juan and Arce. Historian Gerhard Masur described J. M. Díaz, editor of the counterrevolutionary newspaper, as "His Catholic Majesty's royal liar and storyteller," a blunt but generally accurate description.

As political conflict rose in Caracas, the Venezuelan conspirator, Antonio Fernández de León, debarked at Cádiz in March 1809. The Spanish jailed him promptly but briefly. His brother Esteban and his influential protector, Francisco de Saavedra, secured Antonio's release on bond. He journeyed to Seville to defend himself before the Junta Central. Antonio's skillful arguments convinced the junta of his innocence. He charged that the real culprit in Caracas was the captain general. This view pleased the junta, which had already heeded Napoleon's advice and dispatched Vicente Emparán to replace Juan de Casas. Junta members, having studied and traveled in France, admired French culture. If the fortunes of war favored French armies in Spain, the Seville junta could easily and opportunistically switch its allegiance from Ferdinand to the French pretender Joseph Bonaparte. The Junta proved no more intelligent in relations with the American colonies than did Ferdinand VII. Even the notoriously pro-Spanish historian Salvador de Madariaga admitted that the Junta's flawed policies alienated many in Latin America. "Instead of fostering the creation of local Juntas overseas, the Junta Central remained passive and cold towards those actually born there. . . . This tendency to discriminate against the kingdoms overseas was a godsend for the minority of American leaders working for separatism."

As French forces threatened Seville, the Junta Central withdrew to Cádiz, as did the Fernández de León brothers. On November 1, 1809, the junta granted Antonio the title of marques de Casa León. This honor may have come in return for his promise to send food, money, and shoes to resupply starving, barefoot Spanish soldiers. Brother Bernardo remained in Spain as hostage for his brother's good conduct when the new marques sailed from Cádiz in December. Antonio debarked at La Guaira on January 16, 1810.

The new marques found many welcome changes in Venezuela. In May 1809 Capt. Gen. Vicente de Emparán y Orbe (1747–1820) had arrived with other new officials. The captain general had served in the royal navy and then, beginning in 1792, had governed the province of Cumaná for twelve years. Many of the Caracas conspirators, including the brothers Bolívar, Toro, and Montilla, were friends of the new captain general. Fernando del Toro, another friend of Bolívar and younger brother of the marques de Toro, arrived with Emparán as his inspector general of Militias. Antonio's Caracas allies, now with friends in high places, welcomed home the new marques de Casa León.

Casa León quickly published a letter in the February 2, 1810, issue of the *Gazeta de Caracas*. He asked "The Inhabitants of this Province" to contribute supplies for needy Spanish troops battling the French. Ten days later he wrote to his brother Esteban about the volatile conditions in Caracas. "The air is full of intrigue, but I am prudent and keeping myself away from the fire." Esteban likewise tried to keep from being burned by the fires of intrigue in Spain. The French occupied Andalucia and approached Cádiz. The threatened junta appointed a five-member regency and authorized that body to call a Cortes into session. The Cortes gathered in Cádiz on September 24, 1810, and again in 1812. Then the junta disbanded, leaving power to the pro-French regency. The lack of legitimate political authority in Spain offered

Bolívar and likeminded revolutionaries a golden opportunity. Could they take advantage of the power vacuum?

The people of Caracas did not learn of French ascendancy in Spain until mid-April. José Domingo Díaz, a Royalist, described the impact of the news. "Consternation filled the souls of good men. It exalted the audacity of the conspirators." Two commissioners from the regency arrived in Caracas at the same time as the shocking news from Spain. The commissioners apparently met with a few of the independence conspirators. The Bolívar brothers at the Yare estate in the Tuy valley did not share in the excitement. When Caracas mayor José de Llamozas learned of the conversations between the conspirators and the commissioners, he quickly called an extraordinary session of the cabildo. At that meeting, he planned to organize a junta independent from the regency.

Various political factions mobilized. Conspirators went through the streets inviting people to gather in the main plaza. José Joaquín Cortés Madariaga (1776–1826), a canon of the cathedral, maneuvered to serve as one of two representatives of the clergy. Chilean-born Cortés Madariaga had an ambitious and quarrelsome nature and his own secret political agenda. A believer in Federalism and republicanism and thus sympathetic to the more radical Patriots, he had cleverly kept his political views secret and bided his time. When Royalists regained ascendancy in 1812, he was shipped off to prison in Ceuta, Africa, where he remained incarcerated for five years.

The extraordinary session gathered at the town hall early in the morning on Holy Thursday, April 19, 1810. Cortés Madariaga waited at the cathedral for an opportune moment to take action. Two representatives moved to transform the enlarged city council into a governing junta with Emparán as president. Mayor Llamozas sent two messengers to invite the captain general to preside over the debate. Emparán arrived shortly, and Llamozas gave his version of events. He explained to the gathering that French victories in Spain, Ferdinand's captivity, and the lack of central authority in Spain forced them to take action. "These circumstances," said the mayor, "make it imperative that we create a government representative of the people who are now sovereign in Venezuela."

Emparán responded bluntly, "Your statement is false. A central government exists in Spain—the Regency. Two agents of the Regency have come to consult with us. It is now eight o'clock, time to attend mass. Come with me to the Cathedral, and we will discuss the establishment of a junta later." The captain general departed and the hushed assembly followed. As they walked through the plaza, some of the conspiring Patriots regained their wits. "To the cabildo! To the cabildo!" they shouted. Their cries reverberated across the crowded main plaza, where others took it up.

As Emparán neared the cathedral, Francisco Salias grabbed his arm and asked him to return to the town hall. An officer of the Aragua militia told the captain general that the militia stood with the Patriots. Emparán returned to the meeting site, determined to accept the presidency of a governing junta. Just then Cortés Madariaga burst into the room. "It's a pity," he cried, "to see apparently sane men putting the revolution and their lives at Emparán's mercy. His pretended weakness is a sham. He will get revenge later for this outrage which has been done to his authority. You are crazy if you think that you can curb him by making him president of a junta. He can dissolve it when he is ready. Emparán must be deposed! You must create a government with power of its own!"

The captain general tried to save the situation by appealing directly to the people. He stepped out onto the balcony and asked those gathered in the plaza below, "Señores! Do you wish me to rule?" People nearest the balcony shouted "yes." Cortés Madariaga, who had also stepped onto the balcony, signaled the crowd to say "no." Radicals in the crowd cried out, "We do not want you!" "Then I do not want to govern you," replied the proud Emparán. The captain general stepped back inside and handed the baton, symbol of his authority, to Mayor Llamozas. The session quickly declared itself the "Supreme Junta for the Conservation of the Rights of Ferdinand VII."

On April 21 the new Supreme Junta paid Emparán and eight other royal officials their salary plus travel expenses and escorted them to the port of La Guaira. Emparán sailed to exile in Philadelphia. Later in the year he sailed back to Spain and out of history. Had the church canon not intervened and swayed the crowd, Emparán might have become a leader and hero of Venezuelan independence. On such small twists of fate turn the destinies of individuals and nations.

The junta appointed a number of officials. Fernando del Toro became commander of the armed forces. The marques de Casa León served as president of the Supreme Court of Appeals, modeled after the old audiencia. Other provinces, including Barcelona, Cumaná, Margarita, and Barinas, joined with the Caracas junta. Indeed, juntas declared independence throughout Latin America from April through October. Staunch Royalists, however, retained important pockets of power. Peru remained fiercely Royalist. Supporters of the king also held Coro and Maracaibo in Venezuela. Maracaibo, founded in 1571, served as a major seaport, with its strategic location on the west bank of the channel between Lake Maracaibo and the Gulf of Venezuela. Patriot and Royalist forces skirmished throughout the country for the remainder of the year.

Simón and Juan Vicente Bolívar returned to Caracas from their estate soon after Emparán's departure. In May the junta dispatched Juan Vicente and two others to the United States on a diplomatic mission. They carried this letter: "The new government of this Province yearns to draw even closer the ties of its allegiance with the people of North America. The government of the United States of America will be kept acquainted with the new system established in Caracas and of the reciprocal advantages that its commerce will have with us. Our harbors await with open arms all the peaceful foreigners who may call to exchange for our fruit and products all their industry and commerce."

In keeping with its cautious approach, and with an eye to maximizing profit, U.S. policy remained neutral. While selling supplies to the Patriots, the United States also permitted Royalists to purchase arms and ship them to South America. For example, on September 10, 1810, the first agent from the United States to Venezuela, Robert K. Lowry, informed the State Department that the revolutionary government of Venezuela protested a shipment of Spanish arms from Philadelphia to Maracaibo. The Venezuelans carried out discussions and purchased supplies, but Juan Vicente's mission ended in tragedy. He died on the return voyage when a storm sank his ship off the Bermuda Islands. The unhappy Simón had lost yet another close, beloved family member.

Miranda had written a letter urging Venezuelans to send a mission to London. In June the junta appointed Simón Bolívar to undertake this important diplomatic initiative. Some members of the junta opposed his appointment, arguing that he was too young, impulsive, and radical. Bolívar's offer to pay his own expenses swayed opinion in his favor. They also named Luis López Méndez (1758–1841), older and more tactful than Bolívar, as a second envoy. Andrés Bello, a man of letters and a more conservative tutor of Bolívar, rounded out the diplomatic trio.

Vice Adm. Sir Alexander Cochrane, commander of the British Windward Fleet, sent the warship *General Wellington* to transport the three diplomats. They debarked at Portsmouth on July 10 after a month at sea. Bolívar arrived at a very delicate point in English-Spanish relations. Foreign Secretary Sir Richard Wellesley outlined the problem in a letter to his brother Henry, ambassador to the regency at Cádiz: "Make the Regency understand in the clearest terms that His Majesty's government has strained its resources to aid Spain and that this aid must end unless Spain grants British subjects the right to trade with her colonies. Remind the Regency that Venezuela has refused to recognize it, and that His Majesty's government intends to maintain friendly relations with Venezuela. This is a very delicate matter." A delicate matter indeed! England's major concern was commerce. Using relations with Venezuela as a threat, the British might force the regency to relax trade restrictions with its colonies. Wellesley had to balance the desire for opening trade in Latin America with the need for Spanish cooperation in battling Napoleon.

Once settled in London, the Venezuelan trio sought out Francisco de Miranda. The junta's instructions concerning Miranda had been circumspect and ambiguous. Like Bolívar, Miranda had served in the Spanish army. He also served in the French revolutionary army from 1792 to 1798. Bolívar was to regard the older Venezuelan as a traitor to his king. At the same time, however, the junta cautioned against slighting Miranda if his influence might assist their mission. Bolívar would brazenly exceed his instructions and invite Miranda to return to Venezuela.

Because Bolívar, López Méndez, and Bello represented an unrecognized state, Wellesley would not receive them at the Foreign Office. He invited them instead to his London residence, Apsley House, where they convened on July 16, 1810. The conversations took place in French. The foreign minister quickly attacked the Venezuelans. "The actions of the Caracas government," he declared, "are inopportune. They are based on the false premise that Spain is lost. The affairs of Spain have never presented a more favorable aspect." He should have added "for the British."

His brother Lord Wellington remained in Portugal, awaiting the proper moment to attack French forces. Wellesley charged Venezuela with being the only colony to separate itself from the Spanish central government: "Therefore, I must ask you, have the actions of the Caracas government been dictated by resentment against actions of Spanish magistrates, and is the desire of the Caracas government to have those abuses reformed so that it can recognize the Regency, or has the Province of Caracas determined to break all bonds that have united it to Spain and establish an independent state?"

Bolívar replied by reviewing the events in Caracas. He repeated that the Venezuelans had sworn eternal loyalty to their legitimate sovereign Ferdinand VII. Again, Wellesley criticized. "Such action is an act of independence, and a sad blow against Spain. Because of the treaty between Great Britain and Spain, I cannot sanction a separatist movement within the dominion of an ally."

The foreign minister insisted that Venezuelan independence jeopardized and possibly compromised the independence of Spain itself. Bolívar countered that Venezuela was far too small to shape the outcome of wars in the Iberian Peninsula. Bolívar also committed a colossal diplomatic blunder. In presenting his written credentials to Wellesley, he also handed over his confidential written instructions from the junta. As the inexperienced Venezuelan presented his arguments, Wellesley could see clearly that Bolívar's presentation differed markedly from his written instructions.

Bolívar failed to grasp that the most pressing British national interest rested in their alliance with Spain against the French. Current British self-interest did not extend to aiding the Venezuelans, who desperately wanted recognition and material support. Despite the differences and Bolívar's faux pas, Wellesley did not close off contact completely. Additional meetings proved more civil and friendly, but the vital interests of the two parties remained far apart. As with the United States, the national interests of Great Britain remained far more essential to diplomats than did Latin American cries for support.

At Wellesley's request, the Venezuelans framed an unofficial note summarizing their interests. They requested (1) British naval protection against the French as well as aid in defending Venezuela's security; (2) British mediation to preserve Venezuelan peace and friendship with Spain and the Spanish provinces that had recognized the regency; (3) a facilitation and guarantee of agreements undertaken by Venezuela with the Regency; and (4) orders to British officials in the Caribbean to foster commercial relations between British subjects and Venezuela. Wellesley declined to provide a written response. On August 3, however, he provided verbal assurances that their requests had been received favorably.

Miranda took advantage of his vast network of connections to introduce the envoys to many influential people. Miranda arranged a meeting with the duke of Gloucester, the king's nephew. The Venezuelans enjoyed dinner with the duke, who expressed support for their cause. Bolívar also met William Wilberforce, a leading abolitionist, and Joseph Lancaster, a renowned educator.

Some of Bolívar's London encounters did not go well. The Spanish-English language barrier created a scene for the young Venezuelan at a brothel. According to Bolívar, a prostitute misunderstood his amorous request and mistakenly concluded that he was homosexual. She flew into a rage. He tried to calm her with an offering of banknotes. She threw them into the fire. "Imagine the scene," he recalled. "I could speak no English, and the prostitute could speak no Spanish. She thought I was a Greek Sodomite and created a scandal that made me leave faster than I had entered." Thus Bolívar suffered misadventures in sex as well as diplomacy during his London visit.

The envoys, despite failing to secure a treaty with England, did have an impact. Wellesley used their presence to convince the regency to grant English merchants the right to trade with Spanish colonies. British merchants, however, faced stiff competition from the United States. Having completed his mission, Bolívar wrote to Wellesley on August 30 requesting transport back to Venezuela. Miranda also determined to leave England. He sent his papers with Bolívar, who sailed on September 21 aboard the *Sapphire.* The young Venezuelan would never again see Europe. Miranda, after enduring some British-inspired delays, sailed three weeks later aboard a merchantman bound for Curaçao.

Meanwhile in Spain, the deliberations and actions of the extraordinary Cortes gathered at Cádiz offer further compelling evidence on the great gulf that existed between Spaniards and Creoles. Despite the far greater population of the colonies (seventeen million versus ten million for Spain), Americans numbered only 30 of some 280 total delegates. On the second day, José Mexía Llequerica of Quito led Creoles in complaining of the grossly unequal representation of Spain compared with America. Faced with stiff Peninsular opposition on every issue and the political and economic clout of the monopolistic merchant lobby of Cádiz, Creoles clearly understood their second-class status. The delegates sharply rejected the American demand for equal representation. Other American demands for reducing restrictions on trade, the abolition of government monopolies, and for a greater share of offices in the New World all met with rebuff. After a particularly outrageous and insulting attack on September 16, 1811, the American deputies tried to walk out en mass only to be turned back by armed guards.

Bolívar debarked from his 4,655-mile voyage at La Guaira on December 5 and reported to the Supreme Junta two days later. His colleagues remained in London, stranded by the rush of events. López Méndez worked assiduously to encourage British volunteers to fight on behalf of the Patriots. And Bello penned volumes of poetry but gradually became estranged from Bolívar and the Patriot cause. Back in Caracas, Bolívar skillfully shaped public opinion in Miranda's favor in preparation for the Precursor's return. Many Venezuelans distrusted the long-absent Miranda. Some considered him a British collaborator or even an active agent. Thanks to Bolívar's influence, however, a warm reception greeted Miranda upon his arrival.

On December 13, Bolívar "and a great number of the first citizens went down to La Guaira to escort Miranda to his place which he entered about noon on Thursday, mounted on a beautiful white charger." Miranda wore a blue coat, white pants, shiny black boots, and a two-cornered hat, the uniform of a revolutionary French general of 1793. Royalist José Domingo Díaz acidly recalled the day: "I saw Miranda enter in triumph, received as a gift from Heaven, and with the hopes of extreme demagogues founded upon him. He is about 65 years of age [sixty, actually], of grave aspect, of tireless loquacity, always gracious with the scum of the people, always disposed to sustain his pretensions. The most turbulent youth looked upon him as a man of wisdom, the only one capable of directing the government. Moderates looked upon him as a dangerous being, capable of ruining the state."

As the following years of the *Patria Boba* (Foolish Fatherland) revealed, many ambitious politicians would play roles in "ruining the state." The travesties during this first, unfortunate republic would only reinforce Bolívar's belief that Spanish America needed strong, centralized rule and the iron hand of a powerful executive.

PART II

Struggling for

Independence

CHAPTER 4

Disasters for the Foolish Fatherland,

1811–12

The political earthquakes of 1810 shook Spain's American empire from one end to the other, from Mexico to Venezuela to Argentina. Juntas formed throughout the region to debate what course to follow. Ferdinand, their legitimate king, could not rule. A French pretender would not do. Who would rule in Ferdinand's stead? Many Creoles, influenced by Enlightenment values, concluded that legitimate political power rested with them until Ferdinand could reclaim his rightful thrown. More radical voices, including Bolívar, concluded that Creoles should rule themselves without "benefit" of a Spanish king. Happily for the Patriot cause, Royalist bumbling aided them. Even the pro-Spanish historian Salvador de Madariaga admitted the errors: "The only hope for the revolutionists lay in the stupidity of the Spanish authorities. It was justified. Official Spain remained as uncompromising as Caracas, and hardened in 1811."

Spain remained hopelessly backward and out of step with the tides of change. Spanish Royalists feared and condemned Enlightenment ideas, thought of as inviting revolution. Like archconservatives everywhere, many Royalists believed that one could stem the tide of political change by repressing "subversive" ideas. Writing in 1814, Colombian antirepublican José Antonio de Torres y Peña condemned the "spirit of false enlightenment that had corrupted the entire world." The stirrings of empirical science, represented by Alexander von Humboldt and others, inflamed conservative fears.

As during the Counter-Reformation centuries before, Royalist conservatives circled the wagons and waged war on new ideas. As during the Counter-Reformation, the Royalists could not stem the tide of history.

Enough delegates had gathered in Caracas for the first Congress of Venezuela to open on March 2, 1811. They met in the house of the Count of San Javier, then moved to the Monastery of San Francisco. The Junta resigned its power to Congress. Fortunately for Miranda, some parishes had not yet elected their representations to Congress. Members of the influential Patriotic Society (Sociedad Patriótica de Agricultura y Economía) engineered Miranda's election as a delegate from Pao in Barcelona Province.

While the politicians debated, military conflicts ignited between Royalists and Patriots. Royalist naval forces blockaded the Venezuela coast and sailed up the Orinoco River. The Spanish fleet included a schooner, a sloop, two gunboats, two *piraguas,* and four *flecheras.* Ramón Páez (José Antonio's son), in *Wild Scenes in South America,* well described flecheras as rowboats "fifty feet long, very sharp and low to admit of their being propelled by paddles dexterously handled by Indian rowers who, keeping perfect time in the strokes, give in consequence greater impetus to the flecheras; hence the name from *flecha,* an arrow. Manned by fifteen or twenty rowers on a side, they look like huge centipedes skimming swiftly over the water."

They harassed Barrancas on the banks of the Orinoco River near Cumaná. At six o'clock on the morning of April 8, 1811, the fleet lay only a pistol shot from thatched-roof houses on the riverbank. Their guns bombarded the town, and flaming arrows from the piraguas and flecheras set fire to the thatched roofs. Patriots rushed into the river and upset some of the boats. Royalists had to swim for their lives. The spirited counterattack forced the squadron to return to its base in Puerto Rico.

On July 3 another Royalist force, numbering more than a thousand men, appeared off the Caribbean coast of Cumaná, capital of the province of the same name. A hastily assembled troop of two thousand Patriots defended the coast with such zeal that the Royalist fleet again withdrew to Puerto Rico. Royalist agents in Caracas enlisted some Canary Islanders in an anti-independence conspiracy. They planned to steal weapons from the San Carlos Barracks, murder political leaders, and take over the city. Canary Islanders and Royalists in Valencia were to act on the same day. Congress, blissfully unaware of the conspiracies, seated the articulate Miranda on June 22. Bolívar and Miranda quickly enlivened the discussions by promoting the spirit of independence among Venezuelans. Miranda emphatically argued that Congress should declare independence now. Opponents

demurred, countering that they had been elected to preserve the rights of
Ferdinand VII. They warned that Congress lacked the authority to take the
drastic step suggested by Miranda.

On the evening of July 3, young but resolute Simón addressed the Patriotic Society in his first major political speech. Like Miranda, he expressed
impatience with delay and demanded bold action.

> What we desire is that the union be effective, so that it may give us life
> in the glorious struggle to achieve our freedom. To unite and do nothing,
> to sleep in the arms of apathy, was yesterday but a disgrace—while today
> it is treason. The National Congress is arguing issues that should long
> since have been settled. . . . It is also said that great enterprises should be
> planned over a period of time. Three hundred years—is that not time
> enough . . . ? Let us fearlessly lay the cornerstone of South American lib-
> erty; if we hesitate we are lost.

Goaded by the more radical voices, Congress voted independence on
July 4, 1811. Ten days later, Bastille Day, the Patriots displayed a new national
flag of bold yellow, blue, and red horizontal stripes that Miranda had brought
to Venezuela. Bolívar and Miranda seemed to fulfill Bonpland's prophesy
that the revolution would produce sons worthy of leading Venezuela to independence.

Action followed words the following day. "July fifth was the fatal day,"
recalled unsympathetic and dismayed Royalist José Domingo Díaz. "Turbulent young men, armed with daggers, compelled Congress to declare independence. . . . This dismal day was the saddest of my life. Those young
men, in the delirium of their triumph, dashed coatless through the streets
of Caracas, tearing down Spanish flags, insignias, and portraits of Ferdinand
VII, while honorable men remained in their homes, scarcely daring to look
out their windows."

Independence declared, however, was not independence won. On the
afternoon of July 11, residents in northwest Caracas noticed Canary Islanders congregating in a field near the barracks of San Carlos. Some carried
cutlasses, blunderbusses, and sheets of tin to shield themselves. A few sat
astride mules, a mount as common as horses in the mountainous Venezuelan terrain. At three o'clock they shouted, "Long live the King! Death to
traitors!" They fired, forcing bystanders to hit the ground. Patriots threw
stones at the force, wounding several. Troops from San Carlos arrived and
arrested the troublemakers, but problems were far from over. In their po-

litical zeal, proponents of independence overlooked how quickly Spanish forces based in the Caribbean could deploy to Venezuela's long coastline. Santo Domingo in Hispañola (now the Dominican Republic) lay only 578 miles from La Guaira.

According to the Royalist Díaz, Patriot forces then shot sixteen of the prisoners. They decapitated the bodies and placed the heads in various locations on the outskirts of the city. "All of those excellent men," lamented Díaz, "were worthy of a better fate." Another witness, Francisco Javier Yanes, places the number decapitated at ten. Whatever the exact toll, a horrendous decade of butchery and bloodletting had begun.

Although Royalists in Caracas met with disaster, the conspiracy in Valencia succeeded. The marques del Toro again showed his lack of military prowess. The executive council asked Miranda to replace him at the head of the Patriot army. The old revolutionary agreed to take command on one condition—that Bolívar not march with the Aragua militia. The executive council granted Miranda's request. Bolívar protested, saying that if his militia marched without him, he would be considered a coward. The council reversed its decision, and Bolívar left with the vanguard commanded by the marques del Toro.

What had happened since Miranda's triumphal return to Caracas to create such a deep rift with Bolívar? The Spanish apologist Salvador de Madariaga would have us believe that their relations remained amiable, even "affectionate." "Let us then," he writes in his biography of Bolívar (p. 172), "dismiss all the stories of dissensions between Miranda and Bolívar." On the contrary, major issues divided the two. The rash Bolívar, for example, favored immediate expulsion of all Spaniards. Centuries of discrimination had earned for the Spaniards nothing but opprobrium in Bolívar's eyes. The eminent historian E. Bradford Burns in *Latin America: A Concise, Interpretive History* provides the long-term data of the colonial era. "Of the 170 viceroys, only four were Creoles—and they were sons of Spanish officials. Of the 602 captains-general, governors, and presidents in Spanish America, only fourteen had been creoles; of the 606 bishops and archbishops, 105 were born in the New World. Such preference aroused bitter resentment among the creoles. One distinguished representative of the Creoles, Simón Bolívar, stated in 1815, 'The hatred that the Peninsular [Spaniard] has inspired in us is greater than the ocean which separates us.'" The more moderate and cautious Miranda, whose own father was a Spanish Canary Islander *(canario),* believed that *peninsulares* had the right to remain in Venezuela.

Bolívar was not alone in his alienation from Spaniards. The extreme prejudice, discrimination, and nepotism of José de Gálvez (1720–87) and the Bourbon court alienated many Creoles. Of 266 Crown appointments to Spanish American audiencias between 1751 and 1808, Creoles garnered only 24 percent, while 200 (76 percent) went to Peninsulars. After suppressing New Spain, Gálvez, minister of the Indies, turned his attention in February 1776 to the whole of Spanish America. He appointed hordes of Spaniards, often corrupt, who monopolized governmental positions to the exclusion of Creoles. As historian John Lynch noted, "in the decades after 1750, Spanish Americans saw their hard-won and often costly advances reversed by a new colonial state that was more ruthless than its predecessor but not more respected. This government was deaf to representations; none received a favorable response, and their only result was to underline the futility of protest."

Temperament, ego, and ambition also divided the two men as two powerful and very different personalities came into conflict. Miranda, cool and mature, approached problems at deliberate speed. He considered the fiery, impulsive Bolívar to be a "dangerous youth." The two ambitious men also viewed each other, correctly, as rivals. Both sought glory, and neither wished to share center stage. Indeed, a deep ideological rift also divided the men. Miranda had observed in 1799 that "we have before our eyes two great examples, the American and the French Revolution. Let us prudently imitate the first and carefully shun the second." No one would have ever accused Bolívar of prudence or preference for a less radical path.

Although born and raised in Caracas, Miranda distrusted Creole aristocrats in general and the young, brilliant, impetuous Bolívar in particular. Perhaps his Canary Islander father contributed to these views. Even Danish-born Gen. H. L. V. Ducoudray Holstein, whose animosity toward Bolívar is well known, pointed out the distrust aroused by Miranda among many Creoles. Miranda's "constant correspondence with the English government through Curaçao, and his frequent interviews with the commanders of English men of war, who delivered him numerous letters from England, rendered him suspect; and many Venezuelans believed that he had treacherous views against his country. His conduct multiplied the number of his enemies, and he became increasingly unpopular. He answered various interesting questions in a dry and short manner. He preferred English and French officers to his own countrymen—saying that these were ignorant brutes, unfit to command, and that they ought to learn the use of the musket, before they put on their epaulettes." Such views and actions would hardly endear the Precursor to someone as fiercely nationalistic and proud as Simón Bolívar.

The personal antipathies probably widened during Miranda's stay as a guest in Bolívar's home. The young man may have found Miranda's personal habits (such as picking his teeth) offensive. Much more serious, as the famous precursor of independence, the slow, deliberate, arrogant, overweight, white-haired old man threatened to reduce Bolívar's glory. Miranda had lived comfortably by his wits and charm during his forty years of absence from Venezuela. In his old age, he appeared badly out of step with the ardent, active young zealots of the Patriotic Society. Unhappily, such personal and political conflicts would mar the independence era throughout Spanish America and plague the new nations thereafter.

Del Toro and the vanguard left Caracas on July 15 and marched west without incident about fifty miles to Maracay. (Most distances given between towns are as the crow flies. In reality, particularly in mountainous regions, the actual distance traveled might easily be twice as much, owing to twisting, up-and-down roads and trails.) Twelve miles west of Maracay, the vanguard defeated Royalists at the pass of Mariara. The force then proceeded west twelve miles to Guacara and eight miles farther to the fortified hill of El Morro, which guarded the entrance to Valencia. Valencia, Maracay, and Caracas lie in a straight east-west line, Caracas seventy-six miles from Valencia.

Del Toro attacked the hill, but Royalists drove him away. He retired to Maracay on July 19. That day, Miranda left Caracas with about three thousand men. Two days later they arrived in Maracay, where Bolívar paused to establish a hospital. Two envoys arrived from Valencia to propose reconciliation, but Miranda rejected the offer. On July 22 he marched his army to Guacara, where he again received a delegation from Valencia. This time the delegates offered to surrender and Miranda accepted.

At dawn on July 23, Miranda moved his army, now numbering about four thousand, toward Valencia. Desperate Royalists there had armed and mobilized the city's pardos, the mixed or mulatto population. This action would precipitate dangerous racial schisms in Venezuela that magnified the social conflict and bloodshed in coming years. Spanish scientists Jorge Juan and Antonio de Ulloa, who visited the Americas in the 1740s, observed that "to be born in the Indies is sufficient for one to hate Europeans. This mutual antipathy reaches such an extreme that in some ways it exceeds the unbridled fury of two nations, completely at odds, who vituperate and insult each other." In a petition to the king, composed on November 28, 1796, the all-white city council of Caracas offered clear insights into the perilous state of Venezuela's race relations. Their protest also highlighted the already deep split between Spaniards and Creoles, a reality seriously underestimated by historians Salvador de Madariaga and Jaime E. Rodríguez O.

Objecting to the possibility of people of color purchasing honorary white status, the council complained that "this calamity stems precisely from ignorance on the part of European officials, who come here already prejudiced against the American-born whites and falsely informed concerning the real situation of the country. One of their errors is the policy of protection for mulattos and other infamous people, who exploit this favor by ingratiating themselves with officials." The council explained that "the pardos, mulattos, and zambos (all more or less the same in common usage) are descended from Negro slaves introduced into this country for labor on the land. . . . In addition to their infamous origin, pardos, mulattos, and zambos are also dishonored by their illegitimacy, for if they are not themselves bastards, their parents almost certainly are. . . . The ignorance of senior European officials and their prejudices against Americans are not the only defects of government. Another problem is the influence and power the pardos have acquired through the establishment of militias led by officers of their own class, a well-intentioned measure but one that experience shows will lead to the ruin of America."

Overall, whites made up less than one quarter of the population, with people of color (pardos, free blacks, runaway slaves, etc.) counting for well over half. Indians and slaves accounted for about 10 percent each. As the Patriots approached the city, however, the enemy unexpectedly opened fire, so Miranda's force attacked and overran the fortress of El Morro, pursuing fleeing Royalists back into the city. The attackers soon controlled the plaza, while the Royalists retired to two strong positions: the pardo barracks and the Convent of San Francisco. Miranda ordered Fernando del Toro and Bolívar to attack the positions with infantry, cavalry, and artillery. Intense fire greeted them, striking del Toro's horse and then the commander's legs. Heavy fire killed or wounded nearly all artillery officers and soldiers, while the cavalry and infantry suffered lighter casualties.

The cautious Miranda did not dare face the army of Spanish naval captain Domingo Monteverde. Instead, he withdrew to Guacara under cover of darkness. His July 24 report to the secretary of war glossed over the militia's heavy losses. He stated that "our losses in men have not been great but they have been heavy among the principal leaders. . . . I would be remiss in my duty if I did not name other officers who, while they did not shed their blood, offered it no less than the others for the glory of their country." Miranda commended several officers, including Bolívar and the marques del Toro. Bolívar had fought bravely and well, and his courage and ability on the battlefield contributed strongly to his rising political star. The young Creole seemed destined for glory.

During the next two weeks, Miranda's light troops blockaded Valencia. They stopped water, food, and reinforcements from entering the city. The Patriot army grew as aristocrats arrived with their laborers and foot soldiers. Whites in Valencia deserted the city to join Miranda's forces. Miranda's army, now numbering between three and four thousand, attacked the Royalists on the afternoon of August 12. The Patriots faced no more than seven hundred enemy troops. They fought until dark, held their positions overnight, and renewed the attack at dawn. At ten o'clock the enemy proposed surrender terms that Miranda rejected. Fighting continued until noon, when the pardos surrendered. Again, Miranda reported only a "small number of our dead and wounded in this vigorous action." Other sources disagreed, placing casualty figures much higher. By one estimate, the Patriots suffered eight hundred killed and fourteen hundred wounded.

Bolívar and other young Creoles could not fail to compare unfavorably the casualties under Miranda with those of the marques del Toro in his campaign against Coro. Del Toro had lost only 2 to 5 percent of his army. Congress apparently agreed and called Miranda back to Caracas to defend himself. The charming Miranda eloquently defended himself against all charges. Three charges related to having caused unnecessary bloodshed. Congress also charged that he had forced Valencians to contribute 200,000 pesos to his war chest without proper authorization. Miranda had also announced a number of times that he would not obey orders of Congress or the executive power. He intended to march with his army to Santa Fe de Bogotá and unite with Colombian revolutionary Antonio Nariño (1765–1823). A prosperous Bogotá merchant and journalist, he represented one of the many leaders of independence strongly influenced by Enlightenment ideals. A distinguished liberal intellectual and early proponent of independence like Miranda and Bolívar, Nariño had already faced the wrath of the Spanish Crown. In 1794, he secretly translated and distributed copies of *The Declaration of the Rights of Man,* earning him a prison sentence. Sentenced to ten years of hard labor at a Spanish prison in Africa, he escaped in Cádiz and then made his way to France and England. He returned two years later to New Granada to continue plotting and agitating. In a pointed comment to the viceroy, penned on July 30,

1797, he asserted that "the people are everywhere discontented." Like Miranda, he would be called the "Precursor" by his countrymen for his early support of independence.

Nariño suffered additional arrests and imprisonment, ending up in jail at Cartagena. There revolutionaries freed him, and, in September 1811, he made the 414-mile journey back to Bogotá to become president of Cundinamarca. An advocate of strong central government, Nariño often found himself in opposition to military and political leaders who favored a loose federation. Through power of his personality and the sword, he eventually defeated the Federalists, assumed dictatorial powers, and united Patriot forces in repelling the Royalists.

In July the Venezuelan Congress had offered land and opportunity to European immigrants. Venezuela already had received some French immigrants in 1810, following the British capture of the French Antilles. One of the first British subjects to respond was Gregor MacGregor (Hasbrouck spells the name McGregor), a Scot who appeared in Caracas with a letter of recommendation from the governor of Trinidad. In April 1819, MacGregor took Portobelo and held it for nearly three weeks before Spanish forces dislodged him. Over the years, many French, Scottish, and German immigrants served ably with the Patriot forces. Unemployed veterans from both sides of Waterloo would join ranks to aid the Latin American Patriots.

For his part, MacGregor would show flashes of bravery and initiative, fighting bravely and well. However, owing to later financial dealings, his legacy would smack more of opportunism and adventurism than commitment to the Patriot cause. In 1820, he planned a settlement that he called Poyais, which is on the Miskito Coast of the present-day province of Olancho in Honduras. He had operated in the area in league with the French privateer Louis Aury and other privateers. He paid a local potentate a pittance plus whiskey and baubles for a land grant of some seventy thousand square miles. With the backing of London financiers, but with no official government authority, MacGregor promoted his colonization scheme in Scotland. In February 1823, forty-three hapless colonists arrived at a deserted site that they named Saint Joseph's. A month later another 160 people joined them, but harsh conditions, disease, and conflict quickly doomed the colony. By mid-year, the survivors had retreated to neighboring British Honduras (Belize). MacGregor eventually served prison terms in England and France, cold comfort to the hundreds of lives lost or shattered by his schemes. After his checkered career, the charity of the Venezuelan nation provided him with a home in Caracas until his death on December 4, 1845.

During the last four months of 1811, Congress prepared Venezuela's first constitution. While critical of Miranda's military leadership, Bolívar strongly supported his political program. Despite their differences, Bolívar worked through the Patriotic Society to further Miranda's political agenda. Both sought to persuade Congress that Venezuela needed a strong centralized authority. To their dismay, however, the constitution, signed on December 21, 1811, did not reflect their thinking. It provided for a loose confederation of states and a triple executive. Like many new Latin American nations, Venezuela borrowed heavily from the Federalism embedded in the Constitution of the United States. Some sections from the U.S. document appear verbatim in the Venezuelan constitution. Unfortunately, Venezuela's resulting political structure functioned more like the equally ineffective U.S. Articles of Confederation.

Military conflict continued apace with the political wrangling. Royalists again entered the Orinoco in September 1811 with a fleet of twenty-six vessels. (The Orinoco River formed the southern boundary of the Patriot provinces of Cumaná, Barcelona, Caracas, and Barinas.) Aided by Royalists of Guayana Province, the fleet captured all Patriot ports and continued unchecked up the Apure tributary to attack San Fernando. There, however, all the manpower of Barinas Province awaited, and Patriots drove the Royalist fleet back to the Orinoco.

Patriot women as well as men wished to serve the new Republic. The women of Barinas sent a petition to the governing triumvirate, asserting that they could not remain indifferent to the fate of their country. Since all men had been sent to San Fernando, the women wondered why the government had not called on them to defend the province. "We are not afraid of the horrors of war, of cannon. . . . We wish to enlist and supplement the military forces which have departed for San Fernando."

Venezuela's new officials, however, had little interest in promoting equal rights for women. Their official reply read: "The Government is deeply grateful to members of the Fair Sex for this expression of their sentiments, born of a true love of the Patria which they can best serve by occupying themselves with those duties which are considered most useful." Despite this official sexist rebuff, women played a vital role later in Bolívar's armies and in his life.

North of Barinas, Royalists gained momentum in Coro and the western part of Caracas. Juan de los Reyes Vargas, an Indian leader, exercised almost messianic influence in Siquisique (in western Caracas Province). He urged that Royalists attack Siquisique. Domingo Monteverde, a brutal but daring marine captain, landed with 320 men and joined forces with Reyes Vargas. Monteverde and his well-armed force left Coro on March 10, 1812. Before he arrived at Siquisique, however, Reyes Vargas had surprised and imprisoned the Patriot troops. On March 23 their combined force of 720 men surprised Patriots at Carora. They captured more artillery, muskets, and munitions. Monteverde killed some of the inhabitants, imprisoned the rest, and sacked the city.

When Diego Jalón at Barquisimeto heard of the Carora defeat, he rounded up troops and prepared to march against Monteverde. Nature intervened in a deadly, dramatic fashion. On Thursday, March 26, 1812, a massive earthquake struck northeastern Venezuela. The quake swallowed up Jalón and his soldiers, along with their provisions, weapons, and munitions. Friends dug the injured Jalón from the ruins and carried him to San Carlos.

The devastating quake zigzagged through the heart of Patriot-held territory from Barquisimeto and Mérida in the west eastward through San Felipe, El Tocuyo, Caracas, and La Guaira. Thousands of people died in churches, crowded on Holy Thursday, and dozens of Patriot-held towns and cities lay in ruins. Four thousand people died in the churches of Caracas; ten thousand in the whole city; and another ten thousand in the surrounding environs. More of the injured later died.

Bolívar in Caracas during the earthquake of 1812.

The Royalist Díaz witnessed the destruction. He left his house in Caracas at four o'clock in the afternoon. As he neared the plaza of San Jacinto, the earth shook and rumbled. He ran toward the middle of the plaza. Balconies from the Post Office fell at his feet. He saw the church of San Jacinto collapse. As he stood alone in the midst of the ruins, he heard groans from the church. "I climbed over the ruins and entered. I saw about forty persons dead or dying under the rubble. I climbed out again, and I shall never forget that moment. On the top of the heap I found Don Simón Bolívar in his shirt sleeves. Utmost terror or desperation was painted on his face. He saw me and cried these impious and extravagant words: 'If nature oppose us, we will fight against her and force her to obey us.'"

Had this statement not been recorded by an avowed Royalist, it would be suspect. However, one must ask why would Díaz, who detested extremists, put such forceful, memorable words in Bolívar's mouth? The theatrics also fit the volatile Bolívar's personality. The square quickly filled with terrified survivors. Some priests thundered that the quake was the wrath of God. Indeed, the destruction seemed greatest in areas controlled by Patriot forces. Had God, as the priests argued, punished those who had rejected his anointed King Ferdinand VII? Bolívar would have none of this Royalist theology. He threatened one of the priests and forced him down from the table that served as his pulpit. Many terrified, penitent survivors, however, renewed their allegiance to God and king. A Royalist reaction swept the land. Bolívar's dream of independence lay shattered and dashed amidst the ruins.

Many members of Congress hurried from Valencia to Caracas to burn or bury their dead. Patriot leaders tried to help the destitute and counter the growing religious backlash. Meanwhile, Monteverde swept in unchallenged from the west. Patriot garrisons deserted en mass, and inhabitants rushed to welcome him. He moved south from Barquisimeto to Araura. He dispatched detachments southwest to Trujillo and Mérida while he marched southeast to San Carlos. Miguel Ustáriz and Miguel Carabaño tried to defend the city. Their cavalry, however, deserted to the enemy, so they fled to Valencia, taking the injured Jalón with them.

A second, even stronger quake shocked Venezuela on April 4, raising the total death toll beyond twenty thousand persons. Most of the damaged buildings would have to wait fifty years for repair, giving Caracas a forlorn, desolate air for decades. The rump Congress relinquished full powers to the triumvirate and adjourned to face the new calamity. On April 23 the triumvirate named Miranda *generalísimo*, subject to no law except the supreme one of saving the Republic. Miranda traveled east to La Victoria, where he established headquarters in La Trinidad, the marques de Casa León's fine villa.

The U.S. Congress, in a gesture both humanitarian and self-interested, appropriated fifty thousand dollars for relief to the earthquake victims. As Tennessee congressman John Rhea explained, the interests of the United States "required them to cultivate amity and conciliate the South American provinces." All or most of the provisions, including much-needed flour, fell into Royalist hands, however, netting them a handsome profit and doing nothing to help the needy victims.

Monteverde capitalized on the natural disaster and by April controlled the entire west of the nation. The triumvirate fled from Valencia to La Victoria in the face of his advance. Miranda rode toward Caracas to secure money and troops. On the way he stopped at San Mateo, where he appointed Bolívar civil and military governor of Puerto Cabello and subsecretary of its revenues. This appointment forced Bolívar to live in the town, further marginalizing him from the major theaters of operation.

Republicans clung to the fine city of Puerto Cabello, their most important seaport, lying on the north coast directly north of Valencia. Thanks to its well-protected, deep-water harbor, the town flourished during the colonial era as a center for smuggling. According to local legend (probably apocryphal), it received the name *Cabello* (hair), because a single hair could hold a moored vessel to the dock in the smooth-as-glass harbor. Its fort, San Felipe, held many important Royalist prisoners. It also contained most of the state's store of weapons and munitions. Bolívar would have preferred action at the front against Monteverde, but the wily old Miranda did not want competition in that theater. Bolívar reluctantly accepted the appointment and proceeded to Puerto Cabello, unaware of the Royalist intrigue there.

Monteverde entered Valencia in triumph May 3. The next day Bolívar and his escort arrived at Puerto Cabello. The port itself lies on a strait between the town and a narrow peninsula that buffers the town from the Golfo Triste (Sad Gulf) in the Caribbean. This peninsula, shaped like a seven, stretches east about three-fifths of a mile and then turns south to connect with the continent and form part of the west coast of Borburata Bay. Fort San Felipe on the western tip of the peninsula protected the town and served as a prison for the most dangerous enemies of the Republic. Col. Ramón Aymerich had been commander of San Felipe for many years.

A sturdy wall separated the town from Corito, a battery on the northwest corner, running down the west side and across the south, but not on the east or bay side. Bolívar tended to his duties from an inn. He positioned José

Mires and Miguel Carabaño to defend Corito and the wall. Members of the town council and several garrison officers kept Bolívar busy with meetings where they nullified his defense measures. On June 29 Bolívar declared that, owing to the lack of food, all women, old men, children, and invalids must leave town.

Alas for the Patriots, the lack of professionalism among the officer corps again heralded disaster. The next morning Aymerich gave command of Fort San Felipe to Francisco Fernández Vinoni and left to visit his fiancé in town. The treasonous subordinate and his hundred-man garrison released and armed the prisoners. Sailors from vessels in the harbor and men from town increased Vinoni's fighting force to two hundred men. At Corito, Mires heard strange noises coming from the fort. He rowed out in a small boat to investigate. Vinoni yelled at him, "Surrender the city or I will bombard it."

Mires returned to Corito and sent Carabaño to warn Bolívar. A moment later Vinoni fired on the town. Mires answered with his small cannon. Men on the wall peppered the fort with musket shot. Bolívar offered to pardon the "prisoners, officers, corporals, and soldiers who have taken possession of San Felipe" if they surrendered within an hour.

Patriot artillery and muskets fell silent while a messenger rowed to the fortress and delivered the note. Vinoni replied: "The flag of our king, Ferdinand VII, now flies over this fort, and his faithful vassals will defend it to the last drop of blood." He ordered Bolívar, Jalón, and Carabaño to come to the fort to discuss their surrender. Garcés, a Royalist sympathizer, commanded at Solano, a lookout halfway up the mountain behind Puerto Cabello. In the crossfire between Patriots and Royalists, Solano's guns had fired harmlessly in the water instead of hitting San Felipe. Bolívar knew that Garcés was popular with the pardos under his command. He feared that the Royalist might fire on the town if he tried to remove him. At 3 A.M. the next morning, a distraught Bolívar sent a warning and a plea for help to Miranda. "A Venezuelan unworthy of the name has taken possession of San Felipe with the help of prisoners, and is at this moment firing on the city. Nearly all our food and munitions are in the fortress. Royalists have all the vessels that were in the harbor except for our *Zeloso* [a schooner] which escaped. Monteverde is sure to attack. He cannot have failed to hear the cannon. If you do not attack the enemy immediately in the rear, this position is lost. I shall hold out as long as possible."

Instead of reinforcements, Bolívar got even more problems. His outpost of 120 men on the mountain road to Valencia deserted to Monteverde. On July 4 Royalist troops encountered and defeated a force led by Mires who managed to escape to Bolívar. Royalists proceeded to the San Esteban River and cut off the only source of Puerto Cabello's water supply. The next day, Bolívar sent Mires, Jalón, and Montilla with two hundred troops, nearly his entire force, to attack the Royalists. During the half-hour battle, most of the Patriot troops deserted; Jalón was surrounded and captured. Bolívar felt especially anguished by Jalón's loss: "he is worth an entire army." Mires, Montilla, and seven men escaped. The young Bolívar would not forget Vinoni's treachery; he would exact his revenge when the fortunes of war turned against the Royalists.

The guns of San Felipe bombarded the town daily, forcing the inhabitants to flee. On July 6 Bolívar and a few of his men escaped eastward behind the city to the *Zeloso* in Borburata Bay and sailed to La Guaira. The exhausted Bolívar returned to Caracas and poured out his despair over his first military defeat to Miranda:

> My General: Having exhausted all my physical and moral strength, where shall I find courage to take up my pen and write you now that the stronghold of Puerto Cabello has fallen out of my hands? Because of this action, my spirit is crushed much more than all of the province.
>
> General, my spirits are so depressed that I do not feel that I have the courage to command a single soldier. My vanity forced me to believe that my desire to succeed and my burning zeal for my country would serve to replace the talents which I lacked as a commander. I therefore beg you, either place me under the orders of an officer of the lowest rank, or grant me several days to compose myself and to recover the confidence that I lost in losing Puerto Cabello. To this should be added the state of my physical health, for, after thirteen sleepless nights and extreme distress, I find myself almost in a state of [mental] collapse.

The unfortunate Miranda was heading toward his own personal and political tragedy. On May 1 he left Caracas, bound for Valencia. He headed the vanguard of an army that eventually numbered five thousand troops, but many of them were mere teenagers. On May 3 cheers from the inhabitants of Valencia greeted Monteverde. Five days later, Miranda's forces stood ten miles from Valencia. He issued a long proclamation asking the citizens of Valencia to expel Monteverde and reunite with the people of Caracas. Miranda dispatched an advance force to retake Valencia. Three miles from Valencia, the troops deserted and joined Monteverde. Miranda retired eastward with his army and camped at Maracay, twenty-seven miles from Valencia.

On May 18 and 19 Miranda met with the three presidents. Faced with the bleak military situation, they summarily swept away any constitutional vestiges and designated Miranda dictator. Gregor MacGregor, Baron Schombourg, and other European officers drilled the troops. Miranda busied himself writing proclamations, army regulations, letters to British officials in the Caribbean and England, and instructions for diplomatic agents to Bogotá, the United States, France, and England. In a wordy proclamation dated May 21, Miranda declared that he would reorganize and strengthen his army before taking the offensive. This unwise delay gave Monteverde time to occupy the twenty-seven-mile area between Valencia and Maracay.

On the night of June 11–12, Monteverde moved his force to heights that outflanked Miranda's right side, thus forcing Miranda to withdraw eastward fifteen miles to La Victoria. The Precursor then ordered the troops to disarm and clean their guns. Meanwhile, he established his headquarters in Casa León's villa, where he continued his incessant writing. Only MacGregor and his cavalry remained on the alert to contain Monteverde.

Royalist forces ranged the llanos of Caracas, killing Patriots and freeing prisoners. One of those freed, José Tomás Boves (1782–1814), quickly formed his own army of runaway slaves and *llaneros,* the rugged, independent horsemen of the plains. He would become one of the most fierce and terrible of the Royalist avengers. Boves, Eusebio Antoñanzas, and Antonio Zuazola gained control of the vital tropical plains, or *llanos.* The plain covers some 98,000 square miles of eastern Colombia and about 120,000 square miles of adjoining Venezuela. Their victories gave Royalists the bounty of the plains: vast herds of cattle (food), horses (transportation), and mules (money). The latter could be sold at good prices in the Caribbean islands.

Scottish aficionado of equestrian life Robert Bontine Cunninghame Graham left a vivid portrait of the llanos: "A very sea of grass and sky, sunscourged and hostile to mankind. The rivers, full of electric eels, and of caribes, those most ravenous of fish, more terrible than even the great alligators that lie like logs upon the sandbanks or the inert and pulpy rays, with their mortiferous barbed spike, are still more hostile than the land."

The llanos is a vast tropical plain occupying the interior of Colombia and Venezuela. Crisscrossed by many rivers, streams, and swamps, the llanos is also shrouded by forests of dense trees and shrubs *(matas).* To the north and west the mighty Andes mountains rise and bound the plains. Tropical rain forests along the Guaviare and Amazon Rivers bound it to the south. The lower Orinoco River and the Guiana Highlands form the eastern boundary of the llanos.

Two radically different seasons, both extreme and inhospitable, alternate, a dry summer (*verano,* October–March) and a rainy winter (*invierno,* April–September). Thus people and animals must cope with either drought conditions and high temperatures or torrential downpours and mass flooding. The area averages about forty-seven inches of rainfall per year, but virtually all the rain falls within a six-month period. The torrential rains inundate vast low-lying areas that become nearly impassable. The tropical climate of the llanos made infection and disease constant threats to soldiers and their animals. The many rivers held their own dangers, including voracious piranhas, large crocodiles, and electric eels.

Much of the independence fighting occurred in the llanos, sparked by the need to have access to livestock, and the region suffered grave devastation. The number of cattle in the Venezuelan llanos fell from about 4.5 million in 1812 to a quarter of a million a decade later. Between 1814 and 1820 on the Colombian llanos of Casanare, the estimated number of cattle dropped from 273,000 to 50,000, and horses, from 30,000 to 4,000.

Fighting in this tortuous land, Boves and other caudillos headed armies of llaneros. Spaniards and Creoles had raised cattle and horses in the llanos since the mid-sixteenth century. By 1665 hides ranked first among Venezuela's exports. Franciscan and Capuchin priests had established mission villages in the llanos by the mid-seventeenth century. The latter, an autonomous branch of the Franciscans, took their name from the long, pointed hood (in Spanish, *capucha*) they wore as part of the order's habit. The missions generated profits and provided a place for training and indoctrinating Indians. Aside from landowners and priests, most people living in the llanos were nonwhite, Indian, mestizo, black, or mulatto.

As with all cowhands, the llanero always carried a knife or machete. Diplomat Robert Ker Porter termed the knife "an appendage no llanero ever is without, and which amongst the poorest classes, answers likewise for a spear head." Laws in some parts of Venezuela long prohibited llaneros from wearing their shirts outside their pants. Officials imposed this odd dress code to prevent llaneros from hiding their dangerous knives.

Like cowboys everywhere, the llanero subsisted on a rather meager diet. Cunninghame Graham listed the essentials of food and equipment: "Beef is the staple, almost the only food of the Llanero; his ordinary drink is the muddy water of the neighboring stream or the lagoon. His luxuries, coffee, and the rough brown sugar full of lye, known as Panela; his bed a hammock, that he carried rolled up, behind his saddle; his pride, his horse, the companion of his dangers and his toil, sober and hardy as himself."

Llaneros often rode half naked and barefoot in the tropical heat. All carried the indispensable poncho, or *cobija*, well adapted to the vicissitudes of the tropical plains. Venezuelan writer Ramón Páez (son of caudillo José Antonio) described the garment and its utility: "It is fully six feet square, with a hole in the centre to admit the head, and its office is twofold, viz., to protect the rider and his cumbrous equipment from the heavy showers and dews of the tropics, and to spread under him when there is no convenience for slinging the hammock. It also serves as a protection from the scorching rays of the sun, experience having taught its wearer that a thick woolen covering keeps the body moist and cool by day, and warm by night."

English visitor Maj. George Flinter described the llanero technique of wild-cattle hunting, which he observed in 1819. The llanero "at full speed, hamstrings the animal in both legs, which brings it immediately to the ground; he then alights, and, with the point of his spear, strikes the bull in the nape of the neck. . . . He next skins it, takes out the fat, and, after having cut up the flesh in long pieces, brings it to the *hato* [ranch], where it is sprinkled with salt, and hung up to dry in the sun." Needless to say, these riding and killing skills transferred readily into warfare.

As the Patriot infantry sat cleaning their weapons, Monteverde attacked La Victoria on June 20. MacGregor's furious cavalry counterattack forced the enemy to flee in panic, yet the inert Miranda gave no orders. His infantry followed MacGregor, loading their muskets on the run, while the artillery moved its weapons into position. Finally, Miranda, commanding the lancers, threw himself into the thick of the fray. José de Austria, a twenty-year-old second lieutenant, recounted the disappointment of the partial victory: "All advanced, a heroic united front. The Royalists scattered in shameful flight. In that victorious moment everyone yelled to pursue the enemy and complete the splendid triumph; but Miranda, deaf to the clamor, ordered troops to return to their quarters. The exhilaration of having defeated Monteverde and his best troops turned to dismay and disgust."

Miranda enjoyed a two-to-one troop advantage over his enemy. Had he unleashed his youthful horde, they could have annihilated Monteverde's army. As was the custom, surviving Royalist troops would have deserted to the victors. Switching sides was how troops and civilians survived the terrible, bloody independence wars. Miranda got yet another chance to destroy the Royalists. Monteverde and Antoñanzas together attacked La Victoria at dawn on June 29. After a very gory daylong battle, the remnants of the Royalist army fled. Officers pleaded with Miranda to let them move the Patriot army on the double-quick to destroy Monteverde. Paying no attention, Miranda ordered his troops back to their former positions at La Victoria. Another Patriot opportunity squandered!

Meanwhile, Vinoni bombarded Bolívar in Puerto Cabello. Bolívar's early-morning note of July 1 (requesting immediate relief) reached Miranda on the night of July 5 as Miranda and a hundred guests celebrated the anniversary of Venezuela's declaration of independence. Miranda read it and cried: "Venezuela is stabbed in the heart. Yesterday Monteverde had no powder, no lead, no muskets; today he has forty tons of powder, lead in abundance, and three thousand muskets! Bolívar told me that the Royalists were attacking. By this time they should be in possession of everything."

According to José de Austria, after the banquet Miranda made a quick trip to Caracas. During his absence, a movement to depose him spread in the army. Commandant Francisco de Paula Tinoco, Colonel Santineli, and Baron Schombourg numbered among the chief conspirators. Cornelio Mota, a pardo whom Miranda had promoted to captain, was to seize him as he returned to camp. Mota failed to take him, however, and Miranda became aware of his danger. He rounded up the ringleaders and imprisoned them; however, he could not suppress the growing anger and impatience directed against him.

Miranda made many political and military errors. He had offered freedom to slaves who would serve ten years in the Patriot army. However, this measure only alienated slaveholders, many of them Creoles who feared the loss of their property. His person and fame threatened, lacking public support, fearful of further bloodshed, irritated by defections, and fatigued in spirit, Miranda saw his dream and glory fading. Revolution in practice had proved much more trying than in theory. The Precursor could never be the Liberator, but he still ruled as dictator of Venezuela. Grateful Venezuelans would bestow the latter title on Bolívar following the great victories of his so-called Admirable Campaign in 1813.

Miranda summoned his advisors to a meeting on July 12 and reviewed the political and military situation. Nothing remained of the Republic except the thin corridor from La Victoria to Caracas and La Guaira. These cities, however, faced starvation because Royalists had cut off all meat supplies from the llanos. Towns and cities in the northeastern provinces of Cumaná, Barcelona, and Margarita began to declare for Ferdinand in June. They allowed very little food to enter Caracas from the east. All members of the council agreed that Miranda should negotiate surrender terms with Monteverde.

Miranda sent two commissioners to negotiate the surrender at San Mateo. He ordered Casa León to secure an escape route for him. Before leaving Caracas, Casa León called on Antoine Leleux (Miranda's trusted aide-de-camp and possibly his son) and found him packing Miranda's books and other property. Leleux had already placed most of Miranda's papers in the custody of the military commander in La Guaira, Manuel María de las Casas. The commander readied the papers for shipment to the English firm of Robertson and Belt in Curaçao.

Casa León wrote reports to Miranda on July 15 and 16, 1812, and then went down to the port of La Guaira. He ordered Las Casas to prepare the *Zeloso* and three gunboats for immediate departure. Casa León, minister of finance, ordered a customs official to deliver twenty-two thousand pesos in hard money to the English merchant George Robertson (of Robertson and Belt). Casa León returned to Miranda at La Victoria.

On July 22 Miranda sent Casa León to complete surrender terms with Monteverde. The Royalist leader recognized Casa León's peculiar genius and appointed him intendant or fiscal administrator of Royalist Venezuela. Miranda also closed the port of La Guaira and, on July 26, left La Victoria for Caracas. He had not taken any of the officers into his confidence. They knew of the negotiations, but they did not know the terms. Was Miranda running away?

At a council of war, Miranda's officers refused to accept the surrender. They also refused to hand over La Victoria and its supplies to the enemy. They elected Juan Pablo Ayala commander-in-chief and broke into the supply depots. Taking all the arms and supplies their troops could carry, they departed and camped outside Caracas at Antimano on July 27.

Miranda's surrender shocked and appalled Bolívar and many other supporters of independence. On November 16, 1812, Alexander Scott, special agent of the United States, sent a terse, condemnatory assessment to the State Department: "Miranda by a shameful and treacherous capitulation surrendered the liberties of his country. Whether he was an agent of the British Government as he now states, or whether this conduct resulted from a base and cowardly heart, I cannot decide." The secrecy of the negotiations, Miranda's presence in Caracas, and the lack of treaty ratification troubled many. Royalists as well as Patriots fled to La Guaira to escape Monteverde, and Bolívar fled with them. To their horror, they found the port closed. Meanwhile, Monteverde had entered La Victoria, empty of troops and supplies. He pursued the Patriot troops at Antimano, who scattered in retreat. On July 30 Patriot officers reported to Miranda, in Caracas, who told them simply: "You must be tired after all your exertions. Go get some rest."

Miranda left for La Guaira, passing frightened fugitives who clogged the road. Night had fallen before Miranda arrived at the home of his protégé, Las Casas. Miranda immediately opened the port. Capt. Henry Haynes had "opportunely" arrived on the *Sapphire*. Miranda's possessions were already on board, as was George Robertson with the twenty-two thousand pesos from Venezuela's treasury.

La Casas served supper to a motley array of guests, including Bolívar, José Mires, Tomás Montilla, Miguel Carabaño, Captain Haynes, and Pedro Gual (1783–1862). The latter, who would go on to a distinguished career in pubic service, worked as Miranda's private secretary. He had already figured prominently in the Patriot Society, presiding on three occasions. The hour was late when Haynes rose to leave and urged Miranda to board the *Sapphire* immediately. "Come on board with me tonight. The land breeze will soon arise and you will be cool and comfortable. Your books and papers are already there."

Bolívar and others assured Miranda that the land breeze would not arise until ten o'clock the next morning. Miranda hesitated and then decided to stay the night in La Guaira and embark in the morning. A fateful and fatal decision! Haynes departed. Miranda asked to be excused and retired to the room set aside for him. Miranda's dissident officers convened a court-martial. Their deliberations complete, they awakened Miranda and told him he was a prisoner. Some of the dissidents, including the enraged Bolívar, wanted to shoot Miranda as a traitor. Miranda eyed each man who had judged him and muttered: "Slander! Slander! [*bochinche*] These people are only capable of stirring up slander!" Before dawn on the morning of July 31, they escorted Miranda up the steep hill to Fort San Carlos, where they left him in chains, awaiting the Spanish forces.

The horrific act of Patriot officers turning their commander over to the enemy has inspired long, heated debate. Hispanophiles, like Salvador de Madariaga and Jaime E. Rodríguez O., insist that by turning on Miranda, Bolívar also turned on the independence movement. Seeking to save his family fortune and his own skin, goes the argument, Bolívar sought to ingratiate himself to Monteverde by delivering up the big prize: Miranda. According to this version, Bolívar planned to join Wellesley's English troops in Europe and to fight against French forces occupying liberal Spain.

Without question, the shock of losing Puerto Cabello and of then capitulating to the Spanish shook young Bolívar badly. Denial, self-doubt, displaced anger, shame—many emotions must have coursed through his veins. However, given both previous and subsequent actions, it is highly doubtful that

Bolívar was the self-interested quitter that Madariaga and Rodríguez would have us believe. By the end of his life, he sacrificed his entire personal fortune to the Patriot cause. He always followed his repeated defeats and disasters with renewed, resolute action. That perseverance and his ability to inspire loyalty explain much of his success. While his moods could swing wildly from elation to dejection, his determination seldom wavered for long. Miranda might temporize and compromise with the enemy; Bolívar never!

Hispanophiles also underestimate the rift, personal and ideological, that had developed between Bolívar and Miranda. Miranda may have genuinely accepted peaceful coexistence with a liberal Spanish monarchy as preferable to continued savage, internecine violence. Bolívar could not and did not. He would soon declare "war to the death" on all Spaniards who opposed independence, hardly the act of a man reconciled to Spanish liberalism.

Monteverde's troops began entering La Guaira that morning, and Las Casas received orders to close the port. Refugees had already boarded the *Zeloso* and other vessels. Cortés Madariaga, Nicolás Briceño, Yanes, and a hundred Frenchmen, including Pierre Labatut (or Labatud), crowded onto the *Matilda,* a brig that had brought flour from the United States. At ten o'clock the *Sapphire* raised anchor and sailed with MacGregor and other passengers onboard. The warship sailed to Curaçao some 170 miles to the northwest, where officials itemized Miranda's possessions and sent them to London. George Robertson kept the twenty-two thousand pesos, saying that the Venezuelan government owed his firm more than that amount.

The *Matilda* and other vessels started to follow, but guns from La Guaira fired at them immediately. Shots destroyed the cabin of the *Matilda* and sank another vessel. Capt. Alexander Chataing of the *Matilda* transferred Cortés Madariaga, Briceño, and Yanes to another merchant vessel from the United States. Contrary currents and calm winds prevented its escape. Finally, at three o'clock in the afternoon a strong breeze began to blow. When Chataing gave the signal, his crew was to raise anchor, move the *Matilda* beyond cannon shot, and wait for him. If he failed to return that night, they were to sail for Curaçao.

Pierre Labatut saw Chataing's signal, which he gave as soon as he reached the wharf. Within minutes the *Matilda* had moved beyond danger. Two other vessels followed her to safety. That night Chataing returned, and the three vessels arrived at Curaçao four days later. Governor Hodgson confiscated the *Matilda* because it lacked proper papers and because England and the United States were at war. Labatut, Chataing, and other French refugees suffered such bad treatment that they left for Cartagena.

Bolívar managed to escape from La Guaira to Caracas, where antihero Casa León sheltered him for nearly a month. Casa León and Royalist Francisco de Iturbe, a Spaniard and longtime friend of Bolívar's family, obtained a passport for Bolívar. Monteverde issued a pass, but an intemperate outburst from Bolívar prompted him to revoke it. Iturbe pleaded again and Monteverde relented. Given the crushing defeat he had suffered at Puerto Cabello, Monteverde likely saw little threat in the brash, impudent, young Creole. His fateful decision let Bolívar continue toward his destiny as the Liberator of South America. On August 27, he sailed from La Guaira on a Spanish schooner and arrived in Curaçao five days later.

Writing to Iturbe on September 10, Bolívar complained: "My reception was miserable, for no sooner had I arrived than my baggage was confiscated for two very strange reasons: first, because it was in the same house as Miranda's possessions; and second, because the *Zeloso* had contracted debts which I must now pay because I was commandant at Puerto Cabello when the debts were contracted." Bolívar spent six humiliating weeks on the island. Penniless, he lived on the charity of others until the end of October. He finally secured a one-thousand-peso loan and sailed to Cartagena accompanied by a number of other refugees.

The city of Cartagena lies on the Caribbean coast of New Granada (today Colombia), some sixty-two miles southwest of Barranquilla. A major colonial shipping point, the walled city enjoyed the strongest fortifications in the Western Hemisphere. Founded in 1553, the city's protection included the formidable castle of San Felipe de Barajas. The collapse of the colonial fleet system left the city a parasite that could not support itself. Grain from savannas of the Río Sinú (near the boundary with Panama) and meat from other valleys fed its inhabitants. Money from Quito and Santa Fe de Bogotá (capital of Santa Fe Province and of New Granada) maintained its garrison and navy.

Creoles there wanted trade not only with Spain but also with other nations. On May 22, 1810, a Creole junta ousted Spanish officials and declared the port open to all ships. Cartagena followed the example of Caracas in breaking ties with Spain on November 11, 1811. The newly declared Republic of Cartagena would last only five years, and the proud city would pay for its temerity. Spanish forces under Gen. Pablo Morillo retook it after a four-month siege. Many residents died of disease and starvation. In a desperate attempt to escape Spanish rule, Cartagena even declared itself a part of the British Empire. British policy, however, tried to steer a path of technical neutrality and ignored the proclamation.

Fortifications in Cartagena, Colombia. Photograph by Ralph Blessing

The United States also took a cautious interest in the portentous events unfolding in Venezuela. On May 14, 1812, Secretary of State James Monroe instructed Alexander Scott on his duties in Caracas. Monroe ordered the U.S. agent to examine "the state of the public mind in the Provinces of Venezuela, and in all the adjoining Provinces of Spain; their competence to self-government; state of political and other intelligence; their relations with each other; the spirit which prevails generally among them as to independence; their disposition towards the United States, towards Old Spain, England, and France; in the case of their final dismemberment from the parent country, what bond will hereafter exist between them; what form it will take; how many confederations will probably be formed, and what species of internal government is likely to prevail." Alas, neither agent Scott nor anyone else would have answers to these many questions for a long time to come.

Other Spanish American towns also ousted their Spanish officials. On July 20 and 21, a Creole junta in Santa Fe de Bogotá arrested the viceroy of New Granada and his wife and the next month sent them back to Spain. The Santa Fe de Bogotá junta considered itself supreme over all of New Granada. Some provinces and cities recognized its leadership, but not Cartagena. Its junta declared Cartagena's independence from Spain and Santa Fe de Bogotá on November 11, 1811. Soon thereafter Manuel Rodríguez, president of the Republic of Cartagena, solved the city's supply problem. He made Cartagena a privateer base and issued letters of marque at a time when no other bases were available in the Caribbean. U.S. privateers from the Gulf Coast of Louisiana to Charleston and Baltimore soon sent prizes with food, money, and war materiel to Cartagena. Cartagena needed experienced officers to defend her left flank against Royalist Panama and her right flank against Royalist Santa Marta.

Bolívar, although ignored during most of November and December 1812, was not idle. He had time to assess Spain and her American colonies. He concluded that little Spain, half as large as Venezuela, would reconquer all her rebellious colonies unless the provinces of New Granada stopped fighting each other. They had to unite to defeat Monteverde.

Armies from Spain had not threatened New Granada's independence because, in the age of sail, troops from Spain landed first on Venezuela's coast. Monteverde had debarked at Royalist Coro in March of 1812. He had driven to Caracas and overthrown the Republic of Venezuela in less than five months. His army moved through Trujillo toward Mérida. He planned to continue westward and invade New Granada at Cúcuta. He would then march southwest to attack Tunja, meeting site of the Congress of the Federation of United

Provinces of New Granada. The government at Santa Fe de Bogotá, one hundred miles southwest of Tunja, sent an army to compel the congress there to recognize its authority. The political power struggle resulted in a civil war that again threatened the Patriot cause.

In response to the political ferment, Bolívar wrote a long memorial to the citizens of New Granada. A pamphlet signed on December 15, 1812, the memorial became known as Bolívar's Cartagena Manifesto. Venezuela, in Bolívar's view, had committed a fatal error in adopting a weak, federal political organization. Owing to weak government, "every conspiracy was followed by acquittal; and every acquittal by another conspiracy, which again brought acquittal." However, Bolívar's belief in strong, central government and a powerful executive would give rise to charges of dictatorial ambitions. Divisions that would plague Latin America longer after independence already dogged Bolívar's efforts. Besides the lack of unity and the centrifugal forces tearing apart the government, Venezuela faced the reality of Latin America's deep racial divisions. The nonwhite masses did not share the Enlightenment values of their white Creole masters. Thus Royalists recruited mestizos, blacks, and mulattos more effectively than did the Patriots.

Infighting between city, state, and national authorities brought stalemate and dissipated funds and energy. Given the imminent danger from Royalists, Bolívar argued for strong, effective government. His views also provided insight into why he later faced charges of dictatorial rule. "It is essential that a government mold itself, so to speak, to the nature of the circumstances, the times, and the men that comprise it. If these factors are prosperity and peace, the government should be mild and protecting; but if they are turbulence and disaster, it should be stern and arm itself with firmness that matches the dangers, without regard for laws or constitutions until happiness and peace be reestablished."

Bolívar closed by arguing that the time had come for an offensive from New Granada to liberate Venezuela. "The honor of New Granada imperiously demands that she teach these audacious invaders a lesson, by pursuing them to their last entrenchments." Patriot factionalism and regionalism persisted, giving the Royalists their opportunity to strike back at a divided enemy. Venezuelans accurately refer to their first republic as the *patria boba*, the foolish fatherland. It would not be the last display of political foolishness in the region. The experience also strengthened Bolívar's belief that the country needed a strong, central government, presided over by a strong president, to survive.

CHAPTER 5

Victories from Mompox to Araure,

1812–13

After Bolívar's Cartagena Manifesto appeared in print, Rodríguez Torices, president of the Republic of Cartagena, read it and conferred with Labatut, a French adventurer who, thanks to a few quick victories, commanded the Magdalena front against Royalist Santa Marta. Labatut then appointed Bolívar commander of the seventy-man garrison at Barrancas on the left bank near the mouth of the Magdalena River, where, he hoped, Bolívar would be forgotten.

The Magdalena marked the boundary between the provinces of Cartagena and Santa Marta and served as the main highway between the Republic of Cartagena on the coast and the Federation of United Provinces, with its capital at Tunja. Santa Martans had cut communications between Cartagena and the interior at Tenerife, not far upriver from Barrancas, and at small towns farther up the river. Local militia and a few Spanish troops from Cuba garrisoned these towns. These thinly defended towns offered Bolívar an excellent place to test his Cartagena Manifesto.

Despite his humble posting, Bolívar as usual remained very active in love and war. Anita Lenoit, a pretty young French woman in Barrancas, caught Bolívar's eye as he enlisted volunteers, and they became lovers. Bolívar thought he had left her behind when he embarked with two hundred volunteers and sailed south to Tenerife on Santa Marta's side of the river, but she followed him. Bolívar took the Royalists in Tenerife completely by surprise.

They fled north overland to Santa Marta without exchanging a shot, leaving behind boats and military stores. Bolívar occupied the town on December 24. A day or so later, he sent Anita home, promising to return. He then sailed up the Magdalena, taking Royalist villages on the Santa Marta side and freeing Patriot villages on the western side. He entered Mompox (also spelled Mompós), on Cartagena's side of the river, on December 27.

Patriots, no longer isolated from the coast, received him with great joy and gave Bolívar military command of the district. The victory emboldened the young Patriot. "I was born in Caracas," Bolívar noted later, "but my fame was born in Mompox." On December 29, Bolívar embarked five hundred troops and continued his ascent of the Magdalena. His forces entered Banco on New Year's Day 1813. Spaniards had fled the town a few hours before his arrival.

Bolívar pursued the Royalists, who retreated in a northeasterly direction. He defeated them at Chiriguaná, returned to the river, sailed on, and took Tamalameque by surprise. Continuing south, he left the river at the port of Ocaña and marched eastward to the town. On January 8, 1813, he reported to the secretary of the sovereign congress in Tunja, with justifiable pride, that he had opened the Magdalena to navigation in just fifteen days. Congress soon invited Bolívar to open the road to San José de Cúcuta, the natural entry route into Venezuela.

The Republic of Cartagena had benefited greatly from the opening of the Magdalena. President Rodríguez Torices granted Bolívar permission to move against Cúcuta. On February 9, 1813, his advance guard left Ocaña. Six days later Bolívar followed with the rest of his army, which now totaled four hundred troops. Based on earlier records, Bolívar's aide and confidant Daniel Florencio O'Leary (1801–54) would later describe the difficult route. "Thirty miles from Ocaña the ascent begins abruptly, and this spur of the great cordillera presents extremely hard going, made even worse by the frequent storms. All the soldiers were from the burning hot climate of Cartagena and Mompox, and their sufferings were intensified because they were not used to the cold and penetrating mountain air. There were so many hardships, that only Bolívar's inspiring leadership kept them plodding along." Nature often proved as formidable an adversary as the Royalists.

Born in Cork, Ireland, O'Leary served Bolívar faithfully until the Venezuelan's death. In 1817, at just sixteen, the Irishman arrived with other British volunteers to fight for independence. Within a year he gained Bolívar's confidence to the point where he became part of his Honor Guard. In 1820, O'Leary became Bolívar's aide-de-camp, caring for his letters and records and remaining nearly indispensable. He later served as secretary to Antonio José de Sucre, another close ally of Bolívar. After independence was gained, O'Leary returned to Europe and served in the British diplomatic corps, posting to Caracas in 1841 and Bogotá in 1843. The Irishman cared well for Bolívar's papers, and his son, Simón Bolívar O'Leary, later saw to the publication of those voluminous records.

Their passage through the canyon trails had been difficult enough, but as they climbed, the unaccustomed cold and penetrating mountain air inflicted intense suffering. It would not be the last time that the mountain air of the Andes would chill the Patriots to the quick. Bolívar kept them moving and, on the night of February 21, they approached the heights of La Aguada. An outpost of one hundred men guarded the pass to Salazar, San Cayetano, and Cúcuta. Bolívar used a spy to deceive the enemy into believing that in the morning he would attack from the rear and Colonel Manuel del Castillo in the front.

Bolívar again used the element of surprise to drive frightened Royalists into retreat. They fled to Salazar, where Bolívar routed them and occupied the town. He then moved to San Cayetano, where Castillo joined him with 126 men, swelling the Patriot army to about five hundred men. He crossed the Zulia River on the afternoon of February 27 and marched against San José de Cúcuta the next morning. In a feinting maneuver, Bolívar initially attacked with but a small force, holding most of his troops in reserve. Ramón Correa countered the small threat outside the city with eight hundred men, attempting to surround and destroy them, but Bolívar then deployed his main force from the nearby hills. Correa desperately moved his men up the rocky slopes to the left of the rebels, which left Bolívar's troops exposed on the open plain below. Faced with mounting casualties, Bolívar ordered his cousin, Col. José Félix Ribas, on what appeared to be a suicidal bayonet charge up the hill against the Royalists. Against great odds, Ribas prevailed and the Royalists fled in several directions. They abandoned two four-pounders, two stone mortars, 150 muskets, and 4,500 cartridges. The Patriots also captured merchandise sent by merchants from two hundred miles away in Maracaibo to Cúcuta for sale in Royalist New Granada. Bolívar had won his first great victory!

The next morning (March 1), Bolívar pressed across the Táchira River to the small Venezuelan town of San Antonio. Here, in an act repeated many times, he praised his tough, successful troops: "Your liberating arms have entered Venezuela. In less than two months you have concluded two campaigns and commenced a third which begins here. The splendor of your invincible arms will cause Spanish armies to disappear from Venezuela as the darkness is dissipated by rays of the rising sun. All America waits for Liberty and salvation from you, intrepid soldiers of Cartagena and New Granada."

Bolívar left Castillo in command of the army at San Antonio and returned to Cúcuta. The captured Royalist merchandise yielded 33,306 pesos. After paying his troops, he had 10,000 pesos left for his war chest. He added another 5,000 pesos from the sale of cacao and from fines levied on Royalists. On March 4 he sent José Félix Ribas to inform the Tunja Congress and its president, Camilo Torres y Tenorio, that his victorious army, having liberated New Granada, had arrived on Venezuelan soil. After delivering his message, Ribas continued to Santa Fe de Bogotá to request the same permission from Antonio Nariño, who had been elected president of the state of Cundinamarca in September.

Bolívar requested congressional permission to drive the Royalists from Venezuela. The Tunja Congress made Bolívar a citizen of New Granada and promoted him to brigadier general in command of the federation armies. Trouble arose, however, with Manuel del Castillo, his ambitious second in command, who attacked Bolívar in a letter to Congress. He charged that Bolívar had wasted the booty taken at Cúcuta. He criticized as absurd the plan to invade Venezuela. When Bolívar ordered Castillo to march against Correa at La Grita (about sixty miles northeast of San Antonio), Castillo reminded Bolívar that he did not yet have permission to invade Venezuela.

Bolívar had learned of Castillo's charges against him and responded in a letter of April 8, 1813. He defended his actions to Secretary of State Crisanto Valenzuela and the Congress at Tunja, something he would have to repeat often during the independence wars and after. He pointed out that the Royalist general Domingo Monteverde had "achieved the most brilliant successes, because he knew how to take advantage of the favorable circumstances which resulted from the discontent of several Europeans and a few priests, and from the panic which the earthquake caused among a section of the common people. That panic is now incomparably greater in the minds not only of the common people but among the men of understanding and power who direct the multitude. . . . While the first [earthquake] demolished the cities, the second has destroyed public opinion, which fanaticism or prejudice has turned in favor of the tyrants."

Bolívar concluded by assuring the Congress: "I am a soldier and my duty prescribes for me only blind obedience to the government, without examining the nature of its decisions, which doubtless are, and must be, the wisest and the most just, meditated and conceived with that depth and wisdom which characterize His Excellency the President of the Congress, the members of that sovereign body, and the Secretary of State." Whether this statement expressed veiled sarcasm or simple flattery is debatable.

Bolívar understood that he "must not proceed beyond La Grita." However, his powerful, convincing arguments plus strong support from Camilo Torres y Tenorio finally persuaded the Tunja Congress. He received permission to invade Venezuela, but only to liberate the towns of Mérida and Trujillo.

Bolívar did not receive this limited congressional permission until May 7. Six weeks earlier, on March 26, he had read a brief item in a Cartagena newspaper about an uprising against Royalists in the eastern province of Cumaná. In January, Santiago Mariño and forty-five Patriot exiles had rowed across the narrow Gulf of Paria from Trinidad to eastern Venezuela and surprised the Royalists. Bolívar felt both elated and anxious. He was elated because now the Royalists had to fight on two fronts. His anxiety stemmed from his desire to liberate Caracas before Mariño arrived there. Neither Bolívar nor rival officers wanted to share the glory of victory.

Bolívar's "Admirable Campaign," an impressive string of victories, lasted from May 14 until his triumphal entry into Caracas on August 6, 1813. His triumphant run continued through year's end, when he liberated western Venezuela. Bolívar divided his army into two corps, with Ribas commanding the rear guard and Castillo the vanguard. Francisco de Paula Santander (1792–1840), a native of Rosario de Cúcuta, served as Castillo's second in command. Santander had abandoned law school to lead fierce llaneros in guerrilla warfare against Spain. Santander would later fight very well at the Battle of Boyacá in 1819. Thanks to his military prowess, he would serve as Bolívar's vice president in newly independent Gran Colombia beginning in October 1821, ably administering the nation during the president's long and frequent absences.

Political intrigue disrupted the patriot leadership, as it would many times. Castillo resigned his post, left Santander in command of the vanguard, and returned to Pamplona to continue his intrigues against Bolívar. Castillo's actions accelerated troop desertions. By the time Bolívar finally received permission to advance, he had only five hundred men. Fortunately, he had excellent officers—José Félix Ribas, Rafael Urdaneta, Atanasio Girardot, Luciano D'Elhuyar, and Antonio Ricaurte—to command them. His forces enjoyed a well-stocked armory: 1,400 muskets, 140,000 cartridges, and thirteen small field pieces.

Bolívar left Cúcuta and advanced along the road to Caracas. After four days, Cristóbal Mendoza met him in La Grita with good news and Santander with bad news. The good news was that Mérida Province anxiously awaited the liberating army; Royalists had fled for Trujillo. Vicente Campo Elías, a Spaniard who had lived for some time in Mérida, commanded the loyal patriot militia.

Santander delivered the bad news that Castillo and the governor of Pamplona had ordered him to return there with his battalion. As Santander prepared to obey, Bolívar barked: "I command you to order your men to march with me!" Santander, clearly taken aback, nevertheless obeyed the order, but over the next few years, his relationship with Bolívar would slide from friendship to rivalry to bitter hatred and betrayal. Later, when serving as Bolívar's vice president, Santander's power and ambition grew, and the one-time military allies eventually became bitter political enemies, with the liberal Santander criticizing what he perceived as Bolívar's autocratic tendencies and militarism. His ardent Federalism widened the rift, and Bolívar suspended him from office on September 24, 1828. After Bolívar's death, Santander ruled Colombia as president from 1832 to 1837.

His army temporarily united, the triumphant Bolívar entered Mérida on May 23, 1813, where a joyful people welcomed him. His army more than doubled in size when he incorporated the militia of Campo Elías. Bolívar reestablished republican government in Mérida. He also received details about Santiago Mariño's triumphs in liberating the East.

Mariño also enjoyed the service of able officers: the Bermúdez brothers, Francisco and Bernardo; Jean Baptiste Videau (Juan Bautista Bideau), a native of the French island of St. Lucia who had immigrated to Spanish Trinidad before the English captured that island in 1797; and Manuel Piar (1774–1817). The latter was born in Willemstad on the island of Curaçao, the illegitimate son of a María Isabel, a Dutch mulatto. He father was probably Fernando Piar Lottyn of the merchant marine. Alas, his service to the Patriots and his life would come to a tragic end within a few years.

A teenager born in Cumaná, Antonio José de Sucre (1795–1830), would become Bolívar's most trusted and able commander and rise to serve as Bolivia's first president (1826–28). His brilliant victory at Pichincha in 1822 freed much of Ecuador, and his equally impressive win at Junín (August, 1824) and his brilliant strategy at Ayacucho (December, 1824) finally brought victory to the Patriot cause. Shortly before his own death, Bolívar learned the sorrowful news that his beloved friend had died of an assassin's bullet on June 4, 1830.

Francisco Javier Zervériz (also rendered Cervériz or Servériz), Monteverde's military governor of Cumaná, had so terrorized and persecuted the inhabitants of that province that they rushed to support Mariño. He now had possession of the whole peninsula of Güiria, and Piar and Bernardo Bermúdez now occupied Maturín.

On the last day of May, Bolívar sent Girardot with the vanguard to occupy Trujillo. Maracaibo-born Rafael Urdaneta (1788–1845) followed with the center. Because he had been studying in Bogotá, the young soldier first took up the cause of independence in New Granada. He served admirably as Bolívar's second in command and help keep the Patriot cause alive in the Orinoco River basin during the difficult coming years. Bolívar marched with Ribas and the rear guard, and many people along the route told the Patriots of persecutions they had suffered from Monteverde. Antonio Tizcar (Tiscar), who was now in Barinas, and José Yañez, who was in the Apure llanos, had also terrorized the region.

Atrocities mounted on both sides, and the war became more vicious and bloody. Bolívar escalated the violence further by dictating his controversial "war to the death" decree, published in Trujillo on June 15, 1813. In a savage escalation of the conflict, Bolívar decreed death to all Spaniards and Canary Islanders, whom he thoroughly demonized in the pronouncement, "unless you contribute actively to the liberation of America." Bolívar hoped draw clear battle lines and to rally wavering Creoles to the Patriot cause by extending them amnesty.

> Moved by your misfortunes, we have been unable to observe with indifference the afflictions you were forced to experience by the barbarous Spaniards, who have ravished you, plundered you, and brought you death and destruction. They have violated the sacred rights of nations. They have broken the most solemn agreements and treaties. In fact, they have committed every manner of crime, reducing the Republic of Venezuela to the most frightful desolation. Justice therefore demands vengeance, and necessity compels us to exact it. Let the monsters who infest Colombian soil, who have drenched it in blood, be cast out forever; may their punishment be equal to the enormity of their perfidy, so that we may eradicate the stain of our ignominy and demonstrate to the nations of the world that the sons of America cannot be offended with impunity.
>
> Despite our just resentment toward the iniquitous Spaniards, our magnanimous heart still commands us to open to them for the last time a path to reconciliation and friendship; they are invited to live peacefully

among us, if they will abjure their crimes, honestly change their ways, and cooperate with us in destroying the intruding Spanish government and the reestablishment of the Republic of Venezuela.

Any Spaniard who does not, by every active and effective means, work against tyranny in behalf of this just cause, will be considered an enemy and punished; as a traitor to the nation, he will inevitably by shot by a firing squad. On the other hand, a general and absolute amnesty is granted to those who come over to our army with or without their arms, as well as to those who render aid to the good citizens who are endeavoring to throw off the yoke of tyranny. Army officers and civil magistrates who proclaim the government of Venezuela and join us shall retain their posts and positions; in a word, those Spaniards who render outstanding service to the State shall be regarded and treated as Americans.

And you Americans who, by error or treachery, have been lured from the paths of justice, are informed that your brothers, deeply regretting the error of your ways, have pardoned you as we are profoundly convinced that you cannot be truly to blame, for only the blindness and ignorance in which you have been kept up to now by those responsible for your crimes could have induced you to commit them. Fear not the sword that comes to avenge you and to sever the ignoble ties with which your executioners have bound you to their own fate. You are hereby assured, with absolute impunity, of your honor, lives, and property. The single title, "Americans," shall be your safeguard and guarantee. Our arms have come to protect you, and they shall never be raised against a single one of you, our brothers.

Bolívar tried to reassure Creoles that their political rights would be respected; that is, he tried to reaffirm his support for republican government. "The states defended by our arms are again governed by their former constitutions and tribunals, in full enjoyment of their liberty and independence, for our mission is designed only to break the chains of servitude which still shackle some of our towns, and not to impose laws or exercise acts of dominion to which the rules of war might entitle us." Patriot forces did not rigidly enforce this draconian proclamation, but Bolívar's drastic policy of war to the death escalated an already bloody conflict to new heights. Horrifying atrocities by both Spaniards and Patriots marred the entire independence era and set a bloody tone for the newly independent republics. However, terror, especially public terror, had been a longstanding Spanish tactic. Public executions, displaying heads on pikes or in cages, even tearing people limb from limb, extended all the way back to the Spanish Conquest. With a vengeance, Bolívar turned a venerable Spanish colonial tradition against them. Not until an armistice declared in November 1820 would his "war to the death" decree be lifted.

Monteverde had returned to Caracas at the beginning of June after a harrowing campaign in the east. The Spanish dispatched forces to take Maturín under command of Antonio Zuazola, a Royalist with a terrifying, vicious reputation. He supposedly cut off the ears of Patriots and adorned the crown of his hat with them, burned Patriot homes and granaries, and terrorized all he did not kill. Although outnumbered five to one, Patriots defeated the Royalists on March 20. Royalists mounted a second attack on Maturín about a month later only to lose another bloody battle. Hearing of the second defeat, Monteverde sailed east from La Guaira on April 27 with 260 troops from Spain. At Barcelona he collected another two thousand Venezuelan militiamen, along with ammunition, and guns.

Monteverde threatened that he would annihilate the defenders of Maturín as easily as the wind dissipates smoke. The Patriots numbered only five hundred men when Monteverde's army attacked on May 25. According to one Royalist, however, no one in Monteverde's army wished to fight. "Nearly all the European troops that had come to Venezuela perished. Patriots did not shoot the men of color. Monteverde escaped because his *zambo* [Indian-black] orderly protected him." The Spanish forces left behind three cannon, one mortar, muskets, defense equipment, and six thousand pesos. This crushing and unexpected defeat seemed to break Monteverde's spirit. He returned to Caracas in June and wiled away the next month, giving the Patriots time to consolidate their right flank.

Patriot victories continued in July. In one battle, Ribas and Urdaneta took 445 prisoners, about one-third of whom joined the Patriot army. The Patriots built up their war stores with captured Royalist arms and ammunition. The Spanish force of five thousand had completely disintegrated, and Patriots held the entire province of Barinas. On July 9 Ribas attacked a larger Royalist force. Driven back twice, the Patriots charged again, this time capturing cannon and turning them on the enemy. The valiant Ribas had eliminated the Royalist threat to Bolívar's left flank.

Bolívar gathered a force of fifteen hundred men at San Carlos. On the morning of July 29, scouts reported that Royalist Col. Julián Izquierdo had halted at Tinaquillo (halfway to Valencia) to await reinforcements from Coro. Bolívar dispatched his vanguard (Girardot with cavalry, D'Elhuyar with light infantry) at midnight. Urdaneta followed with the rest of the army. On July 31

Bolívar's advance caught up with Izquierdo and attacked. The Royalist troops formed in closed columns and retreated toward the mountains, hoping to escape to Valencia. Girardot and his cavalry harassed the enemy right flank, slowing their retreat. Bolívar realized, however, that the enemy would escape if they reached the mountains before dark. Displaying his quirky military genius and audacity, he ordered two hundred of D'Elhuyar's light infantry to mount double with Girardot's cavalry. Riding two men to a horse, the Patriots galloped around the enemy right. On the plains of Taguanes, the infantry dismounted and charged with cavalry support. The pincer movement of the combined infantry-cavalry column and the rest of the Patriot army cut the Spanish forces to pieces. Colonel Izquierdo fell mortally wounded. Those Royalists not killed or wounded were taken prisoner. On the plains of Taguanes, Bolívar savored a major victory in battle, putting him back on his road to glory.

When Monteverde learned of yet another disaster, the vacillating Spanish commander abandoned his stores and fled with panicked Royalists to well-fortified Puerto Cabello. Bolívar entered Valencia on August 2, while Urdaneta marched on with most of the army to Caracas. D'Elhuyar occupied the heights between Puerto Cabello and Valencia to watch Monteverde and cut his communications with the interior. Bolívar rode east, arriving at La Victoria on August 4, where he found a Royalist capitulation commission waiting to negotiate with him. The Marqués de Casa León (a turncoat but Bolívar's friend) chaired the commission.

The treaty negotiated and signed that day diplomatically ignored Bolívar's decree of "War to the Death!" It granted amnesty to the inhabitants of Caracas, guaranteed security of life and property, and gave permission to leave the country to all who applied for passports within a month. Spanish troops and officers could evacuate the city with honors. They would receive paid transportation out of the country.

A jubilant Bolívar enclosed a copy of the treaty in his letter the next day to the Congress at Tunja. Never bashful and seldom self-effacing, Bolívar proudly trumpeted his military achievements. His remarkable string of unbroken victories, however, would not last much longer.

> By this action, in addition to insuring the principal objective of my mission, which is only to redeem Venezuela from servitude, we have also succeeded in taking the arms and munitions that the enemy possessed and which they surely would have carried off had not flight been their only means of saving themselves.

During the three months that I waged war in Venezuela, I did not go into an action from which we did not emerge victorious and from each encounter, by surprising the enemy through unexpected marches, I obtained every possible advantage, while the valor of my soldiers struck them with terror.

Victories generated vengeance, and anarchy threatened Caracas, where looters sacked abandoned Royalist shops and houses. Respectable citizens armed themselves when they left their homes. Fortunately, Urdaneta and most of the army soon arrived in Caracas, restored order, and prepared for Bolívar's triumphal entry on August 6. Many grateful, elated Caraqueños rode or walked out to meet Bolívar a few miles outside the city. An even greater tumultuous throng greeted him at the city's entrance. The valley of Caracas reverberated with the sounds of artillery salvos, church bells clamoring, bands playing, and people huzzahing.

General Ducoudray Holstein described, with obvious distaste, how citizens prepared "a kind of triumphal car[t]," which he described as "like that which the Roman Consuls used, on returning from a campaign, after an important victory." Bolívar stood in the car, "drawn by twelve fine young ladies, very elegantly dressed in white, adorned with the national colors, and all selected from the first families in Caracas. They drew him, in about half an hour from the entrance of the city to his residence; he standing on the car, bare headed, and in full uniform, with a small wand of command in his hand." His sisters María Antonia and Juana, their children, Hipólita, and Matea waited there for a joyous family reunion. Bolívar danced until midnight at the ball given in his honor. He spent much of his time dancing with Josefina Madrid (or Machado). They soon became lovers.

Simón Bolívar never fathered a child. Like George Washington, he was sterile. Washington, however, unlike Bolívar, never received two thousand love letters from women, documents that may have taken on a strange, long life of their own. "These letters," wrote biographer Hildegarde Angell, "designated by Bolívar for destruction, came home to Caracas in the summer of 1928 in the same tin-lined trunk in which one of his executors took them to Spain a century ago. I trust the Liberator's next biographer may be more fortunate than I was in getting sight of it." Do these tantalizing letters still reside somewhere in Caracas?

The Liberator fully exploited the power and allure of his machismo, the character of a powerful, conquering male (in love and war) so important in Latin American culture. By "conquering" countless women, he adroitly mixed politics with pleasure and enhanced his macho image as well. He also understood and exploited the power of political theater. While his written words might sway the literate minority, his actions, including his triumphal entries, would appeal to the illiterate masses. Likewise his sweeping public proclamations appealed to reason and emotion and became a prototype for countless politicians who followed him. Bolívar became the quintessential "man on horseback," the model of the powerful Spanish American leader who inspired a host of imitators, some for better but many for worse.

On August 9, 1813, Bolívar declared that he would convoke an assembly of noble, virtuous, and learned men to discuss and sanction the type of government that Venezuela needed to cope with circumstances that endangered the Republic. While Francisco Javier Ustáriz drew up a constitution, Bolívar created an interim government. He also dispatched a committee to secure Monteverde's signature on the surrender treaty. If Monteverde agreed to the treaty, he would have to arrange for an exchange of prisoners, then debark, leaving Puerto Cabello in Patriot hands.

Unfortunately for the Patriots, Monteverde had recovered his composure and his courage. He refused to see the commission. Instead, he sent a tart reply saying that he would not consider any proposal that did not return Venezuela to the Royalists. His refusal to deal with the Patriots encouraged Spaniards and Canary Islanders to arouse slaves and free people of color in the valleys south of Caracas. In the pueblos of Santa Teresa, San Francisco de Yare, and Santa Lucia, wrote Yanes, they "robbed, murdered, and committed such acts of violence and abominations that memory shudders to record them, and the pen refuses to describe them." Bolívar's hard-won victories had not brought peace.

Bolívar had to leave the problems of government in Caracas only partially resolved and return to the battlefield. He departed on August 23 to take command of the eight hundred troops moving on Puerto Cabello. They camped eight miles north of Valencia at Naguanagua where the road to Puerto Cabello diverges. The western, or Aguas Calientes, road, thirty miles from Puerto Cabello, offered an easier route because of its lower passes over the coastal mountain range. The more rugged eastern road cut ten miles off the march. Bolívar sent Girardot and D'Elhuyar down the Aguas Calientes road with orders to dislodge the enemy.

Royalist forces held three forts on the mountain spur directly behind Puerto Cabello: Vigia Baja, halfway up the spur; Vigia Alta still higher; and Mirador de Solano near the crest. A salt flat separated the spur from Outer

Town. Puerto Cabello's fortified area, Inner Town, occupied an island connected by bridge with Outer Town. Urdaneta had orders to take Outer Town.

Girardot and D'Elhuyar stormed the spur on August 27. The defenders fled up the slope to the crest while Urdaneta captured his objective, Outer Town. Although lacking artillery, Urdaneta held his position despite fire from the citadel and small boats on either side of Outer Town. Artillery arrived on August 29 and the Patriots silenced the guns of enemy boats. On the thirtieth, Girardot inflicted thirst on the enemy. Puerto Cabello's water supply came from the San Esteban River, which emptied into the sea west of Outer Town. Guns from Vigia Baja fired on boats coming for water, thereby cutting off the port's precious water supply.

On the evening of August 31, Urdaneta's artillery and troops and Girardot's guns at Vigia Baja opened fire on Inner Town. Surprised and bewildered Royalists returned fire and turned the night sky into day. The great noise of this bombardment and Patriot huzzahs convinced Zuazola, the commander at Solano, that the port had been taken. He and his men fled into the hills. Patriots occupied the fort at the crest at dawn and pursued and captured Zuazola on September 2.

Urdaneta, at Bolívar's request, sent a prisoner exchange proposal to Monteverde on September 3. He requested Diego Jalón for Zuazola and four Royalist prisoners for each Patriot prisoner, warning that if Monteverde did not answer within three hours, Zuazola would be hanged, repayment for his gruesome habit of cutting off Patriot ears. The defiant Royalist commander replied: "I will never surrender Jalón, and I will sacrifice two prisoners for every one you kill." War to the death still prevailed. Furthermore, Monteverde probably felt no urge to save his blood-thirsty subordinate. The Patriots hanged Zuazola the next morning, and in reprisal Monteverde ordered some Patriots shot, but not Jalón.

On September 16, twelve hundred Royalist veterans and supplies arrived from Spain. Bolívar's surviving troops, riddled with malaria, could not maintain their siege against now superior forces. Bolívar stationed a few scouts at Trincherón and withdrew the rest of his men to more healthful altitudes. He deployed the remainder of his army in echelon along the road between Naguanagua and Valencia.

The reinforced and reinvigorated Royalists pursued the retreating Patriots. Monteverde pushed southeast with five hundred militia and occupied Bárbula, a ridge dominating the plain of Naguanagua. After two days of reconnoitering, Patriot scouts informed Bolívar that Monteverde had made an incredible mistake. He had divided his forces and left himself seven miles away from his other troops at Bárbula! Three Patriot columns stormed Bárbula on September 30, inflicting heavy casualties. Lamentably for the Patriots, a musket ball hit the gallant Girardot in the forehead and killed him as he raised the republican standard. The valiant colonel, born in Medellín, Colombia, died a martyr at age twenty-two in the battle of Bárbula. In a somewhat macabre but touching ceremony, Girardot's heart was removed and placed in a silver urn before his remains were buried.

On October 3, Girardot's boyhood friend D'Elhuyar and a thousand Patriots took revenge on the Royalists. He shattered Monteverde's army at Trincherón, and a musket ball shattered Monteverde's jaw. D'Elhuyar chased the fleeing survivors back to the fortified part of Puerto Cabello and laid siege to the port. The tough, valiant Monteverde finally seemed broken in body and spirit. His role in the Venezuelan drama would soon draw to a close.

Despite their victories, the Patriots faced continued and varied obstacles. Some Catholic clergy exhorted the people to renew their allegiance to God and His Anointed King. Bolívar needed to rally popular support, so he skillfully used Girardot's tragic death to rekindle the spirit of independence. He declared that September 30, the day of Girardot's death, "shall be a day of mourning forever throughout Venezuela; that his heart shall be born in triumph to Caracas and deposited in the Metropolitan Cathedral; that his bones shall be taken to his native city of Antioquia in New Granada; and that the Fourth Battalion, the instrument of his glory, shall be renamed Girardot Battalion."

In the same spirit and echoing the same theme, Bolívar wrote to the dead Patriot's father, Luis Girardot: "The memory of your son Atanasio will live in the hearts of all Americans as long as national honor is the law of their lives and as long as lasting glory can attract noble hearts." In the long bloody years of fighting yet to come, Bolívar would suffer the loss of many close friends and allies. Miraculously, the impetuous commander would never be wounded in battle. However, political enemies would wound him more deeply than enemy fire ever could.

A corps of drummers led the procession that marched toward Caracas a few days later. Behind them came an army chaplain carrying the urn with Girardot's heart, Bolívar, his staff, and three companies of dragoons. The Admirable Campaign, begun on May 14 at Mompox, had come to a close.

Caracas fell silent on October 14 as the solemn procession marched across the city. They deposited the heart of their fallen hero in the cathedral. Later that day the Caracas town council acclaimed Bolívar as "the Liberator and

Captain General of the Armies of Venezuela." In a letter to the citizens of Caracas, penned October 18, the newly named Liberator expressed his gratitude for the title and the honor. However, he also graciously acknowledged the critical roles played by his commanders, adding that "the other officers and troopers were the true illustrious liberators." He concluded: "I realize how much I am indebted to your own lofty character and, even more, to the peoples whose will you express to me. The law of duty, more powerful in me than the impulses of my heart, enjoins me to obey the wishes of a free people. It is with the most profound feelings of veneration for my country and for you, its spokesmen, that I accept such signal munificence. May God keep you many years."

Santiago Mariño (1788–1854), a rival liberator with tremendous influence in the eastern provinces, threatened Bolívar's supremacy. Since June, Mariño's forces had driven back the Royalists, and on August 3 he had made a victorious entrance to Cumaná. War to the death also marred this front of the fighting. After learning of the fall of Cumaná, a Royalist commander ordered Patriot officer Bernardo Bermúdez killed. His brother Francisco, enraged by the execution, took revenge by slaughtering every Royalist he found.

Although in retreat, the Royalists were far from finished. Royalist Juan Manuel Cajigal in Guayana had two capable, dangerous officers under his command, José Tomás Boves and Francisco Tomás Morales (1781–1845). The latter, a tavern owner in Piritu, Venezuela, served ably under Boves and well beyond. They operated effectively and savagely in the llanos. Cajigal supplied them with arms and munitions from his base at Angostura, two hundred miles up the Orinoco River (today Ciudad Bolívar), and with food from the Caroní Missions.

Boves, born in Gijón on the northern coast of Spain, had been a smuggler for several years before being caught and jailed at Puerto Cabello. After his release, he found his way to the llanos, where he traded in "fruits of the country," including contraband hides. He owned a store at Calabozo, managed by a loyal old Indian. Boves roamed the llanos of Caracas and Barcelona, outdid llaneros in horsemanship, and became their leader, loyal to the Patriot cause. A contemporary described him with "fair hair, an enormous head, large, staring blue eyes, and a broad, flat forehead, a thick beard and a white skin; he was of middle height, capable of undergoing extraordinary fatigue, active, bold, fearless, impetuous, rash, astute, hungry for power, cruel and sanguinary." Unfortunately, a Patriot officer, Juan Escalona, abused and struck Boves, then jailed him for insubordination, probably not without justification. A few days later, on May 21, 1812, Royalists occupied Calabozo and freed Boves, who immediately joined the Royalists and took his violent revenge on the Patriots. He became one of the cruelest and most ferocious commanders in the wars for independence.

In addition to the dangerous Boves, Bolívar faced problems on his own side. He considered Santiago Mariño a rival, but he also needed him. He tried to flatter the younger officer, addressing him in a letter as "Señor General-in-Chief of the Armies of the East." "Both our armies having liberated a large part of Venezuela, we are now able to unite our forces between San Carlos and La Victoria, constrict our enemies, and expel them from Valencia, Puerto Cabello, Caracas, and La Guaira. I take the liberty to invite you to accelerate your movements in order that we may enter the illustrious capital of Venezuela together."

Mariño replied about a month later with a detailed account of his rapid liberation of Cumaná and Barcelona. He added "as soon as I have occupied Barcelona, I will march to Caracas with 4,000 to 5,000 men; and I will soon send five war vessels and a commission to congratulate you on your triumphs." Rival officers during wartime and rival caudillos would vex Bolívar throughout his life. Ultimately, the caudillos would win and political fragmentation, not unity, would characterize Spanish America.

Although battered, Royalists still threatened Bolívar's extended lines on three flanks. Boves and Morales controlled the llanos to the south of Caracas. Royalists to the southwest kept Barinas Province in a state of alarm, as did forces in the west at Coro and Maracaibo. Bolívar countered the western threat with Ramón García de Sena and six hundred troops from Valencia. García de Sena won a victory at Cerritos Blancos but fell ill and yielded his command to Miguel Valdés. Valdés faced the vast Coro frontier and a guerrilla-infested triangle, its base extending from Puerto Cabello to Valencia and its apex at Barquisimeto. Patriot espionage was almost impossible, because most inhabitants supported King Ferdinand. The war for independence had not yet become a war of the masses. While rich Creoles wanted independence, Enlightenment ideals had not reached the poor, uneducated, colored masses. Influential Royalist clergy also worked assiduously to keep the poor loyal to God and His Divine King.

Meanwhile to the east, Boves and Morales recruited more llanero horsemen as they moved west from Barcelona Province toward Calabozo. Tomás Montilla, Bolívar's commander at Calabozo, knew by mid-September that Boves was camped nearby on the bank of a small stream. Despite a warning that it would be difficult to dislodge Boves, Montilla sent out Carlos Padrón with six hundred troops. Early on the morning of September 23, Padrón surprised Boves in bed and scattered his cavalry. Boves's fierce infantry, however, counterattacked and killed nearly two-thirds of Padrón's troops. By noon Padrón had retreated to Calabozo. Montilla had already evacuated, so Padrón followed Montilla north to Villa de Cura, where Vicente Campo Elías, Patriot commander of the Caracas llanos, labored at organizing an army.

Campo Elías left Villa de Cura with one thousand riflemen and two hundred horsemen. Near Sombrero he heard cavalry approaching. He fervently hoped that he heard troops that Mariño had said he would send. He paused and readied for action just in case they proved to be the enemy. With a sign of relief, the Patriots greeted Mariño's reinforcements. Early on the morning of October 14, 1813, enemy artillery greeted Campo Elías at the Mosquitero, a branch of the Río Orituco. Boves, at the head of two thousand horsemen, and Morales, commanding five hundred rifles with two cannons, stood ready for action on the opposite side of the river. Campo Elías formed his line, with infantry in the center and cavalry on both wings, forded the stream, and charged.

Boves attacked the Patriot left wing and threw it back across the stream. He also expected to quickly annihilate the center and right, but the center held behind the seemingly unflappable Miguel Ustáriz, who even managed to seize a cannon. Campo Elías, with the cavalry on the right, boldly seized the other cannon, then together they converged on Morales and Boves. The next fifteen minutes transformed the battlefield into a bloody field of horror for the Royalists. The emboldened lancers of Campo Elías gave no quarter during the battle or after. Boves and the wounded Morales fled south to Guayabal near the Apure, where Campo Elías did not pursue them. The rainy season had turned the llanos into a freshwater sea where Patriot pursuers would quickly become easy prey.

Energized and perhaps maddened with victory, a vengeful Campo Elías occupied Calabozo. Father José Felix Blanco reported the dark events that followed: "As if the blood still seethed in his veins, Campo Elías tarnished his victory by sacrificing the defenseless population to his fury for the blameless crime—if we can call it that—of having allowed their city to serve as headquarters for someone more terrible than he, the matchless Boves." War to the death.

Boves brooded over his defeat as he fled south with but a few llaneros. He had lost his entire army, including most of his horses, arms, cannons, and munitions. Patriot infantry supported by cavalry had snatched his cannons during the time needed to reload them. The loss of the cannons badly disconcerted his troops and gave the Patriots the victory. Boves, bowed but not beaten, learned from his mistakes. In future engagements his cavalry would predominate; infantry would be secondary. When he arrived at Guayabal, Boves tore the iron grillwork from windows and forged the metal into lance tips. He made the shafts of his lances, nine feet or longer, from tough, flexible cane. Ramón Páez, author of *Wild Scenes in South America*, described the dangerous result. In the hands of llanero cavalry, "the lance is a formidable weapon which they handle with great dexterity, from their constant practice with the *garrocha* [a goad with a sharp, iron tip] with which they drive and turn cattle."

Boves, in a circular issued on November 1, called on all llaneros to join him, vowing to pursue "every traitor" to his death. He decreed that the possessions of the dead would be divided among the soldiers who defended the just and holy cause of the king. Capt. Gen. José Manuel Cajigal described the attraction of serving under Boves: "the wicked were able to satisfy their depraved instincts with robbery (officially labeled as 'sacking'), assassinations, rapes, and every type of depredation; while for good men, the only guarantee of personal safety was to enlist in Boves's army." He rounded up mules and exchanged them for what he needed—food from the Caroní Missions and war materiel that Royalist fleets brought up the Orinoco River from Caribbean Islands.

Boves did not stand alone as a fierce, charismatic llanero chieftain. José Antonio Páez (1790–1873) served as one of Manuel Pulido's captains. He would become master of the llanos for the Patriots, a key to their eventual victory in this vital, difficult theater. Independent-minded and nationalistic, Páez later became a formidable political rival to Bolívar. His ambition, personalistic rule, and oligarchic tendencies clashed directly with the ego, goals, and values of the Liberator. He led a Venezuelan separatist movement that destroyed Gran Colombia, Bolívar's unified Republic, and became Venezuela's first president (1831–35, 1839–43), ruling as a powerful, conservative caudillo until 1848. After losing a civil war that year to rival caudillo José Tadeo Monagas (1785–1868), Páez lived in exile until 1861, when he ruled again as supreme dictator, only to be forced to flee two years later. He died in exile in New York City in 1873. Monagas would likewise jockey for political power, with varying success, for several decades after independence.

On November 10 Bolívar moved his army to the pueblo of Cabudare, about three miles from the Barquisimeto mesa. Bolívar could see the Royalist camp on the edge of the mesa. If he climbed to the camp by the main road, his troops would be under fire from artillery. The next morning Bolívar led his troops toward the enemy via a footpath that kept them out of the Royalist line of fire. The Royalists, positioned between the Patriots and Barquisimeto, awaited them.

After the first musket volley, Bolívar's cavalry charged. They drove the Royalist cavalry through Barquisimeto and out the opposite side. As Patriot infantry took Barquisimeto, someone apparently sounded retreat. The confused infantry panicked, threw down their muskets, and fled. Returning cavalry, surprised and shocked at the retreat, also fled, and to their dismay, neither Bolívar nor Urdaneta could stem the tide and restore order. They sacrificed one thousand men. Urdaneta organized the survivors at Gamelotal and marched them to San Carlos. A livid Bolívar renamed the infantry that had been the first to flee the Sin Nombre (Nameless) Battalion and returned in disgust to Valencia.

His forces in disarray, Bolívar had no choice but to appeal for assistance from his rival. He sent a request to "Citizen General Santiago Mariño" on November 14. "We have only 700 infantry in Valencia to hold more than 1,000 in Puerto Cabello, and the inhabitants there are armed from the stores of that plaza. Hasten with aid to that place." With Patriot forces in disarray, the Royalists favored a victory at Barquisimeto, reoccupation of Barinas, and control of all western Venezuela. On November 20 twelve hundred Royalist infantry attacked D'Elhuyar in Valencia. On November 23, Ribas and D'Elhuyar counterattacked on foot. After a six-hour battle, the Royalists retired.

Bolívar arrived with more troops and increased the Patriot force on the savanna to two thousand infantry and three hundred cavalry. Indecisive skirmishes followed on November 24. The next day, however, brought a bloody battle that pushed the Royalists back into high positions the Patriots could not attack. That night, Royalists built bonfires in which they burned as many of their dead as they could collect. With the heights illuminated, they climbed down the north side of the mountain to Puerto Cabello. Bolívar feared that Royalists might try to send a force to Caracas by sea. Bolívar sent Ribas back to defend Caracas. D'Elhuyar remained in Valencia while Bolívar marched to San Carlos, where he met Campo Elías and his troops.

On November 30, Bolívar, with two thousand infantry and one thousand cavalry, launched a drive against the Royalist stronghold in Barquisimeto. He could get no information from the hostile people in the countryside. Thus he had no way of knowing that Royalists had left the town and regrouped at Araure, about fifty miles south of Barquisimeto.

The inclined plain on which Araure is located reaches a crest, the Galera, behind the town. Beyond it, another plain, wooded on both sides, extends to the forest-covered edge of the Río Acarigua. The Royalist commanders had quartered their five thousand or more troops on the Galera. They illuminated the circumference of their camp with bonfires that burned all night. During the night of December 4, however, the Royalists left the Galera.

Bolívar led the main part of the Patriot army directly through the town. Some five hundred infantry skirted the town and climbed the Galera. Unfortunately, hidden Royalists surrounded and annihilated the Patriot force after it descended to the plain. Royalists in battle formation met Bolívar when he arrived with the rest of his army at the Galera. Enemy riflemen and cavalry enjoyed good cover in the woods. A lagoon, with cannon at each end, covered part of the enemy front. Bolívar's infantry formed the front line, with Urdaneta commanding. The Sin Nombre Battalion, armed with lances for want of muskets, deployed to the right. Bolívar remained with the dragoons at the rear.

Surveying his line, Bolívar addressed his troops with rousing words aimed at inflaming their hearts. His infantry and cavalry advanced bravely, ignoring enemy fire. Patriots held their fire until within pistol shot, then Urdaneta's infantry charged the enemy infantry. Royalists pushed back the Patriot cavalry, but Bolívar with his dragoons counterattacked, giving the Patriot cavalry time to regroup and charge again. The tide of battle turned when the terrible lances of the Sin Nombre Battalion broke the Royalist line. The entire Royalist army fled, leaving behind more than one thousand dead, ten cannons, eight hundred to one thousand muskets, other supplies, and six large sacks of silver plus nine thousand pesos. The Patriots suffered eight hundred dead and wounded.

On December 6, the day after the battle, Bolívar reviewed and praised his battle-scarred troops at the pueblo of Aparicio. He lauded the Sin Nombre Battalion, who had redeemed themselves from the disaster at Barquisimeto: "Soldiers! Your valor yesterday on the field of battle won a name for your corps. When I saw you triumph, I proclaimed you 'Victors of Araure'!"

Bolívar assembled his strongest army yet at Araure. Most of his battles before Araure should properly be called skirmishes. They seldom involved more than a few hundred troops. His defeat at Barquisimeto on November 11 involved two thousand or more troops and so could be termed a battle. At Araure, however, Bolívar commanded three thousand troops against some five thousand Royalist troops. He had regained the west. Bolívar next re-

Victory at Araure.

turned to Valencia and turned his attention back to Puerto Cabello. Mariño had sent Piar to blockade Puerto Cabello with a brig, five schooners, and two smaller vessels. Bolívar and D'Elhuyar reestablished a land blockade of the port.

Property owners and Spanish merchants, incensed at the Royalist losses, organized a junta in Puerto Cabello on December 28, 1813. The regency in Cádiz had already lost confidence in Monteverde and named Cajigal captain general. The regency ordered Cajigal to proceed from Angostura to Puerto Rico, where he would gather veteran troops from Spain and retake Venezuela. With the collapse of Napoleon's empire in Europe, the Cádiz regency could throw seasoned troops into the Venezuelan fray.

No one saw more clearly than Bolívar the dangers facing the Patriot forces. In a letter to Mariño, he pushed for political unity and military cooperation. "If we unite all within a single consolidated nation, and at the same time extinguish the embers of discord, we will further consolidate our forces and promote the mutual cooperation of the peoples in support of their natural cause. Divided, we shall be weaker, less respected by enemy and neutral powers alike. Union under a single supreme government will be our strength and will make us formidable to all."

The Liberator also recognized how ephemeral military success could be. He had left much of his liberated area unprotected while he concentrated troops for the Araure campaign. "The enemy," he noted, "did not exploit his advantage at this time; but when he perceives his mistake, he will proceed with greater energy and better leadership in the future." Prophetic words. The terrible Boves, seconded by Morales, stood ready and determined to destroy the Second Republic and the Liberator.

PART III

Spain's Reconquest of Its Colonies

CHAPTER 6

Boves and Royalist Resurgence,

1814–15

Bolívar's victory at Araure on December 5, 1813, liberated for a second time western Caracas Province and Barinas. It would mark the high point of the Patriot cause for several years to come. First, European events turned against the Patriots. In December 1813 a defeated Napoleon made peace with Spain, freeing up Spanish energies and troops for the New World. On April 11, 1814, the pretender Joseph Bonaparte abdicated the Spanish throne, but a month earlier he had sent Ferdinand VII back to Spain. For some Creoles, the restoration of their "desired" king marked the end of their struggle. Not so for Bolívar.

"The Desired One" immediately showed his colors. On his way to Madrid on May 4, he dissolved the Cortes and all of its acts, effectively killing the halting steps Spain had made toward reform and constitutional, representative government. He ordered regents, ministers of state, and a number of deputies arrested and proclaimed that he would never swear allegiance to the Constitution of 1812. By the time he had reached his capital, he had imposed a system on Spain more tyrannical than his father's had been. Each day intolerance against and persecution of liberals increased. The poorly educated, poorly advised, politically inept, vacillating, procrastinating monarch would contribute immeasurably to the suffering of his subjects in Spain and in America. Granted, Spain stood in an unenviable position, so perhaps even a more able monarch would have fared poorly. However, in Spain,

Ferdinand rewarded cowards who did not fight against the invading French and dismissed guerrilla leaders who had valiantly fought. His "purification boards" *(juntas de purificación)* set about identifying any suspected traitors in Spain or the colonies. Zealous Royalists shot nine suspected Republic supporters from Cartagena in February of 1816. Such kangaroo court proceedings alienated even more Spaniards and Creoles from "The Desired One's" rule.

As historian Jaime E. Rodríguez O. put it, with tremendous understatement, "Fernando VII proved unequal to the task of unity of the worldwide Spanish Monarchy." In *Spain and the Independence of Colombia*, Rebecca A. Earle shows that Ferdinand and his underlings shared responsibility for Spain's failures: "Spain never developed a coherent strategy for responding to its revolted colonies, and attempted to pursue simultaneously a collection of often contradictory policies." She continues, "Spain, then, not only lacked a coherent policy for counter-revolution, but also failed to carry through the plans that it succeeded in putting into operation."

Likewise, the colonial heritage from Spain, liberal or conservative, proved unequal to the task of undergirding the foundations needed by the new American nations. Given all the adversities, Spain did put up a remarkable battle to retain its New World holdings. However, partisan, personal, and ideological conflicts within the Patriot ranks probably contributed as much to extending the bloody independence wars as did Spanish resistance. The king also restored the hated Inquisition, suppressed by the Cortes the previous year, and used its powers to persecute independence leaders. The repressive institution finally ended with the liberal upheaval of 1820. Any claim that Spain and its colonies could be reconciled under a fictive veil of common liberalism went up in smoke.

In Venezuela the year 1814 brought defeat and dissension to the independence movement and to the Second Venezuelan Republic. Bolívar faced challenges to his leadership on many fronts. Rival commanders deposed and sought to kill him. Most damaging, José Tómas Boves, with his "Legion of Hell," the llanero cavalry, recaptured most of the plains.

By May, 1815, Bolívar had lost his bid to bring the province of Cundinamarca under his control. Losing in a power struggle to rival caudillo Manuel del Castillo, he bid his army farewell and sailed into exile on the island of Jamaica. Bolívar's dream of a strong, united South America crumbled, as it would again and again, under the strains of localism, divisive political ideologies, and competing political ambitions.

Shortly after the Royalist defeat at Araure, Boves moved north from

Guayabal with fifteen hundred lancers and five hundred infantry. On December 14, his cavalry destroyed a Patriot force of eight hundred at the cattle corrals of San Marcos. Boves entered Calabozo and ordered his troops to behead eighty-seven white women there. He also ordered the execution of thirty-two more people who were absent or in hiding. He then divided the property of the slain among his lancers, an incentive that worked well in attracting and keeping soldiers. Boves would make the independence struggle a war of class and race. Regrettably, a host of self-interested caudillos would adopt his vicious model and perpetuate it through the nineteenth century.

What made the llaneros so willing to fight behind Boves? During the Patria Boba in 1811, Venezuela's republicans had passed the *Ordenanzas de los Llanos* to extend their social and economic control over the unruly plainsmen. These rules outlawed most of the llaneros' life and livelihood: no wild cattle hunting, travel only with an official passport, a requirement for permanent employment as a ranch peon. These specious laws flew in the face of two centuries of llanero practice. Denied their traditional pursuits, llaneros flocked to Boves, who offered booty, adventure, and freedom.

Sacking, pillaging, and confiscation of property served to help finance the war. Some Patriots followed Bolívar because he paid them with property grants. Boves, opposed to private property, rewarded his llaneros with pillage rights. Many soldiers had no clear ideological commitment to the Patriot or Royalist cause. These "guerrilla bandits" changed sides, sometimes several times, depending on which side offered the better opportunities for pillage.

Richard L. Vowell, an English officer serving the Patriots, observed llaneros at work in 1818: "Although usually styled and considered herdsmen, their habits and mode of life were in reality those of hunters; for the cattle, which constituted their sole wealth, being perfectly wild, the exertions requisite to collect a herd, and to keep it together in the neighborhood of a farm-house, were necessarily violent and incessant."

Boves had little trouble equipping, training, feeding, or paying his llaneros. His troops had their own horses and weapons, and they knew how to fight. Cattle of the plains supplied them with beef, milk, and rawhide. As payment, they enjoyed the right to kill and plunder. If defeated in battle, the wily llaneros dispersed quickly over a wide area and regrouped later at a prearranged spot. They lived to fight again, so their enemies could rarely win a decisive victory.

Bolívar faced dismayingly powerful Spanish opposition. The merciless Boves achieved the amazing feat of enlisting some eight thousand llaneros.

He attracted this large force despite the very sparse population of the plains. Boves dominated the plains south of Valencia and Caracas. Other Royalists inflamed the population of all the Apure against the Patriots of Barinas. Royalists in Coro enjoyed large stores of war materiel from Puerto Rico and veteran troops from Spain.

Among the Patriots, Rafael Urdaneta had twelve hundred infantry and a few dragoons at Barquisimeto. He had to cover the Coro frontier as well as Barinas. Juan Escalona had a garrison of only 150 men at Valencia. Luciano D'Elhuyar led three hundred infantry in his Puerto Cabello siege line. Campo Elías had three thousand raw recruits at Villa de Cura (north of Boves at Calabozo). Ribas in Caracas led five hundred infantry and two hundred cavalry. All told, the Patriots had only six thousand troops, spread thinly in the long mountain arc from Barinas to Caracas. This military vulnerability plus Patriot infighting and rivalries would play into Spanish hands.

Recruiting and campaigning depleted Bolívar's manpower base and diminished the food supply for towns inside his lines. Royalists, however, soon shortened the western end. Rich Creoles faced impoverishment. Their peons, fighting for the Patriots, could not produce food or other crops. English control of the seas kept Bolívar from getting weapons and munitions from the outside. His agent Juan Toro sailed from La Guaira on January 11, 1814, hoping to find help in the United States. The British governor at St. Thomas, however, sent him back to La Guaira. In May, Bolívar dispatched two agents to London. The British again detained them at St. Thomas and sent them back to La Guaira.

Great Britain, the preeminent naval power of the nineteenth century, held the Danish, French, and Dutch islands in the Caribbean and would not permit traffic in arms. Her reward for this action would be economic control of Spain's recaptured colonies. Britain already had an economic stranglehold on Portugal's colony of Brazil. Moreover, Britain was at war with the United States. As historian C. S. Forester noted, "She was gathering her strength to bludgeon America into submission, and the British cabinet was organizing as great an effort as they believed the British taxpayer would endure."

The one bright spot for Venezuelan efforts in the United States came from the skilled propagandist Manuel Torres. In October, 1814, William Duane, publisher of the Philadelphia *Aurora*, provided Torres with letters of introduction to prominent politicians, including Secretary of State James Monroe. Duane described Torres as "a man of practical experience and [of] principles and views perfectly in the Spirit of our Government." Indeed,

Torres's activities attracted Royalist attention to the point that they attempted to assassinate the Venezuelan. With his publications and personal meetings, Torres kept the Patriot cause before the American people.

Pushed by propagandists like Torres and its own economic interests, the United States did not ignore events in South America. The State Department dispatched a number of special agents to the region to monitor events. Those serving in Gran Colombia from 1816 to 1818 included Christopher Hughes; Charles Morris; Baptis Irvine, a journalist of considerable experience; Joseph Devereux; and Comdr. Oliver H. Perry, hero of the Battle of Lake Erie. Irvine, sent in early 1818 to demand indemnity for two American vessels seized and sold, failed in his mission. Perry made better headway, but he contracted yellow fever while descending the Orinoco River and died at Port of Spain, Trinidad, on August 23, 1819. Perhaps owing to George Washington's warning against foreign intrigues, the United States' posture ranged from neutral to aloof concerning the travails of its South American neighbors.

Faced with adversity on all sides, Bolívar needed the help of his rival caudillo Santiago Mariño. Bolívar urged Mariño to help create a unified administration for the whole country. Bolívar wanted a strong central government with Caracas as the seat of power. "Divided, we will be weaker and less respected by both our enemies and the neutral countries. Unification under a single government would strengthen us and make us productive for all," wrote the Liberator.

Mariño, who considered himself dictator of the East, preferred to preserve his power and autonomy through a federation with Bolívar. At one point, Mariño, in full military uniform in preparation for a party, stood in front of the mirror and asked his attaché: "Antonio, I am young, rich, handsome, General in Chief at the age of 25! What do I lack?" To which his attaché responded, "Prudence, my General, Prudence." These two dictators, able, ambitious, and young, also held antithetical political philosophies of Centralism versus Federalism. This deep political schism would torture much of Spanish America and give rise to a vicious cycle of civil wars long after independence.

Mariño could not be too intransigent, because he realized that a Royalist defeat of Bolívar would threaten him. He dispatched troops in time to help Campo Elías defeat Boves at Mosquitero. He ordered Manuel Piar with eight small vessels to blockade Puerto Cabello by sea. Mariño had concentrated troops at Aragua de Barcelona to attack Boves from the plains. He did not move his army westward, however, until the third week of January, 1814.

Bolívar wrote Mariño from Valencia on January 3, 1814. He explained that Puerto Cabello could fall within two weeks because of the lack of food. "We are about to assault with land forces," he said, "but all our efforts will be wasted if Piar leaves and supply ships reach the Royalists." Mariño ordered Manuel Piar to continue the blockade, but the officer did so only halfheartedly. Spanish vessels entered and left port freely. Piar soon gave up command of the squadron and returned to Mariño to take command of land troops. Mariño succeeded in gathering about four thousand men by incorporating many "pardoned sons" of Venezuela into his army. Villagers soon learned that, unlike the Royalists, Mariño did not assassinate noncombatants. Many Venezuelans, lacking the ideological fire of a Bolívar, wanted only to survive, so they would opportunistically join either side.

Meanwhile, Bolívar moved his forces south to defend Barinas. While José María Rodríguez and four hundred men held Ospino, Urdaneta returned to Barquisimeto for more troops. The bloodthirsty Royalist José Yáñez laid siege to Ospino on January 31 with six hundred infantry and nine hundred lancers. Three days later Urdaneta received 350 reinforcements. In the battle of February 2, the Patriots killed Yáñez, but most of his troops escaped and regrouped at Guanare. A far greater threat to Urdaneta was the arrival at Coro on February 4 of Capt. Gen. Juan Manuel Cajigal (also rendered Cagigal) from Puerto Rico with supplies and reinforcements for Col. José Ceballos. With these fresh troops and the support of the inhabitants, Ceballos threatened Barquisimeto from the north, and Calzado from the south, but, on February 11, Urdaneta received Bolívar's order to send him troops to help defend San Mateo against Boves.

Rafael Urdaneta pulled in his lines and sent Bolívar 600 infantry and fifty dragoons. These forces reached San Mateo only a few hours ahead of Boves. Urdaneta now had only 650 infantry and a few dragoons. The two sides fought the first battle of La Puerta for two hours on February 3. Boves suffered a wound, but his relentless lancers slaughtered the Patriots. Campo Elías and a few of his men escaped to Valencia, while Boves repaired to Villa de Cura to allow his wound to heal.

Royalists under Francisco Morales attacked La Victoria early on the morning of February 12. He surrounded the city with eighteen hundred infantry and twenty-five hundred cavalry. Ribas kept Royalist cavalry from being effective, but by 4:30 in the afternoon he faltered. One-third of his men had been killed or wounded. Father Blanco, fighting with Ribas, tells us that he "saw no hope of salvation for as our lines diminished, enemy lines were replenished." Then the lookout reported a cloud of dust on the San Mateo road.

Campo Elías arrived with 200 infantry and 200 cavalry. Montilla and 150 cavalry broke the line so Campo Elías could enter La Victoria. Patriots shouted "Campo Elías" like a war cry. The tired, dispirited Royalists fled in the face of the reinforcements. Patriots pursued them, both sides taking no prisoners and giving no quarter. Royalist casualties ran twice those of the Patriots. However, Ribas did not press the advantage, so Boves and his llaneros lived to fight another day.

Almost immediately, Ribas had to return to Caracas to quell the Royalist threat there. Royalist guerrillas dominated parts of Caracas as well as the road from Caracas down to La Guaira. Royalists alerted friends and relatives of Spanish prisoners at La Guaira and in Caracas to storm the jails, release them, and massacre the Patriots. With no Patriot reinforcements nearby, Bolívar cold-bloodedly ordered the prisoners killed. Patriots executed more than eight hundred prisoners on the bloody days of February 13–15, 1814. War to the death still reigned. Neither Royalists nor Patriots held a monopoly on inhumanity and massacres, and each atrocity only inspired more.

Patriots under Ribas defeated Royalists at Charallave, about thirty miles south of Caracas, on February 20. When Ribas entered the town of Ocumare, however, he found three hundred cadavers in the church—men, women, and children who had taken no part in the fighting. The Spanish also waged war to the death and took no prisoners. Bolívar, meanwhile, returned to San Mateo to counter the threat of Boves and his seventy-five hundred troops, half of them cavalry. Patriots initially blocked Boves as he tried to cross the Aragua River in front of San Mateo. Boves retired to the hills south of the river where he could survey the narrow valley and look across at Bolívar's mile-long line of nearly three thousand men. Patriot troops occupied a cluster of huts and the hill of El Calvario (Calvary) behind them on the left end of the line. Artillery occupied the center, with six seven-inch howitzers and ten small cannons. Bolívar's left end covered the sugar works and his manor house, Casa Alta, on a hill behind the mill. The manor house also served as the Patriot ammunition dump.

The battle began at dawn the next morning on February 28. Morales attacked the center, but he could not prevail against the withering artillery. The Patriot left drove Royalists south, but they recovered and pushed the Patriots back to the sugar mill. Boves then hit the Patriot right and soon had possession of the straw huts on the plantation. Bolívar sent Campo Elías to assist, and, a short time later, he suffered a mortal wound— a grave loss for the Patriots. After hours of close fighting, Patriots dislodged

Royalists from the positions they had gained. After more than ten hours of fighting, Boves retired to his camp in the hills. Patriots did not know that a musket ball had pierced his thigh. Boves left Morales to continue the siege while he returned to Villa de Cura to let his wound heal. Puzzled by the lack of activity over the next several days, Bolívar asked a prisoner why there was so little action. He replied that the men wanted to fight only when Boves was leading them, and that he was recovering at Villa de Cura.

The Liberator recognized that the death of Boves would remove a huge obstacle to his independence struggle. He dispatched Manuel Sedeño (also rendered Cedeño) on this mission. He had not gone far before his twenty-man escort mutinied. Loyalties often did not run very deep, and Boves, even wounded, merited his terrible reputation. A humiliated Sedeño returned to San Mateo, and soon Boves learned of his failure. He taunted Patriots with leaflets that said "I will pardon all those who will join my hosts, even that one who told Bolívar that I was prostrate at Villa de Cura, guarded by only a few lancers."

During the lull in the fighting at San Mateo, a messenger from Caracas warned Bolívar that Royalists again threatened the capital. The wily Bolívar dispatched three hundred infantry and one hundred lancers, banners flying in full view of the enemy, east on the road to Caracas. Morales thought they were the vanguard for an attack on his right. He moved his troops to strengthen that end and kept them on the alert all night while the Patriot force marched on to Caracas. There confusion and terror reigned among Patriot supporters.

As he prepared for the second battle of San Mateo, Boves had good intelligence reports. He knew that he had only a couple of days to destroy Bolívar before Mariño arrived with reinforcements. He also knew that Bolívar had precious barrels of powder stored in Casa Alta, a vital element of war that Boves lacked. During the night of March 24, Morales with eight hundred men climbed the mountain behind Casa Alta. Antonio Ricaurte commanded that end of Bolívar's line. At dawn on March 25, lines on both sides saw Morales and his column descend the mountain and approach Casa Alta. Fear clutched the Patriots as they saw Ricaurte run to the sugar mill. Suddenly a huge roar reverberated through the valley. Clouds of smoke and tongues of flame covered the area. Patriots and Royalists were both stunned. How could either side prevail without powder? The battle continued without much energy on either side until later afternoon, when Boves retired to the hills. Unable to overrun the Patriots before Mariño's arrival, he let his troops relax for five days. Then he marched to head off the reinforcements at the bone-littered entrance to the gorge, where Boves had wiped out the army of Campo Elías on February 3. Mariño passed through the gorge and deployed his troops at Boca Chica (Little Mouth), the narrow end. Infantry occupied the hills to right and left, while troops under Leandro Palacios commanded the center.

The next morning Patriots and Royalists clashed repeatedly at Boca Chica. On his third attack, Boves deployed his men on the hills some distance from Boca Chica and set fire to the dry grass. Boves expected the fires to burn toward the Patriots, but the wind shifted, thus threatening the Royalists. Mariño's brave ex-slaves from Cumaná, unmindful of the hot turf, fired at Royalists and forced them back. After a temporary respite, Boves returned yet again, and the battle raged until late afternoon when the Royalists fled.

His officers begged Mariño to mobilize his entire army to destroy Boves. Mariño refused, arguing that his horses were tired and that he lacked ammunition. Judging by the weakness of enemy fire, however, Boves also lacked ammunition. Going back to Miranda's failures, Patriot forces repeatedly failed to push on to greater victory. Another opportunity lost! Father Blanco observed dejectedly: "Far from taking advantage of this great opportunity, we began a shameful retreat by way of the Pao Mountains to La Victoria, during which many men and horses disappeared. Before beginning this movement, I accompanied Mariño on a tour of the battlefield. We found only 80 cadavers. As usual, Boves' horses had dragged them away; but the fatalities we caused that day were extraordinary."

As in Caracas, Patriots in Valencia faced adversity. Since the previous August, Royalist factions had robbed and killed anyone leaving Valencia without an armed escort. They had removed all possible sources of food in the neighborhood. Only a few sacks of corn remained stored in the citadel—that part of Valencia that Gov. Juan Escalona had surrounded with protective ditches, parapets, and stockades. It included the plaza and eight blocks of houses. Within this area, Escalona had deployed eighteen pieces of artillery.

On March 26, a desperate Bolívar ordered Urdaneta: "Defend Valencia to the death. All our elements of war are there. Send 200 men to strengthen D'Elhuyar's siege line so Royalists cannot send ammunition from Puerto Cabello to Boves." The obedient Urdaneta sent the requested troops, which left only 280 men to defend the city. On March 28, four thousand Royalist troops entered Valencia, but they could not take the citadel for lack of artillery.

Patriots drank their last drop of water on March 31. To make matters worse, during the night of April 2, Boves arrived with one thousand fierce lancers. However, his cavalry, so deadly on the plains, stood useless against entrenched artillery. Boves warned the Royalists of Bolívar and Mariño's advance, so they retired to San Carlos.

Valencia had run out of food by the time Bolívar entered. Royalists had burned many houses, ruined churches, and looted jewelry. They had used churches for stables and barracks. The next day Bolívar rode to La Victoria, about fifty miles east of Valencia, where he received Mariño on April 5. What did those two soldiers—young, ardent, and ambitious—say on finding themselves face to face, with swords in their belts? For the moment, at least, adversity cemented temporary cooperation.

The two bold Caesars agreed that the Royalist army at San Carlos must be destroyed, that Puerto Cabello must be retaken, and that Boves must be kept from creating another army in the llanos. Their immediate problem was food, and this caused a division of forces. Bolívar remained in Valencia to intensify the siege of Puerto Cabello, scrounge for food, and look after the government of Caracas. Ribas raised a few hundred troops in Caracas to hold Boves if he returned before the liberators were ready to deal with him.

Mariño left Valencia on April 11 with twenty-eight hundred hungry men. Francisco Bermúdez and Manuel Valdés commanded thirteen hundred infantry from the East; Tomás Montilla, seven hundred from the West; and Sedeño, eight hundred cavalry. Diego Jalón, emaciated and ragged, but happy to be freed from a Royalist prison, went with the infantry. Only a few days before, Royalists had released him from Puerto Cabello. On April 16 Mariño confronted Royalists at dawn on the plain of Arao in front of San Carlos.

Spanish Col. José Ceballos, as usual, waited for his opponent to form his line of battle: infantry in the center; cavalry on both flanks; Mariño in the rear with reserves; and Urdaneta with cavalry to protect the rear guard. Throughout the day the Patriots engaged in many bloody skirmishes. Late in the afternoon Royalist cavalry broke Mariño's line and routed the Patriots. Survivors dispersed in the hills and escaped to Valencia. Ceballos and Col. Sebastian de la Calzada did not pursue. They waited in San Carlos for Cajigal, charged with bringing troops and supplies from Coro. He arrived on April 30 and took command of the Royalist army with six thousand men.

When Bolívar learned of Mariño's defeat at Arao, he withdrew most of D'Elhuyar's troops to Valencia. Then the Liberator returned to Caracas, where he enlisted two thousand men and boys to reinforce Valencia. During the next two months, the cooperation of the two liberators produced an army of five thousand, the largest and best organized the Republic had yet achieved.

Although larger, the Patriot army continued to suffer from the divisive forces of localism, political dissension, and desertions. On May 20, Escalona discovered that Bermúdez's infantry was about to desert and return to Cumaná. A column of two hundred men had already gotten away, only to be captured and brought back. As an object lesson, Mariño lined up his entire army to witness the execution of every fifth deserter.

Meanwhile in New Granada, Antonio Nariño had driven the Spanish from Popayán, but in May of 1814 Royalists defeated him at Pasto. The commander surrendered himself but not his army. The Spanish imprisoned him for four years in Cádiz, but that did not end his contribution to the independence cause. Spanish liberals released him from prison in 1820, and he immediately returned to fight beside Bolívar. The following year Nariño served briefly as vice president of Gran Colombia.

Torrential rains fell as the Patriots left Valencia on May 26. They marched southwest nine miles and camped at Tocuyita. The next day they marched another six miles and camped on the plain of Carabobo. They stacked their muskets in the only house on the vast plain in order to keep them dry. Bolívar, Mariño, and their chief officers remained on horseback all night, vigilantly watching for desertions or a surprise Royalist attack.

On the morning of May 28 they advanced and formed two lines a cannon-shot from the enemy. Infantry, commanded by Rafael Urdaneta, stood at the front line with Francisco Bermúdez on the right, Florencio Palacios in the center, and Manuel Valdés on the left. Bolívar, Mariño, and Ribas formed the second line. Leandro Palacios and reserves stood on the right; Mariño, with cavalry, and Bolívar, with dragoons, in the center; and Jalón's infantry on the left. Cajigal deployed almost his entire Royalist cavalry on the hill flanking Bermúdez, with two infantry regiments on the plateau and the rest of his cavalry on the hill flanking Valdés.

The first battle of Carabobo began shortly after noon on May 28, 1814. Urdaneta's infantry advanced, charged the enemy center with bayonets, and broke it. Royalist cavalry on Bermúdez's flank raced around him to the rear, where Patriot cavalry decimated them. The Royalists tried in vain to contain the insurgents then fled westward. Even the bold Bolívar dared not pursue. His forces had suffered severe losses and they lacked weapons. The rainy season had just begun, making travel difficult to impossible on the swampy plains. Even Liberators had to respect the dangers and power of the llanos.

Boves was in motion from Calabozo toward Villa de Cura when Bolívar left Caracas on June 12 with his secretary, a chaplain, and a few aides. They arrived the next day at the gorge, where the second battle of La Puerta was about to begin. Mariño had his army in an advantageous position halfway through the gorge. He held a good, strong defensive position capable of withstanding cavalry attack. On a hill to the left he positioned nine pieces of artillery. Mariño's infantry took the center, with cavalry on the right. Jalón faced Boves with the bulk of his cavalry.

Unfortunately, Bolívar took command and rashly ordered an advance onto the plains where Boves's cavalry held a great advantage. Each army had about three thousand men, but Mariño's battle-weary troops still suffered the debilitating effects of dysentery. The relentless Boves destroyed the Patriot army in less than three hours.

The Royalists spared none of the wounded. They executed all prisoners except Jalón. The inventive Bermúdez, surrounded by llaneros, threw them his handsome cape. While they fought over it, he escaped eastward across the Caracas llanos to Barcelona. Bolívar, Mariño, Ribas, and a few other officers fled to Caracas. Boves invited Jalón to lunch the next day at Villa de Cura. When Boves had finished eating, he ordered Jalón beheaded.

After the battle of Carabobo, Bolívar had sent Urdaneta west against Ceballos and Calzada. Urdaneta was at San Carlos in mid-July when reports arrived that Bolívar had evacuated Caracas and that Morales and Boves were pursuing him and Mariño. Urdaneta's officers included Father Blanco, the Scot MacGregor, and José Antonio Anzoátegui (1789–1819). The latter, born in Barcelona, Venezuela, had been a leading figure in the Patriot Society of Caracas. He fought at Guiana in 1812 and suffered Spanish imprisonment after the fall of the First Republic. Released the following year, he became an invaluable ally to the Liberator.

Bolívar went to Caracas to confer with government officials, especially Casa León, collector of revenues and director of the economy. What better choice could Bolívar have made to deal with a depressed Caracas than this pragmatic, capable man? Patriot recruiting agents found only empty pueblos. No one wanted to serve in the Patriot army.

On July 9 Bolívar held a war council. His officers agreed that Archbishop Narciso Coll y Pratt and Casa León should be left behind to bridle the fury of Boves. Bolívar led eastward out of the city a mass of twenty thousand women, children, and "worthless men," along with the remnant of his shattered army. The governor of Trinidad reported the grim demographic reality. "Caracas and La Guaira according to the Census of 1810 had a population of 55,000 souls now have only 7,500."

Following his victory at La Puerta, Boves turned his attention back toward Valencia. Now armed with ample munitions, the Royalists besieged Valencia. After twenty-one days of horror, starvation and stench from the dead forced Escalona and his ninety sick defenders to surrender the citadel. The ever-creative Boves held a macabre, sadistic victory ball where he forced the women of Valencia to dance and sing while Royalists killed their husbands, sons, and brothers.

Terrified refugees from the valleys of Aragua and Tuy filled Caracas as black Royalist sympathizers committed acts of violence against all whites in those valleys. Bolívar sent Pedro Gual from Caracas to plead with the English admiral at Barbados to help prevent a massacre in Caracas. Gual boarded an English schooner and, like previous emissaries, soon found himself stranded in St. Thomas. He and two other agents stranded there bought a brig and sailed to Cartagena.

Caracas could not sustain a siege. Food was scarce, the West was exhausted and lost, and only a few officers and troops remained. Bolívar struggled mightily with how to handle the coming disaster. The wealth of Caracas churches—wrought silver and jewels—filled twenty-four boxes. Bolívar sent them to La Guaira, where a Patriot fleet carried them to Barcelona. On July 13 Boves and Cajigal started together for Caracas. They had not gone far when Boves let the captain general know that he, Boves, ranked as supreme commander. Cajigal returned to Puerto Cabello and sailed to Spain to report this gross insubordination. Ambitions and divisions also plagued the Royalist side. On July 16 Boves met with the archbishop, Casa León, and a retinue of followers outside the city. They entered the city and heard mass at the cathedral.

The always adaptable Casa León wisely made himself indispensable to Boves. The marques had been in difficult positions before, but none as dangerous as this one. He could lose his head at the slightest whim of the llanero chieftain. He showed Boves secret account books that proved he had protected the property of Royalists. The wily marques survived. Boves made him political governor of the city. Casa León did help restrain Boves during the few days that he remained in Caracas, but Boves could not abide city life. After ten days in Caracas, he left for the llanos. With a base in Calabozo he raised yet another army. By the end of August he again rode east across the Caracas llanos to exterminate the Patriots in the provinces of Barcelona and Cumaná.

On August 2, when Bolívar and his exiles arrived at Barcelona, Mariño was in Cumaná. He had secured supplies and munitions in Margarita and had sent young Antonio José de Sucre with men and supplies to join Bermúdez in the llanos at Aragua de Barcelona. There he concentrated his troops, hoping to destroy Morales. Bolívar marched southwest with his army and joined Bermúdez, who now had about three thousand troops. Bolívar disliked Mariño's defense plan but did not insist that he change it. Mariño ruled as supreme commander of the East. Bermúdez, his lieutenant, served as the superior officer at Aragua de Barcelona.

The battle of Aragua de Barcelona began on the morning of August 17. As the hours passed, Morales compressed the defenders into a smaller and smaller area. Running perilously low on ammunition, Bolívar and four hundred men escaped to Barcelona. Brave, hotheaded Bermúdez fought on until most of his men had been killed. Then he broke through the enemy line with Sucre and a few others and fled on horseback east to Maturín.

Morales and his troops beheaded all civilians in Aragua and the surrounding forests. The Royalist Díaz tells us that 3,700 Patriots met a violent death; another 730 wounded were taken prisoner. The Royalists lost 1,011 killed and 832 wounded. Most of the wounded died later. All of the 6,000 casualties, Patriot and Royalist, were Venezuelans. Bolívar had declared his war to the death against Spaniards in the hope of uniting Venezuelans. So far, his policy had failed; Venezuelans still killed Venezuelans, as they would continue to do after achieving independence.

Morales entered Barcelona on August 20. His troops hunted and killed refugees who fled to surrounding areas. Mariño held a war council, with Ribas, Valdés, Leandro Palacios, and D'Elhuyar present. Piar did not attend. He had made himself master of the port on the island of Margarita. Tempers flared when Ribas attacked Mariño's plan to evacuate Cumaná, ship munitions and the church wealth to Margarita or Güiria, and sustain resistance there. Ribas declared that the Patriots should hold Cumaná whatever the cost. Most of the officers sided with him and deposed Mariño. The council ended abruptly after learning of Morales's approach to the deserted city of Cumaná. The terrified inhabitants had already filled all available vessels and sailed for the islands.

Ribas and most of the officers fled east to Cariaco. Mariño sent eight thousand musket cartridges to Bermúdez at Maturín. Bolívar arrived in Cumaná on August 25. The next day the two liberators sailed the forty-three miles to Margarita Island, carrying the church silver and jewels. The crossing took two days, enough time for Bolívar and Mariño to learn more about the importance and needs of the navy. They now understood why

José Bianchi, an Italian serving in Venezuela's navy, complained that his vessels, in very bad condition, had not been overhauled in more than a year. Furthermore, the debts Bianchi had contracted to supply the navy had not been honored. His crews (mostly Italian, French, Corsican, or Portuguese) clamored to be paid. With scarce rations and no pay or prize money, crew members often deserted at the first opportunity.

The squadron anchored outside the harbor on Margarita on August 28. Refugees from Cumaná had already told Piar that officers and troops had turned against Mariño. The liberators sent envoys to tell Piar that Mariño had named him as commanding general of Margarita. Piar responded, "Why did you not bring me men and money?" Bolívar sent an aide to reason with Piar, but he jeered and declared Bolívar and Mariño outlaws. The two liberators had yet another ambitious rival to contend with.

The desperate Bianchi could get neither food nor water for his squadron. He and the liberators dispatched one vessel loaded with refugees to St. Thomas, another to Ribas at Carúpano, and left one at Margarita. Then they divided the church wealth and the remaining vessels. Bianchi took eight boxes of silver and jewels and three vessels to St. Bartholomew. Bolívar and Mariño, with sixteen boxes of silver and jewels on two vessels, sailed to join Ribas at Carúpano.

While they crossed the channel, Ribas declared that Mariño and Bolívar had deserted the Republic. Another rival; yet more dissension! He declared himself supreme chief of the West and Piar supreme chief of the East. When Bolívar and Mariño arrived at Carúpano on September 3, Ribas arrested Mariño and demanded that Bolívar turn over the church wealth and supplies onboard their vessels. With few options, Bolívar delivered the sixteen boxes of silver and jewels and the supplies.

Bolívar issued a "manifesto to the People of Venezuela" on September 7 to defend himself and to rally support. His writing took on an uncharacteristic tone of fatalism.

It is malicious stupidity to attribute to public men the vicissitudes which the order of events produces in a state. It is not within the power of a general or magistrate, in times of turbulence, of shock, and of divergent opinions, to check the torrent of human passions, which, agitated by the forces of revolutions, grow in proportion to the force which resists them. And even when grave errors or violent passions in the leaders cause frequent injury to the Republic, these very injuries must, nevertheless, be weighed fairly and their causes sought in the original source of all misfortune—human frailty—and the control of Destiny over all events.

Bolívar concluded with an exhortation:

> Yes, Compatriots, your virtues alone are capable of combating success-
> fully this multitude of madmen who do not understand their own inter-
> est and honor. Freedom has never been subjugated by tyranny. Do not
> compare your physical forces with those of the enemy, because spirit and
> matter cannot be compared. You are men; they are beasts. You are free;
> they are slaves. Fight, and you will win. God grants victory to the perse-
> vering.

Ribas then permitted Bolívar and Mariño to board their vessel and sail out
of the harbor to Cartagena. For the second, but certainly not the last time,
Bolívar had to flee his beloved Venezuela.

On September 19, Bolívar, Mariño, and the other refugees debarked at
Cartagena. Factionalism divided Patriots in the city. Col. Manuel del Castillo,
who would challenge Bolívar's authority, led the victorious faction. As the
liberators departed for Cartagena, Piar arrived at Carúpano with two hundred men determined to kill both Mariño and Bolívar. Patriot infighting
proved to be a great ally for the Royalists and a prime cause of the destruction of the Second Venezuelan Republic. The second "foolish fatherland"
would perish like the first.

Mariño, D'Elhuyar, and Pedro Gual (he had been in the city for some
time) were content to remain in Cartagena. Bolívar, however, anxiously
wanted to unite forces with Urdaneta and report to the Congress at Tunja.
An Englishman in Cartagena wrote to a friend in Jamaica on October 5,
"Col. Robertson and Bolívar are to leave here this evening . . . 2000 of Bolívar's
army are at Cúcuta, on the borders of Venezuela and in this State, which he
again joins, bent on pushing his fortunes once more" (*Royal Gazette*, October 8–15, 1814).

Bolívar would soon face political disaster. Patriot forces in Venezuela faced
military disaster. The bloody Boves marched from Barcelona to attack Patriot forces at Cumaná. In the battle outside the city on October 11 and 12,
Boves annihilated the defenders. He sacked the city and beheaded the inhabitants, then advanced on Maturín. Ribas joined with Bermúdez to
counter the Royalist threat to Maturín. They marched west on November 1
to confront Morales at Santa Rosa, some ninety miles from Maturín. They
had not gone far, however, when a scout reported the approach of Boves.
Bermúdez wanted to turn north against Boves; Ribas preferred to continue
west. More dissension. Neither would go with the other. Bermúdez stub-

bornly rode toward Boves with only twelve hundred men, while Ribas returned to Maturín.

On November 9 Boves's terrible lancers attacked and overwhelmed Bermúdez and his cavalry in the hills of Magueyes. Bermúdez and a few survivors escaped back to Maturín. Strangely, Boves did not follow up his victory. He remained inactive for two weeks. Was he depressed? Did he have a prescience of doom? He finally rode south on November 22 and five days later joined with Morales at Urica, just sixty miles west of Maturín.

Meanwhile in Maturín, Ribas and Bermúdez renewed their dispute. Ribas insisted that they take the whole army to Urica and reconquer Venezuela in a single gallant battle. Bermúdez and other officers argued that they should wait in Maturín and let Boves attack. Ribas left with part of the army and the two best officers, Pedro Zaraza and José Tadeo Monagas. (The latter would survive the wars of independence and go on to become a caudillo and, in 1846, president of Venezuela.) Bermúdez grudgingly followed Ribas, but many disgruntled officers and their cavalry remained behind at Maturín.

Bolívar sailed up the Magdalena River until he arrived opposite Ocaña on October 27. On November 12 he approached Tunja, and Urdaneta's troops, "delirious with joy," came out to meet him and escorted him into the city. Urdaneta called a review of the troops that afternoon at Bolívar's request. Bolívar addressed the men:

Soldiers! My heart swells with happiness at seeing you, but at what cost! At the cost of discipline, of subordination which is the first virtue of a soldier. Your chief is the worthy General Urdaneta, who laments as I do, the excess to which you have been carried by your affections. Soldiers! Do not repeat such acts of disobedience. If you love me, prove it by your loyalty and submission to your chief. I am only a soldier like you, who comes to offer his services to this sister nation. For all of us, our native land is America; our enemies, the Spaniards; our motto, independence and liberty.

The soldiers cheered Bolívar, Urdaneta, and New Granada. The next day they continued the march and entered Tunja on November 22. Two days later Bolívar gave an accounting to Congress of his success in the 1813 campaign, of the establishment of the Second Republic and of its fall before the terrible onslaught of Boves and Morales. Camilo Torres y Tenorio, president of Congress, interrupted: "General, your country is not vanquished while you have a sword. With it you will return to redeem Venezuela again from her oppressors. The Congress of New Granada will give you its protection because it is satisfied with your record. You may have been an unfortunate soldier but you are a great man."

Congress placed Bolívar in command of all troops. He would successfully use force to make Cundinamarca enter the union. He would fail, however, in bringing Castillo to heel in Cartagena. Manuel de Bernardo Alvarez was now dictator of Santa Fe de Bogotá. Bolívar halted near Bogotá and sent a letter on December 8 to Alvarez. The note included both threats and conciliation.

> I offer absolute immunity of life, property, and honor to all the inhabitants of your capital, both Americans and Europeans, if by agreement with me, or by amicably joining the general government, the spilling of blood and the use of force can be avoided. Let those tremble who would wage war against their brothers, who come to liberate them. Let those tremble who would battle the army of Venezuela united with that of New Granada; let the tyrants tremble, since they alone would take up arms against these saviors of their country. But no one need tremble before the armies of the union, when these are received with the honor that is their due.

Alvarez refused to negotiate with the Liberator, but four days of house-to-house fighting forced him to surrender on December 12.

Meanwhile Boves continued his reign of terror in Venezuela. Ribas and Bermúdez arrived at Urica on the morning of December 5 and found the enemy ready for battle. Zaraza and Monagas charged and destroyed the Royalist right wing. Boves, seeing his strong column enveloped, prepared to leave the center when a Patriot lancer killed him. The seemingly invincible Boves was dead at thirty-two. As Irish-born Patriot Daniel Florencio O'Leary noted, "of all the monsters produced by revolution in America or elsewhere, José Tomás Boves was the most bloodthirsty and ferocious."

Despite the loss of Boves, the Royalists countered effectively. "Then," Monagas tells us, "the enemy center and left charged our line, enveloped and completely defeated it." Ribas and Bermúdez fled almost alone to Maturín. Monagas and Zaraza took refuge in the llanos to the south, where they became guerrilla chiefs in control of large areas above the Orinoco River.

Morales pressed on and attacked Maturín on December 10. Ribas and Bermúdez held out until the next day and then escaped in different directions. Royalists caught Ribas near Tucupido, where they killed and decapitated him. They fried his head in oil and took it to Caracas, where it remained as a grizzly warning in an iron cage hanging at the entrance to the city. With grisly humor, they topped the head with the red cap that Ribas usually wore perched jauntily over one eye.

When Morales entered Maturín on December 11, he ordered a general slaughter by the sword. Refugees, the last survivors from Caracas, Barcelona, and Cumaná, filled the city. Royalist historian Díaz wrote: "All that breathed ceased to exist on that terrible day. Many of the chief families perished there, even to their slaves. There also Morales seized the 16 boxes of jewels and silver which Bolívar had delivered to Ribas."

At the invitation of the electoral college of Cundinamarca, the Congress of Tunja moved to Santa Fe de Bogotá on January 13, 1815. Now calling itself the Union Congress, the assembly represented eleven states. The Union Congress named Bolívar captain general of the union armies and approved his plan for defense of the frontiers. Bolívar would take Santa Marta and enter Venezuela via Río Hacha and Maracaibo. Urdaneta and Santander, with a second army, would enter Venezuela by way of Cúcuta. A third Patriot army would deploy south to take Popayán and Pasto.

Bolívar established his authority in Bogotá, but disorder prevailed in Cartagena. Gov. Pedro Gual had managed to prevent civil war in Cartagena, but Manuel del Castillo had advanced to the walls of the city and kept supplies from entering. Hoping to maintain peace and establish friendly relations with Castillo, Gual opened the gate to him on January 18, 1815. There was no bloodshed, but nine days later the electoral college, at the point of Castillo's bayonets, named Juan de Dios Amador governor. Castillo intended to execute political rivals Luciano D'Elhuyar and Gabriel Piñeres, but Gual persuaded him to exile them to the United States.

Most of Bolívar's army had already descended the Bogotá plateau and embarked on the Magdalena River at Honda. Bolívar left Santa Fe de Bogotá on January 24 to join his troops at Cartagena. When he debarked at Mompós (about one hundred miles from Cartagena as the condor flies), Tomás Montilla and Father J. Marimón y Enríquez, president of Congress, greeted Bolívar with two letters from Gual. Gual sought the Liberator's good offices in restoring peace to troubled Cartagena. Bolívar answered with a forthright and revealing note on February 9, agreeing to try to work with Castillo.

> You ask me, "Can I not be the mediator in a reconciliation that I heartily wish to see established?" Let me reply with another question: Can I subordinate the interests of my country to base and violent passions? Can I

listen to talk of vengeance, and lend a deaf ear to the voice of reason? Can I despise a friend who offers me the friendship of an enemy? No, no, no, dear Gual.

I pursue the glorious career of arms only to garner the honors it affords, to free my country, and to merit the blessings of its peoples. Why, then, would I care to tarnish the laurels with which fortune favors me on the field of battle and allow myself to be carried away, like a woman, by emotions truly feminine?

Bolívar remained at Mompós for forty days while communiqués passed back and forth between the various political factions. It became evident that Castillo would never cooperate, so Bolívar marched his army of two thousand men toward La Popa—the high hill overlooking Cartagena. La Popa commanded all the land approaches to Cartagena. From there Bolívar could divert caravans to feed his army with food intended for the city. Castillo countered by sending men to poison La Popa's water tanks. The ubiquitous Englishman in Cartagena wrote to a friend in Jamaica (*Royal Gazette,* April 1–8, 1815): "Bolívar's army have no water, but what is brought with immense labour from the interior. A few skirmishes have taken place between the outposts in which Castillo's force had the advantage."

When poison and desertions had reduced his army to five hundred men, Bolívar asked for an interview with Castillo. The two enemies met at the foot of La Popa on May 8. They signed a peace pact agreeing to cease all hostilities. Castillo's victory and power were short-lived. Two months later Spanish Gen. Pablo Morillo (1778–1837) laid siege to the city. The Royalists took the city in December and executed Castillo. Here, as later, Morillo showed himself to be unbending, ruthless, and bloody. Like many Royalists of his time, he erroneously believed that a Royalist Venezuela could be reconstituted by force. By 1820 he had learned to his sorrow that Spain's declining political and military fortunes dictated a far different future. He would negotiate an armistice with Bolívar, then request and receive reassignment to serve the Spanish Crown elsewhere.

Bolívar resigned his military commission and agreed to sail to Jamaican exile, 530 miles across the Caribbean. He returned to his army and said:

The Government of the United Provinces placed me at your head for the purpose of breaking the chains of our enslaved brothers. No tyrant has been vanquished by your arms; they have been stained by the blood of brothers. I leave you. The salvation of the army has imposed this penalty upon me. Your existence and my own are incompatible here. I prefer yours. Your welfare is mine, my friends, my brothers—everyone's in short, for upon you depends the republic.

The Second Republic and the independence cause lay in ruins. Royalists had shot dozens of captured Patriot leaders, including ex-president of Congress Camilo Torres y Tenorio. Only a few flickers of hope remained. Zaraza, Monagas, and other Patriots waged guerrilla campaigns in the llanos, filling the power void left by the death of Boves. Urdaneta kept the cause alive as he withdrew the Army of the West to New Granada. To Bolívar, languishing in Jamaica, glory and victory seemed distant, unreachable goals.

CHAPTER 7

Regrouping in Jamaica,
1815–16

Bolívar sailed to Jamaica on the English brig of war *Descubierta* and debarked at Kingston on May 14, 1815. On May 19 he wrote a long letter to his English friend Maxwell Hyslop, "merchant of Jamaica." After a brief account of his conflict with Castillo, Bolívar detailed the military weakness of New Granada. The Patriots had only twenty-five hundred men in Cartagena. This small force could not regain the Magdalena Valley from Santa Marta and restore communications with Bogotá. The Patriots numbered only a thousand men under arms in the province of Pamplona. This force could not garrison Cúcuta and defend the fourteen-hundred-mile boundary between Venezuela and the New Granadan provinces of Pamplona and Casanare. Likewise, they had but five hundred troops in Bogotá and sixteen hundred troops in Popayán to hold the southern frontier against Royalist Pasto and Quito.

His military and political reversals had plunged the always mercurial Bolívar into yet another fit of depression. Having been willing to fight and die for his country, he now felt that he served it best by leaving.

> The renunciation of my command, of my fortune, and of my future glory
> required no effort on my part. It is so natural for me to prefer the welfare
> of the Republic to all else that, the more I suffer in its behalf, the greater
> the inner satisfaction my soul receives. I will never again be a general. I

will depart and live far from friends and countrymen. I shall not die for my country. But I shall have rendered it a new service by bringing peace in my absence. Were I to remain here, New Granada would divide into parties, and the civil war would be eternal.

Rapidly changing conditions in Spain gave Bolívar further reason for gloom. Having brought Spaniards under his heel by abolishing the liberal Constitution of 1812, Ferdinand VII set about organizing an expedition to do the same to his rebellious subjects in America. He assembled 10,500 veterans of the campaigns against Napoleon, the largest Spanish army ever sent to the Indies. With great reluctance, thirty-seven-year-old Gen. Pablo Morillo accepted command of the army. His war-weary troops had neither the energy nor desire to fight in America. They would certainly not relish a "war to the death" in Venezuela. After sundry delays, the 12,254 troops departed Cádiz on February 17, 1815, on twenty warships and fifty-nine transports. They believed their destination to be Buenos Aires. For reasons of security and morale, Morillo did not enlighten them until well at sea. Poor morale, short supplies, disease, and disillusionment would plague Spanish forces for the duration of the conflict.

Furthermore, Morillo clashed with Francisco Montalvo, who became viceroy of New Granada on April 28, 1816. As Rebecca A. Earle notes, Morillo "regarded Montalvo as a shining incompetent, inept and inexperienced with both the nature of the country he headed and with warfare in general." Montalvo's sword, according to Morillo, remained "a virgin after its long career; it will have no other merit than that of having belonged to an owner who lived for a long time." Montalvo held Morillo in equal contempt. Like the Patriots, Royalist officers and bureaucrats suffered from deep personal and ideological divisions that hamstrung their effectiveness.

The seventy-four-gun *San Pedro Alcántara* served as the Royalist expedition's flagship. They anchored at Puerto Santo to the windward of Carúpano on April 3. The new troops joined Morales with an army of five thousand men ready to regain Margarita from Juan Bautista Arismendi. Morillo and Morales both sailed to Margarita and anchored at the port of Pampatar on April 7. Bitter disagreements and distrust would continue to mark the unhappy relations between these two Royalist officers.

Arismendi (1775–1841), born in La Asunción on Margarita Island, supported independence early and fought in the 1812 Guiana expedition. He returned to Margarita, spoke on behalf of the Patriot cause, and found himself jailed as a result. After Patriots wrested the island from Spanish control in 1813, he became governor. Daunted by the huge expedition, however, Arismendi surrendered, but the brave, stalwart José Francisco Bermúdez (1782–1831) refused to surrender. The latter would go on to an illustrious career, commanding the Army of the East, fighting in the Battle of Carabobo (1821), and commanding the department of Orinoco. He and some friends boarded the *Golindrina* and sailed unscathed through the Spanish squadron, screaming insults at the Royalists. Three small vessels filled with refugees also escaped from Margarita and sailed directly west for Curaçao.

Morillo reestablished royal authority on Margarita and left a garrison there. En route from Margarita to Caracas, however, disaster struck the Royalists as a sudden explosion sank Morillo's flagship. The Spanish lost one million pesos intended for salaries; a large store of fortification artillery; eight thousand muskets and an equal number of swords, pistols, and uniforms; more than four thousand pounds of powder, bombs, grenades, bullets; and the personal equipment of the officers.

Unhappy Venezuela would have to support Morillo and his army. He spent several months seizing private property and selling it at auction to rebuild his war chest. The eastern sector of Venezuela, especially the area of La Güiria and Maturín, became a constant headache to him. He thought the Patriot chiefs from there had escaped to Trinidad, so he sent a list of names to Governor Woodford demanding that he deliver the refugees listed therein. Bermúdez headed the list.

According to Woodford, Patriots in Trinidad did not present a threat. "The alarm of Don Pablo Morillo," he wrote, "as to the preparations or assembly of refugees along the coast of Trinidad with a view to attacking Guayana is at present groundless." Meanwhile, Bermúdez sailed to Cartagena and other privateers continued building a secret stockpile of war materiel in Trinidad. Patriot privateers continually harassed Morillo's shipping. Late in July he learned that José Padilla, with two gunboats and seventy-four men, had captured the Spanish corvette *Neptune* after it had passed Cartagena on its way to Panama.

The able Padilla captured the new governor for Panama and his family, ten other officials and their ladies, 274 Spanish soldiers, two thousand muskets, and other war materiel. The ubiquitous Englishman reported that "the muskets taken in this vessel have their accouterments complete. The troops and crew were also completely armed and accounted. The easy conquest of this corvette proves the little relish which Spanish troops have to encounter the Americans."

Padilla, a pardo, was born in 1778, the same year as Morillo. A native of Riohacha, a town in the Colombian province of Guarjira, he grew up in a poor family. The poverty of his home and his own spirit of adventure prompted Padilla to join the Spanish navy. He began his sea career as a cabin boy, but the British captured and imprisoned him at the battle of Trafalgar. He escaped in 1808 and returned to New Granada. In 1811 Padilla found himself in command of a gunboat belonging to the squadron of Cartagena. When Bolívar tried to enter Cartagena, Padilla again suffered imprisonment for championing the Liberator. After Bolívar sailed to Jamaica, Padilla was released, but he could not forget that Castillo and Amador had put him in prison. After rising to the rank of major general, Padilla would be executed on September 25, 1828, for turning against Bolívar.

Castillo unwisely did nothing for the defense of Cartagena during the summer of 1815. He married a beautiful young girl and remained at home, receiving his officers in a haughty manner. A strange feeling of optimism pervaded the city, fueled by a steady stream of plunder brought in by privateers. Renato Beluche (born of French and Italian parents in New Orleans in 1780), Charles Lominé (a Frenchman), and other privateers sent in or brought in prizes laden with food and war materiel.

The rest of New Granada remained uneasy. Patriots had no communication with Cartagena, and their armies needed weapons and ammunition. The Union Congress at Santa Fe de Bogotá sent agents to England to buy war supplies. They enlisted the help of Pierre Louis Brion (rendered into Spanish as Luis Brión), a Jewish Dutch merchant and outfitter of ships from Curaçao. Brión chartered the *Dardo,* an English corvette of twenty-four guns, and transported his cargo, bought on English credit.

Brión sailed from London with "15,200 muskets, 2,500 musket locks, 400 carbines, 200 sabres, 200 pairs of pistols, 200 quintals powder, three printing presses, and a complete armament; the whole on account of the United Provinces of New Granada." When the *Dardo* arrived at the island of St. Thomas, Brión wrote to Bolívar in Kingston, Jamaica, asking for advice on the situation in New Granada. Brión wanted to dispose of his unpaid-for cargo to best advantage. Bolívar replied on July 30: "New Granada has plenty of money to buy from you everything you bring. The best route for you to take is up the Atrato River as Cartagena now has no communication with the interior, is without money, and has more than enough arms and ammunition."

As Brión approached Cartagena on his way to the Atrato, he decided to find out what was happening in the city. He sailed into Boca Chica, the narrow pass by which ships enter the bay, and fired a salute to Fort San Fernando. Brión dropped anchor on July 30 and became the guest of H. L. V. Ducoudray Holstein for the next five months. Ducoudray commanded the forts in the area. Born in Denmark, he had fought nearly twenty years under the tricolor of France. Wounded and left for dead in Spain, he lived to escape to Cartagena.

Ducoudray's career with the Patriot forces points up two of their central weaknesses: factionalism and personal ambition. In the first major power struggle he confronted, Ducoudray had sided with the Castillo faction against Bolívar. He, Luis Aury, and other officers, however, became disgusted with Castillo's inaction as Morillo and Morales converged on Cartagena. They also tired of, in Ducoudray's words, "his tyranny and haughty manners." Aury, a French privateer, soon became commander of the naval forces of the Republic of Cartagena.

Ducoudray would switch his allegiance to Bolívar and become for a time his chief of staff. However, the "foreigner" *(extranjero)*, as foreign officers were called, remained very critical of the Liberator's character and actions. His *Memoirs of Bolivar,* published in 1829, is a litany of harsh criticism of his commander's vanity and jealousies. Over time, he says Bolívar became "much more vain, ambitious and bold." However, he also revealed his own deep-seated prejudices: "General Bolivar, who like the greatest part of his countrymen, the inhabitants of Caracas, is very dissembling, and very dexterous in finding out various secret means to intrigue, and to gain his aim by numerous windings and doublings . . . always anxious to save his reputation and zealous to preserve his authority."

About the time of Brión's arrival, Morillo debarked eighty-five hundred troops at Santa Marta—five thousand Spanish veterans and thirty-five hundred Venezuelans accustomed to the heat and humidity of the coast. Morales and the Venezuelans crossed the Magdalena River, then marched toward Cartagena through swamps and thickets to encircle the city on its land side. Observers on the schooner *La Popa* reported these enemy movements but erroneously believed that the approaching rainy season would protect them. They felt confident that Morales could not approach with cannons because of the soggy conditions. Inhabitants of the area fled before Morales and found refuge within the walls of Cartagena. The city now had eighteen thousand mouths to feed.

Morillo, meanwhile, had established a sea blockade of the walled city and the eight-mile-long island of Terra Bomba, that, with the island of Barú, enclosed the Bay of Cartagena. Morillo could not take the four forts that

Renato Beluche, Patriot privateer.

controlled the Boca Chica entrance to the bay. He did, however, take all of Barú except Fort San José, and he sent a fleet of light gunboats through Pasacaballos, a canal dug by Spaniards two centuries earlier through mangrove swamps on the south end of Barú.

Aury kept Morillo's gunboats from entering the bay until October 3, when he ran out of gunpowder. He begged Brión to let him have ammunition from the *Dardo,* but Brión refused. Morillo's gunboats entered the bay through Pasacaballos and connected with the land forces of Morales. Aury returned up the bay twelve miles to the anchorage in front of Cartagena. He went into the city amidst rumors of treason against Castillo. At one o'clock on the morning of October 9, Ducoudray, Aury, and other officers declared Castillo a traitor, arrested him, and put Bermúdez in command of the city. As Morillo's fleet tightened the blockade, people in the city began to die of starvation, one hundred a day, then two hundred, then three hundred. With no place to bury the dead, cadavers piled up in the streets.

In early November, Renato Beluche in *La Popa* beat off two Royalist schooners, entered Boca Chica, and anchored at Fort San Fernando with a cargo of food. Brión and Ducoudray told him that only Bolívar could unite the Patriots. In a letter of November 11, he urged that Bolívar come to Cartagena:

> Dear General, an old soldier of acknowledged republican sentiments invites you to come and place yourself at the head of the government of Cartagena where Bermúdez acts with great weakness and apathy. I engage, by the influence which I have here in Boca Chica and in Cartagena, to put in execution this change of government without the least bloodshed, and pledge my life for all the consequences. Captain Pierril [Renato Beluche] who commands *La Popa* has orders to take you and your friends to Boca Chica.

Beluche in *La Popa* and Brión in the *Dardo* evaded the blockading squadron in mid-November and sailed to different ports. Beluche made for Kingston, and Brión, for Aux Cayes (in Spanish, Los Cayos, now Les Cayes) on Haiti's southern coast. Brión's cargo would be safe from confiscation in the neutral country of Haiti. Bolívar could prepare to invade Venezuela from Haiti without international complications.

The Great Powers had not yet recognized the Republic of Haiti, established in 1804 after a successful slave revolt initiated in 1791 by Boukman and other slave leaders against French masters in Saint-Domingue. Then Toussaint L'Ouverture brought vision and leadership to the slave revolt and turned it into a drive for independence. Writing in the *American Historical Review* (February, 2000), Franklin Knight succinctly put Haiti's independence into broader perspective.

> The genesis of the Haitian Revolution cannot be separated from the wider concomitant events of the later eighteenth-century Atlantic world. Indeed, the period between 1750 and 1850 represented an age of spontaneous, interrelated revolutions, and events in Saint Domingue/Haiti constitute an integral—though often overlooked—part of the history of that larger

sphere. These multi-faceted revolutions combined to alter the way individuals and groups saw themselves and their place in the world. But, even more, the intellectual changes of the period instilled in some political leaders a confidence (not new in the eighteenth century, but far more generalized than before) that creation and creativity were not exclusively divine or accidental attributes, and that both general societies and individual conditions could be rationally engineered.

Meanwhile, the stench of putrefaction in Cartagena, unbearable by December, tellingly and terrifyingly illustrated the high cost of independence. Six thousand persons had died and many remained unburied; some fled the misery and horror and died outside the city walls. Bermúdez, his supporters, and their families planned to sail away with Aury's squadron. First they sent more than two thousand surviving poor outside the city. Soon a messenger arrived with a letter from Morillo. "I am authorized by the laws of war to drive these poor people back into the city, but I cannot because of their misery. I will keep them, but the city must surrender within three days."

More than two thousand walking skeletons boarded the thirteen vessels of Aury's squadron on the night of December 5 and sailed past Royalist batteries down Cartagena Bay to Fort San Fernando at Boca Chica Pass. The enemy fired only a few token shots at the squadron, producing a few casualties on some vessels. The Patriots had not surrendered, but they were evacuating, and Morillo wanted them to get away. He would have fewer mouths to feed and fewer cadavers to bury or burn.

The ragtag Patriot squadron anchored at Fort San Fernando on December 6. That day and the next, officers and their families boarded the vessels with food from the fort. The squadron could not sail until the wind changed on December 9. On the open sea, winds increased to gale force, separating the vessels. Three passengers rode unseen and unwelcome with the refugees: hunger, thirst, and death. Only a few hundred refugees survived to debark from the four vessels that made it to Los Cayos in Haiti. Another Patriot soon joined them—José Padilla.

While Bermúdez and others planned their escape from Cartagena, Padilla planned his revenge against his one-time jailers Castillo and Amador. The privateer *Cometa* stood at anchor in Cartagena. Padilla knew that privateer's English captain planned to sail with Aury's squadron. Castillo and Amador learned of the planned departure and booked passage on the *Cometa* for themselves, their families, and friends. They also loaded their considerable portable wealth.

The Castillo party's property included "6 trunks and 10 bags of wearing apparel; a trunk containing 30 bars of silver, value $2,475; 3 bars of gold, value $3,888; doubloons and dollars to the amount of $1,330; several remnants of silk and a pound of sewing silk; a dirk, its silver sheath; and other articles he does not recollect." Amador sent on board trunks filled with his family's clothes, silver, and jewels. He personally carried two thousand dollars in silver currency.

The *Cometa* sailed down the bay on the night of December 5–6 with Aury's squadron after 106 days of siege. One of the shots from Royalist batteries hit the mast, but the ship managed to escape with the other vessels. On the night of December 10, the *Cometa* put in at the island of Old Providence "to repair the mast, and there landed the passengers, their property and effects remaining on board as the master said they would be ready to sail for Kingston in 3 or 4 days." Passengers had scarcely left the ship when the captain had their trunks opened. José Padilla assisted in counting the money. According to the testimony of Amador, the money, bullion, and jewels of the seventy-six passengers amounted to the considerable sum of 100,000 pesos.

To complete his revenge, Padilla and a party of seven men came on shore and robbed the passengers of all they carried. Padilla stood by while one of his men put a pistol to Castillo's breast and "robbed him of 6 doubloons which he had in his pocket." They returned to the *Cometa*, fired several cannon shots back at shore, and sailed away.

A few days later another English vessel took Castillo, Amador, and the others to Kingston, where they complained to the English authorities. When Padilla sailed into Kingston, Castillo and Jamaican authorities boarded it with a warrant and searched Padilla's trunk. They removed "some remnants of silk, the pound of sewing silk, and the dirk with a silver sheath" belonging to Castillo. Castillo and Amador remained in Jamaica, but Padilla found a way to get to Los Cayos and Bolívar.

Renato Beluche found an unhappy Bolívar in Kingston when he delivered Ducoudray's apologetic plea, penned back in November. The past six months had not been pleasant ones. William, duke of Manchester, governor of Jamaica, had initially received him cordially and granted him interviews. The once wealthy Bolívar, now penniless, lived on loans from his friend Maxwell Hyslop. He worked incessantly to convince British authorities that the time was ripe to outfit an invasion fleet to strike Venezuela.

Despite his surface cordiality, Manchester offered nothing concrete to Bolívar. On the contrary, the Kingston press regularly published the governor's edict that strictly prohibited all and every person and persons whomsoever, being owner, commander, or mariner, on board any ship or vessel, or boat whatsoever, from navigating, or attempting to navigate, any ship, vessel or boat, out of any port, harbor or creek whatsoever, in this our island, having on board any arms or ammunition, without license first obtained for that purpose, from under the hand of the governor or person executing the functions of governor for the time being, under pain of our highest displeasure and of such pain and penalties, etc.

This prohibition appeared regularly in Kingston's *Royal Gazette* from mid-1815 through February 1817.

English merchants, like Hyslop, did not want to miss any future trade advantages. Manchester and the British government did not want to miss any opportunity to dominate Spanish America. Manchester may have been the "Gentleman of the Island" who wrote to Bolívar on August 29, 1815, asking for his opinion on the future of Spanish America.

Bolívar penned a lengthy reply, more than eight thousand words, to the "Gentleman" on September 6, 1815. His so-called Jamaica Letter began by reviewing the traumas his country had suffered "from the time of her discovery until the present at the hands of her destroyers, the Spaniards." The Liberator vowed "the time has come at last to repay the Spaniards torture for torture and to drown that race of annihilators in its own blood or in the sea." He attacked absolutism and monarchy and chided the European powers for not supporting the Patriot cause.

The Jamaica Letter includes exhortation, prophesy, history, criticism, and reasoned political discourse. Bolívar boldly declared:

> Success will crown our efforts, because the destiny of America has been irrevocably decided; the tie that bound her to Spain has been severed. The hatred that the Peninsula has inspired in us is greater than the ocean between us. It would be easier to have the two continents meet than to reconcile the spirits of the two countries. . . .
>
> Because successes have been partial and spasmodic, we must not lose faith. In some regions the Independents triumph, while in others the tyrants have the advantage. What is the end result? Is not the entire New World in motion, armed for defense? We have but to look around us on this hemisphere to witness a simultaneous struggle at every point.

Bolívar's overview of Spanish America in 1815 revealed the broad, hemispheric vision that would still guide him a decade later. In contemplating his bitterness toward Spain, one must remember that the mother country deployed more troops to fight in Venezuela than to all the rest of the colonies combined. Buenos Aires and other La Plata provinces never really fought a war for independence from Spain. Spain, smaller than Venezuela, lacked the manpower and naval power to coerce the distant southern part of the South American continent. The United Provinces of the Río de la Plata simply had to purge their territory of a small Spanish garrison. Then they sent armies to Upper Peru (Bolivia), "arousing Arequipa and worrying Royalists in Lima. Nearly one million inhabitants there now enjoy liberty." Across the Andes, "the territory of Chile, populated by 800,000 souls, is fighting the enemy who is seeking her subjugation; but to no avail." Peru, with 1.5 million inhabitants, "suffers the greatest subjection and is obliged to make the most sacrifices."

The 2.5 million people of New Granada, "the heart of America," "are actually defending that territory against the Spanish army under General Morillo, who will probably suffer defeat at the impregnable fortress of Cartagena. But should he take the city, it will be at the price of heavy casualties, and he will then lack sufficient forces to subdue the brave inhabitants of the interior."

Events in "heroic and hapless Venezuela," Bolívar wrote, "have moved so rapidly and the devastation has been such that it is reduced to frightful desolation and almost absolute indigence. . . . Nearly a million persons formerly dwelt in Venezuela, and it is no exaggeration to say that one out of four has succumbed either to the land, sword, hunger, plague, flight, or privation."

Bolívar next turned his attention to New Spain (Mexico plus Guatemala, which then also included Honduras, El Salvador, Nicaragua, and Costa Rica). According to German naturalist Alexander von Humboldt's estimate, New Spain had 7.8 million inhabitants in 1808. "Since that time, the insurrection, which has shaken virtually all of her provinces, has appreciably reduced that apparently correct figure, for over a million men have perished. . . . There the struggle continues. . . . In spite of everything, the Mexicans will be free." Puerto Rico and Cuba, with 700,000 to 800,000 souls, "are the most tranquil possessions of the Spaniards, because they are not within range of contact with the Independents. But are not the people of those islands Americans? Are they not maltreated? Do they not desire a better life?"

In his Jamaica Letter, Bolívar proved something of a prophet. He anticipated that "Buenos Aires will have a central government in which the military will have the upper hand. Chile will have the most stable government.

The rich in Peru will not tolerate democracy, nor will the freed slaves and pardos accept aristocracy. The rich will prefer the tyranny of a single man to avoid the tumult of rebellion."

In other cases, the Liberator fell victim to wishful thinking. He predicted that Venezuela and New Granada, including Quito and Panama, would become one great nation. "How beautiful it would be," he dreamed, "if the Isthmus of Panama could be for us what the Isthmus of Corinth was for the Greeks! Would to God that some day we may have the good fortune to convene there an august assembly of representatives of republics, kingdoms and empires to deliberate upon the high interests of peace and war with the nations of the other three-quarters of the globe." Alas for Bolívar, the future held political fragmentation and civil war, not unity, for Spanish America.

Bolívar expected that the Mexicans would at first establish a representative republic. "If the dominant party is military, or aristocratic, it will probably demand a monarchy." He correctly envisioned confederation for Central America, although the arrangement would be short-lived. "Because of their magnificent position between two mighty oceans, they may in time become the emporium of the world. Their canals will shorten distances throughout the world, strengthen commercial ties between Europe, America, and Asia, and bring to that happy area tribute from the four quarters of the globe."

Manchester remained intransigent and unimpressed with Bolívar's vision of the future. Who would give a fig for this puny little beggar who had twice failed against Spain and now suffered in exile because his presence wrought such dissension among the Patriots? Manchester concluded that the fires of independence had burned out: "the flame has absorbed the oil."

The English gentleman was mistaken. The flame burned with greater intensity, fed by the oil of Bolívar's dream of glory. On September 27, the exiled "beggar" read an article about New Granada's population, resources, and dissensions in a Kingston daily, the *Courant*. The next day he replied to the arguments in a letter to the editor of the *Royal Gazette*. He summarized the true causes of civil war in New Granada.

Virtually every republic that has inspired great veneration among the human race has borne within it the seed of fatal discord; hence it has been said that dissension is often the measuring-rod of liberty, and that the enjoyment of a liberally constituted government is commonly found to be in direct proportion to the enthusiasm of the parties and the clash of political opinions.

What free nation, ancient or modern, has not suffered dissension? Can you point to a history more turbulent than that of Athens or Rome or England or the United States of North America?

Our discord had its origin in the two most productive sources of national disaster: ignorance and weakness. Spain cultivated the first with superstition and perpetuated the second with tyranny. In our former situation, we were kept in a condition of almost total insignificance.

Furthermore, we were abandoned by the entire world. No foreign nation ever aided us with its wisdom and experience, defended us with its arms, or encouraged us with its resources. This was not so in the case of North America during her struggle for independence. The three most powerful nations of Europe, all colonial powers, helped her win independence. Great Britain has not taken reprisal against the Spain which fought against her in the war that cost the former her colonies.

The United States of North America which, through her commerce, could have supplied us with war materials, did not do so because of her war with Great Britain. Otherwise, Venezuela could have triumphed by herself, and South America would not have been laid waste by Spanish cruelty or ruined by revolutionary anarchy.

Bolívar asserted that Patriot guerrillas in eastern Venezuela and in the llanos along the Orinoco River "are battling with such force and violence that, having seized all the inland provinces, they now stand ready to attack the ports and drive their enemies into the sea." The Liberator exaggerated. Patriot guerrillas had not seized all the inland provinces, although they had enlarged their enclaves. Bereft of his sword, Bolívar continued waging a propaganda war with the pen. He hoped to convince English authorities that aiding a Patriot expedition to Venezuela would result in great rewards for their empire.

Bolívar had twice borrowed a hundred pesos from Maxwell Hyslop. On December 4 he again requested a loan because his landlady hounded him. "This accursed woman," Bolívar said, "now demands more than a hundred pesos for extras. She is such a gossip and so perverse that I do not want her to drag me before a judge for so little, and be there exposed to her insolence and outrages. I do not have a *marvedí* and beg you to send me a hundred pesos."

The Liberator's distress and humiliation in Jamaica did not end until Renato Beluche arrived on Sunday, December 9, with the letter from Ducoudray. Beluche summarized recent events, including the horror in

Cartagena. He invited Bolívar to join the Patriot forces at Aux Cayes. Bolívar declined the invitation, offering the same reason that he had given a week earlier. "I am ready to serve my country; but while the feelings of Cartagena's inhabitants are not in perfect accord, my presence there might cause disputes and difficulties. I should not then be of any help, even within the range of my authority." Bolívar, however, could not sit on the sidelines. He decided to make the two-hundred-mile journey to Haiti.

That same Sunday night a tired Félix Amestoy, Bolívar's paymaster, went to Bolívar's room to await him, laid down in his hammock, and fell asleep. The Kingston *Royal Gazette* (December 16–23, 1815) reported the dramatic events. Pío, Bolívar's slave, entered the dark room "and feeling a man in the hammock, whom he took for his master, plunged his knife into the neck of his supposed victim, when the unhappy man sprung up and struggled with the negro until he received a second and mortal wound in the left side near the back." Amestoy cried out and the assassin was apprehended.

Following a coroner's inquest the next day, Pío appeared in slave court. He confessed that some Spaniards had offered him two thousand pesos to murder Bolívar. The paper noted that "this is the third time General Bolívar's life has been attempted by some of the lowest description of Spaniards, and each time he has had a hair breathed escape. We sincerely hope the abettors of this horrible transaction will be found out, so as to be brought to justice." Where did Bolívar pass that fateful night? He may have been sleeping with a French woman, as some biographers say. He may have boarded *La Popa* and slept there. At any rate, Pío's trial delayed Bolívar's departure. Found guilty, Pío was executed and decapitated, after which officials placed his head on a pole for display in Spring Path.

On December 18 a determined Bolívar sailed for Cartagena to restore unity and leadership to the Patriot cause. However, en route he learned of the city's tragic fall, so he changed course for Haiti. Bolívar wrote a letter of introduction to Alexandre Pétion (1770–1818), president of Haiti, on December 19. Pétion, a veteran of the island's difficult struggle for independence, had founded the Republic of Haiti in 1806 and been elected president in 1807, 1811, and 1815. His achievements, wrote the Liberator, had inspired him and many other Patriots. Alas, neither Pétion nor Bolívar would realize the full extent of their dreams for their respective nations. "I will hasten to present myself," Bolívar wrote, "as soon as possible after arriving at Aux Cayes."

La Popa anchored at Aux Cayes on Christmas Eve. No vessels with refugees from Cartagena had yet arrived, but Brión greeted the Liberator. He told Bolívar they had stored their munitions safely in Haiti's arsenal at Aux Cayes: "15,200 muskets, 2,500 musket locks, 400 carbines, 300 sabres, 200 pairs pistols, 200 quintals [20,000 pounds] powder, and 3 printing presses."

Bolívar departed for the capital, Port-au-Prince, ninety-five miles distant, arriving on New Year's Eve. On New Year's Day, 1816, Haitians celebrated the twelfth anniversary of their independence. Robert Sutherland, a prominent English merchant and Bolívar's friend, asked the Venezuelan to be his guest. Bolívar accepted the invitation. Sutherland, President Pétion's friend and adviser, exercised great influence in the country. He lived in the presidential palace, and his commercial firm operated from an antechamber. He arranged an interview for Bolívar with Pétion on January 2. After the interview, Bolívar wrote to Brión: "The President impressed me, as he does everyone, very favorably. His countenance reflects the kindness for which he is well known. I have asked that the schooner intended for you be sent to Aux Cayes." Pétion could assist Bolívar covertly through Sutherland, thereby avoiding diplomatic complications for his young country.

Why did Sutherland and Pétion agree to help Bolívar? Privateers meant profits for merchants like Sutherland and might bring a measure of prosperity to Haiti. Beluche, Lominé, and other privateers brought their Spanish prizes to small ports east of Aux Cayes on the south coast of Haiti. They unloaded captured cargoes and sold them to merchants for a fraction of their value.

With Spain occupying Cartagena and France at peace with England and Spain, privateers could no longer obtain Cartagenan or French commissions. If Bolívar gained a beachhead on Venezuelan territory, he could establish an admiralty court that could issue valid letters of marque. Privateers who flew the Venezuelan flag could legally capture Spanish prizes and bring them to Haiti, where merchants and officials could continue to enjoy the lucrative, if slightly tainted, trade.

Bolívar left Port-au-Prince with Pétion's promise that he would extend all possible aid to the Patriots. What an uplifting change from the inhospitable Manchester on Jamaica! The Haitian president levied a single but extraordinary condition. Bolívar must proclaim all slaves emancipated in Venezuela and other countries he had liberated. Nothing came without a price. Back at Aux Cayes, Bolívar found that the four schooners had arrived with refugees. Haitian authorities permitted the ships to stay only a few days. The pathetic Patriot schooners debarked a total of six hundred famished men, women, and children. So wretched was their state that two hundred of them soon died. Survivors could barely stand on their feet. Haitians took them into their homes and helped them regain their strength. Louis Aury was one of the few passengers allowed to disembark. "He requested me," says Ducoudray, "to take command of the squadron [two schooners] in his absence. Mr. [Carlos] Soublette attempted to criticize some of my orders while I was in the cabin." Dissension again rumbled through the Patriot ranks.

Carlos Soublette (1789–1870) and Ducoudray despised each other. While the latter would disappear into the mists of history as a mere footnote, the former would go on to hold many high offices, including service twice as president of Venezuela (1837–39, 1843–47). Soublette, able and honest, would later ally himself with Páez and other conservative oligarchs. Ducoudray had the unfortunate habit of berating publicly those who lacked his knowledge of military science. He had humiliated Soublette in this fashion before they left Cartagena. Even-tempered Soublette had made no reply. Ducoudray recorded in his memoirs: "My friends told me of the murmurs of said Soublette. I came on deck and reprimanded him again, in the presence of more than a hundred persons, and Mr. Soublette again received this reprimand without replying a single word." Theirs would not be the only conflict in Haiti.

Another foreign officer, Col. Gustavo Hippisley, described Soublette as "a very handsome figure of a man; about twenty-five years of age; tall, thin, and well proportioned; remarkably neat in his dress and appearance; half cast by birth and complexion; he is about five feet ten inches in height; rather a handsome and European style of countenance; black hair and large mustachios; a smile more then prepossessing; a general lover, amongst the female part of the province, by whom he is well received."

The Patriot survivors desperately looked for comfort and leadership, especially when Aury and Brión began to quarrel. Aury wanted divided leadership, including a piece of the power for himself. Their spat continued when Bolívar returned to Aux Cayes on January 21, 1816. Bolívar immediately asked Pétion to intervene, explaining his fear that divided authority over the exiles would doom his expedition. Bolívar's letter, convincing as usual, gave both Sutherland and Pétion ample details of the Aury-Brión conflict. Pétion ordered the governor of Aux Cayes to collaborate closely with Bolívar to ensure a successful expedition.

Several of Bolívar's friends advised him to legitimize his position as supreme chief by gathering the most notable refugees. A distinguished assembly of Venezuelans, New Granadans, and others met on February 7. The assembly included Brión, Aury, Ducoudray, Bermúdez, MacGregor, Piar,

Soublette, José Antonio Anzoátegui, Mariño, Mariano Montilla, and the eminent New Granadan orator (and botanist), Francisco Antonio Zea y Díaz (1776–1822). Zea, like Antonio Nariño, had been arrested in 1795 for translating and distributing copies of "The Declaration of the Rights of Man" and spent some time imprisoned in Spain as a result. Absolved in 1799, he conducted scientific studies in Europe before returning to Venezuela in 1815.

Bolívar opened the meeting with a speech in which he analyzed the Patriot situation. Ferdinand VII's government in Spain lacked the manpower and resources to subjugate all America. Therefore, the Liberator reasoned, the Patriots must take advantage of this weakness. He urged that they invade Venezuela and aid rebellion there before Morillo became strong enough to take all of New Granada. He also informed the assembly that they must elect a supreme chief and decide where they would locate their first base on the mainland.

Brión jumped to his feet and seconded Bolívar's call for a single authority. "General Bolívar is a suitable man for such a command." Zea, other Granadans, and Venezuelans spoke in like manner, but Aury argued firmly against giving Bolívar unlimited power. He suggested a committee of three or five persons that would share authority. He also urged that the expedition sail to Old Providence, and, from that island base, drive the Spaniards from Cartagena.

Brión predictably attacked both of Aury's proposals. He also stated that he would provide ships and credit to Bolívar as commander in chief but to no one else. Brión then forced the issue of leadership by putting a direct question to Mariño and the others: "Do you consent that General Bolívar, as captain-general of the armies of Venezuela and New Granada, shall be our only commander—yes or no?" Mariño reluctantly voted "yes," as did most of those present. Only Aury, Bermúdez, and two others voted "no."

Immediately after the election, Aury presented a bill for advances made to the government of Cartagena. The bill covered the costs of the evacuation and repairs on two vessels in his fleet that belonged to Cartagena. The sum due him, he said, totaled twenty-five thousand pesos. He agreed to accept the Cartagenan schooner *Constitution* as payment for his claims. After consultation, Zea and other Granadans agreed to cede Aury title to the ship.

When Bolívar heard of this proceeding, he reprimanded the Granadans. He declared the transfer null and void and tore it to bits. Such disputes would give rise to four challenges to duels among various Patriot leaders, including Bolívar. Haitian authorities intervened in some cases to enforce the country's antidueling law. An inflammatory handbill appeared on March 8, 1816. "Citizens and countrymen—You are advised that commandant Mariano Montilla has arrived in this town, and applied to have the honor to be admitted among us. All those who know well the intriguing and dangerous character of this man, will, I hope, join me to oppose his admission into the army. Signed T. M. Hernández, captain of the body guard of his excellency the captain-general of the armies of Venezuela and New Granada." According to General Ducoudray Holstein, a not-always-reliable and never impartial witness, Bolívar actually authored this public slander against Montilla. Some of the group became so frustrated with bickering and delays that they abandoned the mission. The resourceful Aury would not be foiled so easily. He took his case to the president of Haiti in Port-au-Prince, who decreed that Aury must be reimbursed for the advances he had made.

Having pacified Aury, the Haitian president ordered that the *Constitution* be placed at Bolívar's disposal. He further instructed his officials "to prevent the sailing from Aux Cayes of any vessel that does not belong to General Bolívar's Expedition." The mulatto leader proved decisive in consolidating the leadership of Bolívar, a wealthy Creole. Such cross-class and cross-race cooperation would ultimately bring success to the Patriot cause. An anxious, impatient, reinvigorated Bolívar resumed his path to glory.

CHAPTER 8

From Optimism at Aux Cayes
to Disaster at Ocumare, 1816

The year 1816 looked much brighter to Bolívar than had the previous one spent languishing in Caribbean exile. Bolstered by the vote of his supporters at Aux Cayes, he moved quickly to organize his followers. Acknowledging his critical support, he promoted Brión to captain of the navy and upgraded 118 infantry and cavalry officers. He promoted Mariño to major general and Soublette to colonel of cavalry. Bolívar named Zea secretary of the treasury for the Confederation of Venezuela and New Granada. According to Ducoudray, Bolívar appointed him chief of staff and promised to promote him to field marshal as soon as they entered Venezuela. The promotion never came, and the two men ended up bitter enemies.

Bolívar had a very young staff, mostly in their early thirties. The youngest officers, Carlos Soublette and José Antonio Anzoátegui, were only twenty-seven. The former probably owed his standing more to Bolívar's romantic interest in his sister than to any special military skills. Nonetheless, he would go on to a successful military and political career, albeit as the Liberator's enemy by the late 1820s. Ducoudray exaggerated when he recorded a staff of five hundred majors, captains, and lieutenants. Historians put the figure lower: Paul Verna listed only 272 officers; Vicente Lecuna no more than 250. Ducoudray hit closer to the mark, however, when he said that the officer corps initially commanded no more than fifty soldiers. Ducoudray recalled in his memoirs that "[e]ach general had his aide-de-camp, a secretary, servants, and many their mistresses or wives. Each lady has either her mother, sister, or some other friend male or female, servants, and a good deal of baggage, which greatly embarrassed the maneuvering of the vessels. There were besides a number of families, emigrants from Venezuela, who had embarked at Aux Cayes in spite of the entreaties of Brión, who was against the admittance of any female on board the squadron."

Mariano Montilla, Bermúdez, and Aury did not appear on the list of officers. The dissident Montilla had already sailed to the United States, but later, in 1819, Bolívar would successfully bring him back into his fold. Ignoring the officer's history of opposition, Bolívar would ask him to serve on his staff, thereby turning a foe into an ardent supporter. Bolívar could be cold and uncompromising, but he could also exercise flexibility and forbearance. Bolívar would not accept Bermúdez for service because of his refusal to vote for Bolívar as supreme commander. A miffed Bermúdez convinced Pétion to let him sail to Venezuela. The Haitians let Aury sail to his native New Orleans soon after Bolívar's expedition left Haiti. However, like Montilla, Bermúdez would later accept the Liberator's call to return to service.

The bay of Aux Cayes saw lots of activity, with many small vessels coming and going. When corsairs could make a landing on islands like St. Barts or St. Thomas, they picked up Patriot refugees and transported them to Haiti. José Padilla in the schooner *Patriota* brought some thirty dragoons of Caracas to Aux Cayes. The Liberator's main romantic interest, Josefina Machada (or possibly Madrid), also made her way to Haiti and in so doing delayed the fleet's departure for two days. "Señorita Pepa" had been among a dozen maidens dressed in white robes who greeted the victorious Liberator on his entry to Caracas on August 6, 1813. She became not only his lover, lasting far longer than most, but also a very influential adviser.

Jean Baptiste Bideau, a mulatto privateer from St. Lucia who happened to be at St. Thomas, offered the Liberator a letter of sage advice. He suggested beginning the conquest in Guayana, Venezuela's largest province. It had cattle, mules, and the food-producing Caroní missions and had not yet suffered from the war. Many of the inhabitants, according to Bideau, secretly opposed the Spaniards. They would declare for independence as soon as Bolívar presented himself with a thousand men.

The Patriot cause also attracted a new champion in the United States, fiery Sen. Henry Clay (1777–1852). A Virginia native, Clay entered the Senate in 1806 representing Kentucky. He had publicly expressed support for Spanish American independence as early as January 1813, but the War of 1812 hamstrung American policy toward its southern neighbors for several years. Indeed, in his "Letter from Jamaica" Bolívar recognized the deleterious impact of the conflict between Great Britain and the United States. The latter, "which, through her commerce, could have supplied us with war materials, did not do so because of her war with Great Britain."

In January, 1816, Clay asked Congress "how far it may be proper to aid the people of South America in regards to the establishment of their independence." He supported a strong military for the United States, "if necessary, to aid in the cause of liberty in South America." He urged creation of an "American system" of republics to counter threats from Europe's Holy Alliance. He also anticipated the spirit of the Monroe Doctrine (1823) by asserting that "I consider the release of any part of America from the dominion of the Old World as adding to the general security of the New." Like many others, Clay considered expanding American commerce and blunting European influence in the Caribbean as important foreign policy goals. Although he had little concrete knowledge of events in Spanish America, Clay espoused views that would become official policy within a decade.

Royalist Gen. Pablo Morillo, unaware of the hostile popular undercurrent, felt so sure of Guayana that he deployed only a few troops to defend it. Moreover, Bideau knew that black Venezuelans had regained the port of Güiria on the Gulf of Paria. They also controlled the river port of Maturín, some distance up the Río Guarapiche (a branch of the Río San Juan that empties into the Gulf of Paria). The black supporters could assist Bolívar after he landed his army and war materiel at Guarapiche.

Bolívar discussed Bideau's plan with Mariño and Piar. All three saw merit in the proposed strategy, but even more encouraging news from the island of Margarita distracted them. Margaritans, led by native son Juan Bautista Arismendi, had risen en mass in December and forced the Spaniards to take refuge in the forts of Santa Rosa, Pampatar, and Porlomar, and within the fortified line of La Asunción. Royalists foolhardy enough to venture forth suffered defeat after defeat. This island rebellion obliged the Royalists to deploy more troops and five vessels to blockade Margarita. Greatly encouraged, Bolívar and his council voted to sail the 824 miles to Margarita. They planned to establish an admiralty court there where commissions could be issued to privateers. Once in control of Margarita, they could launch their next strike on Caracas or, as Bideau suggested, move on Guayana.

Admiralty courts and privateers played crucial roles by providing logistical support for the independence movement. By issuing letters of marque, admiralty courts gave privateers legal sanction to strike Royalist shipping.

The sale of the prizes taken generated profits for privateers and merchants and yielded much-needed materiel for the Patriots. Pétion, Sutherland, and Bolívar depended on the support of privateers. Privateers, in turn, could only operate with prize money to pay their crews and prevent desertions. "No prey, no pay," went the old refrain. As the Patriots mobilized, Renato Beluche had not remained idle. During the past three months he had captured six prizes. He and Lominé landed at Aux Cayes toward the end of March for two reasons. Their Cartagena commissions had expired and Bolívar's expedition prepared to sail. Necessity combined nicely with economic opportunity.

There were eight schooners in Bolívar's fleet, including Sutherland's *La Fortuna;* the *Constitution,* with Jean Monier commanding; Beluche's *La Popa;* and Lominé's *Jupiter.* Judging from the captains' names of the other four schooners, they were privateers. Each enjoyed an ample stock of ammunition and muskets from the accumulated arsenal at Aux Cayes. Bolívar had thirty thousand pounds of lead, thirty thousand pounds of powder, four thousand muskets with bayonets, and a printing press.

Many of the privateers renamed their vessels, as they customarily did with new legal commissions. Lominé changed the name of his recommissioned ship from *Jupiter* to *Felix.* In a politically astute move, Beluche renamed *La Popa* the *General Bolívar.* The best armed and fastest of the schooners, it served as the flagship. Brión, Bolívar, and Ducoudray took over the cabin when they boarded her. The former, like many officers of the time, reveled in smart uniforms, often multinational in flavor. Admiral Brión wore "an English hussar jacket and scarlet pantaloons, with a broad stripe of gold lace down each side, a field marshal's uniform hat, with a very large Prussian plume, and an enormous pair of dragoon boots, with heavy gold spurs of the most inconvenient length."

The small fleet sailed from Aux Cayes at the end of March to renew the liberation of South America. As they approached the island of Beata, a fast-sailing pilot boat hailed the *General Bolívar.* The Liberator learned that his mistress Josefina had arrived at Aux Cayes with her mother and sister. Would the fleet return for them or sail on without them? The prospect of delay and disruption annoyed Brión and Ducoudray and rightly so. Bolívar's delays and dalliances with Josefina turned what should have been a ten-day voyage into a month-long trial.

Brión and Ducoudray also operated out of enlightened self-interest. If Señorita Pepa came on board, she would move into the cabin with Bolívar, and they would be reduced to sleeping on the open deck, like Beluche. They finally agreed that Josefina could travel with the expedition if she stayed off the flagship. Bolívar appointed Soublette as Josefina's escort, and Captain Monier sailed the *Constitution* back to Aux Cayes for Josefina, her mother, sister, and all their baggage. When the *Constitution* returned to the fleet, Bolívar dressed himself elegantly. Everyone on the flagship watched intently as he departed to visit Josefina. He remained a day and a night and then returned to the *General Bolívar*. Bolívar mixed love and war throughout his life, but his dalliances often sorely tried the patience of even his most ardent supporters. Bolívar seemed fully capable of making both love and war.

The fleet sailed on and soon the lookout sighted a small vessel. Lominé in the *Felix* gave chase and came alongside the vessel off Punta Salinas near Santo Domingo City. As grappling hooks from the *Felix* bit into the vessel, the ship's crew jumped overboard. Two priests who could not swim remained onboard. Not one to overlook any profit, Lominé exchanged the priests for two cows, and the fleet sailed on. After passing Santo Domingo and Puerto Rico, the fleet began island-hopping to pick up Patriot refugees, food supplies, and crewmen. Those with money bought chickens and fresh vegetables at the Dutch island of Saba. Then the fleet followed the line of the Lesser Antilles, making a great arc so that it could approach the north coast of Margarita from the east. The Royalists would never expect an attack from that direction.

Days passed into weeks and weeks into a month as the fleet sailed along at a leisurely pace. At nightfall on May 1, the watch sighted the Testigos Islands. The following dawn the fleet changed its course to due west. By seven o'clock they sighted the islands of Los Frailes east of the northern tip of Margarita. Two hours later the watch sighted a big schooner and a brig, the two main Spanish vessels blockading Margarita. The outnumbered Royalists quickly retreated. The schooner, a swifter vessel, soon left the brig behind. Lominé in the *Felix*, followed by two others vessels, chased the schooner. The remainder of the fleet followed the *General Bolívar*. Beluche soon saw that he faced the enemy brig *Intrépido*.

As the vessels drew within cannon shot of each other, Beluche's gun crews leaped into action, but enemy cannons answered. The *Intrépido* carried Royalist troops bound for Margarita, some of whom jumped into the rigging and fired their muskets. Most of the shots went wild, but one hit Brión in the head. Patriots carried the wounded officer below, where most of the passengers, except Bolívar, followed. Ducoudray bravely handed out muskets to other officers and issued orders. Bolívar climbed into a long boat and from this sheltered vantage point watched the naval battle of Los Frailes. Beluche and his crew, old hands at boarding and taking over another vessel, deployed grappling hooks and swarmed onto the *Intrépido*. The Patriots seized the quarterdeck and drove to the hold those Spaniards who had not already jumped overboard.

Later that afternoon the vessels that had chased the enemy schooner returned with another prize, the *Rita*. When Beluche expressed admiration for the ship's long slim lines, Bolívar awarded the prize to him. That same day Bolívar promoted Brión to admiral and Beluche to commodore. Soublette, who bravely protected Josefina one mile away from the battle, became adjutant-general-colonel. Bolívar did not promote Ducoudray, who perhaps exhibited too much heroism and leadership for the Liberator's taste. The vindictive Danish soldier would not forget the slights and foibles that the Liberator exhibited.

The morning after the naval battle Bolívar's fleet sailed into the harbor of Juan Griego on the northwestern coast of Margarita. A *flechera*, carrying Arismendi, drew alongside the *General Bolívar*. Arismendi climbed on board, complimented Bolívar and his officers, and invited them ashore. That afternoon Bolívar and some of the officers joined Arismendi at his headquarters at Villa del Norte.

The next day Bolívar landed welcome muskets, ammunition, and cannons for one battery for the Margaritans. On May 7 the leading civil, ecclesiastical, and military leaders of Margarita gathered. Arismendi stressed the need to concentrate the direction of the war and the destiny of the Republic in one leader—music to the Liberator's ears. Then he added: "The patriots who escaped to Aux Cayes have elected Bolívar to be their supreme chief. I, too, recognize General Bolívar, and I earnestly entreat you to do the same." Those assembled gave unanimous approval, and Arismendi proclaimed Bolívar commander in chief of the Republics of Venezuela and New Granada. Bolívar ordered the flag of Cartagena lowered from his vessels and replaced by the Venezuelan flag. He also established an admiralty court at Juan Griego. Each of his vessels "was duly commissioned and authorized by the Republic of Venezuela to capture all vessels, their cargoes and all other property belonging to enemies of said republic." The faith of Haiti's politicians and merchants in Bolívar seemed destined to pay off handsomely.

Bolívar sailed with his fleet and five additional flecheras, determined to drive Royalists from the fort at Porlamar. On May 17 his vessels approached the fort, but intense cannon fire kept them too far away to land troops. Bolívar lacked the troops to force the issue by land, so the expedition returned to Juan Griego. On May 25 the fleet sailed from Margarita, anchoring in front of Carúpano late in the afternoon of May 31.

The next morning troops under Piar and Soublette debarked on the beach. Patriots took possession of the town of Carúpano in less than two hours. Bolívar recounted the smashing victory in a letter to his friend Maxwell Hyslop. "In consequence of the occupation of Carúpano by our troops, the Spaniards have abandoned from Cariaco to Güiria, and our communications to Maturín are expedited by land and the Golfo Triste." Republican colors flew in Carúpano, and only a few Patriots had been wounded. In their hasty flight, the Royalists left behind a great quantity of provisions, including a well-armed and equipped brig and a schooner laden with merchandise.

Ducoudray, the professional soldier ever concerned with order and discipline, stood horrified when he saw the hungry victors, who had nearly starved on Margarita, gorging on food they found in the stores. He wanted to ration the food and asked Bolívar for permission to station guards at the stores. The politically savvy Bolívar preferred not to intervene. "The guards would be the first to take what they wanted and the attempt would be useless. When the food is all gone, we will tighten our belts until fortune smiles on us again." Bolívar would exhibit his fascinating blend of fatalism and intense optimism repeatedly during the independence wars.

Bolívar did reserve large stores of valuable cacao beans (processed into chocolate) that could purchase other necessities. Loaded on two schooners and sent to St. Thomas, the cacao purchased additional supplies. At the end of June the two schooners returned from St. Thomas "with others laden with all kinds of goods and a great number of passengers, foreigners as well as emigrants from Venezuela, who are going to join the Independent Army."

Meanwhile, Mariño and Piar, chaffing under Bolívar's command, asked permission to go to Güiria to begin the liberation of Guayana. Bolívar gave them permission, deploying twenty officers, two thousand stand of arms, ammunition, and flecheras to convoy them along the coast. A shocked and disturbed Ducoudray warned Bolívar that Mariño and Piar would set themselves up as independent dictators in the east.

Bolívar took one of his many calculated risks. He did not wish to alienate the two rivals, because he needed able officers. Perhaps Mariño and Piar could march to the Orinoco from Maturín and gain vital control of navigation on the mighty river. Then Patriots could push the enemy north into the sea and penetrate south to the heart of New Granada. Mariño made Güiria his base; Piar moved toward Maturín. Royalists offered little resistance.

Mariño and Piar established communications with some of the Patriot guerrilla chiefs, and their bands steadily increased as Venezuelans fled to them to escape Royalist oppression. Forced contributions to Morillo's war chest, Royalist troops quartered in homes, and forced conscription alienated many Venezuelans. (Similar complaints had inflamed North American sentiment against the British forty years earlier.) Each guerrilla chief had between two hundred and five hundred men. Some had more than one thousand, mostly cavalry. Spanish cavalry and infantry always outnumbered the Patriot guerrillas but could never destroy them. The guerrillas mounted more and more strikes, but the chiefs all needed still scarce weapons and ammunition.

Meanwhile back at Carúpano, the rift between Ducoudray and other officers widened. Ducoudray refused to pay court to Josefina, and officers whom he reprimanded gathered at her house and worked to frustrate his every action. Bolívar refused to support Ducoudray's efforts to impose stricter discipline on the officers and troops. This added further insult to the prior injury when the Liberator refused to promote him. An exasperated Ducoudray resigned from Bolívar's army, sailed to Haiti, gathered his wife and children, and left for the United States. In 1829 he published a venomous attack, his *Memoirs of Simón Bolívar*. Despite his visceral dislike of the Liberator, some of his observations provide valuable firsthand information on conditions and problems inside the Patriot ranks.

Bolívar faced yet another critical situation; he now had only six hundred troops. Some of his men had died; others had gone with Mariño and Piar. Royalists had twice that number concentrated at Cumaná for a land attack against Carúpano. Twelve Spanish vessels prepared to attack by sea. Bolívar had rashly depleted his fleet and supplies to outfit Mariño and Piar. Furthermore, one of Bolívar's best captains, Lominé, had sailed the battered *Intrépido* to New Orleans for repairs. Crews on the remaining vessels, inactive and unpaid for two months, became restless. Brión, recovered from his head wound, wanted to leave Carúpano before the Patriots depleted all their rations. He lacked the ships and men to battle the Spanish fleet, and Bolívar could not mobilize enough men to attack Cumaná. The Patriots could not even feed the troops that Brión transported to Güiria and Maturín. Bolívar thought of his coffee and cacao plantations in the valley of San Mateo. A landing on the coast at Ocumare would shorten the distance to San Mateo and other valleys leading west to New Granada and east to Caracas.

Josefina, along with other women and children, boarded the *Indio Libre* while troops boarded other ships. The expedition sailed for Ocumare on July 2. They had barely departed when the enemy took possession of Carúpano. Four days later the Patriot fleet reached the port of Ocumare.

Bolívar and his men disembarked and marched to the town. As the Liberator noted in a letter, "at midday on the 6th we occupied Ocumare without firing a shot." He immediately proclaimed the emancipation of slaves and invited all free men to join him.

Bolívar complicated matters for Mariño and many others with his proclamation freeing the slaves. The Liberator had honored his pledge to Haitian President Pétion. Mariño quickly faced an inrush of slaves from the English island of Trinidad who fled to freedom in Güiria. Ralph Woodford, governor of Trinidad, demanded that Mariño return the escaped slaves. The Patriots desperately wanted English assistance, and the runaway slave issue alienated the British.

Woodford dispatched Kenneth Mathison to Venezuela to report on conditions there. On July 27 Mathison reported the good news that Bolívar and Mariño had abandoned the former policy of general massacre of Spaniards, the vicious "war to the death" decree issued June 15, 1813. He expressed the hope that the Spaniards would do the same and added: "This young man Mariño appears to have established a greater degree of order and subordination than I have before observed among the Independents in their former temporary success. He has about 500 men. They have erected 3 blockhouses with 4 guns each, capable of containing 300 men, for the protection of Güiria. They subsist on Indian corn, plantains, and fresh fish, all of which they have in abundance."

Bolívar also dispatched Maj. Francisco Piñango to round up recruits. Piñango marched east along the coast, enlisting ex-slaves. Bolívar gave Soublette command of most of the troops. He ordered the force to cross the coastal mountains and gain control of Cabrera Pass east of Valencia. After recruiting more men and promoting rebellion in the valleys of Aragua, they were to advance east to Maracay. Bolívar planned to march with Piñango's recruits directly south from Choroní over the mountains, then join Soublette at Maracay and march on Caracas. Fate, however, decreed otherwise.

Anxious for profits, crewmen unloaded the Patriot's arms and munitions on the Ocumare beach. They loaded their ships with tropical fruits and foodstuffs that they planned to sell at Curaçao, just a short sail off the coast. Brión left only three vessels behind, two transports and the *Indio Libre*. The fleet's departure initiated a series of several Patriot disasters. On July 6, when Bolívar debarked at Ocumare, Francisco Morales arrived at Valencia with his Royalist troops. Morillo had sent him from New Granada to reinforce Caracas. Like the Patriots, Royalists faced problems of poor troop morale, insubordination, and desertions. Back in May, Morillo had complained that his troops in Caracas "are deserting in flocks." On the night of July 6 Soublette left a garrison at the pass of La Cabrera and advanced east to Maracay en route to San Mateo. A concerned Bolívar sent an urgent note to Soublette on the morning of July 9: "To date I have received only one message from you, dated on the 7th from the mountain-top, but I know nothing of your operations all day yesterday. I must emphasize the necessity of frequent communications; without them we shall forever be in uncertainty and doubt, thereby causing embarrassment and delays in planning." Indeed, uncertainty, doubt, embarrassment, and worse would characterize the following days.

Also on July 9 Soublette read an intercepted letter claiming that General Morales had seven thousand troops at Valencia. The planted letter, meant to frighten Soublette, certainly achieved its purpose. In reality, Morales had but six hundred troops, but a terrified Soublette dispatched a runner to ask Bolívar for help. He then abandoned his positions at Maracay and Cabrera and retired to the foot of Ocumare Mountain. Morales and his modest force attacked the next afternoon. Soublette repulsed him and withdrew to the crest of the mountain, while Morales camped in the ravine below. Bolívar marched, too late, to reinforce Soublette on July 13. He had only 150 men, each burdened with a keg of ammunition on his shoulder.

Morales attacked and defeated Soublette before Bolívar could arrive with the ammunition. Soublette and his remaining forces retreated to Ocumare, where Bolívar discussed the next move with his officers. Bolívar proposed marching east along the coast to Choroní, incorporating Piñango's ex-slaves, and then marching directly south over the coastal mountains. There they could contact guerrillas and with their help move east through the llanos to join Mariño and Piar. Confusion and disagreement clouds the accounts of ensuing events. According to Bolívar critic Salvador de Madariaga, neither MacGregor nor Soublette wanted Bolívar to accompany them. As the Royalists' prime target, he made a dangerous traveling companion! If the Liberator sailed east with the war materiel, Morales would not know where he might strike next. The Royalists would remain at Ocumare until they learned where Bolívar had debarked, thus giving the Patriot army a better chance to escape from Morales and from the Royalists at Caracas.

In contrast, biographer Gerhard Masur wrote that "the officers begged him to sail," but Bolívar rejected their plea. According to this version, his officers feared that the Liberator's capture or death would cripple the independence movement. Bolívar rejected their advice and insisted upon remaining with his troops. Whatever the precise circumstances of the fiasco, the fall of Ocumare represented Bolívar at his arrogant worst. He overestimated

Patriot sentiment in the area and seriously underestimated Spanish resistance and the obstacles he would face. He may have once again wiled away valuable time in a love tryst. Soublette would write the following of Bolívar: "Marc Anthony, unmindful of the danger in which he found himself, lost valuable time at Cleopatra's side."

Bolívar went to the port of Ocumare to order the embarkation of arms and munitions still on the beach. The Patriots, however, fearing that the *Indio Libre*'s commander would abscond with the arms, refused to load them on the brig. Small boats carried women and children to the brig. Meanwhile, boats from two transports hastily loaded war materiel. In this midst of this beachside chaos, Bolívar's aide Isidro Alzuru came running from town, crying that everything was lost. Morales had scattered the Patriots, occupied Ocumare, and deployed a detachment marching on the port. Royalist deception again worked to deceive and demoralize the Patriots. Alzuru had simply lied, and he later defected to the Royalists. Soublette's actual message said that Royalists had camped in the mountains and lit their campfires two leagues from the Patriots. On the evening of July 14, the Liberator, his mistress, and a few officers departed by sea. Whatever the specifics, the events at Ocumare unfolded as an unqualified disaster. Bolívar tersely reported the unhappy outcome in a report of August 21 to General Arismendi on Margarita. "We lost 200 men, dead and wounded, and a portion of our troops was cut off in the retreat." Many deserted, and, in their haste, the Patriots lost most of their supplies. The Liberator promised Arismendi that "Your Excellency may rest assured that all the young cattle we can load in our merchantmen and fighting ships will be sent" from the llanos. In exchange, Bolívar requested "all the arms that you do not absolutely require for the defense of the Island, for we need them badly, to place in the hands of men who wish to give themselves to the cause of liberty." When Royalists entered the deserted town of Ocumare, they recovered a valuable booty: one thousand guns, sixty thousand rounds of ammunition, and a bounty of other supplies that Pétion had given Bolívar.

With women and children onboard, the *Indio Libre* prepared to sail. Bideau lowered a boat for Bolívar. The three vessels remained off port during the night waiting for a favorable breeze. In the morning, Bolívar ordered the two transports to follow the *Indio Libre* to nearby Choroní, where he planned to rejoin his troops. The ship captains pretended to do so but instead turned northwest and headed for the nearby Dutch island of Bonaire. The *Indio Libre* sailed in pursuit, but the transports anchored at Bonaire well ahead of the brig. It would not be the last mutiny Bolívar would suffer.

Fortunately, Brión's fleet also lay in the harbor at Bonaire. Backed by the *General Bolívar,* the *Constitution,* and the *General Arismendi,* Brión took possession of the arms and ammunition on the transports. He had the cargo loaded on the *Diana,* and Bolívar departed on that vessel to Choroní. He found it occupied by the enemy, so he continued east to Chuao. There spies told him that Gregor MacGregor's Patriot troops had skirmished with the enemy and then marched inland to the llanos.

With no troops to join, Bolívar sailed back to Bonaire and met with the estranged Bermúdez. With Pétion's help, Bermúdez had secured passage for Margarita, but Arismendi, following Bolívar's instructions, had not permitted him to land. He next sailed to Carúpano, found Bolívar had just left, and followed him to Ocumare. In response to a message from Bermúdez begging to join him, the Liberator replied curtly: "Your presence creates discord. I cannot let you or your companions land. Later, when the Republic is tranquil, you can come among us." On Bonaire, Bolívar remained adamant, so the scorned Bermúdez sailed on a schooner to Güiria and joined Mariño.

Admiral Brión at this time gave Bideau command of the Margaritan navy, consisting of the *Indio Libre,* the *Diana,* and flecheras that Brión hoped to get from Arismendi. A few days later, however, the governor of Curaçao ordered Brión to leave Bonaire within twenty-four hours with all his vessels. Bolívar boarded the *Indio Libre* and, with the *Diana,* headed for St. Thomas. Brión, commanding the *General Bolívar;* Beluche, the *General Arismendi;* and Jean Monier, the *Constitution,* sailed west and harried the coast. All three vessels, however, needed repairs, so they soon turned north for New Orleans. En route Brión wrecked the *General Bolívar* at the Isle of Pines (now the Isle of Youth), forty miles off the coast of Cuba. Skillfully posing as an English officer who had lost his frigate, he persuaded the Spanish commandant to loan him men and four boats to rescue his crew from the Gulf of Batabano. Brión and his crew sailed southeast to Savana-la-Mar near the western end of Jamaica. They arrived the third week of September, burned the four boats, and left the surprised and chagrined Spanish crewmen to shift for themselves on the British-controlled island.

Like Brión, Bolívar endured his own unpleasant odyssey. At St. Thomas the *Indio Libre* anchored on August 7 to debark women and children, including Josefina, her mother, and sister. The press noted Bolívar's disgrace. An August 8 letter in the Kingston *Royal Gazette* asserted that "Brión is quite disgusted with the conduct of Bolívar."

Bideau and Bolívar left St. Thomas and sailed back to Margarita. Finding the Spanish fleet blockading that island, they continued to Güiria, where
Bideau cast anchor on August 21. Unfortunately for the Liberator, Bermúdez
had arrived at Güiria two hours earlier. He, Mariño, and other rival officers
refused to acknowledge Bolívar's authority. Woodford reported that Bolívar
"was for some days kept in concealment by St. Jago Mariño, in consequence
of attempts by Bermúdez and others to take his life, and a general dissatis-
faction expressed by the negroes, which compose the armed force of that
place, at his having returned without his army." When Bolívar did depart,
he had to fight his way to the beach, sword in hand. He left in hopes of
averting civil war and returned to Haiti to again ask Pétion's aid. Rivalry
and dissension among its leaders would plague the Patriot cause during the
independence wars and long after.

In Bolívar's absence, José Antonio Páez and other Patriots continued the
fight in the llanos. In less than three months since the fall of Cartagena the
fierce Morillo had retaken New Granada. Men, women, and children fled eastward to escape his persecutions, as the Royalist still maintained his war to the
death. Thousands of refugees crossed the Andes, sailed down the rivers, and
gathered at Villa de Arauca. Urdaneta, Manuel Valdés, and other officers met
and elected Francisco de Paula Santander commander in chief. The newly
arrived Granadan émigrés, however, ignored him; they considered Páez, "Tio
Antonio" (Uncle Anthony), the man best qualified to lead them.

General O'Leary, with his characteristic sharp eye for detail, described
the llanero chieftain.

He was of middle height, robust and well made, although the lower
portion of his body was not in due proportion to his bust. His chest and
shoulders were broad; his thick, short neck supported a large head, covered with dark, crisp, chestnut hair; his eyes were brown and lively; his
nose straight, with wide nostril; his lips thick and his chin round. His
clear skin showed his good health, and would have been very white had
he not been sunburned. Caution and suspicion were the distinctive traits
of his countenance. Born of humble parentage, he owed nothing to his
education.

In the presence of those he thought better educated than himself, he
was silent and almost timid, and abstained from taking part in conversation. With his inferiors, he was loquacious, and not averse to practical
jokes. He was fond of talking of his military exploits. Entirely illiterate,
he was quite ignorant of the theory of the profession that he practiced,

and did not know the simplest terms of the art. . . . As a chief of guerilla warfare, he had no rival. Bold, active, brave, and full of stratagems, quick to conceive, resolute and rapid in his movements, he was always most to be feared, when he commanded but few followers.

The formidable Páez suffered from epilepsy, but his attacks only added to his mystique. Sometimes in the heat of battle, he fell from his horse, helpless, glassy-eyed, and foaming at the mouth. At those times, his body-guard, Pedro Camejo, a large Afro-Venezuelan called "El Negro Primero" (The First Black), would rescue Páez. This large black man, who wielded a very large machete, had once looted for the Royalists, but became the llanero general's devoted protector.

Royalists, holding fortified San Fernando on the Río Apure, dared not attack Páez and his ferocious llanero cavalry on the plains. He led his army and the émigrés to the Lower Apure just as fast as the accompanying women and children could walk. *Juanas* (Janes, camp followers) often nursed wounded Patriots and on some occasions took up arms. Páez left the women and children at Araguayuna protected by cavalry. With his remaining force, he pushed the Spaniards back and by September controlled the plains south of the Apure River. Manuel Valdés then moved his troops into the plains north of the Apure.

Even away from the fighting, Bolívar remained active. He knew that the independence forces needed supplies. Piar had between two thousand and three thousand men under his command in the llanos of Maturín, but he needed arms and ammunition. Miguel Valdés, commanding five thousand New Granadans and men of Barinas, and Páez, protecting thousands of refugees, also needed weapons. Bolívar hoped that English merchants would give him credit and that his Haitian benefactors would extend more aid. On September 4, Bolívar wrote a long letter to Pétion admitting the misadventures and miscalculations of the past five months. He explained that all his officers needed arms and munitions. "Since I have none to give them," Bolívar wrote, "I have come to you to solicit anew for my country."

Pétion replied sympathetically after just three days. "With more sorrow than I can say, I read the deplorable events which compelled you to abandon *Tierra Firme* [the Mainland]. So it is, in great and in small things; a mysterious fatality warps the wisest scheme, unforeseen reverses mock every precaution and destroy the best laid plans. If I can do anything to mitigate your pain and sorrow, you may count on all that is within my power. Hasten to this city. We will confer."

In Port-au-Prince, Bolívar asked Robert Sutherland for money to cover immediate expenses. There he received the bad news that Brión had wrecked the *General Bolívar*. With typical aplomb, he resolved to regroup and sent new instructions to Brión. "President Pétion is always our protector. Hasten to join me and sail with me to Venezuela." The Liberator had unfinished business to complete. For the second time, however, he had to fight the Royalists from Haiti, not on his beloved Venezuela's soil.

Throughout his life, the mercurial Bolívar alternated between abject depression and boundless optimism. In today's parlance, we might consider him bipolar. According to Mental Health.net, bipolar disorder is "a depressed mood or a loss of interest or pleasure in daily activities consistently for at least a 2 week period. This mood must represent a change from the person's normal mood; social, occupational, educational or other important functioning must also be negatively impaired by the change in mood." On other occasions, the bipolar person exhibits "hypomania—a state in which the person shows a high level of energy, excessive moodiness or irritability, and impulsive or reckless behavior." Symptoms may include "inflated self-esteem or grandiosity, decreased need for sleep, more talkative than usual or pressure to keep talking, flight of ideas or subjective experience that thoughts are racing, attention is easily drawn to unimportant or irrelevant items, increase in goal-directed activity (either socially, at work or school, or sexually) or psychomotor agitation, excessive involvement in pleasurable activities that have a high potential for painful consequences," including "sexual indiscretions." In repeated episodes, the Liberator seems to have swung wildly between these two extremes and exhibited many of these symptoms. This driven man probably faced as many personal as public demons during his eventful life.

CHAPTER 9

Frustration from Jacmel to Guayana,

1816–17

Bolívar's search for credibility, credit, and supplies in Haiti proved slow and frustrating. He chafed at being away from the real action. Back in Venezuela, the indomitable and perhaps not completely sane Gregor MacGregor kept independence hopes alive. On the night of July 14, when Bolívar fled Ocumare, Soublette, MacGregor, and their small band of Patriots filed quietly out of town and moved east over low mountain spurs to Choroní.

The troops recognized MacGregor as their commander, and he led them south over mountains and through valleys. Having reached the llanos, they turned south and east in search of guerrilla chiefs. As MacGregor and Soublette had predicted, Pablo Morales failed to pursue them. Royalists worried mostly about where Bolívar would strike next. Guerrilla chiefs Pedro Zaraza in the Caracas llanos and José Tadeo Monagas in the east both recognized MacGregor as commander in chief. He now had an army strong enough to battle northward through Barcelona Province.

MacGregor received a warning on September 3, 1816, that Morales, belatedly pursuing him, had occupied Santa María de Ipire in Zaraza's territory. Zaraza departed to observe the Royalists, while MacGregor and Monagas marched toward Barcelona and entered the coastal city on September 13. MacGregor immediately informed Arismendi, Piar, and Mariño that he had possession of Barcelona, but that he needed help against Morales and his more than one thousand troops. Arismendi had no men to spare, but he did send supplies. Mariño and Bermúdez, in possession of the Peninsula of Paria, had laid siege to Cumaná when MacGregor's plea arrived. Mariño sent no help, but Piar viewed this as a great opportunity. He had come from Maturín to help Mariño but disliked his subordinate position, so he immediately sent 250 to 400 men overland to Barcelona. He went by sea to get there as quickly as possible.

Piar outranked MacGregor, so he assumed command of MacGregor's Ocumare Division, the cavalry of Monagas and Zaraza, and his own men—an army of twelve hundred to thirteen hundred men. As Morales approached Barcelona, Piar marched his army out of Barcelona on the afternoon of September 26. The battle of Juncal began the next morning with Piar and his troops on the Patriot left. Royalists cut Piar off from his troops. Thinking the battle lost, Piar fled back to Barcelona. The more resolute Monagas, Zaraza, and MacGregor, however, inflicted such heavy losses that the Royalist survivors fled in terror. MacGregor and Monagas pursued and wiped out more of Morales's army until Piar called off the pursuit. The frustrated Morales satisfied himself with killing civilians.

Patriots now controlled Barcelona Province, but discord among the officers again threatened their success. Jealous of Monagas, Piar relieved him of his command and replaced him with Zaraza. MacGregor, disgusted with Piar and the endless Patriot infighting, left the country. The Scot later made considerable money selling commissions and recruiting in Europe for the Patriot army. Although he had shown great courage in battle, MacGregor ended his days scheming, exploiting, and profiteering.

Francisco Olivier had recently arrived from Margarita in the *Diana*. He had put in at Barcelona for the latest news from the continent before sailing to Haiti. Olivier informed Monagas, Zaraza, and the other officers that Arismendi wanted Bolívar to return as their supreme chief. The oft-divided officers finally agreed on something. They needed a supreme chief, and Bolívar was the only man to whom they would all submit. Zea and Olivier departed to meet Bolívar at Port-au-Prince.

In his letter, dated September 22, 1816, Arismendi reminded Bolívar that in all ages founders of republics "have had to encounter that most fearful of dangers, but armed with constancy, they bear up against all opposition." After reviewing past events, Arismendi said that time had revealed the wisdom of Bolívar's grand design and that all ranks—the people, generals, and troops—wanted him to return as their leader. "The country calls you; it is imperious in you to submit. In such a case not a moment is to be lost, and celerity is of the utmost consequence. My uneasiness will not cease until I witness your Excellency among us."

Later in the day, Bolívar wrote urging Brión back into the fray: "You will see that they call me, and that our affairs are going very well. Now we must hurry. Get all the boats you can, arm them so that we can land on the coast with a squadron." The next day Bolívar again urged Brión to hurry with him to Venezuela, where "the people and generals are our friends." News of the victories in Venezuela only increased the Liberator's impatience. Furthermore, Royalists lacked the strength to keep a base at Pampatar on Margarita and at the same time force Mariño and Bermúdez to raise their siege of Cumaná. Forced to give up either Pampatar or Cumaná, they chose to sacrifice the former. Royalists evacuated on November 13, leaving Patriots in control of the entire island.

Bolívar ordered Brión to recruit all the troops he could and to offer letters of marque to all privateers who would sail with the Patriot squadron. The merchant Sutherland now knew that a Patriot squadron could enter the Orinoco and sail upriver to vast herds of cattle, mules, and horses on the llanos. Livestock was better than money in the Caribbean islands, so Bolívar began to get substantial credit from Sutherland.

Bolívar signed three promissory notes to Sutherland in Port-au-Prince on December 4. He pledged his government in Venezuela to pay the British merchant two thousand gourdes (one gourde equaled one peso at the time) for his schooner *La Fortuna,* used in the Aux Cayes expedition, and nine thousand gourdes for rations and supplies for the army and navy. A third note promised two thousand gourdes a month for his transport *La María.* Two days later Bolívar rode to Jacmel, where he signed another note for 2,530 pesos for 506 cartridge pouches.

When Bolívar arrived at Jacmel, he expected to find Brión ready to sail, however, Brión, had remained at Aux Cayes. Finally Bolívar sent the *Diana* to Aux Cayes to fetch his naval commander. Why had the naval officer procrastinated? Had the wound he received in the head six months earlier in the battle of Los Frailes made him gun-shy? Had wrecking the *General Bolívar* shaken his confidence? Brión, a merchant, not a seaman, actually knew little about navigation. A captain always maneuvered the ship on which he sailed. Regardless of his misgivings, Brión sailed, along with Zea and Bolívar on the *Diana* in mid-December. A Haitian warship escorted the vessel, whose name had been changed to honor *General Mariño.* The Jacmel expedition arrived at the port of Juan Griego, Margarita, on December 28, where jubilant Margaritans welcomed the flotilla.

From Margarita, Bolívar sailed to Barcelona, arriving on the last day of 1816. He informed the Patriot chiefs of his arrival in a letter addressed to "the Bravest of the Brave of Venezuela." "With what joy did I learn of the deliverance of those so dear to me . . . ! My happiness lacks only the pleasure of embracing you. I shall ever look forward to that memorable day; and especially so, if you add the titles of conquerors of Guayana to the many laurels that you have earned in the past. . . . Once that is done, however, will you not return to break the shackles of our other brothers who are still suffering the enemy's tyranny? Yes, yes; you will fly with me even to rich Perú. . . . Fortune cannot win over those whom death cannot intimidate. Life is only precious insofar as it is glorious." From that day forward, despite more setbacks, Bolívar's confidence remained unshakable.

Brión, meanwhile, had all the muskets, powder, and supplies unloaded from his squadron and transported from the harbor seven miles up the Neverí River to the city of Barcelona. Then he returned to Margarita with most of the vessels. Antonio Díaz remained to protect the port with his flecheras. The sea held no dangers for this Margaritan. He made the old Dutch harbor east of the mouth of the Neverí his base, protected by El Morro, a fort at the tip of a small peninsula.

Bolívar, Arismendi, and seven hundred infantry marched west from Barcelona on January 8, 1817, headed for Caracas. They had advanced only thirty miles when disaster struck. A Royalist detachment, entrenched behind a cactus parapet, attacked and killed two hundred Patriots. Bolívar and Arismendi retreated to Barcelona and learned that Brig. Gen. Pascal Real had concentrated a force ready to march on the city. A desperate Bolívar dispatched Soublette in a flechera to Mariño with an urgent plea for help. "It is useless to try longer to take Cumaná if Barcelona is lost." Bermúdez, allied with Mariño, had no desire to go to Barcelona, where Bolívar might again refuse to receive him, as he had in Bonaire. Mariño argued with him: "Can we let those Goths triumph over Bolívar? Can we let Arismendi and our friends perish?"

Mariño left Antonio José de Sucre with a few troops at his siege base and dispatched his army in two divisions, accompanying one by sea. Bermúdez led the other overland. Bolívar dug trenches and raised parapets around the area from the plaza and church all the way to the Convent of San Francisco. The defenses enclosed fourteen blocks of Barcelona. Within this area he mounted cannon removed from his vessels and the fort El Morro. Antonio Díaz and his quick, able flecheras fought off Spanish attempts to land cannons. For a change, Bolívar enjoyed an ample supply with guns and ammunition. He had stored all his war materiel in the convent, which he now called his "Casa Fuerte" (Strong House).

Real's Royalist forces crossed the bridge into the city and took possession of squares adjacent to Bolívar's fortified area. Residents retired to the Patriot area, taking all their food with them. Lacking artillery, Real could not dislodge them. Patriot gunfire and severe hunger prompted many of his troops to desert. At this point, Real received an audacious, pointed note from Bermúdez that simply read: "Retire! I, Bermúdez, have come!" Mariño's arguments had prevailed! Bermúdez and his forces had arrived at Pozuelos, a few miles east of the city. Real retired on February 8. When Bolívar and Bermúdez met, they eyed each other for a long second, then embraced, finally ending their long, bitter estrangement. From that moment, Bermúdez became one of Bolívar's staunchest allies. Mariño arrived the next day with the rest of his army.

Real soon regrouped but could not prevail over both Bolívar and Mariño. While he waited for siege artillery, Real made his headquarters southwest of Barcelona at El Pilar. There he could cut off Bolívar's main food item, cattle being driven north from the llanos. A Spanish squadron tried several times in February and early March to cut off all supplies by sea. Each time, the tenacious Antonio Díaz drove them away. Nonetheless, Bolívar and Mariño, facing a serious food shortage, now had to get their troops out of Barcelona. North American companies profiteered by selling arms and supplies to both sides, although not without criticism. On February 5, 1817, the *Aurora*, published by William Duane in Philadelphia, criticized New York and Baltimore merchants for supplying Royalists with "all sorts of arms, accoutrements, stores, and munitions. Shall the resources of this *republic* be applied in this manner to support the cause of *tyranny?*"

Bolívar had no horses or pack mules to transport the bounty of guns and ammunition stored in Casa Fuerte. Mariño marched southwest to the area between Aragua and El Chaparro (in the present state of Guárico), an abundant source of horses and cattle. Guerrilla chief Pedro María Freites volunteered to remain in command of the garrison and protect the three hundred residents within, mostly women and children. Bideau remained with Freites, and Bolívar left to combine operations with Piar in Guayana.

Unlike Real, Royalist Col. Juan Aldama, only two days west of Barcelona at Píritu near the coast, had siege guns. His guns battered down the walls of the entrenched area of Barcelona on April 7. His troops immediately decapitated nearly all the Patriots, including Bideau, but temporarily spared Freites and the governor of the city. The Spaniards took them to Caracas and beheaded them there. A few Patriots, including Freites's brother Raimundo, escaped in the confusion. They fled to Mariño at Aragua and told him of the disaster at Barcelona. Mariño tried to persuade his officers to march east to reassert his dominance of Barcelona and Cumaná Provinces. He did not wish to march south to strengthen Bolívar and Piar in Guayana. His astute officers detected his real motivation—distaste of serving under Bolívar. Bermúdez, Arismendi, Manuel Valdés, and later Soublette deserted Mariño and headed south to join Bolívar and Piar.

Guerrilla chief Manuel Sedeño occupied a mesa in front of Angostura on the south bank of the Orinoco. His forces kept any cattle or grain from reaching that city, the capital of Guayana. Piar had possession of Capuchin missions farther down the river and east of the Caroní tributary. The friars had no weapons, but Spanish forces at Guayana la Vieja (Old Guayana) protected them, as well as the Indians who herded mission cattle and worked the plantations that produced grain, other foods, and cotton.

Guayana la Vieja stood on the south bank of the Orinoco, just a few miles from its delta. J. H. Robinson, an English officer, described the area in his journal published in 1822: "The village of Old Guayana," he wrote, "consists of about 50 houses, the appearance of which is extremely poor and miserable in the extreme. It is situated in a valley close to the river's edge, and on each side stands a fort, one of which has three guns." In February, Piar had worked to establish a land blockade to starve the Spaniards within Guayana la Vieja. His cavalry and infantry marched directly east from the Angostura mesa to Carhuachi. Patriots had occupied all the missions by the middle of February and had imprisoned twenty-two friars in the monastery of Carhuachi. Piar gave command of the missions to Father Blanco late in March and returned to the mesa near Angostura to welcome Bolívar.

With New Granada pacified, Pablo Morillo moved east to San Fernando de Apure, a fortified port city not far from where the Apure empties into the Orinoco. Morillo sent Gen. Miguel de la Torre down the Apure and the Orinoco with eight hundred troops in twenty-six launches to strengthen Royalists at Angostura. La Torre anchored there on March 29. Within a few days Piar knew of La Torre's movements downriver toward Guayana la Vieja. Bolívar and Piar conferred. La Torre's objective might be to regain the missions. On the other hand, he might simply need to secure cattle and grain. Piar raced overland to protect the missions. In early April 1817, Bolívar gathered forces commanded by Arismendi, Valdés, Zaraza, Bermúdez, and Soublette.

When his retinue camped at Ipire on the night of April 18, Bolívar wrote confidently to Brión: "We have enough men to save the Republic. Those with me incorporated with those of Guayana will total at least 2,500 infantry and more than 1,500 cavalry. It is inevitable that Angostura will fall within

8 days. You must come quickly with all your naval forces." On May 13 Bolívar repeated his instructions to hurry and also authorized Brión to contract for more supplies to be paid for with cattle, horses, mules, and cotton from Guayana.

Patriot positions in Guayana had improved during the weeks of Bolívar's absence. As Piar raced east on April 5 to protect the missions, he passed La Torre's flotilla coming downriver. The Patriot forces crossed the Caroní and camped at San Félix not far from Guayana la Vieja. La Torre's Royalist force disembarked on April 9, seeking horses and food, but now Piar blocked his way. The next afternoon La Torre marched halfway to San Felix and camped for the night. He continued his march the next day and confronted Piar late in the afternoon, but Piar's army quickly enveloped the Royalists. As Piar recorded in his diary, the Royalists "fought like men worthy of a better cause, but they were completely routed." La Torre lost more than one thousand men, but he and the remnant of his army managed to slip away under cover of darkness.

Bolívar again faced both military and political challenges. He had to consolidate his authority over his officers and try to organize an effective government. By May 2, 1817, Bolívar, Arismendi, Bermúdez, Valdés, Zaraza, and Soublette had arrived at the Patriot camp in front of Angostura. Historian Vicente Lecuna dates the beginning of Bolívar's effective government from this date. By year's end Bolívar would consolidate military control over his officers and civilian rule over the Third Republic of Venezuela.

The Liberator still faced dissension within his own ranks and tried to pacify the rebellious Piar by naming him general in chief. He urged Brión at Carúpano to rush his fleet to the Orinoco River and ordered Arismendi to round up blacksmiths and carpenters to build flecheras and other boats. One squad cut timber for the boats from forests between San Felix and the right bank of the Caroní. Other crews built the boats near the timber supply. Bolívar dispatched Bermúdez to help Sedeño besiege Angostura and then rode east.

Bolívar passed Guayana la Vieja and stopped at the cove of Cabrián to examine the forts under construction. These posts would protect Brión's fleet after it came through the main channel of the Orinoco delta. Bolívar wrote more letters urging the very cautious Brión to hurry. Unfortunately, Brión seemed to be conspiring with Mariño. The English corvette *Brazen* had anchored at Pampatar on April 25, depositing just one passenger, José Joaquín Cortés Madariaga. The politically astute Chilean priest, so instrumental in pushing the Caracas declaration of independence in 1810, persuaded Brión that the British government and other powers would recognize the Republic of Venezuela once a regular government had been organized. Brión and Cortés Madariaga sailed to Mariño at Cariaco where, on May 8, Mariño, Brión, Zea, and eight others agreed to organize a Patriot government. They elected Bolívar and two other officers to serve as an executive council, with Brión as admiral and Mariño as general in chief of the armies. The ambitious, scheming Mariño had succeeded in gaining military ascendancy over Bolívar, and even stalwart friends Zea and Brión seemed to be turning against him.

Brión sent reports of the "congress" to Bolívar from Carúpano on June 5. "I find myself in continual embarrassment," he said. "I believed it my duty, as a republican jealous of our holy cause, to proclaim in Cariaco on May 11 that we were a federal government. You can imagine every thing was done in order." Bolívar did not accept the legitimacy of the so-called congress. His patience exhausted, he dismissed Mariño for this third attempted rebellion against the Liberator's authority. Brión carefully failed to mention that Sucre, Urdaneta, and thirty other dissenting officers and their troops had left Mariño and proceeded via Maturín on their way overland to join Bolívar in Guayana.

Bolívar learned on May 27 that Morillo had arrived at El Chaparro with several thousand troops, who, by forced marches, headed toward Guayana to aid La Torre. Bolívar became apprehensive about the Capuchin friars. Loyal to Spain, they might incite their mission Indians to free them and aid Morillo. Mainlines of traffic passed through the area from Carhuachi (where Piar had imprisoned the friars) to the mouth of the Caroní River. Bolívar ordered the friars removed south several miles to the mission of Divina Pastora (Divine Shepherdess), where Jacinto Lara and another officer took custody. What happened next is not completely clear, but it appears that Lara, recently arrived at Carhuachi, did not know that a mission by that name actually existed. He interpreted the order to mean that he should send the friars to their heavenly home and shot all twenty-two of the Capuchins. This unfortunate act, abhorrent even to nonbelievers, further tarnished the Patriot cause and provided ammunition for Bolívar's enemies. Did "war to the death" know no limits?

Neither Bolívar nor La Torre knew that Morillo had changed the direction of his march. Gen. José Canterac had arrived at Cumaná with a division of twenty-eight hundred Spaniards to reinforce Morillo. On June 5, Brión (who had returned to the Liberator's fold) notified Bolívar that Canterac had anchored at Cumaná. "I am ready to join you," wrote Brión, "with my squadron of 4 brigs, 6 schooners, 2 *feluccas,* [fast, narrow sailing vessels], 1 *balandra* [sloop], 9 *flecheras* and gunboats. I bring cannon, mortars, grenades, shells, muskets, powder, and uniforms."

The cautious Brión initiated no action unless he sensed easy victory. Even with numbers and arms on his side, he moved very carefully. Brión's squadron passed through the Macareo Channel on July 7 in two divisions, five Margaritan flecheras, with Fernando Díaz leading and Antonio Díaz in the rear. Several hours behind them came Brión with the rest of the fleet. A flechera escort sent by Bolívar waited for the second division while the Díaz brothers proceeded upriver. Suddenly, by the island of Pagayos, a Royalist light squadron of eleven large boats fell upon Fernando Díaz. The Spaniards killed all onboard his flechera and also took the next two boats. The Royalists stopped petrified, however, when a scream split the air and galvanized the Patriots into action. Antonio Díaz leaped on an enemy flechera brandishing his side arms. His inspired crew did the same, quickly killing all who came within reach of their blades. Their wild yells seemingly stunned the Royalists to inaction. At the end of the battle of Pagayos, Antonio had retaken two of his flecheras, sunk one enemy boat, and captured several others. He personally cut off the heads of an impressive number of Royalists, savagely avenging his brother Fernando's death.

The Royalist captain fled with the few boats he had left, while Antonio's badly battered boats headed for Maturín, about one hundred miles southeast of Barcelona, for repairs and to replenish the crews. Antonio's victory opened the Orinoco to the Patriots and broke the spirit of starving Royalists at Angostura. They prepared to evacuate to Guayana la Vieja and wait for help from Morillo.

When the two thousand Royalist marines and soldiers and eighteen hundred inhabitants began to move, Bermúdez alertly kept up a continual fire. The Spaniards boarded thirty vessels, twelve of which were armed with ninety cannons, and sailed downstream. The next day Bermúdez occupied the city of Angostura and began distributing meat to those left behind. On July 19 the Royalist armada anchored at Guayana la Vieja under protection of its forts. Flecheras from San Miguel went out to harass the Royalists and captured one gunboat. The Royalists disembarked and waited in vain two weeks for Morillo. Many were at the point of death from starvation because Bolívar's squads kept cattle or other food from reaching the town. Finally La Torre gave the order to evacuate; Royalists loaded cannons from the forts onto some gunboats and on August 3 sailed downriver.

Arismendi and his troops occupied Guayana la Vieja. Bolívar and his troops hurried to Cabrián to protect Brión's fleet. Sixteen armed Royalist vessels in two columns approached Brión's fleet. Transports and lesser vessels veered to the left and warships to the right in front of Cabrián. Squads of sharpshooters had already joined Brión as he advanced obliquely to meet the enemy. Guns at the forts and infantry onshore provided additional cover.

As the fleets closed in, a shot from Brión's vessel killed and wounded many on the Royalist flagship. Rafael Rodríguez, with Patriot flecheras, fell on the enemy's rear, boarding and capturing several vessels. Transports slid past the battle and moved downstream. Three of Brión's vessels advanced on the enemy line that dissolved and fled behind the transports. The strong current helped them escape through Boca Grande. They reached the open sea on August 4 and sailed to the English island of Grenada, some 360 miles northeast of La Guiara. Although starved and defeated, the Royalists lived to fight again. Brión, always concerned about business arithmetic, took stock at the end of the battle. The Patriots captured fourteen war vessels with seventy-three cannons and lesser guns, 3,300 muskets, abundant munitions, 160,000 pesos in gold and silver, and 300,000 pesos in copper. The value of the captured loot totaled a million pesos. Most of the 1,731 captives wisely agreed to join the Patriots.

Dissension among Patriot officers, however, continued to plague the cause. Piar had begun the conquest of Guayana brilliantly and had recognized Bolívar as supreme chief, but then again turned against the Liberator. Rumors reached Bolívar that Piar had invited officers to disavow his authority and had vowed to wage a race war against whites to make pardos and mestizos the ruling class. Daniel O'Leary observed that, "referring to his own origin, which he had through vanity tried to hide until then, Piar made friendly gestures toward the colored people for the first time." During the first days of July, Piar had left the mission area and entered Angostura with Bermúdez on July 18. Bolívar ordered Bermúdez to have Piar report to him, a prisoner if necessary, at his San Miguel headquarters. Upon hearing these orders, Piar fled on July 26 to join the rebellious Mariño at Maturín.

Bolívar commissioned Sedeño to apprehend Piar. Sedeño found him at Aragua de Cumaná on September 27 with seventy troops who did not know that Piar had deserted Bolívar. When Sedeño explained his mission to the troops they refused to obey Piar. Sedeño captured Piar and took him to Angostura for trial. Bolívar instructed Soublette to act as prosecutor against Piar, charging him with insubordination to the supreme authority, conspiring against order and pubic tranquility, sedition, and desertion.

The court-martial began on October 4, with Brión presiding and six officers sitting in judgment. Piar could not be tried by his peers, because he alone held the rank of general in chief of the armies. Lt. Col. Fernando Galindo conducted the defense, and Capt. José Ignacio Pulido served as secretary. Nine witnesses offered depositions against the prisoner. At the close of the trial Soublette solemnly pronounced the verdict: "Manuel Piar has conspired against society and against the government; he has disobeyed it, has deserted and taken up arms against subalterns of the Supreme Chief. For all of which I decree for the Republic that he be condemned to death." Given his status and military successes, Piar believed he would receive clemency, but Bolívar signed the death decree. On October 16 a firing squad executed Piar in the public square of Angostura for desertion, rebellion, and treason.

Some enemies branded Bolívar a racist for executing Piar, a mulatto, while not taking the same harsh action against the Creole Mariño. The Liberator defended his action this way: "The death of General Piar was a political necessity which saved the country. The rebels were disturbed and frightened by him. . . . All came under my command. My authority was established, and civil war and the enslavement of the country were avoided. Never was there a death more useful, more political, and at the same time more deserved." Perhaps in Bolívar's view, inciting a possible race war presented a much graver threat to the republic than almost routine mutiny against his authority.

In the ever-loyal O'Leary's eyes, "Bolívar's firmness assured the future of the Republic. The proclamation with which he announced this event is an eloquent monument of tender sentiments, good judgment, and moral values. . . . Piar had been planning on a civil war that would inevitably have brought about a state of anarchy and the sacrifice of his own comrades and brothers—in effect, opening the grave of the Republic with his own hands. This could not be tolerated. Bolívar's final words touched on the confidence that the soldiers should have in him as their leader and comrade-in-arms. General Mariño undoubtedly deserved the same fate as Piar, except that he was less dangerous, and a single example was enough."

Bolívar did indeed pursue a very diplomatic approach to Mariño, who styled himself the liberator of the East. The entire province of Cumaná recognized Mariño as general in chief of the armies. Even General Ducoudray Holstein, among Bolívar's most venomous critics, recognized why the Liberator might treat Mariño and Piar differently. Bolívar "pardoned, and most graciously recalled Mariño to his former rank and command, rightly judging that Mariño without Piar would never impede him or his views, whatever they might be."

The intrigues of Piar and Mariño had forced Bolívar to postpone his campaign. A few days before the execution of Piar, Bolívar sent Sucre to soften Mariño's resistance and to win over the dissidents to serve under Bermúdez. The Liberator instructed Sucre to "attempt to complete his reconciliation with the government." Sucre met with Mariño on November 3 and told him that Bermúdez was marching to relieve him of his command. When Mariño angrily protested his replacement, Bolívar replied simply and directly: "If your resistance continues, you will never more be a citizen of Venezuela but a public enemy. If you wish to quit the service of the Republic, say so and I will give you a passport to leave the country." An angry, still rebellious Mariño left for Margarita, swearing he would return at the head of an army to again take command. Bermúdez retorted, "By God, I will be the first to plant a ball in his chest if he comes back."

Sucre understood that Bolívar and the Patriot cause needed both the hotheaded subordinates, Bermúdez and Mariño. Sucre caught up with Mariño before he reached the coast and persuaded him to ask Bolívar's permission to go to Margarita. Bolívar accepted this request as Mariño's submission to the central authority. Bermúdez skillfully won over Mariño's followers; indeed, he gained the respect and submission of all the Patriot factions in Cumaná. In a proclamation to his troops dated January 26, 1818, Mariño would grandly swear his loyalty to the Liberator. "If by a mischief ever to be regretted we have until now been considered as dissatisfied, and have under this character attracted public attention; it is now, and from this moment, our most scared duty to become a model of submission and obedience to the supreme chief! My sincere wish is, that the whole universe may be convinced of the sincerity of our intentions, and find in us the most faithful supporter of our government."

In addition to Piar and Mariño, Bolívar had to deal with another independent, ambitious caudillo, the leader of the llaneros, José Antonio Páez. After his Cariaco Congress in May, Mariño had sent an envoy urging Páez to also recognize him as supreme chief. A few days later two of Bolívar's envoys requested that Páez recognize Bolívar as supreme chief. In his autobiography, Páez recorded that he received all three envoys with respect and acknowledged the need for a supreme chief. He declined, however, to recognize either Mariño or Bolívar as filling that role, preferring to visualize himself as supreme chief. He had access to one million cattle and five hundred thousand mules and horses in the Apure. Some forty thousand of the horses grazed in his pastures, broken and ready for campaigning. The llaneros of the Apure had placed all these resources, as well as themselves, at the disposal of Páez. They had recognized him as supreme chief. How could he place himself and his men under the authority of someone his rugged troops had never seen?

In his apology to the Liberator, Páez asked: "Who can make these men believe that there is anything superior to brute strength? They despise anyone who cannot compete with them in this respect. Who can tell them that they should transfer their allegiance to the *patria* [fatherland], a word that has no meaning for them?" Páez, however, knew what *patria* meant. On July 31 he wrote Bolívar recognizing him as commander in chief.

Bolívar referred to the letter from Páez in his answer from Angostura, dated September 15, 1817. He showered flowery praise on Páez for his nobleness of sentiment, generosity, energy, and patriotism. Bolívar also offered more tangible inducements. The occupation of Guayana had enhanced the Patriot cause with foreigners, "especially the English who had barely learned of the triumph of our arms when their merchant vessels appeared laden with all kinds of produce." Even officers whose loyalty wavered could appreciate the potential profits from trade.

Three weeks later Bolívar sent Páez five stone mortars, two small cannons, other equipment, and two volumes on infantry tactics. "These," he wrote, "are for the better instruction and discipline of the Brave Infantry of Páez." In return, he asked that Páez send him twenty-five hundred mules and "to collect everything that can be sold to pay for the elements of war that we are buying and will buy. Within fifteen days a strong force will march from here to end the siege of San Fernando."

Bermúdez continually harassed the Royalists with guerrilla tactics, seeking to gradually drive them from Cumaná. The attrition forced Morillo to dispatch more and more replacements so that the eastern front seriously drained his manpower. A correspondent for the *Boston Recorder* (January 27, 1818) described the formidable Bermúdez as strong enough "to make the tyrants in his vicinity bite the dust or dive headlong into the sea." The Patriots faced their own difficulties. The enormous expense of equipping the divisions of Bermúdez in Cumaná, Zaraza in the Caracas llanos, and Monagas in the Barcelona llanos had exhausted the resources of Guayana. Very few mules remained. Five weeks had passed since Bolívar had asked Páez to send him pack mules, but none had arrived. "Please," wrote Bolívar to Páez, "send in the shortest time possible the mules I have requested."

The issue of mules was not inconsequential, nor were all mules of equal importance. In a letter to Santander, penned September 13, 1820, the Liberator opened with this forceful demand: "I hear from Trigos that my bay mule, which I left with you in Bogotá, is being kept by one Olaya at Juan Díaz. If this is so, have her brought back and well cared for. [Manuel] Manrique's mule is not fit to carry fodder for my bay, and there is to be no such exchange. That is why I did not order her to be sent to him." In 1998, a number of scholars of Latin America stressed the importance and utility of mules to Bolívar in an online discussion forum called H-LatAm.

The mule is the preferred mode of transportation for crossing the Andes mountains today as it was in the times of Bolivar. Mules are by nature excellent climbers, they have more resistance and can carry heavier loads. Today, mules are as important to the Andes farmer as it was hundreds of years ago. At least in my country, Colombia, coffee farmers, potato growers and farmers in general use the mule for cargo and for secure transportation across the Andes. Bolivar probably used the mule to transport material and in 'El Coronel No Tiene Quien Le Escriba,' novelist Gabriel Garcia Marquez talked about how conquistadores sometimes rode the mules in order to give their horses some rest before battle or after a long and strenuous climb.—Stefano Tijerina

Due to Colombia's topography, mules were and are highly valued for transport. During colonial times and up to today, good mules have been more expensive than horses. They were/are preferred for riding because they are much more surefooted, strong and hardy than horses, especially in the slippery and muddy flagstoned "caminos reales." While Bolívar used "Palomo," his horse, in battle and for making triumphal entries into towns and cities, using mules for riding was the perfect way of avoiding an accident and conserving the strength of Palomo, especially in the high mountain passes where the thin air can kill overworked horses due to the rapid change in altitude.—Santiago Giraldo

Mules are more nimble-footed than horses and were especially valuable for traversing the Andes. Mules were the means to travel from Quito to Guayaquil until the completion of the railroad. Mules have been important to armies for centuries. I am sure most commanders used them at some point.—George Lauderbaugh

The National Park Service has a herd of mules at Grand Canyon, Arizona. They are used to take adventurous tourists to the bottom of the canyon because they are more sure-footed and less temperamental than horses and because they supposedly provide a smoother ride. Mule breeding is still a going industry in some areas of this country. In sixteenth-century New Spain bishops and other important people often rode on mules for the reasons mentioned above.—Stafford Poole

If you have driven a horse, like I have, through the Andes for a week, switching to riding a mule is the most comfortable feeling. This is nothing new, San Martin also rode a mule through the Andes and in the Spanish Army in California a mule was worth twice the price of a horse. The mule was especially welcome when crossing the Santa Barbara mountains. Warning: if there is mud, stick to the horse.—Carlos Lopez

Well, the bottom line is—have you ever ridden a mule? Some of them can be quite large and they can be much safer on mountain trails. I can remember decades ago when Luis Ospina Vasquez would mount some of us aspiring historians to ride in Colombia—mules were preferred. So if Bolivar had a large mule, he could still look quite magnificent—especially since he was kind of short in any case. Yet another pressing issue remains to be discovered—are there famous mules in Bolivar's history whose names have been forgotten?—Ann Twinam

The issue of mules aside, Bolívar needed to mobilize on the political as well as the military front. On October 30 he decreed that the Third Republic of Venezuela needed a Council of State with three departments: State and Treasury, four members; War and Navy, five members; and Interior and Justice, four members. He assembled the principal officers and citizens in the Government Palace of Angostura on November 10. He gave the assembly an account of the legislative powers of the first two republics and declared Angostura the capital until Caracas could be taken. (A grateful Venezuela later would change the name of Angostura to Ciudad Bolívar.) Then he appointed Zea president of State and Treasury, Brión president of War and Marine, and Juan Martínez president of Interior and Justice. Thirteen men, with Brión serving as president of the council, would govern while Bolívar campaigned. If he should be killed or taken prisoner, the council would become the supreme power.

Bolívar left Angostura on November 23 with 750 troops. He intended to combine forces with Zaraza and destroy Morillo. Antonio Díaz's light fleet transported Bolívar and his troops up the Orinoco. Two days later they debarked at Cadenales. Bolívar sent Zaraza south from Chaguaramas along the Río Manipiro to the Río Santa Clara. He was to bring with him all the mules and horses from that area. "I will occupy Ospino [Espino]," Bolívar wrote, "when I know that you are near that pueblo. From this point it will be easy to march upon Calabozo, Caracas, or San Fernando."

Unfortunately for Bolívar, La Torre's troops had occupied Calvario, eighty miles west of Chaguaramas. His scouts reported Zaraza's movement south along the Manipiro. Following night marches, the Royalists routed the Patriots at their camp at La Hogaza, a cattle ranch. Pedro León Torres gathered what remained of Zaraza's cavalry and part of his infantry, then marched to San Diego de Cabrutica and set about recruiting more troops. Bolívar returned to Angostura to prepare for the next, hopefully more successful, campaign.

Bolívar sent Urdaneta to advise Páez to avoid any confrontation with the enemy until Bolívar arrived. He ordered Bermúdez in Cumaná Province to make Soledad, just north across the Orinoco from Angostura, his base so that he could guard both Cumaná and Guayana in Bolívar's absence. The Patriot river fleet had increased to thirty-nine vessels, but Bolívar, impatient to continue up the Orinoco, had to await the arrival of more powder and shot from Margarita. While he waited, James Rooke, a former British army major, arrived. Married to a beautiful mulatto woman from St. Kitts, the tall, strapping Rooke would become aide-de-camp to the Liberator and a gallant fighter. He was a precursor to organized expeditions of some four thousand unemployed officers and troops from England and other European countries who would aid the Patriots.

Great Britain suffered from drought, unemployment, low wages, strikes, and riots when the Napoleonic Wars ended in 1815. The mass withdrawal of British forces from Europe further aggravated the economic situation. Six thousand officers and men had been dismissed from the army by the end of 1817. Another thirty-three thousand had been mustered out the following year. The Royal Navy made similar reductions. Contracts offered by Luis López Méndez sounded positively glowing to many of the unemployed officers. The English soldiers found it easy to believe that they could achieve brilliant careers in Venezuela. Contracts promised promotions of one grade, pay equal to the same grade in the English army, a bonus on arrival, and other attractive benefits. British merchants and manufacturers, anxious to open new markets, equipped military expeditions on credit. British speculators purchased surplus war supplies in European markets and established a base for their sale on Trinidad. War profiteering on Spanish American independence offered many attractive opportunities.

The five ships of the first expedition left England at the end of 1817. One vessel wrecked near the Ushant Rocks and sank with 190 officers. Misfortune also dogged the four remaining ships. Maddening calms followed the storms, food and water ran short, tempers flared, and mutiny threatened. The expedition finally managed to reach St. Barts in the Lesser Antilles. No one met the volunteers who knew either their destination or what they were supposed to do next. They soon heard the disheartening news of many Patriot defeats and that Bolívar lacked funds to pay his own troops. Royalist squadrons also posed a threat to the British vessels. Consequently, many volunteers deserted and wandered among the islands, hoping to find a way home. Others, however, finally arrived in Angostura ready for action in early 1818. To Bolívar, the European troops provided much-needed manpower, expertise, and an important psychological boost. The help from Europe, long-sought by the Precursor Miranda and others, had finally arrived.

PART IV

Patriot Resurgence, Spanish Collapse

CHAPTER 10

From Frustration on the Llanos
to Victory at Boyacá, 1818–19

A strained but effective cooperation between José Antonio Páez, the crude caudillo of the llanos, and Simón Bolívar, the cultured Creole of Caracas, marked the year of 1818. Páez met the Liberator for the first time this year. In his autobiography, he recorded a striking portrait of Bolívar in his prime.

> His two principal distinctions consisted in the extreme mobility of his body and the brilliance of his eyes, which were black, lively and penetrating as those of an eagle. His skin, though burned by the sun of the tropics, still preserved its clearness and its luster, in spite of all the many and violent changes of climate he had undergone in his campaigns.
>
> His temperament was gay and jovial. In private life he was most agreeable, impetuous and dominating when he had some important enterprise in view; thus he united both the courtier and the warrior in himself. He was fond of dancing, gallant and much addicted to ladies' society, and skilful in the management of his horse. In camp he kept his spirits up with witty jokes; but on the march he was always somewhat restless, and tried to fight against his impatience by singing patriotic songs. He was perhaps too fond of fighting, but whilst the battle lasted he was always calm.

In December 1817 Bolívar began preparations to depart Angostura for another campaign. During the last week of the year, Anzoátegui, Santander,

Col. James Rooke, other officers, and an honor guard of more than seven hundred men boarded ships. Bolívar boarded on December 31 and the fleet sailed that afternoon. Prevailing winds carried them westward. On New Year's Day 1818, the ships anchored on the south bank of the Orinoco opposite the mouths of the Pao. Anzoátegui and his troops debarked, while Díaz sailed to the north bank to meet Monagas, Pedro León Torres, and Valdés.

Díaz ferried Monagas and his 700 men (dismounted cavalry and infantry), Torres and 635 infantry, and their animals to the south bank. Díaz returned to the north bank for Valdés and his infantry and sailed westward on January 5. Anzoátegui and the honor guard marched westward along the south bank. Monagas, Torres, and their troops followed, and Sedeño with 700 cavalry and 632 infantry brought up the rear.

As the fleet lay anchored at Caicara on January 17 a scout reported that Royalist troops under Rafael López had Zaraza pinned down. West of Caicara the Orinoco turns south before combining with waters from the Apure and the Arauca. The fleet sailed beyond the mouths of the Apure and Arauca to the island of Urbana and awaited the marchers. Anzoátegui's troops had hiked more than three hundred miles; Sedeño's men about four hundred miles. The fleet ferried them across the Orinoco and up the Arauca to a landing one league from the cattle ranch of Cañafistola. The headquarters of Páez stood nearby at San Juan de Payara. Royalists thirty miles to the north at San Fernando de Apure remained blissfully unaware that three thousand Patriot infantry and one thousand cavalry had arrived at Cañafistola.

On January 31 Páez rode to his first meeting with Bolívar. The two dismounted and embraced. They stood about the same height, five feet six inches. Bolívar marveled at the lionlike head, the fair, sunburned skin, the broad shoulders, and the massive chest of the twenty-seven-year-old master of the llanos. Páez saw black eyes, penetrating and restless like those of an eagle, hands and feet as dainty as those of a woman, and a slight body that was never still.

Much later the llanero recalled his impressions of the meeting in his autobiography.

> Hardly had he seen me, from a good distance off, that he got on his horse to go out to receive me. When we met we both dismounted and gave one another a warm embrace. I told him that I thought it of good augury for the Patriot cause to see him in the llanos, and hoped that from his talent and experience we should find out new means of using the

resources that we put at his disposition, to launch the thunderbolts of destruction against the enemy.

With a generosity that characterized him, he answered me in flattering words, dwelling upon my constancy in resisting the dangers and the hardships of all kinds with which I had had to wrestle in defense of the Fatherland, and assuring me that by our mutual efforts we should be able to finish with the enemy who was oppressing us.

Bolívar moved his army to San Juan de Payara, where Páez presented his troops. The newcomers enjoyed a few days of welcome rest. On February 6 about five thousand Patriots headed for Calabozo, one hundred miles to the north. They first had to cross the Apure, patrolled by enemy gunboats. Bolívar asked Páez, "How are we going to cross the river?" Páez replied by calling out "To the water!" to fifty men of his guard who rode without cruppers and with cinch girths loosened. Fifty centaurs slid their saddles to the ground without dismounting and plunged into the water. Páez recorded their tactics in his autobiography. "Sliding off to one side, they allowed their horses to swim without encumbrance, supporting themselves with one hand upon the animal's haunches, while with the other they guided them by means of a halter. The heads only of the leaders and their steeds rose puffing and snorting above the water." Surprised Royalists had time to fire only a single round before llaneros boarded their gunboats on all sides. Most of the enemy jumped into the water to escape.

The Patriots wiped out Morillo's outpost at Guayabal and advanced over the plains without meeting a single patrol. They camped near a woods on February 12. Páez and Bolívar had the entire force marching through the woods before daybreak. At sunrise they reached a sun-scorched plain. In the center stood a town surrounded with a mud wall built as a defense against Indians. "That wall," wrote English officer Richard Longville Vowell in his 1831 memoir, "was considered by the natives to be so strong, that they called the city Calabozo, or the dungeon. The plain on which it stands is very level, and nearly bare of grass."

A reconnoitering party found part of Morillo's cavalry foraging on a verdant plain three miles south of Calabozo near Misión de Abaja. His infantry had remained in the Mission. Páez, Sedeño, and Monagas attacked and routed the cavalry. General Ducoudray Holstein, always eager to undercut Bolívar's accomplishments, gave this account of the action. "When the cavalry of the Patriots approached near Calabozo, on the 12th of February, they met with a foraging party of seventy or eighty men, who had sallied from

Calabozo, and made a halt before a watering place to water their horses. They had dismounted, and the horses were without saddle or bridle. The men had on their short jackets, and no swords or other arms, so that it was impossible to defend themselves. They were all killed except two, who jumped upon their horses, and escaped into Calabozo, and reported the news to their general, Morillo, at his head quarters." With few cavalry left, Morillo knew that he had to retreat. He planned to move north sixty miles to Sombrero, because in the foothills his infantry would be superior to cavalry. He had a choice of two routes, northeast via the Río Guárico or northwest via El Rastro. The latter village, only nine miles from Calabozo, had water and food. Bolívar left a small patrol to reconnoiter enemy movements and led his army to El Rastro.

Late that night Morillo and residents of Calabozo began to withdraw toward Sombrero. Morillo led the way on foot via the Río Guárico. The few horses he possessed carried the sick and wounded. Most of Morillo's army managed to escape, but Bolívar battled the Royalist rearguard and occupied Calabozo. Patriots refreshed themselves with Royalist stores of food and wine before pursuing Morillo. Despite the welcome rest, both men and horses remained tired.

The Royalists rested near a stream at Sombrero. Bolívar approached with an exhausted force—tired infantry, cavalry, and horses, all suffering from thirst. Royalist fire riddled the Patriots ranks as they ran to drink from the stream. Morillo then zigzagged north, unharried by Patriot forces. He rested his army during the last week of February at Villa de Cura, incorporated reinforcements, and alerted Royalist commanders of the Patriot presence in the llanos.

Llaneros warned Bolívar that their horses were too tired to pursue. Their officers urged that the army retire for rest at Calabozo. In addition, Páez wished to complete the liberation of San Fernando. Bolívar yielded to these pressures and returned to Calabozo. He wisely avoided trying to dictate to Páez for fear of alienating him. The Liberator needed Páez, along with his llaneros, horses, and cattle. Páez soon took San Fernando with no casualties on either side as the starving Royalist garrison evacuated without a fight.

Unfortunately for Bolívar, at Calabozo llaneros began to desert after Páez left. Bolívar notified the llanero chief of the alarming attrition. "The army has almost melted away. The whole brigade of Colonel Vásquez deserted last night so that hardly 100 men remain with him. General Cedeño's are also beginning to desert, and last night some soldiers left from General

Monagas' division. I cannot send troops after them, for I do not trust those who remain. They would probably not return. The deserters go toward San Fernando."

Meanwhile, Royalist pincers began to close on the Patriots. La Torre moved a day's march west from Caracas to keep Bolívar from reaching the capital. Morillo sent Morales with two divisions to clear Cabrera Pass. On March 14 Morales cut two hundred Patriot carabineers to pieces, took their horses, and pushed on to Maracay. Zaraza, Monagas, and Anzoátegui fled to Villa de Cura.

Bolívar, preparing to fight La Torre, learned of the disastrous Patriot defeat at Cabrera Pass. Recognizing the danger of Royalist reinforcements, he also withdrew south through Villa de Cura. The Patriots passed through the Quebrada de Semen to its wide end, La Puerta, and stopped on the night of March 15.

Morales, leading Morillo's van, lost hours thanks to a torrential downpour typical of the rainy season in the llanos. He did not reach Villa de Cura until early on the sixteenth. Bolívar and his army formed on the uneven terrain of La Puerta, and the two armies clashed at sunrise. Vowell described the scene. Royalists, dressed in Spanish uniforms, had a martial appearance "and a decided advantage, in the confidence which it inspired in them when they saw the ragged appearance of the patriots. Many of them were nearly stark naked, their firearms were old and in bad condition. Some muskets were without locks, and were apparently carried for show, until the fall of a few friends or foes should give their owners the opportunity of exchanging them for more effective weapons."

Combatants fought a long, bloody battle at close quarters. The wadding fired from muskets singed their clothes. Col. James Rooke, who had arrived in 1817, suffered two wounds as he followed closely behind Bolívar. Rooke said later that it seemed that Bolívar wished to die on the field, so utterly careless did he appear of his life. The Liberator never wanted for courage.

The two sides repeatedly took and retook positions. Morales faced a precarious situation when Morillo galloped up at sunset with fresh cavalry. The charge caused the Patriots to waver as cavalry cut them down on all sides. Suddenly an unidentified Patriot thrust his lance through Morillo's middle. The lance had to be pushed out from behind, and Morillo almost died. Col. Ramón Correa took command and decided to await reinforcement from La Torre. The welcome break gave Bolívar time to retire to El Rastro and regroup with Páez, who arrived on March 21 with nine hundred llaneros.

On the afternoon of March 22 La Torre learned to his amazement and consternation of the Patriot concentration at El Rastro. He retreated north to Ortiz pursued by Bolívar. On March 26 Patriots tried to dislodge La Torre from the heights. The Patriot cavalry, however, could not operate on the rough hilly ground. La Torre returned to Villa de Cura, while Bolívar marched to Calabozo. Páez and his lancers rode west to the plains of Cojedes near San Carlos.

A week later the Liberator marched to rejoin the llanero chief. Bolívar arrived at Rincón de los Toros on April 16, unaware of the scrutiny of Col. Rafael López and his five Royalist squadrons. López learned the camp password either from Bolívar's captured servant or from a deserter. He then dispatched Tomás de Renovales to kill Bolívar as he slept.

Renovales and a division of forty men approached Bolívar's outpost late at night. When they encountered Santander making the rounds, they gave the password and Renovales said that he and his patrol had to report to Bolívar immediately. Santander pointed to a clump of trees where Bolívar and three other men had slung their hammocks. Renovales detailed two men to each hammock. They fired their muskets into the hammocks, stabbed them with bayonets, and escaped, believing that they had killed Bolívar and his companions.

The attack did indeed kill two and wounded a third, but Bolívar was not one of them. "Providence," wrote Royalist historian Manuel Torrente, "disposed that Bolívar should quit his bed, because of urgent necessity, a few moments before sunrise which casual incident saved him from death." It would not be the last time that the Liberator narrowly escaped assassination.

López and the Royalists advanced in battle formation at dawn. They killed or wounded most of the Patriots and took some prisoner. Bolívar had thrown away his helmet and uniform so the Royalists could not recognize him. Some of his own men fled right by him, failing to recognize their leader. Leonardo Infante, however, killed López and gave Bolívar his horse. Bolívar, Infante, and a few survivors escaped south to San Fernando. Meanwhile, La Torre destroyed most of Páez's army on the plains of Cojedes. Morales defeated Sedeño and entered Calabozo on May 20, giving the Royalists control over the vital llanos and its critical resources.

Once again, the Patriot cause seemed doomed. They had lost all the horses from the Arauca and the Apure, all the arms and ammunition, and almost all their infantry and cavalry. Bolívar remained in San Fernando during the first three weeks of May. He fell ill—feverish, exhausted, depressed, unable to mount a horse because of boils on his thighs. He knew, however, that he had to create yet another army. He boarded a launch on the night of May 23 and early the next morning returned downriver to Angostura.

Historians have long debated the Patriot disasters of 1818. Some argue that Bolívar should have stayed to control the llanos instead of making the foolhardy thrust toward Caracas. He lost virtually his entire army and as many as three thousand horses. On the other hand, he made the Royalists loath to leave the mountain valleys, not knowing where Bolívar might strike next. Morillo, suffering from a serious lance wound, had little stomach left for fighting the rebels. Thanks to a fortuitous call of nature, the indomitable Bolívar escaped assassination and lived to regroup and continue his struggle.

The United States, a very interested outside party, also pondered what course to take. On March 24, 1818, Henry Clay requested that Congress appropriate eighteen thousand dollars to send a minister to the provinces of the Río de la Plata. A month later, Secretary of State John Quincy Adams made clear the conditions under which the United States would recognize a new Spanish American republic: "It is the stage when independence is established as a matter of fact so as to leave the chances of the opposite party to recover their dominion utterly desperate." Obviously, with the series of Patriot setbacks of the year, Bolívar could not expect recognition from the hemisphere's first republic.

As the Liberator pondered the future, the arrival of two English officers with skeleton forces complicated matters. They arrived at San Fernando in May as Bolívar prepared to leave for Angostura. Col. Gustavus Hippisley, with the First Venezuelan Hussars, and Col. Henry Wilson, with the Second or Red Hussars stood ready to fight. (The latter should not be confused with a much more capable officer, Col. Belford Wilson.) But given the recent Patriot disasters, where would they fight? Who would command them? According to Vowell, Bolívar "left it to the option of the foreigners whether they would return to Angostura with him, or remain in the Apure with Páez." Discipline among the British troops collapsed; encouraged by Wilson, they got drunk, looted, and refused to follow Hippisley's orders.

The brazen Wilson, possibly an agent provocateur employed by Spain, led a drunken group of officers to declare they would no longer serve under Bolívar. Wilson proclaimed Páez captain general of the army. Páez wisely rejected the treasonous act and dispatched Wilson to Bolívar along with a report on his activities. The Liberator had the Englishman arrested in Angostura and imprisoned, but he escaped and returned to England.

After the incident, Bolívar pointedly reminded Páez: "The gravity of the crime of which General Wilson is accused has caused his arrest. Military discipline, social principles, and the honor of the Nation and the Government of the Republican make it imperative that exemplary punishment be given the author of such an execrable infraction. Swift punishment is the only way to curb lawlessness and military sedition." Fortunately, other of the British recruits proved more loyal and professional than Hippisley and Wilson. One of the Red Hussars, Daniel Florencio O'Leary, requested permission to join Bolívar in Angostura. Páez delayed answering but finally let him go. O'Leary told Soublette, chief of staff in Angostura, that he wanted to serve with a Creole corps so that he could learn Spanish. Soublette assigned him to the infantry corps that Anzoátegui was organizing. Within two years, O'Leary would rise to serve as Bolívar's aide-de-camp. His astute observations, recorded in memoirs and correspondence, would become invaluable historical sources for independence-era Venezuela. He would return as Great Britain's minister to New Granada from 1844 until his death a decade later.

The temporary lull in fighting gave Bolívar time to mobilize on other fronts. Recognizing the importance of the pen as well as the sword, he established a weekly gazette, *El Correo del Orinoco*. The first edition of this voice of the revolution appeared on Saturday, June 27, 1818. A trio of distinguished intellectuals, Francisco Antonio Zea, Dr. Juan Germán Roscio, and José Luis Romero, served as editors. Bolívar planned to use the newspaper to broadcast Patriot victories.

He sent a letter on August 18 to Zaraza describing the new publication: "It describes the critical situation of Royalist forces in New Granada, so few in number that they have to move men from one point to another, leaving many areas unguarded. Republicans are successful in Buenos Aires, Chile, and Peru. Guayaquil, Quito, and Popayán will be liberated." Bolívar also wanted his countrymen to see the broader political context. "Andrew Jackson has taken Pensacola. Spain, threatened by the United States in Florida, at war with her colonies, embarrassed by the Portuguese, is without money, without ships, not able to send a single man to America. The Russian ships that Ferdinand recently bought dare not cross the ocean." Despite the present military setbacks, the Liberator saw the tide of world politics turning against Spain and in favor of independence.

Ferdinand's isolation from his colonies and Morillo's weakness in Venezuela rekindled confidence in Bolívar. He determined to invade New Granada, where he had the advantage of inside lines. He named Santander commander of the liberating vanguard and governor of the New Granadan border province of Casanare. Santander faced a tall order. He had to gain the confidence of guerrillas in Casanare, unite them under his command, harass Royalist units, and recruit inhabitants for an advance with Bolívar's army to Santa Fe de Bogotá.

Santander departed Angostura during the last week of August 1818. His four flecheras carried one thousand muskets, clothing, and munitions. Bolívar recruited in Guayana and the Barcelona llanos. Páez raised troops in the llanos of Barinas. Richard Vowell recalled the difficulties they faced in the llanos: "It was necessary for all who accompanied Páez to be able to swim well, for the plains were by this time inundated in many parts, and all the creeks that intersected them were now broad and deep. These plains are covered in every direction, as far as the eye reaches, with a long coarse grass which affords pasture to innumerable herds of wild cattle and horses."

After Páez returned to Achaguas, he gave Vowell and other Englishmen permission to secure much-needed clothing in Angostura. Recent arrivals from England had been formed into a regiment called Bolívar's dragoon guard commanded by Colonel Rooke. Chief of Staff Soublette ordered Vowell and the other English troops to join Rooke's dragoons. They would sail to the mouth of the Pao River and join Monagas in the upper llanos of Barcelona.

Despite their victories on the battlefield, problems also plagued the Royalists. Morillo had fallen from his horse in Caracas. Despite his injury, he presided over Royalist rebuilding and preparation, replacing his many causalities with new recruits. By the end of the rainy season, Morillo's generals had restored their divisions to fighting capability. In a letter to Madrid, he also complained bitterly that "from a Power friendly to Spain, come the considerable means our enemies possess to wage war on us." "The army of Bolívar," he claimed, "is mostly composed of English soldiers, Guayana is garrisoned by Englishmen; more than 1,500 men of the same nation have come to Margarita, and the warships, the numerous parks of all arms, the munitions, the clothing, the food, all the elements of making war and fighting for independence have sailed from the harbors of the King of Great Britain."

Morillo had reason to complain, not only of the English but also of the Germans and the Irish. Quixotic Spanish policy occasionally considered asking Great Britain to mediate between Spain and its wayward colonies. In May 1819, Morillo addressed a proclamation (written in eccentric English) to British mercenaries serving under Bolívar.

Englishmen: to you I address myself who are already acquainted with that famous personage whom you no doubt (while in England) compared to Washington at least, but now, having seen the Hero of this despreciable [sic] republic, his troops, his Generals, and the Wiseacres who compose his government, you must be convinced of having been most shamefully imposed upon. You are serving under the command of a man in every respect insignificant, and have joined an horde of banditti who are famed for the exercise of the most barbarous cruelties, which are so averse to your national character, that you must abhor them. He who retains the least spark of honour and justice cannot remain united with such a band of ragamuffins, who are abhorred by the very country that gave them birth whose soil they have sullied with crimes of all descriptions.

With Napolean's defeat and the cessation of European conflicts, an estimated six thousand British soldiers would volunteer to fight on behalf of the independence forces in South America. Had this large force of professionals mobilized in Spanish America together, independence might well have come much more quickly. However, slow travel, death at sea, distrust by some Creole officers, as well as lack of organization and funds blunted their impact. John Devereux (or d'Evereaux), an Irishman whose father had been hanged in the rebellion of 1798, secured a contract from Bolívar at Angostura to raise an army of his countrymen. He had been forced into exile and had become a citizen of the United States. Along with Gregor MacGregor, hero at Ocumare and Juncal, and James England ("British Legion," a.k.a. "Albion Legion"), Devereux ("Irish Legion") played a key role as a recruiting agent in Europe. England offered prospective officers one-third more than equivalent rank in the British cavalry plus monetary bonuses and land after independence had been won. England proved more capable as a recruiter than as a line officer. Following mediocre service in Venezuela, he secured permission from Urdaneta to return to Margarita, where he died of fever on December 13.

Writing to Santander on December 22, 1819, Bolívar expressed high hopes for the arrival of well-trained, experienced professional soldiers from Europe, but he also expressed exasperation over the lack of arms. "I must have 10,000 guns in Cundinamarca or I shall go mad. I shall dispatch them before a month is out, in spite of all the world. I did not find a single musket here because nothing had arrived from Margarita, thanks to the upsets that our arrangements commonly meet with; the d'Evereux division had taken those that were here. He should arrive at any moment with the rest of the 5,000 men whom he promised for this year; several regiments had embarked by September and must by now have arrived at Margarita, but we do not know this for certain."

Promises of riches and rank drew thousands of unemployed soldiers to Margarita and then to the mainland, where they confronted a very different reality. The British army had discharged more than thirty thousand men into a depression-ridden economy, flat after being fueled by decades of warfare. Many on the first voyages perished, and the survivors landed, famished and ill, at Margarita, in the midst of a yellow fever epidemic. Some 750 of the recruits died of disease without ever firing a shot on behalf of the Patriot cause. Penniless, some sold their belongings just to buy food. The hearty survivors, however, well reinforced Bolívar's forces.

After his recruiting success, for which he earned $175 per soldier, Devereux bided his time in Dublin until a rival challenged him to a duel. Preferring to live and recruit another day, he departed for Liverpool, where he sold officer commissions for even higher prices. He arrived safely at Margarita some two months after the Irish Legion departed and after the epidemic had passed. All told, the energetic Irishman recruited about twenty-one hundred soldiers for the Patriot cause. His lack of clear orders and malfeasance accounted for much of the suffering and deaths of his recruits. Despite never actually serving in battle with the men he recruited, Devereux lived out his life in the United States, thanks to a pension. Following his death in 1854, a grateful Venezuela, perhaps unaware of the specifics of his career, buried him with honors in their National Pantheon of Heroes in Caracas.

Some of the European officers and enlisted men would end up with Páez and his one thousand cavalry armed with lances. His infantry, armed with muskets, numbered very few, so Bolívar sent Anzoátegui with the honor guard to bolster Páez's meager infantry. Indians from the Caroní Missions comprised most the guard's one thousand men. A few British also served, including O'Leary, now speaking Spanish and forever taking notes. Anzoátegui and the honor guard sailed on October 22 and debarked near San Fernando de Apure about a month later.

Páez and Anzoátegui informed Bolívar that they needed at least one thousand more infantry. In response, Bolívar dispatched Sedeño with his two hundred to three hundred infantry. He ordered Felipe Santiago Estéves to load his river flotilla with supplies for troops he would embark at the mouth of the Pao. Bolívar and an artillery corps sailed with Estéves on December 21. One week later they took on board 437 recruits sent by Monagas. Later

Rooke arrived with 140 British and llanero troops. The fleet caught up with Sedeño at the mouth of the Arauca on January 11, 1819. On the seventeenth at San Juan de Payara, Bolívar reviewed his Army of the West, now swelled to eighty-eight artillery, twenty-four hundred infantry, and twenty-six hundred cavalry. The irrepressible Bolívar, having recovered from the earlier losses, stood ready to fight again.

The Liberator had depleted the East of manpower in order to constitute his new army. He warned Páez to avoid serious engagement with Morillo. He ordered the llanero chief only to harass the Royalists until the rains returned. Leaving Páez with all the cavalry, Bolívar led the infantry and artillery. They encamped at a Capuchin mission on the right bank of the Orinoco, not far from the Arauca's mouth. Bolívar left the troops in camp while he made a quick trip to welcome additional British troops arriving at Angostura. He also had to install Venezuela's Second Congress. The difficult dual roles of military campaigner and politician would burden Bolívar throughout the independence era.

Deputies from Casanare had not yet arrived on February 15, 1819, when the *jefe supremo* (supreme chief) opened the Congress of Angostura. *El Correo del Orinoco* (February 20, 1819), the official Patriot newspaper, glowingly described Bolívar's discourse as "so full of interest and so moving, that neither citizens nor strangers could hold back their tears. The words with which he concluded declaring the Congress installed, and acknowledging in it the National Sovereignty, excited the most glowing enthusiasm, especially when he grasped his sword and said with extraordinary energy: 'My sword and those of my illustrious companions in arms are always ready to sustain Its August Authority—Viva el Congreso de Venezuela!' These words, repeated many times by the assembly, were followed by a salvo of artillery."

The next day the assembly elected Bolívar as president of the Republic and Zea as vice president. Bolívar warned against aping Anglo-American political models and pushed for a strong central government with a hereditary senate and a "moral power." The Congress rejected these notions, but the Liberator now had a constitutional underpinning to his powers. The gathering included a few representatives from New Granada, in keeping with Bolívar's hopes for a united South America.

Leaving Congress to debate, Bolívar returned to his military duties, promptly dispatching more than half of the new British troops from Angostura to Urdaneta at Margarita. The remaining 450 British and 100 native troops sailed with Bolívar in March when he left Angostura. His *flecheras* stopped at the Capuchin mission near the mouth of the Arauca, loaded more troops, and continued a short distance upriver. April 1 found Bolívar camped with Páez on the south bank of the river. Morillo camped above them on the north bank of Queseras del Medio. Bolívar considered it time to repay the Royalists for last year's losses on the llanos.

Bolívar had been absent from the Apure-Arauca theater for two months in early 1819. During that time Páez had simply harassed Morillo, but, as he approached San Fernando, Páez laid out an extraordinary plan. He instructed his men to send women, children, and old men south of the Arauca and beyond the Cunaviche swamps. The llaneros planned to burn their homes and lure the Royalists to certain death in the swamps. Llaneros well understood that their great horseback mobility provided the best defense.

The troops dutifully burned their homes, followed the charismatic Páez, and let Morillo's divisions cross the Apure to San Fernando unimpeded. Royalists camped on the savanna of San Fernando on January 30. Páez's llaneros, unencumbered by baggage, moved rapidly. They withdrew slowly, however, letting Morillo keep them in sight. Long grasses, marshes, and channels delayed Morillo's infantry, artillery, and logistical support.

Llaneros kept up their scorched earth policy. They rounded up their few remaining cattle and set fire to grasses behind them. They encircled Morillo's camp at night so that his troops dared not forage when they bivouacked. Royalist horses weakened, unaccustomed to the coarse grasses. Morillo's troops became ill, the common plight of outsiders traveling the tropical plains. The Spaniards and natives of the hill country had no experience sleeping in the open air among swamps. They had never lived on beef alone, with neither bread or salt.

Morillo followed Páez all the way to Cunaviche before admitting to himself that he was overmatched against the llaneros in their infernal swamps. He turned back on March 8 and crossed the Arauca to Achaguas (an island formed by the Arauca and branches of the Apure). Bolívar's flecheras were leaving the Capuchin mission to join Páez on the south bank of the Arauca.

Early on the morning of April 2 Páez sent 150 llaneros, including Juan José Rondón, westward and across the Arauca. Ninety llaneros halted while Páez galloped toward Queseras del Medio with three squads of twenty men each in extended line. Their dust cloud fooled Morillo into believing that he faced the entire Patriot army. The Spanish troops formed for battle, infantry in the center and cavalry on either side. As Morillo advanced, Páez and his sixty llaneros retired in perfect order.

Morillo sent mounted carabineers after Rondón's squad. Páez ordered Rondón to wheel about, rush the Spaniards, then retreat. When the Spanish troops saw Rondón coming, they dismounted to fire. Writing in 1929, Páez biographer R. B. Cunninghame Graham well described the action: "Like lightning the wild horsemen were amongst them, slaughtering them with the lance. The night, the wild yells of the Llaneros, and the dust that hung in a dense cloud, mingled with the smoke of the artillery, completed their defeat. The cavalry all turned and fled; the infantry retreated on a wood and the artillerymen, in their anxiety to save their lives, abandoned all their pieces on the plain. Morillo under cover of the night withdrew his army to his headquarters at Achaguas, influenced most probably by the fear of panic spreading through his ranks."

Rondón raced back to Páez with both wings of Royalist cavalry pursuing and converging in one mass. Morillo's infantry could not fire with their own cavalry in front of them. Páez turned his troops, enveloped Morillo's cavalry, and killed four hundred. Morillo's infantry sought refuge in the woods, where nightfall saved them. The Patriots suffered only two killed and six wounded. The event would become famous as the battle of Las Queseras del Medio, a victorious Venezuelan version of the charge of the Light Brigade.

Morillo retreated to the northwest and took stock. In this campaign, Richard Vowell notes, the Spanish general "lost a considerable number of his best troops by sickness, as well as by constant skirmishes, in which the patriot army suffered little." Páez followed up and captured most of the Spanish supplies. Morillo had to destroy most of his powder "for want of beasts to carry it." The Royalists camped briefly above the Río Guanare Viejo. On May 7 Morillo divided his army, sending La Torre west with one column to the town of Barinas. He charged La Torre with preventing Patriot movement into New Granada via the Barinas-Mérida-Cúcuta corridor.

Morillo marched east with the other column to Calabozo to wait out the rainy season. In a letter to King Ferdinand VII in Spain, the Royalist commander described his adversary Bolívar. "Nothing can compare with the untiring activity of that leader. His fearlessness and his talents entitle him to his place at the head of the revolution and of the war; but he possesses as well, from his noble Spanish strain and his education, also Spanish, qualities of elegance and generosity which elevate him far above all who surround him. He is the revolution." He continued, "Bolívar is an indomitable soul whom a single victory of the smallest nature is enough to make master of five hundred leagues of territory."

Bolívar had left his camp south of Queseras del Medio on April 4, marching his forces west along the south bank of the Arauca. On April 15 he camped to let his wind-whipped, dehydrated infantry rest. He crossed the Arauca on April 23 and marched west then north to get away from the scorched plains. The Patriots needed a base on the road to Casanare to remount the cavalry and restock supplies. About the middle of May, Páez brought Bolívar an infantry squadron, Bravos de Páez, and cavalry squadrons. Páez accompanied Bolívar as he moved north to the cattle ranch of Cañafistola near the deserted village of Setenta.

From his Royalist base at Tunja, Gen. José María Barreiro guarded the border between New Granada and Venezuela. Barreiro also placed detachments at mountains passes on trails descending to Casanare. Inhabitants fled before him as he came down the passes and entered a deserted Pore on April 9. Santander recorded an unsympathetic description of the action. Barreiro continued along the foot of the mountain "to where I was the day before and entered Palmar on April 14 soon after I left. My outposts skirmished with his reconnaissance, he returned to Pore, and then made a shameful retreat to Tunja. He has suffered many desertions, and has seen with his own eyes that he cannot conquer Casanare."

Bolívar praised Santander and revealed his plan for "an operation against the interior of New Granada. I do not know the day, nor have I decided the method of executing it. I am only indicating it to you so you will concentrate your forces at the most favorable point." Only Santander and perhaps Páez knew of Bolívar's daring objective. The Liberator assembled his officers for a council of war on May 23. They met in a deserted hut at Setenta. Bolívar had no table on which to spread his maps and no chairs for himself and the others. In traditional llanero fashion, they sat astride cattle skulls, bleached white by the intense tropical sun and rains.

Bolívar reviewed their sobering situation: "Most of the army is naked. We have no medical supplies, no transports for war materiel. Sickness and misery will be fatal to the infantry if we winter in the llanos." Then Soublette read Santander's upbeat letter. When he finished, Bolívar sprang his audacious plan: "Now is the time for a surprise invasion of New Granada." Three officers immediately agreed, but others raised objections. After further cajoling, they all approved the bold plan to strike at the heart of New Granada.

The Army of the West broke camp on May 27 and headed for Guasdualito. Juanas and children accompanied the troops. The force entered Guasdualito on June 3 and rested while Bolívar answered letters and dictated orders.

During this critical time, Páez began exhibiting increasing independence, particularly when Bolívar ordered him into action outside the llanos. "March with the cavalry you have here in Guasdualito toward Cúcuta, cut Barreiro's communications there with Venezuela, open them with me, and send detachments toward Mérida to observe enemy movements." Páez decided not to obey Bolívar's orders. To those around him he explained, "Campaigning in the mountains with my llaneros is as impossible as seizing the sky with our hands." Bolívar ordered Páez to send up three hundred mounts with the army's rear guard. Páez had sixteen hundred good horses, but he complied only halfheartedly by sending his most marginal mounts. The test of wills between the two egotistical leaders would continue well after independence.

On June 4 Bolívar marched south and crossed the Arauca into the New Granadan province of Casanare. He waited in the town of Arauca until his entire army had arrived. When he saw the rear guard with the horses Páez had sent, his jaw dropped and his temper flared. "You have 1,600 good horses," he wrote to Páez immediately, "and I was moderate in requesting only 300 of them—which you have promised to send. It seems strange that when they arrived they were 200 lean and mangy mares."

Bolívar left Arauca with thirteen hundred infantry and eight hundred cavalry. Anzoátegui commanded four infantry battalions: Rifles under Arturo Sandes; Bravos de Páez under Cruz Carillo; Barcelona Battalion under Ambrosio Plaza; and James Rooke's British Legion. Two regiments from the Alto Llanos of Mérida and Caracas rounded out the army.

The Patriot army, along with women and children, waded waist deep across the flooded plains of Casanare. They strained mightily against the thick mud sucking at their feet. Cattle, mules, and horses floundered, many drowning before they could be extracted. Sucking leeches and biting fish tortured humans and animals alike. Clothes rotted after a week of such difficult travel.

The gaunt troop arrived at Tama, where Santander met them. He added welcome plantains and salt to their meager diet. O'Leary attributed almost mystical powers to simple salt. "It made the soldiers forget their pains and dream of great things." Despite the hardships, neither fatigue, discomfort, nor danger seemed to deter the young, energetic troops.

Young troops, young officers. At age eighteen, O'Leary may have been the youngest. Bolívar, at thirty-five, was the oldest. Soublette, Anzoátegui, Santander, Rooke, and Rondón ranged from twenty-seven to twenty-nine. With typical insight, O'Leary left thumbnail sketches of many of the Liberator's officers:

General Soublette, the chief of staff, then twenty-nine years old, who was united to Bolívar by bonds of blood and friendship. In the whole course of the war he always occupied positions of trust. I have already spoken of Santander, the commander of the vanguard division, whose able performance of his assignment in Casanare was recognized by the government in expressions of satisfaction. General José Antonio Anzoátegui, the commander of the division designated at the rearguard, was born in Barcelona in 1789. His extraordinary valor and fearlessness earned for him the esteem of Bolívar and of his companions, despite his surly and unpleasant disposition. He hated Santander with his heart and soul, but out of respect for General Bolívar he concealed this profound dislike as far as he was able. Colonel Rooke, who was in command of a brigade of Anzoátegui's division, had a personality diametrically opposed to that of his commander. Pleased with everyone and with everything, and especially with himself, he seemed to be satisfied with the life he was living and not at all indifferent to it. Such men were the principal commanders of the small army with which Bolívar accomplished the emancipation of one of the most important sections of Spanish America.

Barreiro maintained a strong Royalist garrison at Salina de Chita. He had stationed troops at passes north and south of Pisba but none on Pisba. He saw no reason, because no one could cross Pisba during the rainy season, and only a few hearty Indians managed the feat during the rest of the year. The Patriots rested four days at Tame, crossed more swollen rivers, and entered Pore, located on the eastern flank of 13,000-foot-high Pisba, on June 22. Bolívar's army marched 360 miles to Pore, averaging more than 20 miles a day. Death and desertions decreased the number of troops to 1,850 men. Santander's infantry and cavalry, however, brought the total to 3,000. Having survived the swamps of the llanos, the Patriots next faced the frozen heights of the Andes Mountains.

Departing from Pore, the llaneros and Britons entered an unknown wilderness world of icy mountain peaks. Each time they climbed a crest, another loomed ahead. As the air became thinner, lungs felt as if they would burst. *Soroche* numbed brains, paralyzed limbs, and produced violent vomiting. Soldiers pummeled each other to shake off the lethargy of mountain sickness.

Rains intensified the cold. Each dawn strong winds gusted down from the icy peaks. Lowland horses from the llanos died, as did the last of the cattle. The unshod mounts from the plains found the rocky mountain trails

Bolívar and the Patriot forces crossing the Andes Mountains.

difficult going. The beefeaters of the llanos managed to survive on a new diet. Friendly mountaineers gave them chickens, pigs, and *arepas* (flat fried corn cakes).

Santander's New Granadans, on shod horses accustomed to the mountains, took the lead. As they approached Paya on June 27, they knew that a garrison of three hundred Royalists held Trincherón. This fortified position above Paya commanded the roads to Pisba and to Labranza Grande Pass south of Pisba. According to O'Leary, this mighty garrison could hold off an army double that of the Patriot's three thousand men.

Lt. Col. Antonio Arredondo and Santander, however, worked out clever tactics. Arredondo and his battalion climbed around the Royalists without being detected. They attacked from above; Santander, from below. The garrison fled Trincherón to Labranza Grande. The mountain natives conscripted into the Spanish army had little desire to fight their brothers.

This rout of Royalists at the gate of Pisba, the "Thermopylae of Paya," electrified Santander's Granadinos; Bolívar's tired, depressed Venezuelans; and their British allies. The Patriots now believed that they could accomplish whatever they set out to do. One more mountain crossing and they would descend into the very heart of New Granada.

On June 30 Bolívar proclaimed: "Granadinos! An army of Venezuela united with the bravos of Casanare, under the command of Santander, marches to free you. The cries which Spanish tyranny has forced from you have reached the ears of your Venezuelan brothers, and the ears of the British Legion from more remote climes. They have come to help free you."

Santander sent half a battalion of light infantry to broadcast Bolívar's proclamation throughout the valleys west of Pisba. To facilitate troop movements, Bolívar divided the rest of the army into four divisions. Each division would cross Pisba on a different day: Arredondo on July 3, Santander on July 4, with Bolívar, Anzoátegui, and three of his battalions following on July 5. After Soublette had collected sufficient supplies, he would cross with the British Legion and the rest of the cavalry, baggage, and ordnance.

The divisions of Arredondo and Santander crossed Pisba in a day. Darkness, however, overtook Anzoátegui's division. Poorly clothed, the troops and women huddled together for warmth on the western rim. O'Leary dropped beside a circle of men shielding the wife of a soldier in the Rifles Battalion from the howling wind. She was in labor. The next day O'Leary saw the woman, newborn child in her arms, marching behind the Rifles as they descended to the pueblo of Socha. Such spirit and strength would well serve the independence forces.

Socha lay in the valley of the Río Chicamocha (also known as the Río Sogamoso). The river rises near Tunja, where Barreiro had his arsenal, curves east and north and then west to empty into the Río Magdalena. The fertile Sogamoso valley, at an elevation of eight thousand to nine thousand feet, boasted a healthful, benign, springlike climate.

Arriving at Socha on July 2, Bolívar's advance infantry described the hunger and nakedness of the Patriots who were about to cross Pisba. Father Tomás José Romero, the priest of Socha, joined mayor Don José Ignacio Sarmiento in calling all inhabitants to organize a festival. When townspeople gathered at church on Sunday, July 24, they found infantrymen guarding each door. Romero and Sarmiento obliged each person to donate every piece of clothing except the minimum needed to cover his or her nakedness. Men took off their sombreros, ponchos, shirts, and even pants if they were wearing underwear. Women removed their sombreros, *ruanas* (shawl-like cloaks open at the front), sandals, and blouses. Father Romero pardoned all the blessed Patriots for the seeming sin of indecorum. The sacrificed clothing served the Patriots well. In subsequent battles some soldiers fought wearing women's blouses.

Bolívar's troops, fatigued by the march and weakened by the altitude, badly needed rest and relaxation. The whole army feasted on bread and gratefully quaffed *chicha* (fermented corn liquor). They even enjoyed the rare luxury of smoking tobacco. While his troops recovered and acclimated to the heights, Bolívar diverted the enemy with feints and threats. He hoped to check Barreiro until Soublette arrived with the last division and until the cavalry could be outfitted with fresh mounts.

Why did Barreiro not destroy Bolívar's small, weakened army before Soublette arrived? Historian Salvador de Madariaga provides an answer. "The trouble for Barreiro came from the unreliability of his troops. Time worked for Bolívar. He had no base, or rather his base was everywhere, and therefore he could never be said to be actually cut off, while by his movements he threatened to cut Barreiro from Tunja and Bogotá."

Soublette arrived on July 22, meeting Bolívar at his camp at Corrales de Bonza, fifty miles southwest of Socha. Colonel Rooke, in customary good humor, quickly presented himself to Bolívar. The Englishman congratulated the Liberator on how well the army looked. As they conversed, Anzoátegui appeared. Bolívar asked him, "What's new today?" "As if anything could be new," replied Anzoátegui glumly. "Colonel Rooke has just given me the most favorable reports," Bolívar replied. "How can he?" asked Anzoátegui. "He lost one-fourth of his troops and two of his officers in crossing the mountains." "True," said Rooke, "but they were the least fit. The best have survived."

On July 25 Bolívar took action. He moved his army across the Sogamoso on rafts, then marched them south on the eastern side of the hills. Corrales de Bonza lies on the north bank of the Río Sogamoso. The Barreiro camp stood but two miles west on the Hills of Bonza near a bridge over the Sogamoso. Vargas Swamp (Pantano de Vargas), south of the Sogamoso, separated the two camps. Grass-covered hills flanked both sides and the south end of the swamp.

Barreiro appreciated the importance of blocking this attempt to reach Paipa and the road south of the capital at Santa Fe de Bogotá. The Royalists marched across the bridge and turned up the intervening hills at the end of the swamp. They climbed the western slope of Picacho Hill, soon to be known as War Hill. Barreiro sent his van, five hundred infantry under Lt. Col. Nicolás López, to the top of the hill. The Royalists preferred the momentum of a downhill charge.

Santander, with one thousand infantry (four hundred Venezuelans and six hundred New Granadans), marched ahead of Bolívar and the rest of the army. Next came Anzoátegui's division of almost 1,000 infantry (Bravos de Páez, 300; Barcelona Battalion, 300; Rifles, 250; British Legion, 120), and 400 cavalry (Guías de Vanguardia, 100, Rondón's Lancers, 100; Infante's Lancers, 100; Dragoons, 100).

Bolívar, seeing the Royalists on the crest, ordered Santander to charge up the hill. López and his infantry counterattacked forcefully and drove the Patriots back down. Next, Rooke and the British Legion, followed by the Bravos de Páez and Rifles Battalion, charged up the hill. Maj. John Macintosh took command after a musket ball felled the brave Rooke on the first charge. Macintosh led the Legion, bayonets fixed, to the top and pushed the Royalists down the other side. López gathered reinforcements, retook the hill, and again drove the Patriots to the bottom. War Hill earned its new name with a vengeance.

Bolívar shouted out to Rondón, "Colonel, save the country!" Rondón and his cavalry repeated their performance of Queseras del Medio. Rondón and fourteen lancers in extended line galloped toward López. When the Royalists charged, the lancers faced about in perfect order. López thought he was chasing only fifteen men until they again turned about and charged. This time Rondón had the rest of the squadron, with Infante and his lancers galloping behind. The thoroughly confused Royalist infantry quickly fell, easy targets to Patriot lances.

At the same time, Juan Carvajal led the rest of Bolívar's cavalry against Barreiro's cavalry. The Patriots pushed the Royalists back into the narrow path by which they had come. Darkness and torrential rains finally ended the bloody battles of the day. The Royalists, however, had been dislodged from all their positions. Barreiro lost five hundred killed and wounded, almost 30 percent of his troops. The Patriots suffered three hundred killed and wounded.

Both armies returned to their bases. The next day Barreiro dutifully reported the Royalist defeat to Viceroy Juan Sámano: "Bolívar's infantry and cavalry arose from the abyss into which we had thrown them, climbed the hills with fury, and our infantry could not resist them."

In the Patriot camp Dr. Thomas Foley amputated Colonel Rooke's arm, which had been shattered by a musket ball. After the operation, the irrepressible Rooke waved his severed arm about and shouted, "Viva la patria! [long live the fatherland]." "What patria do you mean?" asked Foley. "England or Ireland?" "The patria where I will be buried," replied Rook. He died three days later, and Patriots buried him at Corrales de Bonza. Anzoátegui's gloom deepened. The Liberator would later toast the fallen British colonel: "To him I owe all my good fortune in New Grenada, and to him Venezuela is indebted for the preservation of her president and will hereafter have mainly to attribute her liberty."

Barreiro, dispirited by his heavy losses, posed no threat until reinforcements could arrive from Tunja. The respite gave Bolívar a few welcome days to rest and recruit. Anzoátegui, who had lost the most men, gained eight hundred New Granadans. His short, wiry, long-haired recruits wore typical wide-brimmed hats of gray wool and large woolen ponchos. O'Leary described these "long-haired Sampsons," wrapped in their ponchos, as looking like little men without arms.

Juan Mellao had figured among the brave lancers who charged with Rondón at Vargas Swamp. On Tuesday, August 3, at 3 A.M., Bolívar sent Mellao with one hundred dragoons across the plains to harass Royalist outposts in the hills of Bonza. The chastened Barreiro avoided battle. He retired from Bonza to a position south of Paipa. His forces occupied a hill that dominated the western road leading south to Tunja and Bogotá.

Bolívar's entire army, following Mellao, occupied Barreiro's positions as soon as he had evacuated. The Patriots entered Paipa on Wednesday afternoon. At sunset Mellao's dragoons and an infantry company led the rest of the army back across the bridge over the Sogamoso. They traveled east along the swamp road and turned south to Tunja. Barreiro did not learn until

Thursday of the Patriot army's march south by the eastern road to Tunja. On that same day, Lt. Col. Juan Loño, with reinforcements for Barreiro, left Tunja. They traveled by the western road via Motavita and north to Paipa. Only a few conscripts remained to guard Tunja, so Bolívar entered easily soon after Loño left.

Tunja's garrison and inhabitants welcomed their brothers. They donated food, arms, munitions, and all the clothing stored there. Patriots ate and slept well that night. In the morning, scouts reported Barreiro's approach to Motavita, a few miles northwest of Tunja. He had marched his army down the western road, halting to rest after meeting Loño. The Royalists entered Motavita at noon on Friday, August 6, 1819, and their scouts spotted the Patriot army at Tunja. A Patriot observation corps occupied the crest of San Lázaro, which stood between Tunja and Motavita.

At daylight on Saturday, August 7, the observation corps reported the movement of Barreiro's army. Bolívar's army, in the plaza of Tunja, readied to form the line of march. Bolívar, however, could not dispatch his troops until he knew which road Barreiro would take. Would it be the western road over which an army could march four abreast? Would the Royalists tackle the steep, single-file path directly south to the bridge of Boyacá? The eastern road to Tunja offered a third option.

Barreiro chose the steep, narrow path. It converged with the Tunja road above a bridge over the Río Boyacá (or Río Teatinos) about nine to ten miles southwest of Tunja. Col. Francisco Jiménez, commanding Barreiro's vanguard, halted for lunch above the bridge at two in the afternoon. Jiménez looked toward the eastern ridge and saw Santander's scouts on the crest. Thinking them nothing more than a reconnoitering party, Jiménez ordered his scouts to annihilate them. Santander sent a runner down the grass-covered slope behind him to Bolívar a thousand feet below.

The sides of these ridges rise above the tree line. The highest crests are over ten thousand feet above sea level. Bolívar ordered Anzoátegui, with his infantry at the double-quick, up the slope in line of battle. Lancers and dragoons followed. Barreiro, half a mile behind Jiménez, halted when he saw the bulk of Bolívar's army on the crest, ready to descend on him. Bolívar had chosen the field of battle! Who did Bolívar think he was? Barreiro always chose the field of battle on the crest of a hill or mountain. He ordered his divisions to climb the opposite ridge. Santander raced to the bridge, chased Jiménez south across it, and cut him off from Barreiro.

Patriots enjoyed a modest edge in numbers, 2,850 troops to 2,700 for the Royalists. Both armies numbered about 2,300 infantrymen, but Barreiro had twenty artillerymen and three field pieces. Bolívar had no artillery. Barreiro had 350 cavalry; Bolívar, 500. At the bridge Santander had 900 infantry and 100 dragoons. Jiménez had 600 infantry and 100 dragoons. Barreiro formed his line of battle with dragoons flanking both ends. Two battalions of infantry stood to his right, one battalion and artillerymen in the center, and a battalion on the left. Dragoons and lancers stayed to the rear.

Anzoátegui formed his line with the Rifles Battalion and the British Legion opposite Barreiro's right. Lancers from the high llanos and dragoons occupied the center. Barcelona Battalion and Bravos de Páez stood opposite the enemy left. Behind them loomed the eight hundred "long-haired Sampsons." Bolívar enjoyed a clear view of the action from his command post high on the opposite ridge and applauded the actions of his better-conditioned troops.

Barreiro made a movement to his right, trying to get to the bridge. Anzoátegui, with Rifles and the British Legion, encircled and forced him back, while Barcelona, Bravos de Páez, and lancers attacked from the front. Dragoons and the "long-haired Sampsons" supported them. After some two hours of fighting, the Royalists, hemmed in on all sides, threw down their arms and surrendered. Barreiro tossed away his sword to avoid the shame of surrendering it to Bolívar. Pedro Martínez of Rifles Battalion took Barreiro prisoner.

Santander's dragoons crossed a ford near the bridge and attacked Jiménez from the rear. Seeing that Barreiro had surrendered, Jiménez also gave up. Just two hours had passed since he had halted above the bridge to enjoy lunch. Only fifty Royalists escaped, fleeing down the royal road to Bogotá. The victory at Boyacá opened the way for the Patriot occupation of all central New Granada.

Two of the fleeing Royalists covered the eighty miles to the capital by Sunday afternoon. They told Viceroy Sámano that Barreiro and Jiménez had surrendered with their forces almost intact. The viceroy could not believe it. By the end of the day, however, other soldiers arrived to repeat the story. The next morning, August 9, Sámano and his cavalry guard fled across the plateau and north to Honda on the Magdalena River. The Audiencia and the rest of Sámano's retainers, unable to find horses in Bogotá, fled on foot.

Sámano transferred command of the capital to Col. Sebastián de la Calzada. Having no desire to confront Bolívar, Calzada also fled south to Popayán. There he expected to get help from the Royalist commander of Quito. The next afternoon, as Bolívar arrived within six miles from the capital, he learned that Sámano and Calzada had fled. The city stood with neither defenses nor government. Bolívar ordered Anzoátegui to pursue and capture Sámano before he reached Honda. Infante, his lancers, Lt. Col. José María Córdoba (1799–1829), and another 150 men went with Anzoátegui. Born in the province of Antioquia, Colombia, Córdoba had joined the Patriot ranks in 1814. His valor moved him quickly through the ranks to captain in 1817, lieutenant colonial two years later, and general in January 1823. He would distinguish himself at the major battles of Boyacá, Pichincha, and Ayacucho. His brother Salvador (1801–41), who rose to the rank of colonel, also fought in many Patriot engagements.

Bolívar entered Bogotá alone an hour before sunset on August 10, 1819. Santander and the van entered the next day. Patriot troops brought Barreiro, Jiménez, and other Royalist officers to the city. Most of Royalist troops joined Bolívar's army, but some did not get the chance. The Liberator learned that the Royalist contingent of prisoners included Francisco Vinoni. He still harbored hatred for the man who had turned over Puerto Cabello to the Spaniards imprisoned there back in 1812. That treachery led to Bolívar's first humiliating military defeat and the collapse of the First Republic of Venezuela. Patriots summarily hanged the traitor and left his body dangling in the plaza of the village of Ventaquemada. The city's residents welcomed their liberators.

Soublette's "Bulletin of the Liberating Army of New Granada," dated Santa Fe, August 11, 1819, recorded the significance of the victory: "The precipitation with which the Viceroy and all his satellites fled at the first news of the Battle of Boyacá did not give them time to save anything of public interest. In the Casa de Moneda we found more than half a million pesos, and in all other storage places enough arms to equip a large army. One may say that the liberation of New Granada has made inevitable that of all South America." The great victory at Boyacá on August 7 turned the tide in Colombia's struggle for independence. The day is now a national holiday on which Colombian presidents assume office.

Meanwhile Anzoátegui marched rapidly to Honda, where he learned that Sámano and most of his men had commandeered boats. They had escaped down the Magdalena to Cartagena, where Royalists remained strongly entrenched. Anzoátegui marched overland north to Nare. He recruited and organized an expedition under Córdoba, a New Granadan, that gained control of Antioquia Province.

With Infante and his lancers as escort, Anzoátegui returned to Bogotá. He wrote his wife Teresa on August 28, recounting the amazing feats of the past months. His words reflect the respect and loyalty that Bolívar inspired in his men:

> My much in mind always dear Teresa
>
> Finally I have a little time to tell you what has happened to your husband since the day he left you in Cumaná, full of anguish and terrified at what Fate might have in store for him. My luck has been better than you might think. The Liberator has loaded me with honors and attentions. In Angostura he gave me the rank of Colonel and named me Chief of Staff of the Venezuelan Army. In this capacity I accompanied him to the Apure where this prodigious man has achieved miracles.
>
> The Liberator had prevailed in every situation and brought to pass the most daring and perilous enterprise—that of invading New Granada crossing the Apure, Arauca, and Casanare during the worst part of winter, and then the Cordillera of the Andes. It is impossible for you to imagine what those days were like from Arauca to Tame, marching through water, swimming from time to time. The llanos were inundated. They seemed to be a sea, like that which you see from your balcony.
>
> Almost all our troops were without shirts and pants, a few had old jackets, and the rest had not a stitch of clothing except a *guayuco* [loincloth worn by Indians]. Only these soldiers who had never been two days in the same place and who almost slept in water or on their horses, only these I tell you, could have made the crossing.
>
> We arrived at Tame in Granadan territory on June 11 where we met the army of General Santander. We halted to reorganize the army, and then headed for Pore and Paya. Climbing the Páramo of Pisba we lost all our horses; and the llanero, that man so terrifying on his own land, was reduced to nothing.

Anzoátegui did not mention that one woman gave birth to a child that horrible night on Pisba. Perhaps he paused in his writing, his mind full of questions. Had Teresa conceived when they were together? If so, his child would have been born about the time he crossed Pisba. Only a suggestion of his usual gloom found its way into the letter as he continued:

> When we crossed the Páramo of Pisba, I and all my companions believed ourselves lost because so many had died, and all of us were sick. Only the genius of the Liberator saved us, aided by the patriotism and enthusiasm of the people in the province of Tunja, especially the women

who—you will not believe this—undressed and gave us their clothes! They made shirts, pants, underwear, and jackets for our soldiers, and gave us everything in their homes that would help us. This was a marvelous resurrection. Life returned to us, and valor and faith. You will read, in the papers I am sending, an account of our victories at Pantano de Vargas and at Boyacá; and of my promotion to General of Division, a title which I lay at your feet, my dear wife.

José

Post-data. We will see each other soon because I have permission to go and embrace you; and this letter with my embraces is for the whole family. Farewell.

The "whole family" included Anzoátegui's four-year-old daughter, Calixta, and Juana, a daughter born while he crossed Pisba—a child he would never see.

After organizing a government for the liberated provinces, Bolívar concentrated on military matters. He dispatched a unit south against Royalists strongly entrenched in Pasto, the southernmost province of New Granada. The Liberator knew that Morillo, upon hearing of the surrender of Bogotá, would send La Torre to reinforce Sámano, who held all of the Caribbean coastal provinces. The Royalists would strive mightily to regain the heart of New Granada. Morillo ordered La Torre to advance into New Granada via Cúcuta.

Bolívar badly wanted another Boyacá in Venezuela. Such a victory near Caracas would liberate Venezuela's capital. Bolívar dispatched Soublette to Tunja and Pamplona. He was to prevent La Torre's entry into New Granada and then join Páez in the Apure. Bolívar still had many obstacles to overcome before he could repeat his success. His troops in New Granada lacked muskets. He found it increasingly difficult to raise troops. Bolívar remained unaware of yet another political problem, civil war brewing in Angostura.

The Liberator laid out his dreams for the future. He told Anzoátegui to build strong battalions, defeat La Torre, take Maracaibo, and advance toward Caracas. Bolívar would prepare another front from the Apure and Angostura. Together their grand offensive would take the Venezuelan capital and consolidate continental independence.

On September 11 Bolívar named Santander vice president of New Granada, then nine days later he departed for Venezuela. Santander became uneasy as the time approached for Anzoátegui to march with his divisions for the Pamplona-Cúcuta frontier. The departure would leave Santander with only a few troops to protect his infant provisional government.

Rumors circulated in Bogotá of a Royalist reaction plotted by Barreiro, Jiménez, and other officers. Many people in the capital liked and admired the Royalist prisoners, especially the handsome Barreiro, known as the "Adonis of the women." Kinship ties played a role as Barreiro was engaged to a local woman whose brother served in Colonel Plaza's company. The fearful Santander, perhaps also motivated by revenge, decided to execute the Royalist officers. The night of October 10, 1819, he ordered them shackled and dragged from their comfortable quarters. Troops escorted them, dragging heavy chains, to a barracks on the main plaza. Barreiro, Jiménez, and two other officers stood in the front rank. Barreiro asked Colonel Plaza, in command, to take the portrait of his fiancé from his pocket. He requested that Colonel Plaza give it to his fiancé's brother. Barreiro, Jiménez, and two others knelt. Patriot troops shot them and the other prisoners in the back. Santander had revealed his true sanguinary temperament. "War to the death" may have ended for Bolívar, but not for Santander.

Anzoátegui and his division marched north the next day. They believed that by the time they arrived at Pamplona, Bolívar would have recruited enough Granadinos to defend the frontier. Then the Venezuelans could return home. They arrived in Pamplona on October 25. Bolívar explained, to their dismay, that they could not yet go home. He still lacked enough forces to defend the frontier without them. On November 14 the Liberator wrote to Santander that Anzoátegui's officers and troops desperately wanted to go home. "Give them every support," Bolívar pleaded, "for the least cause will increase their desperation and may make them desert."

November 14 marked Anzoátegui's thirtieth birthday. Tragically, the warrior who had stood with Bolívar since the days of the Patriotic Society in Caracas, took ill that day and died the next day in Pamplona. His untimely passing left young Teresa widowed and his two small daughters orphaned. Bolívar, shocked by the news, did not have time to grieve. He had to return to Angostura before feuding factions destroyed each other and the young republic. He only learned of the political strife when letters arrived from Angostura on the same fateful day that Anzoátegui became ill.

Criticism of Bolívar had remained veiled and covert until his February departure to liberate New Granada. In his absence opposition leaders charged openly that Bolívar had depleted Venezuela of its manpower. Opponents argued that he had invaded New Granada without congressional permission. They fanned rumors that Bolívar had been killed and that Spaniards were about to attack defenseless Angostura.

Vice President Zea excelled as an orator and parliamentarian; alas, he made a very poor executive, as Bolívar himself recognized. Six months later, writing to Santander on May 30, 1820, he confided that "Zea lacks the firmness to be the leader of a people such as ours, especially in times of revolution. You must destroy this letter, so that Zea may have no cause for resentment against me. I owe him much, but I know his faults." (Obviously Santander did not obey this order.) Zea could not crush the conspiring ringleaders. Many resented the supervision of a teacher who had never fought in any battle. Intrigue brought Zea down. When Zea sent orders to Urdaneta in Margarita to arrest Arismendi for his obstructionism, Urdaneta did so. Arismendi was imprisoned in Angostura. Mariño, now a member of congress, conspired with Arismendi and the opposition. They succeeded in forcing Zea to resign on September 14. Congress elected Arismendi vice president. He promptly relieved Urdaneta and Bermúdez of their commands and named Mariño commander in chief of the Army of the East.

Five days later, on September 19, the *Gazeta Estraordinaria de Guayana* broadcast news of the great Patriot victory at Boyacá. Venezuelans learned of the surrender of Barreiro and Jiménez. Bolívar expressed his satisfaction "with the behavior of every Chief, Officer, and Soldier of the Liberating Army on this memorable day. Our loss consists in 13 killed, and 53 wounded." Zea, who edited the *Gazeta,* must have taken great pleasure in breaking the stories of Bolívar's tremendous military success.

Bolívar debarked at Angostura on December 11. He literally danced through the next three days, embracing and chatting with everyone, soothing irritations, and restoring confidence. The Liberator, fresh from military victory, showed equal political skill. He leveled no recriminations and launched no investigations. "This policy," O'Leary noted, "won for Bolívar as many friends as his deeds of valor had won admirers. Arismendi's faction became a nonentity, and for the first time since Venezuela was raised to the rank of a nation there was but one party—that of defenders of independence."

Arismendi offered his resignation as vice president but Congress refused it. He served a few days longer until new elections were held. Meanwhile, an Extraordinary Session of Congress was announced for December 14. The *Correo del Orinoco* (December 18, 1819) recorded the Liberator's triumphant return to power. The "President of the State" would present to the "National Representatives" his account of the triumphs that the "Arms of the Republic of New Granada" had won.

Congress convened at noon, with Francisco Antonio Zea, the proud New Granadan, presiding. A special committee escorted Bolívar to the Salon of

Public Sessions to the sound of martial music. Three cannon shots announced that His Excellency had left his palace. A twenty-one-gun salute marked his arrival at the Plaza of the Sovereign Congress. Congressmen marched to receive His Excellency. Zea gladly ceded his chair to Bolívar.

His Excellency made a low bow to Congress and said: "Señores of the Legislative Body! On entering this august hall, my first sentiment is one of gratitude for the great honor Congress has bestowed upon me, permitting me again to occupy this Seat, which less than a year ago I yielded to the President of the Representatives of the people." Bolívar recounted what had happened since February. He lauded the New Granadans for aiding the Liberating Army. He spoke of the Granadino desire for union with Venezuela.

Bolívar concluded: "Legislators! The time has come to lay a firm and enduring foundation for our Republic. It is for your wisdom to decree this great social act, and to lay down the principles and terms of the pact upon which this vast Republic shall be founded."

Zea replied: "Excelentísimo Señor, among the many illustrious and glorious days that you have given the Republic, none has been as fortunate as today." Turning to the legislators he said, "Señores, imagination cannot encompass that which the Hero of Venezuela has done since he installed this August Congress." Zea proposed that Venezuela, New Granada, and the province of Quito (Ecuador) be formed into a single, great, independent republic.

After more speeches, Zea appointed a committee to formulate a fundamental law for the new state. They would name the new republic in honor of the discoverer Christopher Columbus. Three days later Congress examined and accepted the committee's "Fundamental Law of the Republic of Colombia." Each representative kissed and signed the document. Then Zea proclaimed, "The Republic of Colombia is born. Viva la República de Colombia!" Later appointed a special diplomatic agent to Europe, Zea did not enjoy much success. He negotiated disadvantageous loans and only gained recognition of his country from one country, the United States. Zea would write a history of Colombia as well as works on botany before his death in Bath, England, in 1822. In 1874, Venezuela honored him by placing his ashes in the National Pantheon.

A new republic needed new officials. Elections had to be held for officers for the Republic and the departments of Venezuela and Cundinamarca (the name "New Granada" was dropped). Elections in Quito would have to await its liberation. Predictably, Bolívar won election as president of Colombia and Zea as vice president. Roscio would serve as vice president of Venezuela, and Santander as vice president of Cundinamarca.

Congress took a number of additional actions before dissolving on July 19, 1820. They officially changed the name of Santander's capital to Bogotá, dropping the colonial "Santa Fe de." (In the 1990s, Colombia would again restore "Santa Fe de" to the capital's name.) Congress also decreed that one year later, on January 1, 1821, a new congress would meet at El Rosario de Cúcuta to shape the final form of the constitution. Bolívar reveled in the popular adulation during this heady time, the height of his military and political glory.

CHAPTER 11

Armistice

Joining with San Martín

to Turn the Tide, 1820–21

In late 1819 Bolívar struggled to map a strategy to retake Venezuela. He felt checked, frustrated by the enemy and the weather. The Patriots remained weak in the Apure, while Morillo stood strong in Venezuela. Any supplies Sucre might send would arrive during the rainy season, and they could not be transported across the flooded llanos. Bolívar concluded that any offensive in Venezuela would have to be delayed.

Where should his next major thrust against the Royalists come? Bolívar wanted to attack Morillo and La Torre, but should he remain on the defensive in Venezuela or take the offensive in Cundinamarca? Santander controlled eighteen provinces in the center of Cundinamarca for the Patriots. Antonio Obando commanded the Army of the South in Popayán Province, keeping Royalists at bay along the Quito border. Before Bolívar could liberate Quito, Peru, and Upper Peru, however, he had to free the Caribbean coasts of Cundinamarca and Venezuela.

The Liberator also had to try to forecast Spain's reactions. Spain might send no more reinforcements to America. Revolts had broken out in Spain against Ferdinand's rule. Privateers blockaded the coasts of Spain and Portugal and prevented ships and troops from sailing to Spanish America. Perhaps the Patriots should simply wait for the Spanish will in the colonies to crumble.

Bolívar could not simply plan; he had to act. He turned his attention to Royalist vulnerability along the Caribbean coast. He had to drive them from the Lower Magdalena and Santa Marta to open a link between Bogotá and the Caribbean. He sent Col. Mariano Montilla to St. Thomas for supplies, carrying thirty thousand pesos to buy food, clothing, and arms for Irish recruits arriving at Margarita. Montilla would create an army of Creole and Irish troops, board Brión's fleet, and harass the coast from La Guaira west to Santa Marta. He would then debark at Santa Marta, penetrate inland, and connect with Urdaneta's army.

Bolívar left Angostura on the day before Christmas of 1819 and sailed up the Orinoco to Páez in the Apure, where he found sickly llaneros and skinny horses. When Manuel Valdés and his Army of the East (two thousand infantry) arrived, Bolívar wanted to attack Morillo. Unfortunately, he lacked sufficient muskets and powder. These vital supplies had to be bought in the West Indies and transported up the Orinoco. Montilla's Irish-Creole army first had to take Río Hacha and Santa Marta on the Caribbean coast and open communications with Bogotá. Until then, arms and ammunition would have to be packed from the Apure across the Andes.

With the Caribbean link opened, the Patriots would enjoy access to the vast stockpile of war materiel on St. Thomas. Privateers constantly replenished stocks with captured Royalist supplies. Santander sent pesos at regular intervals to Bolívar. On January 16, 1820, Bolívar sent Sucre with eighty thousand pesos to buy muskets and powder at St. Thomas.

Bolívar decided to return to Bogotá. He also ordered Valdés to march his army to Bogotá. Valdés took the longer, more difficult route across the plains of Casanare, over the Eastern Cordillera of the Andes, then down to the valleys of the Sogamoso. Vivas and shouts of joy greeted Bolívar when he rode into Bogotá on March 5, 1820. But he found a worried Santander. He had levied taxes on Cundinamarca's salt mines, tobacco, the mint, and on general sales. Taxes for the expensive war effort might make the people hate their liberators more than they hated the autocratic Ferdinand.

Bolívar rode out of Bogotá on March 22 on an inspection tour toward the Venezuelan border. He found Valdés and a very sickly army at Sogamosa. "I am astonished at what has happened here," Bolívar reported to Santander. "In less than four days we have lost fifty men, and more than a hundred have gone to the hospital. The number of deaths is increasing daily. From the symptoms of those who have died, and as a result of our investigations, I am convinced there is a plot here to poison our men or cause them to desert." The survivors, including Valdés, were tough. They had walked more than fifteen hundred difficult miles from Angostura to Sogamosa. Many had died or deserted along the way. Bolívar gave them a new mission that would further test their mettle. Valdés would march his division toward Popayán to drive out the Royalists. Pushing farther south, the Patriots would begin the liberation of Quito.

Valdés marched south, and Bolívar rode north toward Cúcuta. Montilla, meanwhile, marched inland from Río Hacha to meet Urdaneta and his army. Montilla had arrived with supplies at the port of Juan Griego, Margarita, in late February. There he found the Irish soldiers starved and mutinous. The Irish could not speak Spanish, but Col. Francis Burdett O'Connor, born in Cork, Ireland, in 1781, spoke French. Like many of his countrymen, he had been banished for rebellion against English rule in 1798. He offered his services to Napoleon, without success, and then purchased a commission from d'Evereux and arrived with the Tenth Lancers, a regiment of the Irish Legion. He explained to Montilla in French how the Irish had been deceived with false promises into enlisting. They had been on short rations during the passage across the Atlantic. No provision had been made for their reception in Margarita. Hundreds had died of fever soon after landing.

Montilla fed the seven hundred disenchanted Irishmen and embarked them with native troops on Brión's fleet. The expedition sailed on March 7, already a month behind schedule. To save time, Montilla bypassed the Caracas coast and headed straight for Río Hacha. The town lacked defenses, so the inhabitants quickly disappeared when Brión's fleet anchored on the evening of March 12. The next morning the Patriot troops entered an empty town. The frightened inhabitants gradually returned, and José Padilla, a Río Hacha native with the expedition, recruited local marines.

Leaving troops to protect Río Hacha, Montilla and O'Connor marched inland seeking Urdaneta. They had covered about a hundred miles when Montilla learned of Royalist troop concentrations near Río Hacha. On March 25, the Patriots scattered the enemy in a brief skirmish in which O'Connor received a slight shoulder wound. Without cavalry and afraid of being cut off from Brión and the fleet, Montilla returned to the coast. The long-suffering Irish complained again of short rations and asked to be transported to a British colony. Some officers applied to Brión for their pay. He had money, but he gave them nothing. The Irish troops had suffered enough. Montilla went to their barracks to reason with them, but they were in no mood to listen. They demanded that Montilla return them to Ireland. He managed to secure passage for them on four merchant vessels to Jamaica. O'Connor and his lancers, Col. Edward Stopford, and a few other officers loyally offered to remain. Montilla, however, asked O'Connor and Stopford to accompany the disgruntled Irish to Jamaica and turn them over to British authorities.

After most of the Irish had departed, Montilla and the small remnant of his army (one hundred Irish lancers and sixty Creoles) embarked from Río Hacha. They sailed west and staged a sham attack on Santa Marta. Then they sailed up the Magdalena River and took the port town of Sabanilla without firing a shot. Royalists still held about 150 miles of the Magdalena River, with control points at Tenerife, Mompox, and Banco. Montilla sent Father Francisco Paéres Masenet to penetrate enemy territory. He wished to verify rumors that a Patriot force was approaching the Magdalena via the Cauca River. Father Paéres found José María Córdoba. The priest informed him that Montilla was sending Padilla upriver with arms and munitions. Galvanized by this good news, Córdoba led his two hundred men directly east over steep ridges and through dismal swamps.

Writing from San Cristóbal on April 20, 1820, Bolívar explained to Santander of the continuing need for troops. He ordered "that the Army of the South induct as many slaves capable of bearing arms as it may need; and that 3,000 unmarried young men be sent to the Army of the North." The Liberator also explained the rationale for his order to emancipate slaves in exchange for their military service.

> The military and political considerations that have led me to order the drafting of slaves are quite obvious. We need robust, vigorous men who are accustomed to hardship and fatigue, men who will embrace the cause and the service with enthusiasm, men who will identify their interests with the public interest, and men for whom death can have little less meaning than life.
>
> The political considerations are even stronger. The emancipation of the slaves has been proclaimed both *de jure* and *de facto*. The Congress has had in mind the dictum of Montesquieu: In moderate governments, political liberty gives civil liberty its value, and he who is deprived of the latter is necessarily deprived of the former; he beholds a happy society, of which he is not a part; he finds established security for others but not for himself. Nothing is nearer to the condition of beasts than to view free men everywhere and not be free. Men in this position are enemies of society, and, if large in number, they are dangerous.

Notwithstanding his 1816 pledge to Petión, the Liberator had liberated only male slaves who served in his armies. Gradually, however, he edged toward more enlightened racial views. He declared in favor of a "law of the free womb" (emancipating children born to slaves at birth) until 1821 and advocated the complete abolition of slavery five years later. Like most of the "active citizenry" (*ciudadanía activa,* the Creole minority with political rights) of his time, Bolívar feared that anarchy or a tyranny of the majority might result from enfranchising and empowering the nonwhite, rural masses. He also feared the frightful death tolls of the wars for independence that skewed the racial balance even further. As he concluded in his April 20 letter, "In Venezuela, we have seen the free population die and the slave survive. I know not whether or not this is prudent, but I do know that, unless we employ the slaves in Cundinamarca, they will outlive us again."

Word of Córdoba's approach to Mompox panicked Royalists at Banco, who evacuated and fled downriver before the Patriots cut off their escape. Hermógenez Maza and a small river fleet took possession of Banco. Córdoba attacked and occupied Mompox, then, together with Maza, sailed from Mompox downriver to Tenerife. They arrived just as Padilla's Patriot fleet came up from Barranquilla. Maza and Córdoba attacked Tenerife on June 25. Maza captured nine enemy vessels carrying muskets and powder and sank one vessel. Another ship escaped, but Padilla captured it.

Patriots now completely controlled the Magdalena and the Cauca Rivers. This vital strategic link gave the Patriots important logistical, economic, and diplomatic advantages. They could now communicate readily between the South American mainland, the Caribbean, and the rest of the world. Montilla, Córdoba, Padilla, and Maza united for the next two movements. First they would blockade Royalists at Cartagena to prevent interference with their revived commerce. Next they would take Santa Marta and further shrink Morillo's perimeter.

In addition to the successes along the Magdalena, events in Spain conspired to help the Patriots. The *Correo del Orinoco* (Nos. 55 and 63, March 18, 20, 1820) broadcast the startling news of a liberal revolution in Spain. On New Year's Day, Rafael Riego had proclaimed the Constitution of 1812. He led soldiers garrisoned near Cádiz (ready to embark for Venezuela) against the commander in chief of the army. Ferdinand VII had been forced to swear that he would rule according to that constitution.

Bolívar learned of the momentous events in Spain on May 1 while at San Cristóbal. He ordered Santander to print a broadside filled with the weighty news carried by the *Correo.* Bolívar fervently hoped that this shocking news would bring more Venezuelans into the Patriot fold. Bolívar also wrote to independence leaders in Argentina and Chile: "With great pleasure I am sending you copies of the *Correo del Orinoco* which contain documents concerning the uprising of the Spanish Army against the king. Buenos Aires and Chile now have nothing to fear from Spain." He notified Bernardo O'Higgins in Chile that "the army of Colombia is marching to Quito under the command of General Manuel Valdés. His orders are to co-operate with the armies of Chile and Buenos Aires against Lima."

"Everything on military affairs is going divinely for Bolívar," correctly noted a reporter in Angostura on June 5 (*Trinidad Gazette*, October 7, 1820). Bermúdez, Monagas, Sedeño, and Zaraza capably handled land operations in the East. Antonio Díaz and his Orinoco Squadron kept communications open with Margarita. Valdés pushed southward in Popayán and the Cauca, driving the Royalists back into Quito. Patriots controlled the Magdalena, and privateers hounded Spanish shipping in the Caribbean.

In late May new directives from the government in Madrid arrived in Caracas. Royalist officials in the Venezuelan capital wanted the orders obeyed and delivered them to Morillo in Valencia. One ordered every Spanish authority to promulgate the Constitution of 1812. Others instructed the Spanish to seek an armistice with "the Dissidents" and to end the war. General Torres asked Bolívar to suspend hostilities and to lift the siege on Cartagena. The Liberator, smelling success, angrily replied with a tirade.

> Do you believe, Sir, that old and corrupt Spain can still dominate the New World? Do you believe that the government of that nation, which has given the most terrible example of whatever is absurd in the human spirit, can succeed in shaping the happiness of a single village in the world? Tell your King and your nation, Sir, that in order not to bear the stain of being Spanish, the people of Colombia are resolved to fight for centuries and centuries against Peninsulars, against men and even against immortals if they were to side with Spain. Colombians prefer to descend to the eternal abysses rather than be Spaniards.

In reality, Royalists, not Patriots, faced the unhappy task of making concessions. Morillo could barely contain his irritation as he rode to Caracas. First he would face the humiliation of negotiating with Venezuelans against whom he had been fighting a war to the death for years. Second his absolute command would end, because the 1812 constitution provided for separation of powers, executive, judicial, and legislative. It also mandated the separation of civil and military authority. "The most miserable constitutional *alcalde* [mayor]," Morillo fumed, could obstruct the operations of the army by withholding supplies.

Nonetheless, Morillo dutifully promulgated the constitution on June 7 in Caracas. He delayed another ten days, however, before initiating armistice talks. Finally he wrote to Bolívar and the other Patriot leaders: "As it is impossible for reason to be heard in the din of war, a suspension of arms is needed to calm passions for a moment and permit reason to function. Therefore, I have this day ordered the commanders of all divisions of my armed and naval forces to suspend hostilities for one month from the date that patriot commanders do so."

Bolívar did not consider the rainy season the right time to enter into peace negotiations. With the plains flooded, llanero cavalry could not operate effectively. Supplies could not be packed over the Andes to Cundinamarca. True, Patriots had access to foreign markets via the Magdalena, but it would take several months to accumulate adequate stockpiles of arms and powder. Only then would he feel strong enough to dictate terms. He needed the force to convince Morillo that Patriots would never recognize Ferdinand VII as their king.

After considering Morillo's letter, Bolívar revealed his thinking in a letter of June 19 to Carlos Soublette: "The Spaniards are thoroughly convinced that they are impotent against us, and they are suffering every possible calamity that war could inflict upon them; hence, to grant them peace, I say, is to accord them an important victory. They are in the position of Plato's rich man: they have everything to lose and nothing to gain; and we, having nothing to lose, covet all that they possess. The conflict has left us nothing but our lives, and life means nothing to desperate men." The Liberator made clear his terms. "We must offer peace, and nothing more, in return for independence."

The news from Spain also sharply increased desertions from the Royalist armies. Morillo needed the one-month truce. He ordered La Torre to send a messenger to Bolívar and get his acceptance of the truce. Morillo would then send two envoys to negotiate a longer armistice. The messenger found Bolívar with Urdaneta's army at San Cristóbal. The Liberator answered, expressing "the greatest satisfaction" with the one-month armistice. He bluntly warned La Torre, however, that if Morillo gave his envoys any mission "other than the recognition of the Republic of Colombia, Your Excellency will kindly signify to them, in my behalf, that I am resolved neither to receive them nor to hear any proposal." Bolívar gave La Torre a week to reply.

Bolívar wished to delay talks while he consolidated his forces at Cúcuta. From this central location he could march south to Bogotá, northwest to Cartagena, and east to Angostura and Caracas. On July 21 he chided Morillo in a letter: "The Republic of Colombia rejoices to see the dawn of that bright day when Freedom will lay its hand of benediction upon unhappy Spain and when our former mother country will follow us upon the path of Reason." He warned the Spanish commander that "the armistice solicited by Your Excellency cannot be granted in full until the nature of the negotiations committed to [Juan Rodríguez del] Toro and [Francisco González de] Linares has been made known. They will be received with the respect that is due their sacred office."

Despite Bolívar's sharp provocations, Morillo could take no offensive action. The Royalist situation in the east had become precarious. Bermúdez had penetrated the upper llanos of Caracas, the source of Morillo's food supply. Mass desertions forced Morillo to shorten his lines. Indeed, many Spanish troops found little reason to sacrifice their lives for a decadent, distant government. First, Barcelona Province fell without a fight to the Patriots. In August, Royalist garrisons deserted and joined Zaraza. Monagas won over all the Indian villages in the province of Barcelona. The Spanish governor simply sailed away, leaving Patriots in control of the entire province. Patriots also held Cumaná Province except for the capital. Bermúdez had his headquarters in the southeastern portion of Caracas Province.

Bolívar left Cúcuta, 270 miles inland from Cartagena, on August 9 to visit bases on the lower Magdalena River. In late August he reached Turbaco, Montilla's headquarters for his fourteen-month land blockade of Cartagena. Brión and Padilla blockaded Cartagena and Santa Marta by sea. Soon Urdaneta could march on Maracaibo. Now satisfied with his strong strategic position, Bolívar returned to San Cristóbal and wrote to Morillo, expressing a willingness to negotiate an armistice. Such discussions, however, had to include sufficient guarantees for Colombia. He suggested meeting at San Fernando de Apure, 183 miles south of Caracas, and indicated that he would be there by late October.

The Liberator had no intention of going to San Fernando. Urdaneta had fallen ill, so Bolívar sent Colonel Plaza to clear enemy troops from Mérida and Trujillo. Plaza met little resistance from either of the small Royalist garrisons. The garrison in Mérida evacuated the town on September 30, and Bolívar entered on October 1 accompanied by only staff officers. He entered Trujillo soon thereafter and advanced toward Carache on October 11. Bolívar had accomplished his objectives—to dramatize Royalist weakness and to bolster popular support for the Patriot armies. He returned to Trujillo on October 17. Three days later the formidable Indian leader Juan de los Reyes Vargas deserted the Royalist cause and joined Bolívar. The able Reyes Vargas knew the countryside, and his Indians supporters followed him ardently.

Following his long siege, General Montilla, assisted by Padilla, recaptured Cartagena. Bolívar dubbed the city "La Heroica," the Heroic City, for its valiant, costly opposition to Spain. Cartagena survived this difficult, bloody period and again became a major shipping and trading port. After the many battles, the city also became more cosmopolitan, as Jews, Turks, French, Lebanese, Italians, and Syrians immigrated and established themselves as managers and owners of most of the city's hotels and restaurants.

Having consolidated his position, Bolívar now shrewdly prepared to accept an armistice. "It was an excuse for time to regulate the war and was adopted exactly as I had written it. It was a sane, humane and politic treaty which put an end to that horrible butchery of slaying the conquered, of giving no quarter to prisoners of war—Spanish barbarism that the patriots were forced to adopt themselves in reprisal. . . . It was an advantage to us, fatal to the Spaniards. Their forces could only diminish, mine augment and organize." He could always break it later and renew operations against Morillo. In late October Bolívar proposed from Trujillo definite armistice terms to Morillo. He covered his absence from San Fernando with a lie, saying that because of Urdaneta's illness he had to take command of the Army of the North.

> Since I have not received a reply from you to my San Cristóbal letter, let me give you an idea of the terms on which I think an armistice could be based: (1) the armistice will be from four to six months in every department of Colombia; (2) this army will retain the position occupied at the time of ratification of the armistice; (3) the division on the coast will take possession of the cities of Santa Marta, Río Hacha, and Maracaibo—it is at present marching on these cities and they will probably surrender; (4) the division of Apure will have for its boundary all the course of the Portuguesa; (5) the Eastern Army will keep all the territory it occupies at the time of ratification; (6) the division at Cartagena will maintain the positions it occupies at the time of ratification; (7) the division of the South will keep all territory it has taken on the march to Quito and maintain positions at the time of ratification.

Morillo, at Barquisimeto (165 miles west of Caracas), had his own reasons for stalling. He wanted to move his two thousand infantry and two hundred cavalry closer to Trujillo before he negotiated. He found his own excuse for delay. On October 29 he wrote to the Liberator: "I have already sent three commissioners to where you said you would be in your letter of

September 21. They have gotten as far as Calabozo. I will recall them and send them to you to discuss terms, but I do not consider myself authorized by my government to accept those you have outlined in your letter of October 26."

In the days that followed, messengers rode back and forth between Morillo and Bolívar. Padilla and his fleet, working with José María Carreño's land forces, took Santa Marta on November 11. Morillo advanced toward Trujillo. He had arrived at Carache, only twenty-five miles away, when Bolívar warned him, "if you advance any farther, thinking to dictate an armistice, I assure Your Excellency that I will never accept it, and Your Excellency will be responsible before humanity and your nation for the continuation of this bloody struggle."

Had he so chosen, Morillo had sufficient strength to advance. He halted because, like many Spanish officers, he had had enough of war in Venezuela. He wanted to return home to Spain. A dozen times he asked to be relieved of his command. Officials finally granted his request on condition that he first obtain an armistice. Morillo met with La Torre and the three commissioners, Ramón Correa, Toro, and Linares, to determine acceptable terms.

Col. Domingo Antonio Pita delivered the Royalist terms to Bolívar along with the names of the commissioners. Pita suggested that Bolívar withdraw to Cúcuta to ensure successful negotiations. Bolívar refused to evacuate territory he had liberated. He responded to Morillo with bluntness born of strength. "I welcome the prompt arrival of señores Correa, Toro, and Linares that together we may take the first step toward the prosperity of Spain and Colombia. But if these *señores* come charged with the same insulting proposals that you have sent us so many times, nothing will be more disagreeable for me than to receive them."

Morillo immediately dispatched his commissioners to Trujillo. Negotiations opened on November 22. Sucre, José Gabriel Pérez, and Pedro Briceño Méndez (1794–1835) represented the Patriots. The latter would become a close friend and confidant of the Liberator, eventually marrying into the Bolívar family. In two days the commissioners established an armistice treaty consisting of fifteen articles. They agreed that (1) each party would remain in the territory it possessed on that date, (2) neither party would engage in offensive action, (3) plenipotentiaries would be sent immediately to Madrid to discuss peace, (4) the truce would last for six months, and (5) the commissioners would write a second treaty to establish the rules of war and finally end the "war to the death."

The six commissioners signed the armistice treaty on November 25. They sent Morillo a copy of the treaty and an invitation to meet with Bolívar at Santa Ana, midway between Trujillo and Carache. The next day Morillo signed the treaty at Carache and rode to Santa Ana. Bolívar signed the treaty the same day in Trujillo. The commissioners completed and signed a second treaty, consisting of twelve articles. It provided that no prisoners would be shot, prisoners would be exchanged, and both sides would give "Christian care" to prisoners.

Morillo and Bolívar signed the second treaty on November 27. Then Bolívar rode to Santa Ana. As he approached the last hill, Bolívar sent O'Leary ahead to announce his arrival. When O'Leary entered Santa Ana, he saw Morillo and his retinue mounted, ready to ride and greet the Liberator. Morillo wore his dress uniform, resplendent with medals and decorations. His escort included General La Torre, forty-nine officers, and a squadron of cavalry.

Morillo asked O'Leary what kind of escort Bolívar had. O'Leary answered, "He does not have any. Ten or twelve officials are with him and your commissioners." "I was afraid my guard was too small," Morillo said, "but I see my old enemy has outdone me in valor." He ordered his cavalry to retire.

When he saw Bolívar's party coming down the hill, Morillo asked O'Leary, "Which one is Bolívar"? O'Leary pointed to the Liberator. "What!" cried Morillo. "That little man in the blue coat and campaign cap, riding a mule"? That "little man" rode up to Morillo. Both men leaped to the ground and embraced. Then they retired to the house to enjoy a celebratory banquet. Bolívar reported accurately much genial toasting and mutual respect among Spaniards and Americans, a clear sign of the growing Spanish lack of will to fight. "It is not possible," wrote Morillo, "to give an idea of the different emotions, sensitivity, frankness, sincerity and nobility with which their excellencies manifested in a thousand different ways the profound satisfaction they enjoyed at that moment."

Bolívar later wrote to Santander that not a single officer wanted to continue the war. No one, however, hinted that peace could be obtained without independence. Bolívar did not intend to let his ultimate dream of independence slide away. The Liberator reasoned that "the armistice is to our advantage because, with the establishment of uninterrupted communication and with our forces holding good positions in the continuous line of defense, we are in a superior situation to continue operation when the time comes; which, however, I believe will not be necessary, as the greatest advantage of the armistice will, to all appearances, be the end of the way."

Morillo turned over his command to La Torre and, at long last, embarked for Cádiz on December 17. In a letter to Vicente Rocafuerte, Bolívar noted that "Morillo has declared himself my friend and has gone to Spain to win new friends for us. General La Torre, now in command, is married to a relative of mine, and also is my friend, so that the expeditionary army appears to have desires to incorporate with the liberation army, and to prefer a young and beautiful *patria* to one that is old and decrepit." To achieve his dream of glory, the Liberator had to count upon the support and friendship of three high-ranking Royalists, Ramón Correa, Pablo Morillo, and Miguel de la Torre. Unlike some of his own erstwhile officers, they did not fail him.

Bolívar sensed the tide of history turning in his favor. He knew that Spanish authority had collapsed in the United Provinces of the Río de la Plata and in Chile. In the province of Quito, the port city of Guayaquil had declared independence. On August 20, 1820, a fleet and army under Adm. Lord Thomas Cochrane and Gen. José de San Martín had sailed from Valparaíso to liberate Peru.

Along with Bolívar, San Martín (1778–1850) stands as the other great hero of South American independence. He achieved military greatness despite the fact that he suffered from pains in the chest and stomach (occasional coughing up of blood), rheumatism, and other ills. He had to take opium daily. Writing from Chile on July 1, 1822, the opinionated but insightful Maria Dundas Graham remarked unfavorably on San Martín's personality. "San Martin has vulgarly been said to drink: I believe this is not true; but he is an opium eater, and his starts of passion are so frequent and violent, that no man feels his head safe." She met him a few months later in Santiago, Chile.

San Martin's eye has a peculiarity in it that I never saw before but once. ... It is dark and fine, but restless; it never seemed to fix for above a moment, but that moment expressed every thing. His countenance is decidedly handsome, sparkling, and intelligent; but *not open*. His manner of speaking quick, but often obscure, with a few tricks and by-words; but a great flow of language, and a readiness to talk on all subjects.... We spoke of government; and there I think his ideas are far from being either clear or decisive. There seems a timidity of intellect, which prevents the daring to give freedom and the daring to be despotic alike. The wish to enjoy the reputation of a liberator and the will to be a tyrant are strangely contrasted in his discourse. He has not read much, nor is his genius of that stamp that can go alone.

Despite his many health problems, he liberated Chile, invaded Peru, penned Royalists in the mountains, then met Bolívar at Guayaquil to seek help in eliminating them. A seemingly jealous Bolívar would not let San Martín have his army. Because the two leaders met in private, we will never know what prompted San Martín's abrupt departure. He made his "great renunciation," retired from the war theater, sailed to self-imposed exile in Europe, and died there in 1850.

San Martín was born on February 25, 1778, at Yapeyú in what is now the province of Corrientes, Argentina. His father served as governor of the department. His family moved to Spain in 1785, where at age eleven, San Martín became a cadet in Murcia Regiment. Posted to the north African coast of Melilla in 1791, he saw action against Moslems in the port of Orán. Thirteen-year-old San Martín suffered thirty-three days of bombardment, hunger, and insomnia. Terrifying earthquakes intensified everyone's fear and anguish. It may have been during this difficult ordeal that San Martín was first exposed to the use of opium. Moslems indulged freely in opium and hashish and used these drugs as trade items in North Africa and Spain.

San Martín's military career progressed satisfactorily over the years. When Napoleon made his brother Joseph king of Spain in 1808, he entered the service of the Seville Junta. He soon became ill, however, and remained in Seville on sick leave all the next year while Napoleon's armies overran central Spain.

Reassigned to duty on January 24, 1810, San Martín requested a discharge on August 26, 1811, so that he could depart for Lima, ostensibly to aid Royalists there. The regency granted his request. Like Bolívar, however, the Creole San Martín had turned against Spain. Sir Charles Stuart, a British agent in Spain, sent San Martín a false passport, and he sailed to London. There he met influential young men from Buenos Aires, among them Carlos de Alvear. He and his companions sailed from London on the *George Canning*. On March 9, 1812, they arrived in Buenos Aires, a city where rival factions struggled for power.

No one in Buenos Aires knew San Martín, but his companions touted him and his twenty-two-year service record to independence leaders. As a lieutenant colonel of cavalry, he created the cavalry corps that would become Argentina's famed regiment of Mounted Grenadiers. That same year he married María Remedios de Escalada. He also remained active politically, creating the Lautaro Lodge, and pledged to liberate South America of Spanish rule. As in Venezuela, Creoles remained divided on whether their goal was independence or loyalty to King Ferdinand.

On February 3, 1813, San Martín and his grenadiers fought against Royalist forces along the estuary near the Monastery of San Lorenzo. They defeated the Spanish invaders, but a shot felled his horse, and he could not spring clear as it fell. Two men died protecting San Martín before the Royalists fled. At the end of 1813 San Martín journeyed to the northwestern frontier to take command of the Army of the North. Manuel Belgrano's army stopped to loot the Spanish mint at Potosí, 264 miles southeast of La Paz. He loaded mules with 300,000 pesos worth of coins and bullion, diamonds, and disks of gold valued at 400,000 duros, then continued his march. He surrendered his command to San Martín at Tucumán in northern Argentina.

San Martín used part of the money that Belgrano brought to pay his troops. He assigned Martín Güemes, the caudillo from Salta province, and his famous gauchos, to defend the Upper Peruvian frontier, then turned his back on Upper Peru. He complained of a pain in his chest and did not emerge from his quarters for many days. Gen. José María Paz later called this "illness" a ruse so that San Martín could leave a command he did not want. "All the physicians of the army met yesterday to discuss the condition of my health," wrote San Martín to Supreme Director Gervasio Posadas (April 27, 1814), "and they unanimously decided that I should leave promptly for the mountains of Córdoba, for which I beg Your Excellency to grant me a leave of absence to recover."

Posadas granted the request. San Martín petitioned for an appointment as governor of the province of Cuyo. Mendoza, Cuyo's capital, was in the "Garden of the Andes," where vineyards and orchards flourished. Posadas named San Martín governor of Cuyo on August 10, 1814, so that he could recover in a healthful, delightful climate. The peace of San Martín's Shangri-la was shattered when three thousand men, women, and children from Chile fled to Mendoza through the Uspallata Pass of the Andes. These refugees had retreated from Royalist Gen. Mariano Osorio after the battle of Rancagua (September 30 through October 2, 1814).

Pressured by Chilean Patriots, San Martín had to do something. Argentina did not face an immediate threat from Chile, because the viceroy recalled Osorio to Peru and replaced him with a weakling. San Martín spent two full years undisturbed by any Royalist army to recruit, discipline, and provision his army. He recruited some fifteen hundred slaves into his force and, in exchange for freedom, they fought valiantly and well. The work paid off, as did his careful strategy. San Martín's predecessor, Gen. Manuel Belgrano, had unsuccessfully attacked Upper Peru overland from northern

Argentina. San Martín abandoned the northern, overland strategy in favor of an audacious sweep from the south. He would cross the Andes, conquer Chile, and then attack the Spanish stronghold of Lima from the sea. He also pushed the politicians to declare independence for the "United Provinces of the Río de la Plata," which they did on July 9, 1816.

His dramatic crossing of the Andes in January 1817 ranks among the most successful high mountain crossings in military history. He enjoyed excellent intelligence, thanks to cooperation from Bernardo O'Higgins and other Chileans, who also spread false rumors to confuse the Royalists there. The Army of the Andes climbed over six different passes. Each division achieved its objective on schedule. The troops numbered about five thousand infantry, cavalry, and artillery, well armed, well trained, with provisions to last a month. The two key columns climbed through Los Patos and Uspallata and united with superb coordination at Santa Rosa of the Andes. Aided by an audacious cavalry charge led by Bernardo O'Higgins, his two middle divisions won a stunning victory at the Battle of Chacabuco on February 12, 1817.

San Martín and his Army of the Andes could have pursued and wiped out the enemy. However, named supreme director by grateful Chileans, San Martín deferred to O'Higgins (1778–1842) and hurried back across the Andes to Buenos Aires. Early in 1818, Royalists arose again, this time in southern Chile, and advanced almost to the southern limits of Santiago. San Martín's army destroyed them at the battle of Maipú, the decisive battle that completed the liberation of Chile.

Born in Chillán, O'Higgins had been dispatched to England in 1795 to further his education. He met and came under the influence of none other than the Precursor, Francisco de Miranda. After returning to Chile in 1802, he worked to further the goal of national independence. Like the Liberator, he would prove more effective on the battlefield than in the political area. O'Higgins ruled Chile as dictator from February 18, 1817, until January 28, 1823, when dissident Creoles forced him into exile. San Martín remained ill in Mendoza much of the next two years until he sailed with Adm. Lord Thomas Cochrane, later earl of Dundonald, to invade Peru.

Cochrane set sail on August 20, 1820, carrying the expeditionary army from the port of Valparaíso, Chile. They landed on September 8, 1820, some 1,367 miles north at the little port of Pisco, 127 miles south of Lima. San Martín began to spread revolutionary propaganda from this isolated base. Cochrane patrolled the coast and sent a brig loaded with war materiel to Colombia's Pacific port of Buenaventura, two hundred miles southwest of

Bogotá. When the brig arrived, Santander reported to Bolívar (November 17, 1820): "Two deputies came in here for the purpose of entering into a treaty, offensive and defensive, with the government of Colombia against their common enemy."

Things looked suddenly brighter for the Patriot cause, with San Martín at Pisco and wishing to ally with Colombia against Spain. Cochrane's brig had debarked twenty-six hundred muskets and other supplies. Suspicions and rivalries in the Patriot ranks, however, continued to arouse fears. Santander understood that if San Martín moved swiftly he might get north to Guayaquil before Colombian armies got south to that point. Thus he published a not-so-subtle message to San Martín and the general public proclaiming Ecuador a part of Colombia: "Guayaquil is comprehended, as well as Quito, within the limits of Colombia, and as the *uti possidetis* is the basis of the Armistice, now belongs to her, and will probably remain quiet during the period assigned, and enjoying free trade" (*Trinidad Gazette*, January 31, 1821).

Meanwhile, Bolívar renewed his diplomatic efforts with Spain. He learned that commissioners authorized to make a peace treaty had arrived in Caracas from Spain. In response, on January 24, 1821, Bolívar sent two diplomatic agents to Madrid, carrying a rather pointed letter to King Ferdinand:

> Your Majesty has chosen to learn the truth from us, to hear our cause, and, doubtless, to accord us justice. . . . Colombia's existence is a necessity for Your Majesty's peace of mind, and for the welfare of our people of Colombia. It is our hope to offer the Spanish people a second homeland—one that is proudly erect, not bowed in chains. The Spaniards will come to gather the sweet fruits of virtue, knowledge, and industry—they will not come to seize them by main force.

As peace negotiations appeared imminent, events in Maracaibo unfolded in favor of the Patriots. Many prominent citizens, including the governor and military commander, had Patriot sympathies. Francisco Delgado, the Royalist military commander of Maracaibo, was a native of that city. Since late 1819, Patriots had cut Maracaibo off from its natural markets with the interior via the Cúcuta-Pamplona route. With commerce paralyzed, the city suffered, and local merchants clamored for a remedy. They knew that they could expect no help from Spain to regain their lost markets.

Urdaneta, another native of Maracaibo, had stationed José Rafael de las Heras with a battalion of troops at Gibraltar on the southeastern shore of

Lake Maracaibo, on the Royalist side of the armistice line. Delgado proclaimed the independence of Maracaibo on January 28 and immediately reestablished commerce with the provinces of Trujillo, Mérida, and Pamplona. Las Heras took possession of the city on January 29.

Urdaneta reported "the spontaneous action" in Maracaibo to La Torre in early February. With somewhat strained logic, he maintained that the armistice made it lawful to accept a deserter and that Maracaibo qualified as a deserter in a larger sense. Therefore Maracaibo had the right to declare itself part of the Republic of Colombia. La Torre termed the sending of troops to Maracaibo "a public infraction of the armistice." He proposed that Las Heras withdraw his troops to preserve the armistice.

Bolívar learned of the independence of Maracaibo as he approached Cúcuta on February 14. He pondered the matter for five days, then wrote to La Torre: "The efforts of the governor, garrison, cabildo and people of Maracaibo to remove themselves from Spanish domination has created a problem between our respective governments which appears at once difficult and dangerous; but it will entail no consequences if it is resolved by justice and right." Bolívar went on to deftly show La Torre how to justify his acceptance of the loss of Maracaibo.

La Torre could not agree to Bolívar's proposals without the support of Pablo Morales, who commanded seven thousand troops at Calabozo. Rather than wait in Cúcuta for La Torre's answer, Bolívar rode to Trujillo and ordered Urdaneta to establish his headquarters in Maracaibo, organize an army, and prepare to invade the province of Coro when the armistice ended.

Even as he prepared his troops and bases, Bolívar waged psychological warfare against La Torre. He wrote to the Royalist: "Although this might be unpleasant to you, I take the liberty to inform you that San Martín is in Peru and has defeated General [Joaquín de la] Pezuela. He fled from Lima as San Martín entered. This event should make clear to the Spanish government the true state of affairs in America." On March 10, 1821, Bolívar delivered an ultimatum to La Torre: "Each day there is less food because the armistice has limited commerce to the Apure. I can vacillate no longer. I must make peace or fight. If the Spanish commissioners are empowered to negotiate peace, I will meet them and you in San Fernando. If they are not empowered to negotiate peace, I must inform you that 40 days after you receive this note, hostilities will commence according to Article 12 of the Armistice."

La Torre replied the same day that military operations would begin on April 28. "The whole world has its eyes fixed on us," he reminded Bolívar. "It will judge who is responsible for renewing the evils of this fratricidal war." On March 23 La Torre published a proclamation to the "Inhabitants of These Provinces." He admitted that he lacked the authority to negotiate a peace that presaged independence. "Therefore," La Torre added, "in accord with Article 12 of the Armistice I will begin hostilities on April 28, which will be forty days from March 19 when I received Bolívar's letter." By placing the blame on Bolívar for renewing hostilities, La Torre hoped to remain in the good graces of the Spanish government while at the same time letting Bolívar have his way.

Bolívar met with Gen. Antonio Nariño, precursor of independence in New Granada, in Achaguas. Nariño had been taken prisoner after Royalists overran Pasto in May 1814. Imprisoned in Spain until the liberal uprising in 1820, he returned to his homeland. Bolívar hoped that he might help control the angry deputies slowly gathering at the Congress in Cúcuta. Congress had yet to convene and some of the deputies had already exhausted their funds. Many blamed Bolívar, with some justification, for neglecting them.

For his part, Bolívar expressed exasperation with years of political attacks. He vented his frustration in a letter written on April 21, 1821, to a friend in Congress. As Bolívar himself understood, he felt more comfortable as a soldier than as a politician.

> You may be certain that I will never be president; even though I should be named a thousand times over, in the end I will resign. Eight years as head of this republic of ingrates have wearied me. I am tired of being dubbed usurper, tyrant, despot, and I am even more weary of duties that are so contrary to my nature. On the other hand, I believe that special knowledge is required to administer a state—a knowledge that I do not possess and that I find utterly distasteful. You must know that I have never seen an account book, nor have I ever bothered about my household expenses. Neither am I made for diplomacy, because I am extremely guileless and easily excited; I know only the meaning of the word. I do not know anything about anything, but as I am naturally inclined to love liberty and good government, I will fight for my country with the greatest of pleasure, and I will defend the laws, which I believe to be the best in any congress.

In April 1821, Bolívar appointed Nariño as provisional vice president of Colombia. Santander would later defeat him and thus prevent his serving a full term. The gallant Colombian precursor would die two years later, a bitter, disillusioned Patriot, not unlike Bolívar. The Liberator then gave Dr. Pedro Gual, secretary of the treasury (and after March 1821, minister of foreign affairs), a rather extraordinary, brutally realistic, order. He commanded Gual to "use for Congress the funds destined for the army because, in a little while, half the soldiers will have been killed and the other half will need nothing, whether victorious or vanquished."

Nariño arrived in Cúcuta at the end of April, calmed the deputies, and convened Congress even though a quorum of the ninety-five deputies had not yet arrived. These able young men (young because of the high mortality rate) proceeded to write a constitution for Colombia. Priests, lawyers, and landowners predominated as the war theater occupied the generals and colonels.

On April 28 Bolívar directed Urdaneta to move from Maracaibo 141 miles northeast to begin the liberation of Coro, then march as quickly as possible to Guanare. He ordered Páez to cross the Apure and to be in Mijagual (a few miles southwest of Guanare) no later than May 25. All of Bolívar's divisions began operations on schedule. Urdaneta's troops entered Coro on May 11. Bermúdez left Barcelona, 153 miles east of Caracas, on April 28 with about one thousand men. On the morning of May 14, Ramón Correa and his Royalist force retired from Caracas and marched west to La Victoria. That afternoon Bermúdez entered Caracas amidst shouts of "Viva Colombia, Viva la Independencia," ringing bells, and firing artillery.

Bermúdez did not tarry; he pursued Correa. The press of the time reported the outcome. "Correa was confessing and receiving the Communion when the Independents approached La Victoria; notwithstanding which he would not prepare for action until he had gone through the whole of his devotions. When at last dispositions were taken, they were so bad that the Patriots nearly surrounded his forces, upon which Correa commanded them to disperse on the right and the left, and Bermúdez entered Victoria without losing a man, taking many prisoners."

Royalists abandoned the port of La Guaira on May 15 and sailed all their ships of war westward to Puerto Cabello. The next day Bermúdez took possession of La Guaira. La Torre, aware of the loss of Caracas, withdrew from Araure to San Carlos on May 20. Bolívar's van entered Araure two days later. The same day Patriots captured a Royalist messenger. La Torre had told his garrison to abandon Barquisimeto and move toward Valencia, ninety miles to the east. La Torre's move gave up a central position from which he might have prevented Bolívar, Páez, and Urdaneta from uniting. Bolívar advanced his concentration point to San Carlos.

Writing from Guanare, Bolívar addressed a candid letter to Minister of Foreign Affairs Dr. Pedro Gual on May 24, 1821. The Liberator's observations clearly illustrate the vast class gulf dividing Colombia. He also voiced one of his frequent concerns: the lack of preparedness of the masses for political participation. Describing the llanero cavalry fighting for him, Bolívar noted that "they are without hope of gathering the fruit of what they *have won by the lance.* They are obstinate, ignorant *llaneros,* who have never regarded themselves as the equal of men who know more or who make a better appearance. I myself, who have always been at their head, still do not know all their capabilities. I treat them with extreme consideration; and yet this consideration is not enough to inspire in them the confidence and frankness that should exist among comrades and fellow-citizens. You can be sure, Gual, that we are over an abyss, or, rather, over a volcano that is about to erupt. I fear peace more than war, and in saying this, I leave it to you to imagine all that I leave unsaid for it cannot be said."

However, the fruits of independence had not yet been won by the lance. Royalist movements would seem to indicate that La Torre, like Correa, wished to make things as easy as possible for Bolívar. Morales, an irreconcilable Royalist, did not yield so easily. When he heard of the fall of Caracas, Morales left Calabozo with three thousand men. By forced marches he reached La Victoria on May 25 and immediately attacked Bermúdez. Outflanked on all sides, Bermúdez withdrew eastward through Caracas and camped not far away. General Morales entered Caracas amid shouts of "Viva el Rey" and ringing bells.

Páez joined Bolívar at San Carlos on June 7. Urdaneta got as far as Barquisimeto before he became too ill to travel, at which point he turned over command to Col. Antonio Rangel (1788–1821), who moved the troops at San Carlos on June 16. Bolívar organized his combined forces into three divisions commanded by Páez, Sedeño, and Plaza. Informed of the Patriot massing, Morales left Col. José Pereira with one thousand troops to hold Caracas. He marched to join La Torre on the plains of Carabobo, fifteen miles southwest of Valencia. Bermúdez quickly reoccupied Caracas after some resistance on the part of Pereira, who withdrew to La Guaira.

Bolívar's army left San Carlos on June 20. They halted at dusk three days later, ten miles from La Torre's army, and camped on the plains of Carabobo. Torrential rains fell all night, but a cloudless morning sky greeted the Patriot army as it marched to the battlefield. From a high hill Bolívar looked down on La Torre's army lined up for battle. The Royalists had prepared for an attack in the center and on the left but not on the right wing. Bolívar sent Páez, followed by Sedeño, on a wide westward detour. They were to swoop down on the enemy's right and rear. The llanero cavalry cut off La Torre's retreating infantry and took on his cavalry as well. During the battle, Lt. Pedro Camejo (ca. 1795–1821), faithful bodyguard to Páez, perished. Called "El Negro Primero" (The First Black), he had initially assisted Royalists but deserted and switched sides in 1816. Venezuelan folklore records his last words to Páez as "My general, I'm going to tell you goodbye, because I am dead." Plaza readied an attack on La Torre's front and left.

The Second Battle of Carabobo began at eleven o'clock on the morning of June 24, 1821. It ended before noon, with battered Royalists fleeing in all directions. Stalwart British Huntsmen stood fast and delivered withering fire, despite taking heavy losses. Badly outnumbered by the Royalists and never receiving much-needed reinforcement, they pressed forward, engaging the enemy with bayonets after having exhausted their ammunition. One of the officers bitterly complained, "Why Bolívar at this time, and indeed during the period since our first advance, sent us no support I have never been able to guess. Whatever the motive, it is certain that the second and third division of the army quietly looked on while we were being slaughtered, and made no attempt to help us. The curses of our men were loud and deep, but seeing that they must not expect any help, they made up their minds to carry the enemy's position or perish. Out of nine hundred men we had not above six hundred left."

Bolívar's official report the next day exaggerated the great victory over a Royalist force of about five thousand even further. Bolívar inflated the size of the enemy forces by one thousand men, "but this army is no more. At best 400 men may have straggled into Puerto Cabello today. The army of liberty equaled that of the enemy in size, but no more than a fifth of its number decided the battle. Our casualties are by no means severe: perhaps 200 dead and wounded." In reality the Patriots did not count their own losses carefully, but, since the whole army saw action, its casualties must have exceeded two hundred. The British Battalion lost about a dozen officers and one hundred men. Moreover, Bolívar lost two of his division commanders: Plaza and Sedeño. La Torre had fought with about fifteen hundred troops fewer than the Patriots. His army suffered one thousand to twelve hundred dead and wounded; fifteen hundred unwounded prisoners, and seven hundred to eight hundred disappeared. About two thousand Royalists, including La Torre and Morales, escaped to Puerto Cabello, leaving behind considerable military stores in Valencia.

Bolívar entered Valencia before sunset, and the army arrived the next day. Bolívar continued toward Caracas, sending Lt. Col. Diego Ibarra ahead to prepare for his entry. Bolívar's triumphal return to Caracas was tempered by the fact that most of the population had fled. Ibarra found only a few remaining blacks and pardos who received Bolívar with joy. Ibarra journeyed down to La Guaira to offer Pereira an honorable capitulation. Entering La Guaira on July 4, Bolívar arranged transport to Puerto Cabello for about two hundred Royalists, while more than five hundred Royalist troops opted to remain with the Patriots.

The Liberator next rode westward to Valencia on July 9. He tried but failed to negotiate another armistice with La Torre, perhaps owing to stiff opposition from Morales. When Bolívar returned to Caracas on July 30, he divided Venezuela into three military departments: the West with Mariño in command; the Center with Páez in command; and the East with Bermúdez in command. Leaving military matters in the capable hands of these three men, Bolívar returned to the world of politics.

Bolívar arrived at the Congress at Cúcuta on October 3. He had either forgotten his April vow not to accept the presidency or he had changed his mind. Under the new constitution of the Republic of Colombia, Bolívar became president and Santander his vice president. Congress passed a law giving Bolívar extraordinary powers to assure the liberation of territories still held by Royalists. The law also allowed Bolívar to leave the government of Colombia in the hands of Santander. Bolívar persuaded Congress to transfer the republic's capital from Cúcuta 251 miles southwest to Bogotá.

Bolívar and Urdaneta, with some of the veterans of Carabobo, left Cúcuta on October 10 to begin the liberation of Royalist-held territory. Halfway to Bogotá they heard the welcome news that Patriots had taken possession of Cartagena. The wily Padilla had sailed silently through the narrow Boca Chica entrance to Cartagena Bay on the night of June 24, undetected by the forts on either side. Montilla fired on the city from the heights of La Popa and diverted attention from Padilla, whose fleet attacked the Royalist flotilla.

Spanish Gov. Gabriel Torres refused to hear Padilla's surrender proposals. Col. José Candamo, however, approached Padilla and said that he would bring with him all the officers in Cartagena if Padilla would allow them to go quietly about their business. Padilla accepted the proposal on August 29. Candamo and the officers boarded the flotilla. The departing Royalists reported that each man at the garrison had only two ounces of rice and four of flour per day. They confided that the town would have surrendered long before but for Torres, who did not expect to be well treated by the Patriots. Torres did not surrender until October 1.

Bolívar heartily congratulated Montilla on the victory, especially since it freed 4,000 Patriot troops to fight elsewhere. Bolívar ordered the freed troops deployed as follows: "This is the way you are to distribute them: leave 500 veterans in Cartagena; send 2,000 to operate against Portobelo (on the Caribbean coast of Panama); and send Salom with 1,000 men to me, 300 to Santa Marta, and 200 to Río Hacha. You will notice that I said to send 1,000 men, not soldiers, with Salom. This leaves you with 1,000 soldiers to use as needed in Panama."

Royalists at Cumaná, meanwhile, worked out surrender terms with Bermúdez, who took possession of the city and its military stores on October 16. Patriots now occupied the entire Caribbean coast of Colombia except for Puerto Cabello, where an epidemic of "black vomit" (yellow fever) raged. The Spanish warship *Asia* had anchored there in July to allow the debarkation of Juan de la Cruz Mourgeón and a few troops. He was to be viceroy of New Granada after he had pacified Cundinamarca. The *Asia* continued to Vera Cruz with Juan O'Donojú, the new captain general for Mexico. Patriots besieged him at Vera Cruz, and he could not get from that port city to the interior of Mexico. Members of his family began to die of yellow fever. O'Donojú met the Mexican Patriot leader Gen. Agustín de Iturbide on August 24 and recognized the independence of Mexico. O'Donojú later died in Mexico City.

Mourgeón had a little better luck in Puerto Cabello. La Torre could spare only a few officers and troops for duty at the port. He did supply the brig *Hiena,* on which Mourgeón sailed to Panama with fewer than four hundred troops, many infected with yellow fever. The *Hiena* anchored at Chagres on August 2. Mourgeón and the infected troops debarked and crossed the isthmus to the city of Panama. There he conscripted more troops and sailed to the coast of Ecuador with about eight hundred men.

As soon as Mourgeón had departed, Col. José Fábrega and the bishop of Panama called a meeting of leading military, religious, and civil officials. They declared Panama independent and part of Colombia on November 28, 1821. Fábrega also wrote to Montilla in Cartagena asking for help to contain the Spaniards. Montilla replied by sending nearly one thousand troops. A month passed before Santander in Bogotá received Fábrega's news of the "spontaneous declaration of independence" in Panama. Santander assured Fábrega on January 17, 1822, that Colombia would sustain Panama's independence with troops and vessels and accept her as part of Colombia.

Santander, Montilla, and Bolívar clearly understood Panama's strategic importance and commercial value for interoceanic trade. Indeed, King

Charles V of Spain had first contemplated a canal across the isthmus back in the sixteenth century. As long as the Patriots held it, Spain could not send troops and war materiel across the Isthmus of Panama to the Pacific. Thus Spain could not reinforce Quito or Lima. On the other hand, Patriot troops and supplies could be sent across Panama, then shipped south on transports to help Bolívar, Sucre, and San Martín liberate Quito and Peru. Having secured the Caribbean coast, Mexico, and Panama, the future looked considerably brighter for independence forces throughout Latin America.

CHAPTER 12

Delirium over Manuela
and Chimborazo, 1822

With Colombia and Venezuela secure, Bolívar turned his vision south toward the western coast of South America. Bolívar determined to defeat the Royalist bastion at Pasto, 320 miles southwest of Bogotá near the border with Ecuador. That stronghold had defeated every Patriot army sent against it the past ten years. Only winding trails, not roads, penetrated the mountainous province of Pasto that sheltered the town of the same name, the only sizable population between Popayán to the north and Quito 130 miles farther south. Tough, fanatical Royalists inhabited this isolated, theocratic enclave. They believed the king of Spain to be God's regent on earth; Patriots served the Devil. Beginning in December 1821, Bolívar tried forgeries and propaganda to win over religious and political leaders in Pasto. His various ruses all failed. He resigned himself to attacking the mountain stronghold and began assembling an army in Cali. They would march northwest to the nearby port of Buenaventura, then sail the eight hundred miles to join José Antonio Sucre and his one thousand Colombians at Guayaquil, Ecuador. Sucre had found a strong San Martín party there but not the Argentine's army.

Bolívar saw San Martín as a real threat to his own quest for glory, a concern he confided to Santander. "I do not wish to go [to Peru] if glory does not follow me. . . . I do not wish to lose the fruits of eleven years through one defeat, and I do not wish San Martín to see me other than as I deserve to be seen, namely as the chosen son." Sucre furthered Bolívar's interests by deftly convincing the governing junta to place Guayaquil under the protection of the Republic of Colombia. Within months, Sucre would gain victory laurels that would inflame the Liberator's jealousy.

With Sucre's army and his own, Bolívar expected to march inland to the north and liberate Quito, then approach Pasto from the south. A letter from Sucre, which arrived January 6, 1822, changed his mind. Juan de la Cruz Mourgeón had disembarked on Ecuador's far north coast at Esmeraldas with eight hundred Royalist troops, arms, and munitions. He had marched to reinforce Gen. Melchor Aymerich in Quito. Mourgeón's audacity amazed and dismayed Bolívar. He found it hard to believe that Royalists had crossed the seemingly impassable mountains between the coast and Quito. Here was a dangerous and worthy foe!

Mourgeón's armada consisted of an armed corvette, four armed brigs, and three transports. Bolívar had only a single poorly armed brig to protect transports that would carry his Patriot army to Guayaquil. Instead of risking unequal naval conflict, Bolívar decided to abandon the southern ocean route and march overland to Popayán. On February 25 he dispatched Manuel Valdés and Pedro León Torres with 2,850 troops toward Pasto, which Santander ominously called "the graveyard of the brave."

As Bolívar faced serious military challenges in South America, the diplomatic front brightened in North America, where U.S. President James Monroe cautiously moved his nation beyond its longstanding neutrality. On March 8, 1822, he declared to Congress that five colonies, Colombia, Chile, Peru, Buenos Aires, and Mexico, should be recognized as independent nations. He further asked for money to deploy diplomatic missions to the new countries. After spirited debate Congress agreed, and Monroe signed the resulting legislation on May 4. The same month Adams informed Colombia's chargé d'affaires Manuel Torres that Monroe would receive him. Although seriously ill, Torres traveled to Washington, D.C., and met with Monroe on June 18. The United States thus became the first country outside of Latin America to recognize a new Spanish American republic. The Portuguese monarch, operating from Rio de Janeiro, Brazil, had recognized Buenos Aires as independent in 1821. Despite appearing more overtly sympathetic, Great Britain would not publicly announce recognition of any of the new republics until early 1825.

Meanwhile, Bolívar and his staff caught up with the army and skirted mountains in southern Colombia that rose more than three miles above sea level. These high peaks protected the small plateau of Pasto. Two treacherous rivers cut through the province, the Juanambú to the north and the Guatira to the west. Sickness, desertions, and guerrilla attacks reduced the army to two thousand troops by the time it reached the Juanambú River. Bolívar crossed the river and left the main trail, then circled west around Pasto, planning to attack from the south near Consacá. On April 7 he advanced from Consacá to the hacienda of Bomboná.

The Patriots sighted Col. Basilio García and his troops three miles to the east on the Loma de Cariaco, the heights above the Quebrada (Ravine) of Cariaco. A Royalist abatis topped with cannon protected the bridge across the ravine. The Guaitara River, a torrent too deep to be forded, protected García's left flank. The almost perpendicular stone sides of the Quebrada de Cariaco blocked the approach to his right flank.

In late morning, Bolívar sent Manuel Valdés left along the side of the Cariaco. His troops would descend the ravine then climb out beyond the enemy right. Torres prepared to attack the Royalist center with part of his division. The rest of his force descended the ravine to attack the Royalist left. What comes down to us as the battle of Bomboná began at half past three in the afternoon. Within half an hour, withering fire from the well-entrenched Royalists killed or wounded all Patriots who had advanced across the bridge. Torres and many of his troops, who got as far as the abatis, died or suffered wounds.

Patriot fire kept García from sending reinforcements to his right, so shortly before dark, Valdés and his Rifles scrambled out of the ravine and attacked. Escaping Royalists warned García of the attack, but having exhausted his ammunition, the Royalist commander silently withdrew in the darkness. The bloody standoff ended with Bolívar having lost one-third of his men and having failed to push forward to Pasto. Bolívar circled north to Trapiche, midway between Pasto and Popayán. A disappointed and chastened Liberator renounced his goal of taking Pasto and awaited reinforcements from Santander and news from Sucre.

The day of the battle of Bomboná found Sucre about two hundred miles south of Quito. He marched north to outwit Mourgeón and Aymerich, passing high amid active and extinct volcanoes. He did not know that the audacious Mourgeón had died a few days earlier. As Sucre advanced, the enemy withdrew, and friendly inhabitants greeted his forces all along the way. The Ecuadorans well remembered the harsh reprisals of Spanish authorities who crushed their uprising in 1809. Sucre won a small battle on April 21 west of Riobamba in central Ecuador. The town lies one hundred miles south of

Quito, at the base of Chimborazo, a massive peak that soon returned to Bolívar in his dreams.

Sucre rested his army for a day, then they climbed around snow-crowned Cotopaxi, the highest active volcano in the world (elevation 19,341 feet). After four days of grueling effort, they descended to the valley of Chillo on May 17. Scouts reported that Aymerich had retired to a strong position outside Quito. Sucre crossed a ridge that divides Chillo from the plain of Turubamba, Quito's southern pasture. He offered battle on May 21, but the Royalist army did not move. He tried for two days to provoke combat, but Aymerich continued to ignore him.

The city of Quito lies at 9,300 feet in elevation on a terrace of volcanic ash on the southern slopes of massive Mount Pichincha, whose highest peak rises 15,962 feet. Tufts of grass cover the rough, broken sides of Pichincha above the tree line and support large herds of hardy cattle. On the night of May 23, 1822, Sucre began a westward flanking movement. Indians, packing his ammunition and cannon, led the Patriots around Pichincha's skirt. They could look down from the heights upon the city almost a mile below.

Aymerich saw the first companies forming for battle at eight o'clock the next morning. In response, the Royalist commander ordered an extremely unwise frontal attack, forcing his troops to climb laboriously straight up the mountain for an hour and a half. At fourteen thousand feet above sea level, the badly winded Royalists confronted the Patriots. By noon the Patriots had won a resounding victory over the exhausted enemy. Sucre sent O'Leary to propose honorable terms. Aymerich, the last Spanish president of the kingdom of Quito, accepted, surrendering the entire province of Quito, and quickly departed for Spain. He left behind 1,100 troops and 160 officers as prisoners, 190 additional wounded, and 400 dead. Sucre lost 200 killed and 140 wounded in his remarkable liberation of Ecuador.

Since the battle of Bomboná on April 7, Bolívar had sent several letters to García asking without success that he surrender. The third week of May, reinforcements arrived from Santander boosting the Liberator's army to two thousand men, sufficient to dislodge García from Pasto. He marched south from Trapiche at the end of May. On June 5 he met agents from García who told him that the Royalists would capitulate. Three days later Bolívar entered Pasto, and the Royalists officers prepared to depart for Spain. After capturing Pasto, Bolívar received news of Sucre's daring victory at Pichincha. The Liberator did not like being upstaged, especially by a youngster; indeed, he wished to occupy center stage at all times. Instead of rejoicing in a great Patriot victory, Bolívar, revealing the full extent of his gigantic ego, vented his jealousy to Santander.

> Sucre had a larger number of troops and a smaller number of enemies than I. The land was very favorable because of its people and because of the character of the terrain. We, on the other hand, found ourselves in a veritable hell and fought with the Devil. The victory of Bombaná is greater than that of Pichincha. The losses in each were equal, and the characters of the enemy leaders were not. General Sucre did not carry away any greater glory on the day of battle than I, and the surrender he received was not more complete than mine.

Fortunately, Bolívar's jealous outburst did not permanently cloud his judgment. He continued to rely upon Sucre, who would indeed cover himself in glory and become Bolivia's first president. Bolívar reorganized the province of Pasto and dealt skillfully with the bishop of Popayán. He refused to accept the bishop's offer of resignation, thereby winning over a bitter enemy. The Liberator used his considerable charm and diplomacy on many occasions to turn enemies into supporters.

With affairs settled at Pasto, Bolívar and his small escort rode south, where their spirits soared at the warm welcome provided by the inhabitants of the province of Quito. The people of Quito hated the Royalists as much as those in Pasto hated the Colombians. Bolívar entered Quito to the joyous clanging of church bells. Little girls in angel costumes ran before them scattering flowers, and an admiring crowd in the narrow, cobbled streets shouted, "Bolívar! Bolívar!" The elite of Quito showered rose petals over the heroes from their balconies. As the triumphal procession approached the main plaza, a young woman on one of the balconies aimed a laurel wreath at Bolívar's feet. According to popular legend, it hit him in the face. Surprised and taken aback, he glanced up toward the balcony into the beautiful eyes and enchanting figure of Manuela Sáenz del Thorne (1797–1856).

During his busy life, Bolívar would have countless sexual encounters, many brief and immediately forgotten. After his wife's death, he vowed never again to marry, a promise that he dutifully kept. However, his reverence for his wife's memory did not preclude extramarital relations. In Guayaquil, he would have an affair with Joaquina Garaycoa. "I love her devotedly and gratefully," he wrote of the woman he called "La Gloriosa" (The Glorious). Quito's Manuela Sáenz, however, would become his truest love, valued confidante, brave and ardent supporter, and keeper of his archives.

Born in Quito, Ecuador, as the illegitimate daughter of a Spanish gentleman, Simón Sáenz y Vergara, captain of the king's militia, Manuela Sáenz
faced a challenging life in a class, race, and propriety-conscious society. Her
mother, Joaquina Aispuru, was the youngest daughter of a Panama-born
gentleman of Basque ancestry, Mateo José de Aispuru, a lawyer who also
had large landholdings in Quito. Manuela's father owned a flourishing im-
port business.

Manuela lived at the Convent of Santa Catalina after her mother died.
She revealed her strong, independent nature very early. She seemed more
drawn to dancing and smoking cigars than to praying. Her seduction by a
young Spanish officer earned her expulsion from the convent. Simón Sáenz
then took his spirited daughter to Panama, where she met Dr. James Thorne,
a wealthy, middle-aged British merchant who fell in love with her. Manuela's
father provided a dowry, and she and Thorne married in 1817.

Thorne's business interests took them to Lima. Once presented to the
viceroy, the vivacious, beautiful, and flirtatious Manuela became a dominant social figure. Her charm and intelligence won her many admirers. The
Spanish viceroy in Lima favored Thorne, perhaps because his ships brought
military supplies for the Royalist forces. Rosa Campuzano, a blond beauty
from Guayaquil, became her best friend. Together they learned, in the words
of William Samuel Waithman Ruschenberger, a U.S. Navy officer, that "Lima
is the heaven of women, the purgatory of men, and the hell of jackasses."
Observing Lima society, Englishman Robert Proctor less profanely noted
that "the ladies of Lima, who are certainly a superior race of beings to the
males, are in this city of vice and enervation the principal actors. Their
dress very much contributes to assist them in carrying on those intrigues
which their education has taught them to believe to be the chief object of
existence."

The typical walking dress of Lima *(saya y manto)*, according to Proctor,
had "the double advantage of showing a good shape in the most exciting
manner, and of completely securing the wearer from recognition." Using this
fashionable disguise, Manuela, Rosa, and more than a hundred other women
functioned as part of the Patriot underground in Lima. Ruschenberger provided a good description of the dress.

> This dress consists of two parts. The *saya*, the lower part, is a silken petti-
> coat, made in folds or plaits, extending from bottom to top, and of nearly
> the same breadth above and below. It sits closely to the figure, and being
> elastic, from the manner in which it is sewed, manifests the contour of

the figure, and the whole muscular play of the body and limbs. The *manto* is a hood of crimped silk, cut bias or diagonally, to give it elasticity. The bottom part of it is gathered full by a drawing string, and, encircling more than half of the body, sits low enough down to hide the top of the *saya*. This hood, drawn up from behind, over the shoulders and head, and covering the elbows and arms, is folded over the face in such a manner as to conceal all but one eye.

Thanks to this dress, women freely carried messages and printed propaganda hidden under their hoods. Even in broad daylight, they could enter the homes of important Royalists without fearing that someone might carry tales to their husbands.

Some women put their charms to work for independence. Rosa Campuzano flirted with José de la Serna (1770–1832), who became viceroy on January 29, 1821. He had arrived as a general in Peru in 1816, fighting under Viceroy Joaquín de la Pezuela. The latter's decision to try to hold Lima at all costs led to his overthrow. La Serna's fellow officers then acclaimed him viceroy. Rosa's charms had recently persuaded the commander of Numancia Battalion and other officers to defect to the Patriots. Manuela persuaded her half brother José, a captain in that battalion, to do the same. Ultimately, these officers persuaded the entire battalion to join San Martín's army on December 2, 1820. She had been living in Lima but returned to her native city, more than eight hundred miles away, ostensibly to handle legal matters concerning her family's lands. She and two devoted slaves had sailed on an English brig from Lima's port of Callao to Guayaquil. There they mounted horses and rode from Guayaquil to Quito, 165 miles up into the Andes. Don Juan de Larrea welcomed her to his home the night before Bolívar's arrival in Quito (not to be confused with the man of the same name who participated in the independence movement in Buenos Aires). It was from Larrea's balcony that Manuela hit Bolívar with the wreath.

The evening of Bolívar's arrival in Quito, Don Juan gave a ball in his honor. When Manuela appeared in the doorway, Don Juan immediately presented her to Bolívar, who bowed and kissed her hand. The coy Manuela, age twenty-six, curtsied politely but then ignored the forty-year-old soldier. She danced with other men until the Liberator, a man not to be denied, sought her out. At midnight they went to the supper room, returned to dance more, then disappeared. The two spent the next twelve days together in amorous bliss.

The pair quickly mixed politics and love, passions for them both. The Liberator asked Manuela many questions about San Martín. She had fervently supported San Martin's government, for which she received in January 1822 membership in the Order of the Sun. This honorary group included 111 "knightesses" *(caballeresas)*, who displayed proudly a red-and-white silk sash with a gold medal bearing the government's coat of arms and the motto "al patriotismo de las mas sensibles [to the patriotism of the most sensible]." Manuela gained intimate knowledge of the Argentine general and his rule in Lima. She told Bolívar of San Martín's illness and of his delaying tactics. The cautious Argentine had refused to press his advantage and expel the Spanish from the port city of Callao, some ten miles from downtown Lima. Founded two years after Lima in 1537, the port on the Rímac River suffered massive destruction from an earthquake and tidal wave in 1746. The fortress of Real Felipe, built during the city's reconstruction, became the key to controlling the port and Lima. Manuela recounted the miserable condition of his decimated army in Lima. She explained to Bolívar why Admiral Lord Cochrane, later earl of Dundonald, and most of the Argentine officers had left San Martín disgusted and dismayed. Cochrane would later put his considerable naval skills at the service for the Brazilian monarchy.

The Liberator and San Martín, the two military giants of South America, had corresponded ever since the latter's liberation of Chile in 1818. Bolívar hammered on the theme of Latin American unity. Writing on June 22, 1822, from Quito, the Liberator asserted that "the interests of a small province must not interrupt the onward march of all South America. United in heart, in spirit, and in aims, this continent must overlook the petty quarrels of the revolution and raise its eyes instead to peer into the centuries which lie ahead." In one of his last letters to San Martín, Bolívar said that he would mass three armies totaling 10,000 to 12,000 troops, ready to sail from Panama and Guayaquil. Bolívar, however, lacked a fleet to move his men. He depended on San Martín to send the ships, something the Argentine general did not do.

The Patriot blockade of Lima had brought death and disease to the city. Viceroy La Serna evacuated on July 6, 1821, stripping the city of all government bullion and other funds, printing presses, and war materiel. The men of Lima's leading Royalist families accompanied him in flight. One of San Martín's generals warned him not to enter Lima and its coastal pestilence, terming it a death trap where their troops would be decimated. He suggested that San Martín go instead to the highlands, where his troops would be healthy and well fed. Public opinion in the highlands favored the Patriots, and San

Martín could organize an army that would assure him victory. San Martín unwisely chose not to heed the advice, entered the bankrupt city on July 10, and proclaimed himself "Protector of Perú." He faced the daunting task of feeding sixty thousand civilians in addition to his army.

Like Manuela, no shrinking violet, Rosa Campuzano did not waste time. All of Lima soon learned that she had settled in as "La Protectora." The stoic San Martín usually ignored women, but Rosa touched his heart as no other woman ever had. She confided to Manuela that he suffered from rheumatism and sharp pains in his stomach that compelled him to take opium. Both Rosa and Manuela noticed the considerable friction between San Martín and Admiral Cochrane. They heard other officers complain of the ever-cautious San Martín's inaction. This situation became critical in September, when La Serna sent Gen. José de Canterac down from the highlands.

Early on the morning of September 10, San Martín positioned his six thousand troops to drive Canterac's thirty-four hundred into the sea. Patriot chief of staff Juan Gregorio de las Heras and other officers begged San Martín to seize the initiative, but he did not budge. Admiral Cochrane also urged San Martín to attack immediately. San Martín replied curtly, "My measures are taken." Cochrane continued to push for action, but San Martín turned to a peasant and made small talk about the man's family. Then he granted an audience to women who wanted their sons discharged from the army. Cochrane renewed his plea, but the Protector stood firm. "I alone am responsible for the liberty of Peru." Then San Martín took his customary afternoon nap. At four o'clock Las Heras awoke him to say that the army remained under arms. San Martín merely ordered that they should receive their rations.

Some officers threatened mutiny, fully aware that San Martín could have captured Canterac, destroyed the Royalist army, and thus secured Peru's independence. Instead he let Canterac depart with his army intact, carrying everything of value that had been left in Callao. A disgusted Cochrane deserted San Martín and sailed away. Most of San Martín's Argentine officers soon asked for their passports and returned home.

Meanwhile, yellow fever and other diseases decimated the Patriot army camped near Lima. One commander observed acidly: "Since the coastal climate of Peru is fatal to the army, and especially to troops of colder areas, San Martín has incorporated into it all the slaves he found or that presented themselves. This procedure harmed the owners of the slaves, ruined agriculture, demoralized the country, and excited great discontent."

San Martín had taken an inordinately long time preparing earlier movements, such as crossing the Andes from Argentina to liberate Chile. He again spent many months minutely planning a big operation. In addition, during the latter part of 1821, "two months of disease so enfeebled him that he was unfit for any effort." His overall strategy was to join Bolívar's army and finish the war during the summer of 1822. To that end, he issued a manifesto on January 12, 1822: "I am going to Guayaquil to meet the Liberator of Colombia. The rapid termination of the war in which we are engaged, and the permanent destiny which America is rapidly approaching, make our meeting necessary, now that the order of events has made us largely responsible for the outcome of this sublime undertaking."

Guayaquil became another test of wills, egos, and real estate for the Liberator and the Protector. On March 3, the latter wrote to Bolívar, arguing that "we must permit Guayaquil to determine its own destiny and to consider its best interests in order to allow it freely to join the area it should choose." The Liberator wanted to outwit San Martín's agents in Guayaquil by joining the port to Gran Colombia before they built irresistible sentiment favoring annexation to Peru. When he received the letter on July 22, the Liberator replied, sharply disagreeing with the Argentine general and dismissing the call for popular sovereignty. "I do not believe as does Your Excellency that the views of a single province should be consulted in order to determine national sovereignty, for not a part but all the people deliberate in those general assemblies which are fully and legally convoked." Bolívar wished to foil the annexation move without antagonizing San Martín unduly. Thanks to inside information and sage advice from Manuela, the Liberator knew what his tactic should be. He wrote to San Martín saying: "It affords me great satisfaction to inform Your Excellency that the war in Colombia is ended; that her army is prepared to march wherever their brothers may call and, in a very special way, to the land of our southern neighbors."

San Martín received this letter on July 13. He also learned from Guayaquil that the Electoral College would meet on July 28 to determine whether the port and province of Guayaquil would remain independent, join Peru, or join Colombia. San Martín immediately wrote Bolívar to congratulate him on his victories, won with the help of Peruvians (San Martín had sent troops to help Sucre win at Pichincha). Then he said "Peru will receive with enthusiasm and gratitude all the troops Your Excellency can spare. I shall sail from the port of Callao, and as soon as I disembark in Guayaquil, I shall march to greet you in Quito."

The Protector of Peru underestimated the speed with which Bolívar could operate. During the next two weeks Bolívar imposed political organization on the province of Quito. He wore out two or three secretaries at a time dictating myriad decrees, orders, and letters. They had time to recover only when officers, priests, and others interrupted the dictation for consultations. Bolívar also sent instructions for Andrés de Santa Cruz, commander of the Peruvian troops who had helped Sucre win at Pichincha.

A mestizo born in La Paz, Bolivia, Santa Cruz (1792–1865) claimed descent from the royal Incas and had won a large following among the Indians of Peru and Bolivia. A Royalist officer, he had switched sides in 1820. After independence he would govern Peru (1826–27) as Bolívar's lieutenant. In 1829 Bolivians elected him their president, but a rival caudillo ousted him after seven years. Like Bolívar, Santa Cruz would fail in his goal of uniting the South American countries. In 1839 he lost another major battle at Yungay to his enemies, led by Chilean Manuel Bulnes, and sailed to exile in Nantes, France, where he died in 1865.

Bolívar ordered Santa Cruz to march south with Colombian troops as far as Riobamba, where they would separate. The Colombian troops would turn west, join Bolívar at Guaranda, and continue to Guayaquil, ninety-four miles southwest of Riobamba. Santa Cruz and his Peruvian troops would march south eighty-seven miles to Cuenca. After recruiting 250 replacements, they would turn west to the port of Naranjal near the mouth of the Guayaquil estuary. After boarding ships, they would sail south seven hundred miles to Lima. Bolívar put the Peruvian troops on this rather long, circuitous route to avoid a confrontation between Peruvians and Colombians over Guayaquil.

Bolívar and his escort left Quito on July 2 and rode south around and between gigantic volcanic mountains. The army moved slowly, so Bolívar had two days to contemplate. He also climbed part way up towering Mount Chimborazo, which rises 20,700 feet above sea level. The volcano, which has not erupted in historical time, is located in a depression that separates the Western and Eastern Cordillera of the Andes in Ecuador. A veil of clouds always hides its glacier-covered peaks. Until Edward Whymper's climb in early 1880, no one knew that four-mile-high Chimborazo actually had two peaks.

Even before he saw it, the "shining, incredible cone" had been an obsession to Bolívar, who had read descriptions of Chimborazo in Humboldt's *Atlas and Voyages*. One night back in May 1817, after Spaniards had almost captured him along the Orinoco, Bolívar prophesied: "I do not know what

View of Chimborazo, mountain peak in Ecuador. Photograph by
Ralph Blessing

Providence had disposed, but she inspires unlimited confidence in me. We
have arrived at Guayaquil, within a few days Angostura will surrender, then
we will liberate New Granada, and create Colombia. We will hoist our tricolor on Chimborazo and carry our victorious banners to Peru." Within a
few months, the powerful mountain would return to him in a dream.

Bolívar arrived in Guayaquil on July 11, where deep political divisions
rent the city. Proponents of complete independence, of union with Peru,
and of union with Colombia all shouted their messages. Two days after his
arrival Bolívar had his chief of staff proclaim the city under his protection.
Bolívar had three thousand Colombian troops stationed in or near
Guayaquil, and he now controlled popular opinion as well. In theory, an
electoral college would meet later in the month to determine Guayaquil's
final fate. In reality, Bolívar assumed civil and military authority, making
Guayaquil a de facto part of Colombia.

Meanwhile, San Martín sailed north from Callao aboard a Chilean warship, the *Macedonia*, on July 14. The ship made the seven-hundred-mile
voyage in eleven days and dropped anchor off the island of Puná at the
mouth of the Guayaquil estuary on July 25, 1822, one day after the Liberator's

thirty-ninth birthday. Manuel Blanco Encalada, admiral of the Chilean fleet, saluted the *Macedonia* from his frigate, *Prueba,* as he prepared to transport Santa Cruz and his troops back to Peru. When San Martín boarded the *Prueba,* three members of the Guayaquil junta reported on Bolívar's dominating presence in the city.

Incensed and frustrated, the Protector wanted to return immediately to Peru. Bolívar held a commanding position militarily and politically. San Martín needed Bolívar's army to prosecute the war in Peru, but the Argentine general, far from home, had only the weakest of political and military support. Under such conditions he could not have expected to deal with Bolívar as an equal. Four aides delivered Bolívar's brief but flattering greeting to the "Protector of Peru."

> Most Excellent Sir: We have this moment been most pleasantly surprised to learn that Your Excellency has arrived off the shores of Guayaquil. My happiness, however, is clouded by the fact that we shall have time to prepare only a meager part of the welcome that is due the Hero of the South, the Protector of Perú.
>
> I am taking the liberty of sending you my aide-de-camp, Colonel [Ignacio] Torres, in order that he may have the honor of complimenting you on my behalf and of requesting Your Excellency to send back one of my aides to advise me when you will honor us with your presence in the city.
>
> I am extremely anxious to meet with you; such a meeting will greatly redound to the benefit of South America, and will satisfy my most fervent desire to greet personally the father of Chile and Perú in token of sincere friendship.

Initially San Martín determined not to meet Bolívar, so the Liberator immediately sent another request, this time addressing him repeatedly as "friend." "A few hours, as you have said, suffice for military men to come to an understanding; but a few hours will hardly be enough to satisfy the demands of friendship, once it has experienced the pleasure of personal acquaintance with one hitherto cherished only through his name and high repute." San Martín sailed upriver the next morning, July 26. Upon meeting, Bolívar and San Martín embraced for the first and last time. A committee of town women and young ladies also greeted the Protector.

San Martín and Bolívar talked alone for several hours, but, alas, we have no independent record of this historic occasion. Bolívar, operating from his position of strength, would not agree to San Martín's requests. The Protector probably asked Bolívar to send his entire army to fight in Peru. Bolívar would have been loath to do so, with simmering unrest in Guayaquil and strong Royalist sentiment less than three hundred miles away in Pasto. The Protector probably even offered to serve under the Liberator's command, an offer Bolívar refused. The Liberator's immense ego could not accept such a potent rival. Practically speaking, Argentine and Peruvian officers loyal to San Martín might rebel against Bolívar's command. San Martín likely took the refusal as a rebuke, which may have spurred his decision to desert the Patriot cause for exile.

The issue of political organization likely divided the two warriors as well. San Martín believed that a European monarch might unite, preserve, and strengthen the new South American nations. Bolívar utterly rejected monarchism and favored a republic, albeit one headed by a powerful, highly centralized presidency. In a letter of September 26, 1822, two months after the fateful meeting, the Liberator addressed the issue bluntly. "Some are prone to think that it is an easy matter to put on a crown and to have all bow before it. But I believe that the era of monarchy is ended, and, until the day that man's depravity goes so far as to still the love of liberty, thrones will never again be in fashion." Having fought steadfastly against Ferdinand VII, Bolívar would not accept the rule of another European king.

At a banquet held in San Martín's honor, Bolívar tried gamely to dispel the Protector's gloom. He jumped to his feet, raised his glass, and toasted: "To the two greatest men in South America, General San Martín and myself." The obvious lack of humility in the toast did nothing to reassure the Argentine soldier about Bolívar's character. The Protector of Peru could not reply with a similar beau geste. His far less grandiose toast telegraphed surrender to the younger man's strategy: "To the early end of the war, to the organization of the various republics of the continent, and to the health of the Liberator of Colombia." San Martín silently left the party at one in the morning, boarded the *Macedonia,* and sailed back to Peru.

Many years later, in 1840, the old soldier candidly described his negative reaction to the Liberator: "At first sight his personal appearance prejudiced me against him. He appeared to have much pride, which was in contrast to his habit of never looking in the face of the person he was addressing unless the latter was by far his inferior. . . . I was able to convince myself of his want of frankness in the conferences I had with him in Guayaquil, for he never responded in a positive manner to my propositions, but always in evasive terms." At least publicly, Bolívar continued to express admiration for the Protector of Peru. "General San Martín came to see me in Guayaquil, and I gathered the same impression of him as did those who have judged him most favorably."

San Martín's "glorious renunciation" came on September 20 when he proclaimed his farewell to Lima. Ten days later he began the long return trip to Buenos Aires. An old, gnarled apple tree, marked with a brass plaque, stands in the foothills of the Andes near the town of Tunuyan, in Mendoza Province in far western Argentina. According to local legend, as recorded on the plaque, San Martín stopped to rest in its shade on his journey back from Peru. His wife died on August 3, 1823. On February 10 the following year, dismayed by the political conflicts engulfing Argentina, he and his daughter Mercedes sailed to self-imposed exile in France. He died on August 17, 1850, having never returned to America. Juan Manuel de Rosas, the obliging military dictator in Argentina, supported his exile with a modest pension.

San Martín, still embittered in his later years and ever distrustful of the masses, who, in his mind, represented anarchy, praised the strength displayed by Rosas. "Liberty! Give a child of two years a box of razors to play with," he wrote to his friend Tomás Guido, "and see what will happen. Liberty! So that all honest men shall see themselves attacked by a licentious press, without laws to protect them, or, if there are laws, they become illusory. Liberty! So that if I devote myself to any kind of work, a revolution shall come and ruin for me the work of many years and the hope of leaving a mouthful of bread to my children."

Bolívar's aide and close friend, Daniel O'Leary, penned contrasting portraits of the two military leaders, which not surprisingly favored the Liberator. "The Argentine, after being rewarded for his services to Peru, abandoned her cause; the Venezuelan after being banished by his compatriots, returned to Colombia and gave them liberty. The former was born and grew up in poverty and acquired a fortune [not exactly accurate]. The latter inherited a large fortune and died almost in poverty. San Martín accepted the title of Protector of Peru; Bolívar rejected the crown offered to him in Colombia. Both were benefactors of their countries, and both were victims of the ingratitude and persecution of the peoples whom their genius and their courage had redeemed."

Like the Argentine general, Bolívar would later seek to sail to European exile. However, in 1822, he would take a stranger journey, not to Europe but into a dreamworld. One October night at Loja, some 166 miles south of Riobamba, Bolívar had been inspecting Patriot defenses, given that the Peruvian border lay just one hundred miles farther south. After he finished his rounds, he went to bed and a feverish delirium engulfed him. When he awoke, Bolívar wrote "Mi delirio sobre el Chimborazo" (My delirium over Chimborazo) (The earliest known copy of the writing is dated Loja, October 13, 1822. This translation comes from T. R. Ybarra, *The Passionate Warrior,* pp. 252–54).

I came, wrapped in the mantle of the dawn, from where the mighty Orinoco pays its tribute to the god of the waters. I had visited the enchanted springs of the Amazon, and I wished to climb the watch-tower of the world. I sought the footsteps of La Condamine, of Humboldt. Boldly I followed them, nothing could hold me back.

I reached the glacial regions, where the air was so thin that I could scarcely breathe. Never before had human foot trodden the diamond crown placed by the Eternal Father on the lofty brow of the King of the Andes. "Wrapped in this mantle," I exclaimed, "which has served as my banner, I have traversed the infernal regions, crossed rivers and seas, climbed the shoulders of the Andes. Under the feet of Colombia, the Earth has flattened itself, and Time himself has been unable to check the march of Liberty. The goddess of war has been humbled by the light of dawn— wherefore, then, should I not be able to trample upon the white hairs of Chimborazo, giant of the earth; wherefore not; I will!"

Impelled by a spirit of violence hitherto unknown to me, that appeared to me divine, I left behind the footsteps of Humboldt and set out to climb beyond the eternal belt of cloud shrouding Chimborazo. As if driven forward by this unknown spirit within me, I reached the summit; and, as I touched with my head the pinnacle of the firmament and saw at my feet a yawning abyss, I fell in a swoon.

Feverish delirium engulfed my mind. I felt as if inflamed by strange, supernatural fire. The God of Colombia had taken possession of me.

Suddenly Time stood before me—in the shape of a venerable old man, bearing the weight of all the centuries, frowning, bent, bald, wrinkled, a scythe in the hand.

"I am the Father of the Centuries! I am the Guardian of fame and the secrets of life. My Mother was Eternity; the limits of My Empire are the Infinite. For me there is no tomb, because I am more powerful than Death. I gaze upon the Past, the Future, and through my hands goes the Present. Why think vain thoughts, you of the human race, whether you be young or old, sunk in obscurity or cast in heroic mold?

"Think you that this universe of yours is anything, that to fight your way to eminence on an atom of creation is to raise yourselves? Think you that the infinitesimal moments you call centuries can serve for measuring my secrets? Think you that holy truth has been vouchsafed to you? Think you in your madness that your actions have any value in my eyes? All about you is less than a dot in the presence of the Infinite, who is my brother!"

Filled with terror, I replied: "Surely, oh Time! the miserable mortal who has climbed this high must perish! All men have I surpassed in good fortune, for I have raised myself above all. The earth lies at my feet; I touch Eternity; beneath me I feel the throbbing of Hell; beside me I contemplate radiant planets, suns of infinite dimensions. I gaze upon the realms of space which enclose matter; I decipher, on your brow, the history of the past and the thoughts of Destiny."

"Man!" spake Time to me. "Observe! Learn! Preserve before your mind what you have seen, trace for your fellow men the picture of the physical universe, of the moral universe. Hide not the secrets which Heaven has revealed to you! Speak the Truth to mankind!"

The phantom disappeared. Speechless, stupefied, unconscious, I lay for a long time stretched out upon the enormous diamond which served me for a couch. Finally, the ringing voice of Colombia summoned me. I returned to life! Rising to my feet, I opened with my fingers my heavy eyelids, became a man once more, wrote down what I had heard and seen in my Delirium!"

The dream, the images, the audacity fit well with the mystical Bolívar's complex personality when awake. Why should he be different when delirious? He had conversed with Time! Why not? What mortal was his equal? Seemingly purified of his fears and doubts, he resumed the heavy burden of leading his people to freedom. Yet despite the great strides made toward independence in 1822, the Liberator's toil had not ended. Royalists in Pasto again threatened the republic there. Back in Venezuela, Morales had escaped from Puerto Cabello and regained Maracaibo. Chaos threatened in Lima, where rival factions in council of government fought each other, and General Canterac kept the Royalist threat alive in the highlands. Their troops could descend on the coast, raid, and kill, but they could not depart with Patriots in control of Lima and its port of Callao. Furthermore, the Royalists had no ships and Spain could not send them any. Could Bolívar hold Gran Colombia together and free Peru as well, thus finally banishing Royalists from South America?

CHAPTER 13

Final Triumph in Peru, 1823–25

The expected Royalist uprising in Pasto began on October 28, 1822. Bolívar quickly sent Sucre from Quito to crush the rebellions, which he did in November and again in December. When Bolívar arrived in Pasto on January 1, 1823, he offered to pardon anyone who surrendered hidden arms and munitions and swore allegiance to Colombia. Only a few rebels appeared, so Bolívar retaliated with heavy fines on the province and the confiscation of enemy property. He departed for the south at the end of January, stopped briefly in Quito, and rode into Guayaquil on February 5.

The diplomatic scene in Colombia improved as Charles S. Todd, of Kentucky, arrived in Bogotá on a special mission from the United States. This gesture strengthened the ties established in the United States by Colombian chargé Manuel Torres and, later, ambassador José María Salazar. Also in January, the U.S. Senate confirmed another Kentuckian, Richard C. Anderson, as the nation's first minister plenipotentiary to Colombia. However, things did not remain quiet on the political front for long. Developments in Peru soon forced the Liberator to travel there, where he found junta members in Lima warring with each other and with Congress. All the Peruvians shared one thing in common, however, their dislike of outsiders—the Colombian troops. The junta had shipped the troops Bolívar had sent back to Guayaquil, demanding arms, not troops. The disruptions of war had paralyzed Lima's trade and credit. In the unhealthy coastal climate, Argentine, Peruvian, and Chilean troops became sick and demoralized. At the same time, Viceroy La Serna maintained a strong Royalist position from his base at Huancayo and later Cuzco in the highlands, enjoying abundant food and clothing.

The junta adopted San Martín's plan to launch an expedition inland from Arica, the port on Peru's southern coast (today part of Chile). Royalist spies in Lima informed Viceroy La Serna, who ordered Royalist troops down from the mountains toward Arica, where they allowed the Patriots to advance a few miles inland. On January 21, 1823, the Royalists destroyed the best corps that San Martín had assembled and trained; only a fourth of the troops escaped back to the coast.

Angry army officers demanded that Congress throw out the junta and name José de la Riva Agüero president. Congress dismissed the junta, but it selected the Marquis de Torre Tagle instead of Riva Agüero. The next day Andrés de Santa Cruz led the army into Lima and forced Congress to install Riva Agüero as president. Riva Agüero, a Creole about the same age as Bolívar, faced stiff opposition from pro-Spanish members of Congress.

The new president gave Santa Cruz command of the army. He requested help from the Chileans and asked Bolívar to come to Peru. On March 18, 1823, Bolívar sent Manuel Valdés with three thousand troops to aid Riva Agüero. Santa Cruz's emissary urged Bolívar to direct the Peruvian campaign. The Liberator replied, "Very soon the Republic of Colombia will have sent 6,000 troops to her brothers of the South. If the General Congress of Colombia does not oppose my absence, I shall have the honor of being a soldier of the Grand Army of America congregated on the soil of the Incas."

Bolívar recognized the urgent need and opportunity for leadership in Peru, but he also recognized the dangers if he lacked sufficient public support. "Everyone says that unless I go to Peru, the 15,000 men from four American nations will be lost for lack of a leader to command them; for among equals no one is willing to take orders. If Congress permits me to march to Peru, I shall leave immediately." Ever seeing a dark side of the Liberator's actions, General Ducoudray Holstein imputed a baser, more selfish motive. "Instead of remaining in his native country and employing all the means in his power to establish a solid government, we see him, even as early as 1822, seeking a new field for his ambition, a new scene of what he deems his glory."

The Liberator clearly foresaw the political dangers that beset a military leader as forceful, ambitious, and successful as he. "I have the secret fear," he wrote to Riva Agüero, "that my enemies will regard my trip to Lima with envy. There was only one Bonaparte, and our America has already had three Caesars. My three colleagues, San Martín, O'Higgins, and Iturbide, have already suffered an ill fate because they did not love freedom. And I do not wish even a faint suspicion to make me appear like them. The desire to end the war in America drives me to Peru, and the love of my reputation holds me back at the same time. . . . Nevertheless, I am inclined to think that, if it is so destined, my love for my country will triumph." Bolívar sent Sucre to Lima as minister plenipotentiary. Sucre disembarked at Callao on May 2 and found Santa Cruz preparing 5,500 troops for a second expedition to the south. He planned to sail 634 miles south to the port of Arica, march inland 200 hundred miles up into the mountains to La Paz in Upper Peru, follow the royal road back north around Lake Titicaca, and then conquer Cuzco (Cusco).

Santa Cruz sailed south at the end of May just as Canterac's forces descended the 123 miles from Huancayo to threaten Lima. Faced with an invasion crisis, Congress deposed Riva Agüero. Pending Bolívar's arrival, Sucre assumed political and military command of the threatened region. Many families fled Lima for the port city of Callao, where Sucre had three thousand Colombian troops. Riva Agüero and his followers sailed to Trujillo, three hundred miles to the north. Canterac met no resistance when he marched into Lima on June 17. It would be hollow victory, however, for the same day Santa Cruz landed at Arica and began the trek up to La Paz, more than 12,500 feet above sea level. When Canterac learned of the threat from the south to his highland bases, he ordered Jerónimo Valdés with twenty-five hundred troops to assist La Serna. He then evacuated Lima on July 17 to undertake operations against Santa Cruz.

Three days later Sucre sailed south to the port of Quilco to join the three thousand Colombian troops he had sent to aid Santa Cruz. Sucre had advanced inland only a few leagues when he learned of another devastating Royalist victory over Santa Cruz. Only six hundred infantry and three hundred cavalry remained of his fifty-five hundred troops, so the outmanned Sucre withdrew to the coast and sailed back to Callao. Royalists had smashed Patriot forces twice in six months.

Political disaster accompanied the military defeats as dissension in Lima continued to plague the Patriots. A rump congress named Torre Tagle president. Riva Agüero raised an army of three thousand troops in Trujillo, intending to dissolve Congress, and Sucre had not yet returned from the south. On August 3, Bolívar finally received permission from the Colombian Congress to depart for Peru. On September 1, 1823, a salute from the batteries of Callao announced Bolívar's arrival, and all the troops in Lima marched to the Callao road and escorted him into the city. "Lima seemed to give herself up to the most enthusiastic expression of admiration for this successful warrior," observed English visitor Robert Proctor. "Nothing was heard for about a week but addresses to and amusements for him." The Lima congress granted Bolívar supreme political and military authority. As O'Leary described it, "when he entered the chamber, the entire audience burst into wild applause, and all the members of Congress stood up to show their respect." Gen. William Miller summed up the situation: "Torre Tagle retained his title, but such was his admiration of Bolívar and such his fears of Riva Agüero that the power of the president was reduced to a mere phantom of authority."

Manuela Sáenz arrived at Callao from Quito in the middle of September with her two slaves. She returned to her home near the sea in Magdalena de la Mar. Bolívar's headquarters at the viceregal villa stood only a few squares away. Bolívar's staff liked Manuela; she proved good tonic for the Liberator. Bolívar even accepted a remarkable suggestion from O'Leary. He put Manuela on his staff with the rank of colonel, and she took charge of his personal archives. She remained in command at his headquarters when he marched north to deal with Riva Agüero in Trujillo in November. A woman had emerged from the ranks of female spies and camp followers to serve as a Patriot officer.

Bolívar patiently tried diplomacy to bring Riva Agüero back into the fold, but the traitorous Riva Agüero negotiated with the enemy to drive Bolívar, Sucre, and all Colombians from Peru. Bolívar did not want civil war, and he needed Riva Agüero's troops to take on the Spanish. Bolívar did win the allegiance of some rebel officers, one of whom took Riva Agüero prisoner on November 25. Bolívar ordered the rebel to Guayaquil and then to European exile. The Liberator now controlled Peru's northern provinces of Trujillo and Cajamarca.

Bolívar took immediate action to prepare his forces to reverse the recent, demoralizing Spanish victories. First he reversed San Martín's unwise decision to quarter the troops on the pestilential coast. He ordered Sucre inland, where the troops could be well fed in mountain valleys while they trained to fight on mountains and plains. Using lead from the mines of Huamachuco and Cerro de Pasco, Sucre established arsenals and forges where workers forged new lance tips, nails, and horseshoes. Patriots in Trujillo sewed uniforms, while others crafted lance shafts of tough, lightweight cacao wood from Loja, Cuenca, and Guayaquil. The Patriots fashioned llanero lances, twelve to fourteen feet long, far longer than Canterac's lances, which measured only six to eight feet in length. While thicker and heavier, the Spanish lances lacked the flexibility of Colombian lances. The difference in cavalry armament would favor the Patriots.

Colombian reinforcements from Panama and Guayaquil arrived at ports along the Trujillo coast. Francis Burdett O'Connor arrived with the first contingent. Bolívar sent him to Sucre, who dispatched him on an inspection tour of his bases. At Yungay O'Connor watched a German sergeant major, Philipp (Felipe) Braun, drill a squadron of mounted lancers. Braun finished the drill, then called a lancer out of formation. The lancer skillfully put the whole corps through its paces with the greatest precision. Braun assured O'Connor that each of his lancers could do the same.

Meanwhile the United States finally appeared to be coming to the aid of the Patriot cause. President James Monroe delivered his seventh annual message to Congress on December 2, 1823. Embedded in his remarks, crafted with assistance from Secretary of State John Quincy Adams, emerged ideas that would have long-lasting impact on relations between the United States and Latin America. Recognizing the imminent end of Spanish colonialism in Latin America, the Monroe Doctrine asserted that the newly independent nations should "henceforth not be considered as subjects for future colonization by any European powers." The American president drew a sharp line between Old World monarchy and New World republicanism. Monroe then linked the destinies of North and South America: "we should consider any attempt on their part [Europe, including Russia] to extend their system to any portion of this hemisphere as dangerous to our peace and safety." With a few cogent paragraphs, Monroe seemingly served warning to the Holy Alliance that America, North and South, was and would remain in the control of Americans.

Most European powers dismissed the bluster of the upstart republic, but some American politicians wanted to give the doctrine teeth. On January 20, 1824, the ever energetic Henry Clay asked Congress to go on record "that the people of these United States would not see, without serious inquietude, any forcible interposition by the Allied Powers of Europe in behalf of Spain, to reduce to their former subjection those parts of the continent of America which have proclaimed and established for themselves, respectively, independent Governments, and which have been solemnly recognized by the United States." Clay's resolution died of neglect, tabled and ignored for seven months, a harbinger of the direction of American policy. The Senate never considered the resolution at all.

Many Latin American leaders welcomed the belated expression of support from the north. Vice President Santander termed the message "an act worthy of the classic land of liberty" that "might secure to Colombia a powerful ally in case her independence and liberty should be menaced by the allied powers." Furthermore, on December 12, 1823, American minister Richard C. Anderson had arrived in Bogotá. The *Gaceta de Colombia* warmly greeted his arrival saying that he "cannot fail to inspire the most pleasing sensations in the bosom of every friend of liberty." Adams, however, quickly quashed such optimism. Seven months after Monroe's speech, Colombian minister to the United States José María Salazar expressed pleasure "that the government of the United States has undertaken to oppose the policy and the ulterior designs of the Holy Alliance." He then asked, rather pointedly, "in what manner the government of the United States intends to resist any interference of the Holy Alliance," and whether the United States would "enter into a treaty of alliance with her [Colombia] to save America from the calamities of a despotic system."

On August 6, 1824, Monroe dashed Colombia's hopes for such an alliance and revealed the Monroe Doctrine as more rhetorical than substantive. "By the constitution of the United States, the ultimate decision of this question belongs to the Legislative Department of the Government." Adams reaffirmed that the United States would retain its traditional stance of neutrality and that it "could not undertake resistance to them [the Holy Alliance] by force of Arms." So much for help from the sister republic to the north. Writing to Santander on March 8, 1825, Bolívar recognized the disjuncture between words and actions and reflected acidly: "The English and the [North] Americans are only possible future allies, and they have their own selfish interests."

Bereft of meaningful assistance from the United States, the Patriot forces also faced continued internal political unrest, this time in Callao, Peru. On the night of February 4–5, 1824, leaders of the Callao garrison seized and confined all their officers. Their commanding officer had kept the payroll instead of paying the men. The mutineers demanded back pay and free passage from Peru, but Congress did nothing. Royalist prisoners in Callao convinced the mutineers to hoist the Royalist flag. They raised the Spanish flag over Callao and sent envoys to Canterac.

Manuela's slave Jonatás frequently visited one of the mutineers, who warned Manuela. She quickly packed Bolívar's archives, uniforms, gold service plate, and her clothes. When Gen. William Miller learned of a Royalist division approaching Lima and Callao, he hastened with a cavalry corps to meet Manuela. They escaped by night across the coastal desert north of Lima. Torre Tagle opened the gates of Lima to Gen. Juan Antonio Monet as the Spanish again occupied Lima and Callao without bloodshed.

In January Bolívar had lay feverish and almost unconscious for six days at Patilvica. Joaquín Mosquera visited him to see if he could help. He found

Bolívar seated on a rawhide stool, resting his small, bony frame against a wall. Mosquera asked, "What do you expect to do now?" "Triumph," replied Bolívar, optimistic even in sickness. "I am building a strong cavalry. Every good horse in the country has been requisitioned, and I have embargoed all the alfalfa to fatten them. If the Spaniards come down from the cordillera, I will destroy them with my cavalry. If they do not come down, when I have the force to attack, I will ascend the cordillera and destroy them in Jauja."

The Royalist army included 18,000 men. The viceroy expected to open the campaign against Bolívar with 12,000 troops. "All the insurgents had succumbed to the arms of Castile," wrote Spanish historian Mariano Torrente. "The only rebel that survived was the obstinate Bolívar, isolated in a small town; and although he had from 4,000 to 6,000 Colombians and 4,000 Peruvians, they were greatly disheartened and were without resources." (Bolívar reported that he had 7,000 Colombian and 3,000 Peruvian troops.)

Bolívar did not open his offensive until he made certain that Canterac and Jerónimo Valdés could not unite against him. The Spanish faced their own serious political divisions, as rumors spread that Gen. Pedro Antonio de Olañeta (1770–1825) in Upper Peru had usurped Viceroy La Serna's authority. Olañeta had declared against La Serna, a constitutionalist, for not obeying God and King Ferdinand and declared himself the lawful ruler of Upper Peru. La Serna needed Olañeta and his four thousand troops, so he dispatched Valdés with five thousand troops to regain his allegiance.

Olañeta faced problems within his own ranks and family. His nephew, Josef Joaquín Casimiro Olañeta (1795–1860), born in Chuquisaca (now Sucre), served as his secretary. However, the nephew adroitly deserted in 1824, as the Royalist fate appeared doomed, and allied himself with the Patriots. He would later exercise tremendous political power in Bolivia, usually behind the scenes. His Machiavellian activities earned him the dubious nickname "Dos Caras" (Two-Faced).

Bolívar knew of this internal Royalist conflict by the second week of April. He laid out his battle plan. "The rest of this month [April] we will prepare, in May we will march, and in June we will fight." His timetable reflected the Liberator's customary optimism. By the end of May, however, horses had been shod, and each cavalryman had a mule to ride in order to rest his horse. Each division had sufficient supplies for the campaign. The Patriots had a three-hundred-mule train loaded with ammunition. Riders had rounded up a herd of six thousand cattle to feed the army as it moved in three sections to converge at the foot of Peru's mighty Cerro de Pasco, about one hundred miles northeast of Lima.

José de la Mar's Peruvians, based at Cajamarca, nearly three hundred miles away from Cerro de Pasco, had the longest march. Jacinto Lara commanded one division of Colombians; José María Córdoba, the other. Lara positioned his troops along the Río Santa Gorge between La Mar's cavalry and Córdoba's division at Huaras. Each division snaked along the contours of gorges and mountains. The thin air impeded their march, and *soroche* felled entire battalions. As darkness descended, trumpeters along the trail guided the end of the long columns to camp. The cold Andean nights afflicted man and beast. Sucre, however, had prepared barracks, piles of firewood, food for the troops, as well as sheds and forage for the horses. "The horses were covered with blankets the nights we were in the sierras," recalled General Miller, "with the result that they were almost as fat as those of the Royalists fed on alfalfa and maize in the rich valley of Jauja. Most of the horses were of Chilean stock."

All elements of the Patriot army, totaling almost nine thousand men, reached the foot of Cerro de Pasco by late July. More Colombians arrived several days later. Unhappily, old divisions opened among the Peruvian troops, and factions developed. Bolívar, long plagued by internal strife, called together his fractious chiefs. He named La Mar commander in chief of the Peruvian army and Mariano Necochea commanding general of all the cavalry of the united army. Miller served under Necochea as commander of the Peruvian cavalry. The Colombian cavalry had no single commander, but a leader as capable as Felipe Braun commanded each squadron.

On July 29 the whole army assembled on the high plain of Cerro de Pasco, a dizzying 12,400 feet above sea level. Bolívar staged a grand parade in which Córdoba's division marched on the right, the Army of Peru in the center, and Lara's division and Necochea's cavalry on the left. Bolívar, Sucre, La Mar, and other officers reviewed their forces. "The morning sun was temperate," recalled Col. Manuel Antonio López. "The perpetually snow-covered peaks of the Andes diffused its luminous rays in all the rainbow colors, and the arms of soldiers reflecting them made an ideal picture of legions at ease. Music of the bands caused the air to vibrate with martial echoes and inflamed the breasts of these soldiers of liberty. Bolívar saw enthusiasm and assurance on each countenance." Three days later Canterac broke camp at Jauja and marched toward Cerro de Pasco. In response Bolívar marched his troops from Pasco on August 4, leaving the Cerro de Pasco to Jauja road open for Canterac. Bolívar took the road west around the head of Lago de Reyes. This fifteen-mile-long lake between two ranges of the cordillera occupies a broad expanse of lower ground. The road on the eastern side of the lake is level; on the western side the road is craggy and difficult.

Bolívar took the arduous western route because he knew that Canterac would never take it. On August 5 his scouts reported seeing Canterac on the opposite side of the lake, heading north to Cerro de Pasco. Bolívar put nine hundred cavalry in the van, with Felipe Braun's well-trained squadron leading. The main army continued its march south. A greatly surprised Canterac found only a few sick troops and stragglers at Cerro de Pasco. They told him that he must have passed Bolívar, so Canterac reversed direction and raced down the eastern road to prevent Bolívar from cutting him off from his base.

At 2 P.M. on August 6, scouts spotted Canterac at the town of Reyes, seven miles to the east. An hour or so later, Canterac saw Patriot cavalry descending the narrow pass onto the plain of Junín. This plateau stands near the towns of Jauja and Cerro de Pasco at an elevation of nine thousand feet. Canterac deployed about sixteen thousand men to Bolívar's nine thousand. In what is probably unique in nineteenth-century warfare, both sides deployed only cavalry; not a gunshot was fired. Canterac observed that when the cavalry came out of the pass, it would have to skirt the swamp at the southern end of the lake. Mountains to the west would force the Patriot cavalry to move east. An elated Canterac ordered a frontal attack with his cavalry. His seemingly invincible cavalry outnumbered the enemy by four hundred. He dared not take time to get his infantry in battle formation. The delay might let Bolívar snatch victory from him. He sent his infantry down the road toward Jauja on the double.

By the time that Canterac had positioned his cavalry, Felipe Braun had readied his lancers for battle. They lined up along the edge of the swamp, the horses' long tails dangling in the mire. They dropped their reins, leaving both hands free to wield their lances. Miller, followed by Isidoro Suárez, cut through the swamp behind Braun. As he emerged on Braun's left, Canterac, at the head of his cavalry, gave the order to charge at full gallop. Canterac's right wing, somewhat out of line because of the long charge, pulled their horses to a stop fifteen paces from Braun. The Patriot cavalry sat motionless, lances level and ready.

At a signal from Braun's bugler, his long-lanced cavalry sprang at the Spaniards, pierced them in the belly, lifted them two or three feet from the saddle, and flipped them to the ground. Having broken through the Royalist line, they wheeled about and charged the enemy rear. At the same time, the rest of Bolívar's lancers struck the Royalist right. Those Spaniards still uninjured turned and fled, not out of cowardice but because they stood no chance against the long, deadly Colombian lances.

The battle, which lasted a mere forty-five minutes, determined the fate of Peru. Canterac's cavalry had lost its aura of invincibility. The defeat further demoralized Royalist troops and supporters. They could no longer count on intelligence and assistance from people in the countryside. Canterac's troops left more than three hundred horses on the plains of Junín. More important, they lost their confidence in the face of the disciplined, audacious Colombian lancers. The Patriots did not escape unscathed. Lt. Col. Charles Sowerby, born in Bremen of English parents in 1795, suffered two lance wounds and died in the arms of his friend General Miller. General Necochea also suffered a wound, leaving the cavalry under the command of General Miller, who displayed great heroism and leadership that day. José Joaquín Olmedo (1782–1847), Ecuadorian statesman and poet, glorified the Liberator's great victory with his ode *La victoria de Junín* (The victory at Junín), penned in 1825. The poet later served as Ecuador's ambassador to Paris and London after independence.

The defeated Canterac retreated 450 miles south to the ancient Incan capital of Cuzco. Monet left Lima with his troops and joined Canterac. A depressed La Serna sent orders to Jerónimo Valdés to forget about Olañeta and bring all his troops to Cuzco. La Serna and the liberal Spanish officers had supported the movement to restore Spain's 1812 constitution. They left Spain in 1817, having endured three years of the absolute rule of Ferdinand VII. They rejoiced when the 1820 revolution forced Ferdinand to restore the 1812 constitution. They did not know, however, that the French armies of Louis XVIII had invaded Spain in the summer of 1823, nor that on October 1, 1823, the absolutist Ferdinand had abolished the liberal constitution.

The inept monarch and his ineffective underlings had failed their nation badly. But Ferdinand had not yet finished bedeviling his nation. Upon his death in 1833, he left no male heir. Before expiring, he passed over his brother Carlos in favor of his daughter, who became Isabella II. This final machination precipitated the so-called Carlist wars between supporters of the two aspirants, conservatives backing Carlos and liberals behind Isabella. The latter would preside over Spain's disorderly slide until an army revolt forced her into exile in 1868. Ferdinand died deluded and convinced that he could yet recover Spain's lost colonies. Spain's economy declined along with its political leadership. Cádiz, the once vital center of Spanish trade, became a mercantile backwater. By 1824, the city's three hundred shipowners had declined to twenty. Bereft of its rich colonies, Spain's overall economy spiraled downward, not to recover for 150 years.

A nation with a gift for denial, Spain would only slowly, begrudgingly recognize the legal existence of its now independent colonies: Mexico in 1836, Ecuador in 1840, Venezuela in 1845. Colombia would not be recognized until 1881, and Honduras in 1895, shortly before inept Spain would lose its last New World colonies, Cuba and Puerto Rico. The nation, already "beggarly," in Adam Smith's estimation, faced a long political and economic slide that continued into the twentieth century. In the war of 1898, Spain lost its last colonies of Cuba, Puerto Rico, and the Philippines to the United States. A tragic three-year civil war ended in 1939 with the fascist dictatorship of Francisco Franco. Recovery only began slowly, with Franco's death in November 1975.

Ferdinand's actions also had negative repercussions in the New World as internecine warfare broke out between his absolutist supporters and liberal opponents. Ferdinand's absolute government in Madrid could not send help to La Serna and his generals. It could not even communicate with them or with Olañeta in Upper Peru. Olañeta, however, had read in a Buenos Aires newspaper of the restoration of the old regime in Spain. Several weeks passed before La Serna and his generals knew that this restoration had triggered Olañeta's rebellion on December 25, 1823, when he attacked the Spanish liberals. Now, after the rout at Junín, the demoralized troops must have asked themselves: "Why are we fighting? For whom? Why not end this farce and make its last act something we want to remember?" Once again, changing political fortunes in Europe played a strong role in shaping New World history.

Torrential rains forced Bolívar and his army to pause frequently as they moved toward the Chalhuanca valley. They occupied an extended observation line from there to the west bank of the Apurimac River. Cuzco lay east of the Apurimac. Bolívar decided to depart the Chalhuanca valley, return to the coast, besiege Callao, and take Lima from the garrison Juan Antonio Monet had left there. Bolívar turned over command of the army to the capable Sucre and left Sañaico on October 6. Sucre would retake Lima, ably supported by seasoned, capable officers, including Cordóba, Braun (promoted to lieutenant colonel after his stellar performance at Junín), and La Mar. After independence had been won, Braun would ably serve in the Bolivian army, earning the rank of general, until his assassination in 1839.

At Huancayo on October 24, 1824, Bolívar received unhappy news of further political intrigue in Bogotá. Congress had passed a law on July 28 revoking Bolívar's extraordinary powers and transferring them to Santander. The Congress gave as their reason that Bolívar had accepted the dictatorship of Peru. Another dispatch from Santander ordered Bolívar to give Sucre command of the Colombian troops. This order changed nothing in Peru as Bolívar had already placed Sucre in command, not only of Colombian troops but also of the whole united army. Divisiveness again rent the always tenuous Patriot unity.

An angry Bolívar went to seek solace from Manuela. She and her escort had followed three days behind Bolívar as he pursued Canterac. She had stopped in the Jauja valley near Huancayo and remained there during the worst months of the rainy season. Like Bolívar, she understood that Santander had undermined the Liberator's authority in Bogotá. They also realized, however, that until Bolívar could return to Bogotá as president of Colombia, he needed Santander's cooperation. Manuela and Bolívar spent two nights together, then Manuela returned to Lima. Bolívar rode toward Cerro de Pasco to hasten the march of convalescents to Sucre, before turning west to the coast.

The Liberator arrived at Chancay in early November, a port forty miles north of Callao. On November 10 he dictated a friendly letter to Santander, using the charm and diplomacy that had so often turned foe into friend. He informed the Colombian that since the decisive victory at Junín, he had liberated more than twenty provinces without firing a shot. He reassured Santander that Sucre now commanded the army. Three days later Bolívar praised and thanked Santander for the troops he had sent. "If they had not come," Bolívar told him, "Spanish chains would have afflicted Peru for many more years."

A grateful Lima welcomed Bolívar when he entered the city on December 5, 1824. He undertook a typically rugged work schedule that included the first steps toward making his dream of a Pan American Congress a reality. He invited representatives of Mexico, Guatemala (which then included the five current nations of Central America), Colombia, Chile, and the Río de la Plata to meet in Panama in the following year.

Manuela noticed that Bolívar grew increasingly distracted and irritable, and she knew why. Letters from Sucre and others reported the movements of the Royalist and Patriot armies in the Sierras as they maneuvered for position. The final great battle for independence would take place without Bolívar, a stunning blow to his ego and his quest for glory. During the last week of September, La Serna had reorganized his forces. He could not give Canterac top command because of his defeat at Junín and his intense rivalry with Valdés. In a compromise solution, the viceroy named himself commander in chief and made Canterac his chief of staff. Monet, Alejandro González Villalobos, and Valdés served as Royalist division commanders.

By October 24, the entire Royalist army had crossed the Apurimac and camped at Acosvinchos. Sucre's army camped at Lambrana on the right bank of the Oropesa River.

Three major rivers, the Oropesa, Chalhuanca-Pachachac, and the Pampas, drop almost straight down from the west into the Apurimac River. Their collective waters eventually empty into the Amazon. La Serna planned to swing south around Sucre, cross the three swollen tributaries on Sucre's left, march to the plain of Ayacucho near Juamanga, and await Sucre's forces.

Sucre's army crossed the Pachachac as La Serna's crossed the Oropesa. Sucre could move more slowly, thanks to a shorter, inside line. The two armies advanced about a hundred miles as the rains subsided in November. On December 6 Sucre ordered F. Burdett O'Connor to find a position "from which to finish this campaign once for all."

O'Connor climbed a crest and observed the enemy army nine miles to the west on the far side of Acocro Quebrada. He also spotted a suitable plain and scouted it well. The plain of Ayacucho dropped gently west for three-quarters of a mile from the base of Cundurcunca Mountain (Quechua for "condor's nest"). A narrow three-eighths of a mile wide at the eastern end, it broadened slightly to the west. Mountains with steep gullies at their bases flanked the plain to the north and south.

Later that day Valdés, leading La Serna's van, climbed to the crest of a mountain. A mile and a half to the east, he saw Sucre's army on the plain of Ayacucho, more than ten thousand feet in elevation. La Serna, Canterac, and Valdés conferred and agreed that they could not strike from the west. They camped that night on the mountain, believing that Sucre would continue his retreat. The next day, however, Sucre remained on the plain. La Serna circled around the mountains that enclosed Ayacucho. He camped on a height north of Sucre on the night of December 7. The next day he marched around ridges to the eastern side of Cundurcunca. That afternoon Patriots watched the Royalists come from behind the mountain and march to a position halfway down Cundurcunca's side, only a cannon shot away from them. Two hours before sunset, the Royalists descended almost to the plain. What followed looked more like a ballet than a battle. At the sound of bugles, Royalists and Patriots executed movements almost touching each other. The two sides suspended fire at intervals, and various opposing officers advanced and conversed together. As Gen. William Miller recalled, "nothing could exceed the audacious, gallant conduct of troops on both sides." Miller returned in 1826 to London for a time, but then in 1834 came back to Peru and commanded the army. He died in Callao in 1861.

Why this mutual display of bravado instead of a blood-and-guts fight? "Fighting was our recreation," Col. Manuel Antonio López reminds us. "The day of battle was a special day of fiesta for the soldier. The long days of marching tired the body, and the daily routine of camp did nothing for the soul." In reality, both sides recognized that the long conflict had come to an end. Royalists needed to satisfy honor and propriety, but their cause was finished. Spain's long reign in South America had ended.

Both armies slept that night in the open air, two and a half miles above sea level. On December 9 the sound of more than forty bugle and drum corps greeted the sun as it rose over Cundurcunca. Royalist ranks numbered some ten thousand men, while the Patriots fielded fewer than six thousand. They could all be heard at the same time in the Ayacucho amphitheater. Patriot Col. Manuel Antonio López recalled the poignancy of the moment:

> Corps of opposing camps saluted each other courteously; and tumultuous harmony, like strong liquor, intoxicated our spirits. We had no other on which to get drunk.
>
> It was one of those cold but tonic mornings when the air is pure ether, distances are shortened, and the earth is lifted up and bathed in the floating blue of the firmament. One feels that he has wings, and everything is so beautiful that even war loses its horror and death its melancholy. Everyone felt that he was of divine origin, and that nothing was going to take place that would be casual or insignificant.

The battle had an auspicious prelude.

General Monet came down to the Patriot line at eight o'clock. He asked for General Córdoba, to whom he had spoken the night before. Monet requested permission for friends and relatives to cross the line. More than fifty men did so. According to historian Salvador de Madariaga, the two division commanders, Córdoba and Monet, may have discussed surrender terms. The fraternizing lasted half an hour, then the armies ate breakfast. At about eleven o'clock both armies assumed their starting positions. La Serna's formed partway up "the Condor's Nest"; Sucre's, on the plain. Monet's division occupied the center of the Royalist line, Valdés's on the left, Villalobos's on the right. Sucre took the center of his line. La Mar's division stood opposite that of Valdés, and Córdoba's opposite Villalobos.

Impassive Indians, wrapped in multicolored blankets, appeared as bright dots on the heights flanking the opposite armies. A vast sea of varied colors ebbed and flowed below the spectators. Sucre's army had uniforms with blue, green, or flesh-colored trimmings. Royalist uniforms shone even more vividly. The different, brightly colored uniforms of twenty-six or twenty-seven Royalist corps made it easier for the commander in chief to move them about. As López noted, "an artist would have enjoyed seeing those long mobile lines of color that gracefully variegated the straw-green slope of Cundurcunca: the white, blue, green, gray, yellow, terra cotta, flesh and other hues of that dress parade as it executed about turns and evolutions."

Sucre reviewed his line and told his troops, "The fate of South America depends on your efforts today." Monet came down to Córdoba and asked, "Are you ready for battle?" "We are ready," replied the Patriot officer. When Sucre gave the starting signal, Córdoba audaciously dismounted in front of his troops, killed his horse, and shouted: "Forward! Step of conquerors!"

The battle of Ayacucho lasted but two hours. Both sides suffered casualties but not nearly as many as would be expected with such large forces. Monet's center broke first. Patriots wounded La Serna and took him prisoner. After enough blood had been shed to satisfy honor and the verdict of history, the Royalist officers surrendered. The capitulation terms provided that all remaining Royalist forces in Peru would also surrender, including those at Callao. Royalists would be returned to Spain at the expense of the new Republic of Peru. They would draw half pay until their repatriation. Alternatively, Royalists could enter the army of Peru with the same rank. Fortunately, for the Republic's budget, La Serna's army had only a week's march to reach the coast.

Bolívar received Sucre's report of the battle before Christmas. O'Connor would later complain that Sucre failed to "mention the brave and meritorious captains of the Rifles Battalion" as well as many other heroic British and Irish soldiers. Nonetheless, O'Connor became a trusted Sucre ally and took over operations in Upper Peru after his general's death. Later, President Santa Cruz made him a commander of the Legion of Honor of Bolivia. With his severance pay, he purchased a farm near Tarija, retired in 1839, and later took up Bolivian citizenship. He died on October 5, 1871, leaving his memoirs unfinished until his grandson Francisco O'Connor D'Arlach completed the task.

On Christmas Day, the Liberator proclaimed the great victory, decreed honors for the victors, and appointed Sucre grand marshal. "The battle of Ayacucho is the climax of American glory and the work of General Sucre," said the Liberator. He added, with a touch of regret and envy, "posterity will represent Sucre with one foot on Pichincha and the other on Potosí." Sucre quickly fulfilled the last part of Bolívar's prophecy. He pressed on to Cuzco before year's end. He left there on January 9, 1825, marching along the western side of Lake Titicaca, then southeast to La Paz, 325 miles from Cuzco. La Paz sits in a bowl some 12,500 feet above sea level, surrounded by high peaks. Founded in 1548, the city served as a major colonial trade center on the route from Potosí to Lima and as an important administrative center. Sucre, as commander of the liberating army, decreed on February 9 that the five provinces of Upper Peru should send delegates to a general assembly to decide their future. The delegates had three choices. They could vote to join Peru, join Argentina, or become an independent nation.

Units of Olañeta's army in different cities spontaneously proclaimed for independence as Sucre advanced south to Potosí. His army camped in alfalfa fields near Potosí on the night of March 28, 1825. Sucre's patrol reported that Olañeta had left Potosí that morning with four hundred troops. One of the officers who had fled with Olañeta, Col. Carlos Medinaceli, turned against him on March 30. His small force fought that of Olañeta at Tumusla, seventy miles south of Potosí. Olañeta would die of an assassin's attack in April, ending Royalist resistance in Upper Peru.

The recalcitrant governor of Callao, Gen. José Ramón Rodil, prolonged the misery along the coast. Refusing to accept the settlement reached at Ayacucho, he holed up with 2,500 soldiers and 3,800 civilians in the forts of the port city. Well provisioned and well protected, Rodil stubbornly held out against the Patriot siege until January 1826. Reduced to eating their pack animals, cats, dogs, and rats and afflicted with scurvy and typhus, the Royalists suffered mightily. Most of the civilians and 2,095 of his soldiers died in the senseless act of defiance and hubris. After his surrender, Rodil returned to a hero's welcome in Spain, where Ferdinand VII rewarded his inane bravado with appointment as captain general of Cuba and later made him a nobleman.

Thus ended fifty years of Western Hemispheric wars for independence from European colonial powers. Yankee minutemen had begun the battles at Lexington and Concord in April 1775. Bolívar and Sucre completed the task in 1825. All that remained of Spain's once vast American empire were two Caribbean islands, Cuba and Puerto Rico. Royalist commanders still held Callao in Peru, Vera Cruz in Mexico, and the Chiloé archipelago off the coast of Chile. Within a year, however, they too had surrendered.

Grand Marshal Sucre called an assembly for Upper Peru at the colonial capital of Chuquisaca. He then headed for La Paz on July 2 and an assembly opened its sessions on July 10. After considerable debate, the delegates declared Upper Peru an independent state and christened it *República Bolívar* (which soon became Bolivia). This process of political fragmentation would continue among the newly created republics for another decade. Meanwhile, in Lower Peru, another congress had met in Lima on February 10, 1825, and declared Sucre's title to be grand marshal of Ayacucho. The delegates refused to accept Bolívar's resignation as dictator of Peru. The congress extended his dictatorship for one year and granted him a large stipend. Bolívar refused the money but accepted the extended dictatorship. He left Lima on April 11 for a state visit to Upper Peru. He stayed nearly a month in both Arequipa and Cuzco. He also passed a day or two at other cities and towns on his route. On October 5 he entered Potosí, about 170 miles, as the condor flies, north of the border with Argentina.

Two Argentine agents joined the throng that welcomed Bolívar. They proposed that he unite Upper Peru with the United Provinces of Río de la Plata. They also suggested that he use the Colombian army to fight against monarchical Brazil. Bolívar saw clearly that the impending war between the Brazilian Empire and the United Provinces would be a power struggle between two strong, independent American states. They contested control of vital waterways of the Río de la Plata region. Nothing in their clash would arouse the heroic will of his Colombians. No mystique would impel them to risk their lives in battle. The agents tempted him with the glory of returning to Colombia by way of Rio de Janeiro, but Bolívar resisted the lure. Moreover, the Liberator had grown mortally ill. He had a presentiment that his days were numbered. Told that Upper Peru had been renamed in his honor, he responded: "I shall soon die, but the republic of Bolivia will endure until the end of time."

Sucre, the two Argentines, and others accompanied Bolívar when he climbed the famous silver mountain of Potosí on October 26, 1825. On its summit, he planted the flags of Colombia, Peru, and the United Provinces of the Río de la Plata. Turning to those around him, he said:

> We have marched triumphantly from the Atlantic, and after fifteen years of gigantic struggle have overthrown the edifice that tyrants erected during three centuries of usurpation and violence. The miserable drudges of these lords of the world were subjected to the most degrading slavery. How great must be our joy on seeing millions of men restored to their rights by our perseverance and our exertions.
>
> As for me, standing on this silver mass called Potosí, whose rich veins were the treasury of Spain for 300 years, I esteem this wealth as nothing

compared with the glory of having brought the banner of Liberty from the banks of the Orinoco, to plant it here upon the top of this mountain whose womb is the wonder and envy of the universe.

Bolívar's armies had marched some three thousand miles from Angostura on the banks of the Orinoco River to the silver mountains of Potosí. Most of the way they had followed rugged, treacherous zigzag trails. They crossed three chains of the highest, most rugged mountains in the hemisphere. The Liberator clearly understood the immense sacrifices and losses suffered, but he considered the gains worth the cost. Writing to his Uncle Esteban Palacios on July 10, 1825, he reflected: "as for the less fortunate, the fields of Venezuela have been watered with their blood and littered with their bones; their only crime was their love of justice." He asked rhetorically, "'Where is Caracas?' you will ask. Caracas no longer exists. But her ashes, her monuments, the ground on which she stood, have been lighted by the lamp of liberty and covered with the glory of martyrdom. This consolation has healed all wounds; at least this is my consolation and I trust it will be yours."

Writing a century later, Henry Rowan Lemley, a retired major of the U.S. Army, put the Patriot stamina and courage in perspective.

Over these [trails] Bolívar passed on horseback many times, but his last long and meteoric ride to and from the Argentine frontier to eastern Venezuela, perhaps 5,000 miles by the paths he followed and interrupted only by a short voyage from Callao to Guayaquil, is the most remarkable in the annals of horsemanship. Almost immediately he retraced his steps halfway, to Guayaquil, and returned to Bogotá. This was more difficult than it would be to ride from Vladivostok to the Hook of Holland. The marches of his army exceeded in the aggregate those of Alexander to India and of Hannibal through Africa, Spain, and France to Italy, as well as of Jenghis and Kublai Khan and Tamerlane across Asia.

The hard-riding Liberator earned many times over his accurate, if somewhat prosaic nickname, "Iron Ass" *(Culo de Hierro).*

PART V

Political Failure
to Postmortem Glory

CHAPTER 14

Trying to Hold Gran Colombia
Together, 1825–28

Bolívar's star reached its zenith on Potosí. He had directed nearly five hundred battles in fifteen years over an area of three million square miles. He had liberated colonies from Spain that became the nations of Venezuela, Colombia, Ecuador, Peru, and Bolivia. The Admirable Campaign of 1813, the battle of Los Frailes in 1816, and the Orinoco campaign of 1817 stood as high points in his military glory.

The low point had come in May 1818, after the disastrous campaign to retake Caracas. True, Morillo had a lance thrust through his abdomen. Bolívar's infantry, however, had been destroyed, his essential horses killed or captured, his money, weapons, and ammunition exhausted. Everything had appeared lost, but Bolívar's indomitable courage and remarkable vision remained intact. He created a new army that liberated Colombia, Peru, and Upper Peru. Bolívar, a mortal, not a god, suffered natural human ambitions that made him a slave to his own triumphs.

The Liberator left Potosí on November 1, 1825, and rode to Chuquisaca, the Bolivian capital renamed in 1839 to honor Sucre. There he promised to write a constitution to be considered by the Bolivian Congress the following May. On New Year's Day 1826, he explained to the citizens that a sacred duty called him to Lima. "The Peruvian Congress is about to convene," he said, "and I must return the dictatorship which it confided to me."

Leaving Sucre behind as military dictator, Bolívar rode to the port of Arica. He boarded the brig *Chimborazo* and sailed north to Chorillos, near Magdalena del Mar, where Manuela awaited him. Bolívar and Manuela enjoyed two days together before Congress convened in Lima. Congress quickly rejected his resignation as dictator and recessed. The townspeople overwhelmed Bolívar with gifts and adulation. Equally gratifying, people treated Manuela with the respect that they would have given a legal wife.

Many Peruvian aristocrats wanted a monarchy, an empire of the Andes, with Bolívar on the throne. English and French agents also suggested monarchy, as did Páez. The latter sent an agent to Bolívar on October 1, 1825, with the message that conditions in Venezuela resembled those in France while Napoleon was in Egypt. He urged Bolívar to return and save Venezuela as Napoleon had saved France. Bolívar pointedly rejected the Páez plan of monarchy: "Napoleon was great and unique but highly ambitious. Here we have none of this. I am not, nor do I care to be, a Napoleon. I regard these examples as unworthy of the glory that I have achieved. The title of Liberator is superior to any that human pride has ever sought. It cannot, therefore, be degraded. Moreover, our people have nothing, nothing whatever, in common with the French. Our Republic has raised the country to heights of glory and prosperity, endowing it with laws and freedom."

Although professing republican sentiments, Bolívar also revealed to Páez his fundamental political conviction: only a strong central government could survive. "I shall tell you quite frankly that the plan [for monarchy] will not benefit you, me, or the country. I believe, nevertheless, that in the next period in which the Constitution can be revised, appropriate amendments favoring sound conservative principles can be introduced without violating any republic doctrines."

One of Bolívar's harshest critics, General Ducoudray Holstein, considered the Liberator a second-rate Napoleon. In his 1829 memoir, he charged that "Bolívar in his proclamations imitates, or endeavors to imitate the style of Napoleon. He began with a small bodyguard and afterwards greatly increased it, like Napoleon. He is ambitious, absolute, and jealous of his command, like the other. On public occasions he is simply dressed, while all around him is splendid, like Napoleon, and he moves quickly from place to place like him. With respect to military and administrative talents, there is no resemblance between them." The equally critical Colonel Hippisley agreed. "Bolívar would ape the great man. He aspires to be a second Bonaparte, in South America, without possessing a single talent for the duties of the field or the cabinet." Both appraisals are unduly negative, but no one can deny that both Bonaparte and Bolívar pursued their personal glory with unfettered zeal.

María Antonia, Bolívar's sister, heard of the Páez proposal and offered her brother straightforward, astute advice: "Tell them always what you told them in Cumaná in 1814, that you will be Liberator or nothing. This title is your real one; it has extolled your name among the great of the earth; it is the title that will now preserve your reputation built at the cost of untold sacrifice. You should repudiate anyone who offers you a crown, because he is interested only in your downfall." Antonio José de Sucre and Francisco de Paula Santander also opposed the idea of crowning Bolívar, pointing out, rather indelicately, that the impotent leader had no heirs. Santander asked: "After your death, who will succeed? Páez? Montilla? Padilla? I do not want any one of these to be crowned supreme chief for his lifetime."

As he wrote a new constitution for the republic of Bolivia, the Liberator pondered a political structure for Colombia, Peru, and Bolivia. His proposed constitution provided for a strong central government and a president for life. Bolívar wished to have the countries he had liberated accept this constitution, fearing that tyranny and anarchy threatened everywhere, forces that could overwhelm and destroy a weak republic.

Bolívar also feared the tyranny of the colored majority (pardocracia) and limited the franchise, much as did the Founding Fathers in the United States. In the latter country, the electoral college, limited access to Senate seats, strict voting requirements, and other strictures sharply limited and controlled political participation for the first century of national life. Only propertied citizens that "know how to read and write, possess some employment or industry, or profess some science or art, without being subject to another in the category of domestic service" could vote and hold office. He justified the need for strong, centralized rule in a letter to Pedro Briceño Méndez written May 25, 1826. He presented his constitution as steering a middle path between monarchy and anarchy. However, Bolívar's fundamental distrust of republican democratic government, especially a federalist one, shows through clearly.

> In Venezuela I shall try to put an end to the partisan spirit and, at the same time, preach to my friends the gospel of my Bolivian Constitution, as opposed to Federalism and monarchy. This Constitution reconciles extremes and provides the means for insuring domestic tranquility combined with freedom for the provinces.

You will observe that my reasoning is quite republican yet philosophical in belief. The republican aspect was necessary in order to silence the
charge of monarchical ideas which some attribute to me and which others proclaim as being the means to salvation. In Buenos Aires and in Chile
they use this as a pretext to speak of me in horror.

Although he supported remedies different from Bolívar, Santander recognized the troubling divisions and difficulties confronting Colombia. Writing to a friend on May 9, he complained that "the discontent of the military
is spreading because soldiers are distrusted, even scorned, everywhere, partly
because of the bad conduct and worse manners of some of our officers and
partly because ambitious lawyers *(letrados)* want to destroy everyone who
might become a counterpoise." "The anxious clergy," he continued, "is bursting with rage at the liberality of the Congress and at the insults published
daily against them." Furthermore, "the liberated, more numerous than the
liberators, are taking exclusive possession of the countryside, and since there
is a large number of ambitious and fickle lawyers, they are trying hard to
exclude the military, the clergy, and everyone who will not submit to their
opinions and desires for offices and advancement." Santander concluded
with an ominous, accurate prophesy to which he also contributed: "The
fuel is gathered, the elements of disunity are on collision course; at the slightest clash, the spark will leap, and this poor land will burn."

The Bolivian Congress adopted Bolívar's constitution on July 11, 1826,
and elected Sucre as president. Sucre refused a life term but agreed to serve
for two years; he fervently wished to return to Quito and marry Mariana,
his betrothed. Unfortunately, trouble brewed all around. Some Peruvians
continued to resent the presence of Bolívar and his twenty-three hundred
Colombian troops. They plotted to expel what they considered an occupying force. The plotters included one of Bolívar's own officers, the Granadino
Col. José Bustamante (a secret agent of President Santa Cruz). He conspired
to turn Venezuelan officers against Bolívar. Santander, meanwhile, worked
to undercut Bolívar's authority in Cundinamarca and Venezuela.

The General Constituent Congress made some changes in Bolívar's grand
scheme. They added as article 6 that "the Roman Catholic and Apostolic
religion is the religion of the republic, to the exclusion of all other public
worship." In article 78, they also insisted that the president must "profess
the religion of the republic." They also strengthened the requirements for
citizenship, and thus voting, insisting that, to qualify, a man must "know
how to read and write well; this condition will be required only after 1836."

However, the Congress left intact the centralized structure designed by the Liberator. The tripartite legislature consisted of tribunes, serving two-year terms; senators, with eight-year terms; and censors, appointed for life by the president, who exercised broad, discretionary powers.

The vision of Bolívar and the necessities of war had created the Republic of Colombia. Countervailing forces, however, quickly reappeared: historical tradition and geographic reality. Bolívar could delay, but he could not halt the disintegration of Colombia. Páez sparked Venezuela's revolt against the central government in Bogotá. Santander charged that in early 1826 Páez exceeded his authority by drafting troops in Caracas. He charged Páez with insubordination, relieved him of his command, and replaced him with his ally Juan Escalona. The Colombian Senate summoned Páez to Bogotá for trial, but the llanero caudillo refused to go. He made public his defiance of the central government by reassuming command of the army in Valencia on April 30. Two weeks later Valencia made Páez its civil and military chief. Caracas and other cities followed suit. When Páez reported his version of the affair to Bolívar, he laid blame on the "insidious Santander."

Santander needed Bolívar's support against Páez, so he bombarded Bolívar with twenty-three letters between June 6 and October 22, 1826. "You are the one," Santander said in his second letter (June 9), "who can extricate us from the present critical circumstances, and save your daughter from anarchy and civil war. Your presence in Colombia is absolutely necessary." Meanwhile, the Congress that Bolívar hoped would form a League of American States opened sessions in Panama. The Liberator carefully excluded the United States (for fear of angering Great Britain, among other reasons), monarchical Brazil, and black, French-speaking Haiti. Writing on May 20, 1825, he warned Santander to "never forget the three political admonitions that I have ventured to give you: first, it will not be to our advantage to admit La Plata to the league; second, or the United States of America; third, do not attempt to liberate Havana [from Spain]." He pointedly repeated the warning on June 7: "Haiti, Buenos Aires, and the United States, each in its own way, offer great disadvantages. . . . The North Americans and the Haitians are foreigners to us, if only because they are heterogeneous in character." Again on October 21, "I do not believe the [North] Americans should be admitted to the Congress of the Isthmus. Such a step would cause us trouble with Albion."

In his invitation, issued on December 7, 1824, he implored his fellow Spanish American leaders: "Great and Good Friend: After fifteen years of sacrifices devoted to the liberty of America to secure a system of guaranties that in peace and war shall be the shield of our new destiny, it is time the interests and relations uniting the American Republics, formerly Spanish colonies, should have a fundamental basis that shall perpetuate, if possible, those Governments. To initiate that system, and concentrate the power of this great political body, implies the exercise of a sublime authority, capable of directing the policy of our Governments, whose influence should maintain uniformity of principles, and whose name alone should put an end to our quarrels."

As events would show, few of his fellow political leaders shared the Liberator's vision of a united Spanish America. The only delegates present for the June 22, 1826, meeting came from Mexico, the weak confederation of Central America, Gran Colombia, and Peru. Great Britain and the Netherlands dispatched observers. Although not invited, President John Quincy Adams, a recent convert to the importance of Latin America, determined that the United States should send two observers. The agenda of the Panama Congress, he said, included "objects of the highest importance . . . bearing directly upon the special interest of this Union." In language reminiscent of the Monroe Doctrine, he asserted that "America has a set of primary interests which have none or a remote relation to Europe." He urged cooperation with the new republics to the south, "whose political principles and systems of government, congenial with our own, must and will have an action and counteraction upon us and ours to which we cannot be indifferent."

Adams failed to convince leading diplomat Albert Gallatin to attend. Instead, John Sergeant of Pennsylvania and Richard C. Anderson, minister to Colombia, received the call. Opposition in the U.S. Senate, accompanied by rancorous debate, delayed their departure, and ultimately neither attended. Anderson died on the way to Panama, and Sergeant learned that the Congress had already adjourned. It is doubtful that he lamented not traveling to pestilential Panama. So far, the first republic of the Western Hemisphere had been very inept at creating bonds of Pan-Americanism with its neighbors to the south.

The absence of North American representatives left the diplomatic field open to Edward J. Dawkins, agent of the astute George Canning (1770–1827), to further the interests of Great Britain. Viscount Castlereagh's death in 1821 had opened the foreign office to Canning, and he served as foreign secretary for six eventful years. Dawkins effectively promoted British interests and sharply undercut those of the United States. Bolívar may have viewed Britain as a possible protector to the fledgling South American republics.

Canning and his successors, however, found economic expansion, not military obligation, a much more attractive policy toward Spain's ex-colonies.

The Panama Congress adopted four conventions before adjourning on July 15. One provided for "union, league, and perpetual confederation" of the states represented. Another set up a tribunal to arbitrate boundary disputes. An army of the confederation would enforce decisions of the tribunal. Only Colombia ratified the conventions. Newly freed from Spanish shackles, Spanish Americans throughout the region would exhibit an intense distrust of outside political power. Centrifugal forces would tear the region into smaller, squabbling nations, very unlike Bolívar's dream of a large, powerful, grand confederation.

Writing to Páez on August 8, Bolívar delivered a sharp postmortem, framed in classical terms, on the Panama meeting. "The Congress of Panamá, an organization that might have been magnificent if only it had been effective, is not different from that crazy Greek who sought to direct sailing vessels from a rock. Its power will be a shadow, and its decrees mere advice, no more." Bolívar's dream of an American League of Nations quickly died, but it did serve as a model and inspiration that would guide later efforts at cooperation. The 1826 Congress of Panama established a precedent for a later series of Pan American Congresses and for the Organization of American States, founded in 1948.

As Bolívar prepared to leave Lima, officials, crowds of citizens, even a delegation of women, begged him to stay. The electoral college of Lima Province approved the Bolivian constitution on August 16 and offered Bolívar the presidency for life. Bolívar declined, but he did organize a Council of Ministers for Peru, with Bolivian General Santa Cruz as president. Even the ever-loyal O'Leary recognized that Bolívar may have overstayed his welcome in Peru. He defended the Liberator's presence by noting that "the complete confusion into which the country had fallen as a result of the war and the revolution required the help of an expert hand to set matters right." Then, in a slap at the country, he added, "Unfortunately for Peru, there was no one among her native sons who had sufficient prestige to undertake the Herculean task. The situation in Upper Peru was distressing, for the war had not yet ended there, but more to be feared was the horrible specter of anarchy." The Liberator would never successfully resolve this conundrum of dictatorial control versus anarchy, nor would several generations of his successors.

Bolívar and Manuela spent a farewell night together on September 2, and the next day Bolívar sailed from Callao (without the twenty-three hundred Colombian troops). Sucre and Córdoba had warned him not to attempt to retake Guayaquil, as his troops lacked necessary supplies and tropical diseases had decimated their ranks. Political intrigue, for once, worked in the Liberator's favor. Agustín Gamarra signed an armistice agreeing to return Guayaquil to Colombia, so Bolívar and his beleaguered army retook the city without firing a shot. Tuberculosis—which would ultimately claim the Liberator—incapacitated him for a time in Guayaquil.

The Páez revolt in Venezuela encouraged some Guayaquil leaders to exercise similar independence. In August they endorsed the Bolivian constitution, and when Bolívar arrived in September, they proclaimed him dictator. Brig. Gen. Juan José Flores (1800–1864), a Venezuelan born in Puerto Cabello, served as the ranking military officer in Guayaquil. Flores grew increasingly conservative in his political views. Neither Bolívar nor anyone else could know, of course, that Flores would go on to play a key role in the destiny of Ecuador. In 1830 he would lead the secession movement, removing Ecuador from Gran Colombia and becoming the new nation's first president. The centrifugal political forces at work in Spanish America persisted. A staunch conservative who supported entrenched special privileges, he would also lead conservatives in a civil war against Vicente Rocafuerte and the liberals in 1834. Flores served as president twice (1830–34, 1839–45) and remained a political power in Ecuador, but his dictatorial ambitions led opponents to depose him in 1845. He returned in 1860 and served as chief of the army until his death four years later.

Bolívar remained the pivotal force holding Gran Colombia together. Vice President Santander, Secretary of War Soublette, and Secretary of Foreign Relations José Rafael Revenga left Bogotá on November 9, 1826, and rode south to greet Bolívar. They met two days later at Tocaima, fifty-four miles from Bogotá. Given the danger of disunion, both Bolívar and Santander realized that, for the present, they must show public confidence in each other.

Santander returned to Bogotá in two days. Feverish from tuberculosis and plagued by hemorrhoids, Bolívar proceeded more slowly. He had already written apologetically to Manuela, "I am so tired with all this travel and with all the troubles of our country that I have no time to write you long accounts in small letters as you wish me to do." Disease and long years of hard riding had caught up with "Iron Ass."

After an absence of five years, Bolívar and his staff approached Bogotá the morning of November 14. A delegation met them two leagues from the city, and the two groups of riders dismounted. One official impudently harangued Bolívar on the legal order and the laws that had been violated.

Bolívar retorted angrily: "This day is set aside to celebrate the glories of the Liberating army, not to discuss violations of laws!" He abruptly mounted his horse, galloped ahead, and rode into the city nearly alone.

A cold rain fell. Only a few people in the streets greeted him. Many signs, however, proclaimed "Viva la constitución," the very document that Bolívar wanted to change for his own. The Liberator received some modest reassurances at the official reception in the Palace of Government, where Santander, cabinet ministers, the president of the Senate, judges of the Supreme Court, and a host of citizens greeted him. Santander lauded Bolívar's glorious victories in his southern campaigns, and Bolívar praised Santander in reply and assured all that "the Constitution, that gospel of the Colombian people in which are consigned our rights, will prevail."

The reception brought temporary calm to the agitated city. Congress had declared on March 15 that Bolívar had been reelected president and Santander vice president. Their second four-year terms would begin on January 2, 1827. Bolívar, however, could not ride to Venezuela, resolve the divisions created by Páez, and return to Bogotá in only six weeks. Santander suggested that Bolívar assume extraordinary power as provided by article 128 of the constitution. Bolívar could then grant Santander authority to act as vice president after January 2, thus delaying the inauguration of both men. Bolívar pondered his options for five days, then, on November 23, he assumed the presidency with extraordinary powers. Two days later Bolívar mounted up and headed for Caracas, 637 miles away. Santander, cabinet members, and many citizens rode with him for the first day. They spent the night at Santander's hacienda, six leagues from the capital. Most of the cavalcade returned to Bogotá the next day, but a small committee escorted Bolívar for the next two days. Thereafter, Bolívar covered the rest of the long, arduous journey attended only by the officers of his staff.

John G. A. Williamson (1793–1840), new U.S. consul to Caracas, arrived on the scene that same November. A native of Person County, North Carolina, Williamson displayed far more bigotry than political acumen during his service in South America. As is often the case with American diplomats, he owed his appointment to political sway (in this case, Henry Clay's), not to any special talents of his own. However, in fairness, he arrived at a very difficult time. He immediately got off on a bad foot with Bolívar. At a banquet, the Liberator warmly toasted the British but failed to mention the United States, the first nation to recognize Colombia. The slight, or oversight, incensed Williamson, who walked out of the room. Subsequent events, including a long delay in obtaining a passport, only increased the American consul's distaste for Bolívar, a man of "egotizm and Vanity" (spelling was not a Williamson strength either). Later reflecting on Bolívar's life, Williamson concluded that "his ambition ruined him, hurried him from the field of Glory to an obscure grave." Soon the Liberator would rise again from that temporary obscurity to even greater glory.

Bolívar made it to Cúcuta, 250 miles from Bogotá, by December 11. From there he rode two hundred miles to Maracaibo, crossed the lake by boat, then proceeded along the coast past Coro to Puerto Cabello, where he expected that he might encounter the rebellious Páez. On January 1, 1827, Bolívar issued a decree granting a general amnesty to all who had supported the defection of General Páez. He declared that "General José Antonio Páez remains fulfilling the Civil and Military Authority under the name of Superior Chief of Venezuela. Immediately after this decree's notice, my authority as President of the Republic will be submitted for recognition and obedience." "The joy which these proclamations occasioned," wrote British Consul Sir Robert Ker Porter, "cannot be imagined. I never witnessed so sudden a change in any city. The streets before deserted, were thronged with persons of all classes; faces once gloomy and dejected were now all smiles and life."

Even besieged and awash in enemies, Bolívar retained his sense of destiny—and of his own invincibility. Writing to Páez on December 11, 1826, he both boasted and threatened. "With me you have conquered, with me you have won glory and fortune; you must place your every hope and trust in me. On the other hand, General Castillo opposed me and lost; General Piar opposed me and suffered defeat; General Mariño opposed me and went down to defeat; General Riva Agüero opposed me and lost; and General Torre Tagle opposed me and was defeated. It would seem that Providence condemns my personal enemies, whether American or Spanish, to perdition." Páez replied, "from this moment the authority of His Excellency the Liberator is recognized and will be obeyed." Bolívar left Puerto Cabello on January 4 and met Páez at the foot of Naguanagua Mountain. The wary llanero arrived with his bodyguard, but on seeing the Liberator alone, he dismounted, embraced, then both rode into Valencia to enthusiastic cheers.

Meanwhile, people in Caracas lined the streets with poplar and palm branches. They erected triumphal arches decorated with ribbons and flowers and prepared a lavish banquet. On January 8, 1827, many citizens rode or walked west toward Valencia to meet Bolívar and Páez. At two o'clock on the afternoon of January 10, Bolívar and his retinue entered the city gate. Jacob Idler, a Philadelphia merchant, received the two warriors with his

Portrait of Bolívar in 1826.

coach and horses. Both men, "splendidly dressed in their richest uniforms," basked in the adulation of "crowds of rejoicing people, all wild in screaming Viva Bolívar! Viva Páez! Viva Colombia!" Two months of gay balls and parties, visits with friends and family, and his old nurse Hipólita gladdened the Liberator's heart and lifted his spirits. Unfortunately for Bolívar, the vivas would quickly fade away.

The euphoria in Caracas lasted only as long as Bolívar remained there. In Bogotá and Lima, localism and nationalism worked against Bolívar and the unity of Gran Colombia. Col. José Bustamante, probably at Santander's urging, had convinced sergeants of the Colombian troops in Lima to mutiny.

He argued that to get their back pay and return home, they must overthrow their generals and colonels.

During the night of January 25, 1827, Colombian troops surrounded the houses of their commanding officers, then arrested and imprisoned them in the fortress of Callao. The next day the Cabildo met, declared the Bolivian constitution abrogated, and elected Santa Cruz president of Peru. The new president shipped the imprisoned officers north to Buenaventura. Then he persuaded Bustamante that he should embark with his troops for Guayaquil, overthrow Bolívar's government in the departments of Guayaquil and Azuay, and federate them with Peru. Bustamante left with his troops on March 19, bound for Guayaquil.

The brave, resolute, and loyal Manuela had stood alone against the revolt. She rode straight to the barracks and pleaded with the troops to start a counterrevolution in support of Bolívar. Santa Cruz imprisoned her in the Convent of the Nazarenes on February 7, but she managed to smuggle letters to the troops and to her friends in Lima. After several outbreaks among the troops, she received an order to "leave Peru in twenty-four hours or you will be put in the *Casas Matas* [women's prison]." Manuela sailed on a brig for Guayaquil, but Bustamante had already won the port city. He held her incommunicado but then permitted her to depart for Quito. He provided mules to carry her trunks (one of them containing Bolívar's archives) and four Colombian soldiers who accompanied her inland. Ten days of travel brought Manuela to Quito, where she took refuge in the home of her half brother.

News took three months to reach Caracas from Lima, two months from Guayaquil, a few days less from Quito, and almost a month from Bogotá. Before Bolívar heard of Bustamante's revolt and Manuela's forced departure from Lima, he received letters and newspapers from Bogotá that reported Santander's abuse and censure of him. Santander subsidized the biweekly *El Conductor* with government funds, published in it unsigned attacks on Bolívar, and sent 150 copies of each issue to every department.

Santander's attacks became even more vitriolic after he learned of Bolívar's reconciliation with Páez. Bolívar's promotion of Páez to supreme military and civil chief of Venezuela and the promotions of Páez's followers enraged Santander. Equally upset by the chorus of newspaper attacks, Bolívar submitted his resignation to Congress in Bogotá. When he learned about Bustamante's revolt and the ill treatment of Manuela, however, he knew that he would have to return to Bogotá. On June 7 Congress had not yet accepted his resignation, and on the thirteenth Santander renewed his oath to the existing constitution.

A worried Bolívar sailed west from La Guaira on July 5, 1827, but Cartagena's warm welcome five days later lifted his spirits. Padilla gave him a splendid banquet in anticipation of his birthday (July 24) and accompanied him partway to Bogotá. Ever the optimist, Padilla wrote to Santander hoping to effect a reconciliation. "Bolívar thinks you are his enemy. I tried hard to dissuade him of this notion, and I believe that when he arrives in Bogotá you two will be good friends. I am the Liberator's friend and your friend. News of the reconciliation of the two men so necessary for the well-being of the Republic will give me the greatest happiness." They boarded the steamboat *Gran Bolívar,* the first steamboat to ply the Magdalena, at Barranca Vieja.

Soublette and most of the cabinet ministers remained loyal to Bolívar, who still enjoyed substantial support in Congress. Secretary of Interior José Manuel Restrepo recorded in his diary on July 29 that the Senate had refused to accept Bolívar's resignation. Both houses of Congress, however, passed a law ordering a Great Convention to meet at Ocaña on March 2, 1828, to consider changing the constitution. Restrepo also noted that Venezuelan troops concentrating at Ocaña, under Generals Urdaneta and Salom, would attack the rebellious Bustamante in Guayaquil.

Santander, however, feared that the troops at Ocaña would be used against him. He panicked and told Soublette that he was going to lead a revolution against Bolívar. Soublette persuaded him that Bolívar would never use that army to spill blood in Bogotá. Restrepo, Soublette, and many others rode to meet Bolívar as he neared the capital far ahead of the troops. On the morning of September 10, Bolívar sent Restrepo ahead into the city with a request to the president of the Senate that he have Congress in session that afternoon so that Bolívar could belatedly take his oath for a second term as president of Colombia.

Bolívar entered Bogotá that afternoon and rode through crowded streets to the church of Santo Domingo, where Congress awaited him. After mass, he took the oath of office, then reported on the use he had made of his extraordinary powers in Venezuela. He asked Congress to continue in session, and later it approved all of his actions in Venezuela and Peru.

Vice President Santander waited at the Palace of Government to receive Bolívar, along with cabinet ministers, the principal authorities of Bogotá, and a "numerous concourse." All of them felt anxious and uneasy. Would Bolívar humiliate Santander in their presence? Happily, Santander pronounced a short discourse in which he congratulated Bolívar on having taken charge of the nation. Bolívar answered with tact and charm, and the relieved crowd rejoiced, at least for the time being, as the president and vice president maintained their fictive public friendship.

Tired, besieged, sick with tuberculosis, prematurely old, Bolívar sought solace from Manuela, whom he wrote the next day: "Your love revives a life that is expiring. I cannot live without you. Come. Come to me. Come now." About the time that Manuela received this letter in Quito, Bolívar received another informing him that Gen. Juan José Flores had approached Guayaquil with veteran troops on September 29. Bustamante and his associates had fled to Peru, and some of their troops had defected to Flores. Flores peacefully occupied the city and for the present reestablished a government favorable to Bolívar. Flores, however, would later push to separate Ecuador from Gran Colombia.

The opposition press continued to attack Bolívar as well as his candidates in the November election of delegates to the Ocaña Convention, due to meet in March 1828. Taking the political high road, Bolívar had forbidden his officials to meddle in the election process, and they obeyed the order. Bolívar, as a result, had no local leadership to influence public opinion. The great warrior seemingly had no stomach for the trench warfare demanded by partisan politics. Santander, in contrast, waged an effective propaganda war through the press and his local henchmen that made Bolívar anxious about the results, especially in major cities like Cartagena.

All returns had reached Bogotá by the end of December. The tally showed that Santander and a majority of his candidates had been elected. An angry, frustrated Bolívar cried fraud, but he also recognized with despair that "Santander is the idol of this people." According to Col. Belford Hinton Wilson, observing in Bogotá, Santander's victory "has so much affected the Liberator that he has lost all his energy, and even his best friends complain of his ruinous apathy. His enemies of course rejoice at it." Decline in both politics and health came quickly and dramatically to the Liberator.

A few days into 1828, Manuela Sáenz rode into Bogotá. She had left Quito at the end of November with a few loyal officers and a squadron of lancers. Pack mules carried her possessions and Bolívar's archives. Bogotá's streets were deserted, so the travelers asked some Indians in the plaza where they could find Bolívar. The Indian replied that Bolívar was at Quinta, a villa outside the city, where the convoy arrived after dark. Bolívar's emaciated frame, sallow complexion, and thin hair shocked Manuela. As she arrived, he sat in a meeting with his officers to discuss how to prevent the disintegration of Colombia. All of them rejoiced at Manuela's welcome presence, and José Palacios, Bolívar's servant and bodyguard since childhood, glee-fully received her. She quickly assumed command at the villa and labored to keep the machinery of government running.

Soon news from Venezuela dispelled Bolívar's apathy and roused him to action. He learned that Spanish agents from Puerto Rico had infiltrated from Coro south to the Orinoco River and into the eastern provinces. Span-ish ships approached the shores of Venezuela, signaled Royalist guerrillas there, and disappeared. Páez informed Bolívar on January 9, 1828, that Ad-miral Angel Laborde's Royalist squadrons had increased their activities along the coast, apparently signaling another attempt to reconquer Venezuela. When Bolívar received this letter a month later, he replied simply, "I am coming to help you."

Bolívar planned to remain in Venezuela only four or five months. While he prepared to leave Bogotá, Santander concentrated his efforts on control-ling the important Ocaña Convention. Bolívar made a few cabinet changes and departed on March 16, 1828. He traveled the route to Venezuela that he knew so well, the road through Tunja to Cúcuta, riding a little more than thirty miles a day. Two days beyond Tunja, he received the good news from Páez that residents of Coro had suppressed a Royalist revolt there. Laurencio Silva had done the same in Guayana. After Monagas, Bermúdez, and Mariño crushed uprisings in the rest of Venezuela, Laborde and his Royalist squad-ron sailed away in frustration.

The Liberator rested well that night, but the next day brought the bad news that José Padilla had revolted in Cartagena. Recruiting black and mu-latto followers, he threatened to plunge Colombia into a vicious racial war. The political maneuvering continued through March. Santander, bolstered by Padilla's support, used the unrest in Cartagena to launch his own machi-nations against Bolívar. Cartagena, considered the bulwark of Colombia and the key to Cundinamarca, made an impressive political base. In the political shuffle, Bolívar's loyalist Mariano Montilla managed to take com-mand of the military in Cartagena. Padilla apparently got cold feet and fled to Santander in Ocaña. There he also visited O'Leary, who advised Padilla to return to Mompox, which he did.

Bolívar, meanwhile, had changed his route, now turning northwest to-ward Cartagena. At Bucaramanga on March 31, he learned that Montilla had things under control in Cartagena. Bolívar dispatched Col. José Bolívar (a llanero and no relative) to arrest Padilla in Ocaña and take him to Cartagena for trial. Montilla, who did not want Padilla's blood on his hands, disobeyed Bolívar's order and instead sent Padilla to Bogotá for trial.

Bolívar remained at Bucaramanga, only three or four days' ride south of Ocaña, where the convention delegates had gathered. From there he could easily communicate with O'Leary and his minority delegates at Ocaña. As delegates arrived, Santander entertained them at dinner, paid for their lodgings, and showered them with propaganda. Even so, he did not command a majority when the convention opened on April 9. Only 64 of 108 elected delegates attended: twenty-three Santanderistas, twenty-one Bolivarians, and eighteen Independents and Moderates.

A majority of the delegates agreed on the need for constitutional reform but wrangled over the specifics, making little progress, for eight weeks. At one point, an impatient Bolívar unwisely threatened the delegates with military force, prompting a panicked Santander to demand a passport. This heavy-handed tactic further affirmed the opposition view of the Liberator as a ruthless dictator. Discord, bitter attacks, and increasing tension prevented the adoption of a new constitution. Santanderistas rallied to propose reinstating the existing constitution, with article 128 deleted. That article granted the president extraordinary powers in times of crisis. They needed only 43 votes to pass their proposal, but the 21 Bolivarians persuaded one Independent to join them and go home. Once the dissidents had departed by June 10, the rump convention fell 12 short of the 55 required for a quorum (one more than half of the 108 elected). The stymied, failed, discordant convention disbanded on June 11. Bolívar had not prevailed, but he had foiled Santander.

As political conflict increased, anxiety and fear gripped Bogotá. The Cúcuta constitution had been discredited, but no new one had been adopted. Gran Colombia lurched along without a constitutional rudder. Rumors swirled that Bolívar planned to leave the country. There would be no government! To counter such an emergency, Col. Pedro Alcántara Herrán, governor of Cundinamarca, convoked a junta of civil, ecclesiastical, and community leaders in Bogotá on June 13. That junta agreed not to obey any act that might come from the Ocaña Convention. It revoked the powers conferred on deputies of Bogotá Province. Finally, it asked Bolívar to return to Bogotá to assume supreme power. Seemingly, only Bolívar could save the republic.

The Liberator relished his role of savior and rode to accept the offer of dictatorial power. A mighty, fervent welcome greeted him in the capital of Bogotá on June 24. An enthusiastic throng led him to the cathedral, where he attended mass, gave thanks to the Almighty for his safe arrival, and asked for His blessing. At a special pavilion in the Central Plaza, dignitaries praised his government, then everyone accompanied him to the Palace of Government.

Acceptance of the June 13 act poured into Bogotá from capitals and other cities throughout Colombia. Bolívar assumed power full of hope and began to revise the government. First he quickly eliminated the office of vice president and then appointed Santander minister plenipotentiary to the United States to get him out of the country. Biding his time, Santander accepted the post and chose a secretary, but they made no move to leave. Bolívar, increasingly distrustful of his fellow Creoles, appointed many foreign officers to government. He trusted the loyalty of the Europeans over Creoles, but this move further isolated him from the citizenry and made him look like a remote dictator, surrounded by foreign mercenaries, not unlike the unfortunate Miranda in 1812.

Bad news from the south arrived during the first week of July. Gen. Agustín Gamarra had massed a Peruvian army on the Bolivian border. There he waited for plotters to stir up Colombian troops in Chuquisaca. Those troops mutinied on April 18, and as Sucre approached the barracks to quell the uprising, a musket shot shattered his right arm. The wound would cause him serious pain for the remainder of his life. Gamarra invaded Bolivia at the end of April and forced Sucre to resign and take his Colombian troops home. General La Mar, now president of Peru, marched to invade Colombia by land, and a squadron of two frigates and a schooner sailed to blockade Guayaquil. General Flores, deeming these actions a declaration of war, took measures to defend Guayaquil and the Ecuadorian provinces bordering Peru.

A furious Bolívar ordered O'Leary to Lima to negotiate a truce. The question of the boundary between Peru and Colombia also needed to be settled. Bolívar hoped the negotiations would give him time to move troops from Colombia to Guayaquil and the southern border. However, before he could move to reestablish stability in Peru and Ecuador, dramatic events much closer to the Liberator claimed his attention.

CHAPTER 15

Political Decline and Death,

1828–30

Faced with intrigue and uprisings on all fronts, Bolívar would learn on the fateful evening of September 25, 1828, the intensity of the growing opposition to his rule. The evening's events in Bogotá overshadowed the war preparations to the south as the Liberator faced yet another assassination attempt. Back in 1815, on the island of Haiti, Pío, one of his former slaves, had tried to stab Bolívar but mistakenly killed Félix Amestoy, asleep in the Liberator's hammock. Other attempts had likewise failed, but now pro-Santander conspirators plotted to murder Bolívar as he slept at his official residence. Fortunately for the Liberator, the alert and valiant Manuela slept by his side in the Palace of San Carlos.

Earlier in the evening, Bolívar had left a masked ball sooner than expected, unwittingly foiling a planned attack on him. Then, a drunken conspirator revealed the plan to murder the Liberator, forcing the others to act hastily. Thirty conspirators left the home of Santander's secretary of legation at 11 P.M. Pedro Carujo (a Venezuelan), with a squad of artillery, and Agustín Horment (a Frenchman), with a dozen civilians, planned to kill Bolívar. Ramón Guerra would attack the barracks of Vargas Battalion and free Padilla from jail. A third column would attack the grenadiers in their barracks.

Horment quickly killed three sentries at the entrance to the Palace of San Carlos. The conspirator also killed José Palacios's dogs that barked a warning. Andrés Ibarra, Bolívar's aide, heard the commotion and ran down from the second floor, where a saber thrust felled him. Horment searched the first floor while Carujo climbed upstairs. The barking dogs awakened Bolívar and Manuela. The Liberator grabbed weapons and prepared to meet the intruders, but Manuela saved his life by persuading him to dress and escape. The Liberator hastily pulled on Manuela's shoes; his were out for cleaning. He jumped from the balcony just as Carujo pounded on the door. Manuela grabbed a sword, confronted the assassin, and told him that Bolívar was in the Council Room. Carujo marched Manuela in front of his squad as it searched the palace but failed to find Bolívar. When Manuela saw Ibarra in a pool of blood, she tore a strip from her petticoat and knelt to bandage his wound. One of the conspirators hit her and another threatened to knife her, but Horment admonished them in macho fashion, "We are not here to kill women."

Frustrated, angry, and now fearful because of their failure, the conspirators again turned on Manuela. Carujo kicked her, grazing her shoulder and wounding her forehead. He then beat her with the flat of his sword, inflicting injuries that took weeks to heal. As the mob left, loyal Col. William Ferguson entered the palace, despite Manuela's shouted warning. Carujo shot and killed him. The brave, loyal British officer had been promoted in 1826 after his extraordinary service at Pasto. He began his career with the Patriots as a drummer boy for the British Battalion on the lower Apure. Captured and imprisoned for fourteen months at Puerto Cabello, he escaped to Margarita and joined the Irish Legion. Twice wounded, he later made an epic ride, accompanied by Capt. Belford Hinton Wilson, of eighteen hundred miles in nineteen days, to deliver Bolívar's new constitution to Sucre in Chuquisaca, Bolivia. The latter—dispatched by his father, Gen. Sir Robert Wilson of the British Army, to assist the Patriots—arrived just in time to fight at the battle of Junín. Promoted to colonel, he faithfully remained with the Liberator until his death, then in 1832 he served as British consul general in Peru and, beginning in 1849, in Venezuela. Bolívar's will included specific thanks to Wilson's father for his son's excellent service.

Some of the men with Guerra at Vargas Barracks killed Padilla's guard, Col. José Bolívar, freed Padilla, and fled. The Vargas Battalion pursued the rest of Guerra's men. During the confusion, Bolívar and his servant José Palacios had taken refuge under the Bridge of Carmen in the cold waters of the small San Agustín River, one of Bogotá's sewers. Minutes later pursued and pursuers crossed overhead. Shouts of "Viva el Libertador!" rang out, followed by "Death to the Tyrant! Viva Santander!"

Meanwhile, grenadiers repulsed the third column and rode to the plaza, where Urdaneta took command. He restored order and sent squads to find Bolívar and capture the conspirators. One squad crossed the bridge shouting "Viva el Libertador!" Hearing no opposing shouts, José Palacios crawled up the steep bank to scout for enemies. Then he helped Bolívar climb away from the stinking sewer. Three nerve-wracking hours under the bridge left Bolívar cold, wet, numb, and nearly unable to speak. After that traumatic night, he christened Manuela as "The Liberator of the Liberator."

The next day Bolívar loyalists arrested Santander, Padilla, and several others. Córdoba served as interim secretary of war so that Urdaneta could preside over the trials, sentencing, and executions. No one spoke up to clear José Padilla, who, because he was in prison, could not have taken part in the conspiracy. Several conspirators spoke against him, and a sergeant testified that Padilla could have saved Col. José Bolívar from attack, but instead he had seized his sword and escaped. The Bolívar government ordered Padilla, Horment, Guerra, and ten others executed. Padilla, shot on October 2, faced his executioners dressed in the uniform of a division general, which a sergeant stripped off him. Refusing a blindfold, he shouted out "Cowards!" as the firing squad obeyed their orders. Carujo plea bargained for his life in return for testifying against Santander and others. He received a sentence of perpetual exile from Colombia. Bolívar commuted the death sentence of six conspirators to prison terms and granted amnesty to most of the troops involved.

Santander was convicted of having given counsel and aid to the conspirators. Urdaneta sentenced him to be executed and to have his property confiscated. The Council of State, however, recommended that Bolívar commute the sentence to banishment. Members of the council considered Santander guilty of abetting the conspiracy, but they warned that his execution might be viewed as unjust, vengeful, and overtly political. Bowing to the public protests in Santander's favor, Bolívar commuted the death sentence to banishment and instead of confiscation placed his property in trust.

Santander and his supporters had failed to defeat the Liberator politically at the Ocaña convention and now had failed to kill him. He did not, however, abandon his anti-Bolívar activities. Ambition and political philosophy deeply divided the two men. Santander, a dedicated federalist, fervently opposed Bolívar's centralist, authoritarian tendencies. From 1829 to 1832, the exile traveled in the United States and Europe. After Bolívar's death, Santander would get a taste of the life the Liberator had endured. With the dissolution of Gran Colombia, he served as the first elected president of New Granada (1832–37). He ruled competently but suffered plots against his life and had to maintain control by force. Despite their philosophical differences, Santander and Bolívar faced similar, intractable political realities.

Bolívar had little time to savor his narrow escape. Pressing problems demanded his attention on other fronts. Bolívar had dispatched O'Leary south as a peace commissioner to Peru. O'Leary and Flores arrived in Guayaquil on September 13, where they tried to arrange the suspension of hostilities and the negotiation of two major problems. Peru and Colombia disputed the boundary between them, and Peru owed Colombia a considerable debt for expenses incurred during the liberation. Flores estimated that it would take him two months to muster the five thousand troops needed to confront Peru. O'Leary assured Bolívar that a victory in battle would be the best basis for peace negotiations.

With military conflict imminent, Bolívar again called upon the brave, loyal Sucre. On April 28, 1828, while in Bolivia, Sucre had married by proxy a woman from Quito, Mariana Carcelán y Larrea, marquesa de Solando. They had met at a ball in 1822, when he was twenty-seven and she seventeen years of age. They became engaged the following year, but owing to war and politics they had not seen each other since. Sucre had been married before, but his first wife died. Like the Liberator, he had taken many mistresses over the years. Sucre resigned the presidency of Bolivia in mid-1828 and rode to Cobija on the coast. He and Mariana found time for a brief honeymoon. From Cobija he sailed to Callao and then to Guayaquil, where he met O'Leary and Flores.

Arriving in Guayaquil on September 19, Sucre spent the day briefing Flores and O'Leary on the situation in Peru and Bolivia. He told them that President La Mar intended to take command of the Peruvian army and march north to the Colombian border. A squadron under George Martin Guise, an able English naval officer, approached Guayaquil by sea. Sucre left Guayaquil for Quito, anxious to join his wife and to retire from public life. It was not to be. Admiral Guise began the blockade of Guayaquil on September 28. O'Leary and Flores wondered what La Mar would do. He remained with the army in northern Peru, "talking much, doing nothing," reported O'Leary. In November, O'Leary informed Bolívar that Flores had gone to Riobamba to raise an army, leaving John Illingsworth, an English general, commanding at Guayaquil.

Peruvian agents persuaded Guise that if he attacked Guayaquil the port would offer no resistance. The agents were wrong. Guise's guns fired on the city on November 22, but Illingworth returned fire. Shelling continued for two days until a cannonball killed Guise. Bereft of its commander, the fleet broke off the attack.

Bolívar dispatched a special messenger to Sucre in Quito on October 28, 1828, naming him "absolute commander of the south," an appointment that inflamed the jealousy of the ambitious Flores. "All my powers, for both good and evil, I delegate to you. Whether or not you make war or peace, save the south or bring about its ruin, you are the arbiter of its destinies. I have placed all my hopes in you." Sucre plotted how to checkmate La Mar and the Peruvians. The six-month rainy season would soon begin, flooding the low land surrounding Guayaquil, and neither Colombian nor Peruvian troops would be able to cross the flooded plains. Even if Peruvians occupied Guayaquil, they could not threaten the important border provinces of Cuenca and Loja. Here the Colombian army could be well fed, so Sucre chose the plain of Tarquí for the battlefield.

The grand marshal of Ayacucho advised Flores on December 18 that he should await the enemy at the gates of Cuenca. Flores moved his army there. La Mar occupied Loja in January 1829. On Sucre's orders, Illingsworth surrendered Guayaquil and retired north to Daule, where he directed guerrilla operations. Sucre joined Flores at Cuenca on January 27, and a month later the opposing Colombian and Peruvian armies fought nearby at Tarquí. After two hours of battle, half the Peruvians lay as casualties and the other half had fled. The almost invincible Sucre added another splendid battle to his military glory.

Sucre's generous peace agreement, the convention of Girón signed February 28, stipulated that a treaty would be made after Peruvian troops had evacuated Colombian territory. Sucre bade farewell to the army at Tarquí on March 2, 1829, and headed back to Quito. He wrote Bolívar that the crisis was over, that he was tired and going home, and that he hoped Bolívar would relieve him of command. As Bolívar neared Pasto, he received Sucre's request. Sucre was wrong; Bolívar faced yet another political crisis. Col. José María Obando (1795–1861) had declared against Bolívar in Popayán late in September 1828. The illegitimate son of an elite Popayán family, he had been adopted by a member of the Pasto gentry and thus grew up with an air of legitimacy. A Royalist guerrilla officer from 1819 to 1822, Obando switched sides and served as a Patriot officer from 1822 through 1828. After independence, he remained enmeshed in Colombian politics, briefly serving as president in the mid-1850s, until he died in an ambush after rebelling against the government in 1861.

Obando left Col. José Hilario López (1798–1869) in command at Popayán and marched south to Pasto. A native of Popayán, López had joined the Patriot cause in 1814, been captured, and languished in prison from 1816 to 1819. However, he opposed the Liberator's dictatorship and actively participated in Colombian politics, serving as president of the nation from 1849 until 1853. Bolívar learned of Obando's insurrection on November 22, but, unable to leave immediately, he dispatched Córdoba with fifteen hundred troops. The Liberator determined that he would personally punish rebellious Peru. He arranged for a Council of Ministers to rule during his absence and decreed on December 24 that elections for delegates to a constituent congress would be held in July 1829. He also instructed that elected representatives should convene in Bogotá on January 2, 1830, to write a new constitution for Colombia. Having made the necessary political preparations to safeguard the republic, Bolívar rode south to join Córdoba. He progressed more slowly than in prior campaigns, however, owing to his rapidly declining health.

In November, Obando routed the Patriot forces in Popayán, led by Tomás Cipriano de Mosquera. After retaking the city, Córdoba publicly humiliated Mosquera. However, the latter survived to hold a number of important diplomatic and political posts, including the presidency of Colombia. Anxious to push forward into Peru, Bolívar decided to negotiate with the rebellious Obando. He sent two priests with an offer of pardon to any rebels in Pasto who laid down their arms. Obando sent two commissioners to negotiate, then rode to greet Bolívar. They met on March 2 at the bridge over the Río de Mayo. Obando promised safe conduct for Bolívar's armies through Popayán and Pasto on south to Quito and Guayaquil. Still feeling invincible, Bolívar traveled with Obando, with no other protection, for a day and a half. Obando gave Bolívar what he wanted but at a high price. He demanded and got promotion to the rank of general and exemption of the men of Pasto from military service for a year. Unaware of Sucre's defeat of La Mar, Bolívar had given away much to gain little.

Only in Pasto did Bolívar learn of Sucre's victory at Tarquí. He received the news of La Mar's promise to evacuate his Peruvian forces with mixed emotions. He dearly wanted to thrash the Peruvians and force them to submit to his rule. On the other hand, a larger, bloodier conflict had been avoided. The Liberator also learned of Sucre's desire to be relieved of his command. Bolívar ordered all troop commanders to suspend their march southward, then he rode on to Quito to meet Sucre. A sick, emotional Bolívar twice tried unsuccessfully to respond to Sucre's greeting; then they silently embraced.

Bolívar granted Sucre's fervent wish to be relieved of his command. Mariana and Sucre were expecting their first child. Bolívar did not disturb them again when he received word that the Peruvians had broken the Girón Convention, had refused to evacuate Guayaquil, and continued to wage war. The Liberator sent O'Leary to inform the Council of Ministers in Bogotá of renewed hostilities, then he dispatched Córdoba with his division to Quito. An elated and excited Córdoba departed, expecting to receive the command that Sucre did not want. Bolívar, however, spoiling for a fight and another shot at glory, took command personally and ordered the disgruntled Córdoba back to Popayán without his army.

Peruvian politics again interrupted Bolívar's march on Guayaquil. On June 6 two subordinates, Agustín Gamarra and Antonio Gutiérrez de la Fuente, overthrew La Mar's government. Gamarra shipped La Mar to Guatemala, where he soon died. La Fuente, correctly seeing a war against Colombia as senseless and fratricidal, vowed to end hostilities and negotiate an honorable peace. Once again, Bolívar did not have to retake Guayaquil by force. Commissioners concluded an armistice in Piura, signed by Gamarra on July 10; Peru would return Guayaquil to Colombia after Bolívar signed the armistice. The first city founded by the Spanish in Peru (1532), Piura witnessed an end to nearly three centuries of Spanish colonial domination. On July 21 a triumphant Bolívar entered Guayaquil. Unfortunately, he became seriously ill with what he diagnosed as a liver ailment.

Back in Quito, Mariana gave birth to baby Teresa (called Teresita) on July 10, 1829. A somewhat disappointed Sucre, showing the machismo of his day, wrote apologetically to Flores, the child's godfather, that "she gave me a daughter." To Bolívar he wrote, "Unfortunately, I have a daughter instead of a soldier to serve my country." Mariana remained in bed for weeks, with her mother and three sisters hovering around her. Perhaps baby Teresa sensed her father's disappointment. Whenever Sucre approached, the baby cried and Mariana sighed. The marshal of Ayacucho proved to be a nervous, timid parent. He, who had ruled a nation, commanded armies, and stoically endured cries of the wounded and groans of the dying, could not abide the whimpering of his wife and child. To escape, he volunteered to return to politics, agreeing to represent his province in the constituent congress.

Along with the disruptions in Guayaquil and Peru, the Liberator also had a brief, unpleasant encounter with future American president William Henry Harrison (1773–1841). As a strong supporter of President John Quincy Adams, Harrison received appointment as U.S. minister to Colombia. He arrived in Bogotá in February 1829, only to be recalled a month later by

Andrew Jackson, who had defeated Adams's bid for reelection in 1828. Harrison remained minister until his successor arrived in September. The actions and government of Bolívar did not measure up to the American minister's standard of what constituted proper republicanism. The ethnocentric Harrison understood little of the obdurate political and social divisions that faced Bolívar.

After leaving Colombia, Harrison fired off a patronizing letter to Bolívar, declaring that "the strongest of all governments is that which is most free." This chastisement aroused controversy in Colombia but also proved helpful in Harrison's subsequent career. Harrison did nothing to improve Bolívar's already worsening view of the United States. Writing to English chargé Patrick Campbell in Bogotá on August 5, 1829, the Liberator bemoaned "the United States, who seem destined by Providence to plague America with torments in the name of freedom."

Americans elected Harrison as their ninth president in 1840. The nation's oldest president inaugurated up to that time, he delivered a long-winded inaugural address, greeted supporters in a snowstorm, and caught a bad cold. In his address, he again chastised Bolívar, a decade after the Liberator's death. "Caesar became the master of the Roman people and the senate under the pretense of supporting the democratic claims of the former against the aristocracy of the latter; Cromwell, in the character of protector of the liberties of the people, became the dictator of England, and Bolívar possessed himself of unlimited power with the title of his country's liberator." Less than a month later, on April 4, 1841, he died of a cold-turned-pneumonia, the first chief executive to die in office. With him died the fortunes of the Whig Party.

Bolívar himself had to cope with worsening health problems. He poured out his fears and concerns in a long letter to O'Leary, written on September 13, 1829: "My condition is incredible, considering the fact that I have been active all my life. Whether it is my mental powers that have greatly declined or my constitution that has been completely undermined, the fact remains that I do not possess the strength for anything, and nothing in all the world can revive it." Nor had the Liberator's deep-seated doubts about Federalism diminished over the years. "I am less inclined toward the federal form of government. Such a system is no more than organized anarchy, or, at best, a law that implicitly prescribes the obligation of dissolution and the eventual ruin of the state with all its members. I think it would be better for South America to adopt the Koran rather than the United States' form of government, although the latter is the best on earth."

Bolívar recognized that, like his own life, much that he had labored for would also end soon. Pondering the troubled future of the vast territory he had freed from Spanish rule, he concluded that, owing to his precarious health, he had to "relinquish the supreme command forever."

> We all know that the union of New Granada and Venezuela holds together solely because of my authority, which must sooner or later come to an end, whenever Providence, or man, so determines.
>
> The Constituent Congress must choose one of two courses, the only ones open in the present situation:
>
> 1. The separation of New Granada and Venezuela.
>
> 2. The creation of a life-term presidency and a strong central government.
>
> I admit that the existing Republic cannot be governed except by the sword, and yet at the same time I must concede that the military spirit is incompatible with civilian rule.

After signing the peace treaty with Peru, Bolívar rode slowly back north, only to receive more bad news in Popayán of further threats to separate Venezuela from Colombia. He also heard that the Council of Ministers, to secure protection from France and England, had agreed to establish a monarchy in Colombia. French agent Charles Bresson and British chargé d'affaires Patrick Campbell suggested making Bolívar king of Colombia. Upon his death, a European prince would rule, but on that issue the intriguers had rival plans. Bresson wanted a French Bourbon to succeed Bolívar, a prospect that alarmed Campbell, especially when the Council of Ministers seemed to favor it. Bresson attempted to negotiate a marriage contract between the sterile Bolívar and a French princess that stipulated that a Bourbon prince would succeed Bolívar.

England did not want its advantageous trade treaty with Colombia jeopardized by the Bourbons and preferred dealing with three or four smaller, easily influenced nations. At least one English agent, Adm. Charles Elphinstone Fleming, was already abetting a separatist movement in Venezuela. He moved his headquarters from Barbados to Caracas in May, where he entertained Páez and encouraged him to separate Venezuela from Colombia. Many Venezuelans did not need much encouragement to consider secession. Residents of Caracas chafed under the demotion of their city from a major political and economic center during colonial times to a satellite of Bogotá. Slow communications between the two cities—messages might take a month in transit—hampered effective governance. Localism and distrust of outside authority, not Bolívar's call for international cooperation, characterized the worldview of most Latin Americans.

When disappointed, angry, bitter Córdoba heard of the monarchical scheming, he rode down the Cauca Valley toward Antioquia, spreading the seeds of rebellion against the "tyrant Bolívar." He charged that Bolívar expected to rule as king, bound by neither laws nor a constitution. The Council of Ministers in Bogotá learned of Córdoba's rebellion in late September. Minister of War Urdaneta ordered O'Leary and eight hundred veteran troops to wipe out the rebels. Later in 1830 Urdaneta tried to restore a dictatorship under his command, but Bolívar would not support him. He left Colombia in 1831 and later served as Venezuelan minister to Spain and France.

O'Leary fought Córdoba near the mountains east of Medellín on October 17, killing half the rebel troops. Some of the rebels fled, but most of the rest lay wounded, including Córdoba. Col. Rupert Hand found José María Córdoba lying on the floor of a hut and brazenly killed him. Córdoba and his brother Salvador had fought bravely for the Patriots in many battles. As with many other Patriot officers, divisive politics, not battlefield dangers, brought about his downfall. Hand was later tried, found guilty of murder, and sentenced to death, but he escaped from prison.

A popular assembly in Caracas prepared to vote for separation when Bolívar arrived in Popayán on November 21. The next day he wrote pointedly to the Council of Ministers and warned them (according to Robert Ker Porter): "You have gone too far in your negotiations with France and England, suspend all such negotiations; you have usurped the functions of Congress and limited its powers, and I will not recognize your acts. Leave the Constituent Congress free to determine Colombia's future." The ministers indignantly declared that they would resign when Bolívar returned to Bogotá. That suited the Liberator just fine, because he could appoint a new cabinet and immediately suspend negotiations with Bresson and Campbell.

The Constituent Congress called by Bolívar lacked a quorum, so it could not begin work as scheduled on January 2, 1830. Delegates trickled into Bogotá during the next two weeks. Bolívar arrived on January 15 and convened Congress five days later. Congress elected Sucre its president and the bishop of Santa Marta, José María Estéves, vice president. Bolívar then declared Congress installed and left. He did not want to be present when the delegates heard his written message. First he congratulated Congress on behalf of the nation for meeting to draft a constitution for Colombia. He reviewed the successful end to conflict with Peru, but then, with an understandable tone of bitterness, he tendered his resignation.

I fear, and not without reason, that my sincerity will be questioned when I speak to you of the magistrate who is to head the Republic. But Congress must realize that their honor forbids them to consider me for that post, and that mine forbids me to accept it. Would you, by chance, return this precious authority to him who has delivered it to you? Would you, conceivably, to the detriment of your good name, cast your votes for me? Would this not mean that I had voted myself into power? Far be it from you or me to stoop to such behavior.

As is it your obligation to organize the Republic into a well established government, you will find, both within and without your own august number, illustrious citizens who are capable of discharging the office of president with glory and success. All, all of my fellow-citizens, excluding none, enjoy the great good fortune of being held innocent of suspicions; only I am branded as aspiring to become a tyrant.

Do as you will with the presidency, which I respectfully deliver into your hands. Henceforth, I am but a citizen-in-arms, ready to defend my country and obey her government. My public duties are forever ended. I formally and solemnly deliver to you the supreme authority conferred upon my by the express wish of the nation.

The committee named by Congress to frame a reply to Bolívar's message concluded that they could not accept his resignation without a new constitution and new leaders in place. While preparing the new constitution, however, Congress also faced a challenge from Páez, who had declared Venezuela an independent and sovereign state. Ironically, not many months earlier, the llanero leader had suggested to the Liberator that they both wash their hands of politics and retire, "like simple Roman citizens," to his farm in Apure. Writing in September 1829, Bolívar replied that "the idea has much moved me. Would to God I could enjoy private life in your companionship."

An idyllic retirement did not lie in the future. Sucre and Bishop Estéves crossed the boundary and entered a few miles into Venezuela. The military commander of La Grita forced them to recross the boundary, insisting that no representative from Bogotá would be allowed on Venezuelan soil. In response to the secession movement led by Páez, the Liberator cried out in despair: "I have never suffered so much, and I long for the moment when this life, now become so ignominious, may end."

Sucre also dreamed of a happier, more peaceful life. While waiting at Cúcuta for the Venezuelan commissioners, Sucre reminisced about Cumaná, his birthplace by the sea, where divers came up with beautiful pearls. He thought of his wife, with whom he had lived for less than a year. He asked a friend to bring him pearls from Cumaná for Mariana. Then he wrote to her: "I think of you more and more tenderly, and want to be near you. I may be asked to become President of Colombia, but I will not accept. I want nothing more than to live with you in retirement and peace."

In mid-April Venezuelan commissioners met with Sucre and Bishop Estéves but resolved nothing. Both sides realized that they had to take several unpalatable steps. The Bogotá Congress would have to recognize Venezuelan independence. They also had to contemplate Bolívar's expulsion from Colombia, a step demanded shrilly by the Venezuelan press. As Sucre and Bishop Estéves rode back to Bogotá, the southern departments of Colombia under the leadership of Flores declared the independent state of Ecuador. The new republic, which enjoyed little political power or status as part of Gran Colombia, began its independence era under the rule of a Venezuelan general. Accepting the political fragmentation that seemed inevitable, the Constituent Congress at Bogotá agreed to divide Colombia into three states. It approved a constitution for New Granada and accepted Bolívar's resignation. As Bolívar prepared to depart on May 5, Sucre rode into Bogotá.

Bolívar's dream of South American unity lay in shambles. Liberals and federalists adamantly rejected his plan for centralized government and a strong chief executive. Unlike George Washington, his North American counterpart, Bolívar could not make the transition from soldier to statesman. Bolívar could be charming, charismatic, and convincing, but, unfortunately, his gigantic ego and almost fanatical quest for glory clouded his judgment and made him appear a megalomaniac. No longer needing his military leadership and finding his dictatorship odious, even one-time friends turned against him. Unwanted, mortally ill, Bolívar slipped quickly from the center stage of history one tragic day at a time. His friend, Col. Joaquín Posada Gutiérrez, recalled the Liberator's despair. As they walked along a brook, "suddenly, with his hands pressing his temples, he cried in a trembling voice, 'My glory, my glory! Why do they destroy it? Why do they calumniate me?'"

Three days after arriving in Bogotá, Sucre heard mobs yelling in the street and saw them burning portraits of Bolívar. The ever-faithful ally raced to warn Bolívar at his residence, but Bolívar had already accepted his fate, departing for Cartagena and European exile. Sucre wrote to him: "When I came to your house to accompany you, you had already departed. Perhaps this was just as well, since I was spared the pain of a bitter farewell. In this hour, my heart oppressed, I do not know what to say to you. Words cannot express the feeling of my soul. . . . Be happy wherever you may be, and wherever you are you may count on your faithful and devoted, Sucre."

Bolívar received Sucre's letter as he neared Cartagena. He sadly replied on May 26. "Your esteemed, undated letter, in which you take leave of me, has filled me with emotion; if it pained you to write it, what of me, for I am leaving not only a friend but also my country!" Fate struck yet another cruel blow as Bolívar waited in Cartagena for money from the sale of his copper mines. Sucre had ridden through the Berrueco Mountains near Pasto on June 4, on his way to join his wife in Quito. Assassins, likely sent by Col. José María Obando and José Hilario López, shot him down. As Bolívar faced exile, his beloved friend and successor, the self-effacing, loyal, humane Sucre, lay murdered. López received promotion to general.

Sucre's murder did not end the unhappiness of his line. Thirteen months after his death, his widow Mariana remarried to a Gen. Isidoro Barriga. Social custom of the time dictated that a widow wait an appropriate length of time, at least five years, or preferably remain unmarried to honor the memory of her husband. Despite what she called her "torn heart" and "painful feelings that burden my soul," Mariana flaunted custom and paid a high social price in so doing. Much more tragically, in mid-November 1831, a drunken Barriga, standing on the first-floor balcony, playfully tossed two-year-old Teresita into the air. He failed to catch her and she crashed to the pavement below and died. Barriga preceded Mariana in death, so she spent her last years alone. She died at age fifty-six, in Quito, on December 15, 1861, "with fever, having practiced all virtues, especially charity toward the poor, and lamented by almost every one."

The heat and humidity of Cartagena became intolerable to the failing Bolívar. He waited impatiently for money to finance his exile, money that never came. José Palacios and a few friends moved Bolívar to Barranquilla in October 1830 and then inland to nearby Soledad. Joaquín Mier, a wealthy Spaniard near Santa Marta, sent Bolívar an invitation to come to his villa three miles from Santa Marta, where he could rest and regain his health.

Either Mier or Bolívar (the accounts are ambiguous) requested that the prefect at Cartagena send a vessel immediately to Savanilla for Bolívar. No Colombian vessel was ready for sea at Cartagena, but Lt. Comdr. Isaac Mayo of the USS *Grampus* promptly offered his services. He sailed immediately to windward. When he anchored at Savanilla, however, he learned that Bolívar had just embarked on the brig *Manuel,* which Mier had sent for him. The *Grampus* escorted the *Manuel* to Santa Marta.

Both vessels anchored at Santa Marta on December 1. The next day Dr. George B. MacNight, surgeon on the *Grampus,* and Dr. Alexandre Prospère Révérend, graduate in medicine of the University of Paris, examined Bolívar. According to MacNight's diagnosis, Bolívar suffered from chronic lung catarrh. Révérend concluded that he had pulmonary and meningeal tuberculosis. In either case, the Liberator faced a grim prognosis.

The next day faithful José Palacios, his slave and companion since his youth, carried Bolívar in his arms to a carriage that bore him to Mier's villa, San Pedro Alejandrino, near Santa Marta. Bolívar's physical condition had deteriorated badly, but his mind remained clear. He issued his final heart-rending proclamation to "the People of Colombia," dated December 10, 1830. Even as he lay dying, he tried to urge his recalcitrant people toward reconciliation and unity.

You have witnessed my efforts to establish liberty where tyranny once reigned. I have labored unselfishly, sacrificing my fortune and my peace of mind. When I became convinced that you distrusted my motives, I resigned my command. My enemies have played upon your credulity and destroyed what I hold most sacred —my reputation and my love of liberty. I have been the victim of persecutors, who have brought me to the brink of the grave. I forgive them.

As I depart from your midst, my love for you tells me that I should make known my last wishes. I aspire to no other glory than the consolidation of Colombia. You must all work for the supreme good of a united nation: the people, by obeying the present government in order to rid themselves of anarchy; the ministers, from their sanctuary, by addressing their supplications to Heaven; and the military, by unsheathing the sword to defend the guarantees of organized society.

Colombians! My last wishes are for the happiness of our native land. If my death will help to end party strife and to promote national unity, I shall go to my grave in peace.

Toward the end of his life, Bolívar apparently recanted his earlier atheism or at least accepted the final rituals of Roman Catholicism. A parish priest heard his confession and administered the sacraments on December 10. Then Bolívar dictated his will. He had two books from Napoleon's library, Rousseau's *The Social Contract,* and Count Raimund Montecuccoli's *The Art of War,* which he left to the University of Caracas. The former had shaped his political thought; the latter treated an "art" at which he had alternately excelled and failed.

Bolívar left eight thousand pesos to his faithful steward José Palacios. He bequeathed all of his real property to his two sisters, María Antonia and Juana, and to the children of his deceased brother, Juan Vicente. He instructed his executors to deliver the sword that Sucre had given him to his wife, Mariana. Article 10 stated that "it is my will that upon my demise my remains be buried in my birthplace, the city of Caracas."

Bolívar faded quickly. His last coherent words were: "Let's go! Let's go! People in this land do not want me. Let's go! Carry my luggage on board the frigate." The Liberator died at age forty-seven on December 17, 1830. His remains were taken to Santa Marta, where, as an eyewitness reported:

> His body was embalmed, and laid in state for three days at the Custom House, the front of which appeared in magnificent mourning, with a monument therein. It is almost impossible to imagine the anxiety that people manifested to get a view of the remains of the Liberator, the staircase being often impassable, from the number ascending and descending. His funeral took place on the 20th, and so splendidly and with so much order was it conducted, that the inhabitants of Santa Martha, in the midst of the grief that overwhelmed them, were pleased to see so much love and gratitude manifested to so worthy a personage.
>
> The ceremony lasted four hours, and in the Holy Cathedral Church a magnificent and tasteful funeral decoration was prepared, which added greatly to solemnize the scene. The populace flocked there in crowds, to see the last of their lamented leader. The militia behaved with so much discipline, that no regiment of the line could exceed it. The band played two funeral marches, and the Moro fortress fired a cannon every half hour, the bells responding with double force. Such is a faint description of what Santa Martha has done on the irreparable loss of the "Immortal Founder of Colombia." (*Kingston Chronicle*, January 8, 1831)

Manuela outlived the love of her life by twenty-nine years, but her ending would be equally tragic. In one of his last letters to her, the Liberator expressed his love and a warning: "My beloved one, I am glad to tell you that I feel well, but I am filled with your grief and my own over our separation. My beloved, I love you very much, and I shall love you much more if you will now be more reasonable than ever before. Be careful what you do, or you may ruin yourself, and that means both of us." Indeed, the combative Manuela found herself scorned and reviled by his enemies.

Her husband asked that she return to his side. She replied with an un-
equivocal and rather blasphemous "no!" "Do you believe, after being the
mistress of this general for several years, with the security of possessing his
heart, I could prefer to be the mistress of the Father, the Son and the Holy
Ghost, or the Holy Trinity?" She also compared Thorne and Englishmen
invidiously with Bolívar. "Monotony is reserved for your nation in love, for
sure, but also in the rest; who else does so well in commerce and sailing.
Love affords you no pleasure, conversation no wit, movement no sprightli-
ness; you greet without feeling, rising and sitting with care, joking without
laughter, these are divine formalities, but I am such a miserable mortal that
I have to laugh at myself, at you and at all your English seriousness. I will
never be yours again."

After learning of Bolívar's death, she let a poisonous snake bite her in a
suicide attempt. In January 1834, a squad of soldiers evicted her from the
house she had shared with her lover in Colombia. Fighting in Ecuador pre-
cluded return there, so, like Bolívar some two decades earlier, she sailed to
exile in Jamaica. After a year, and without government permission, she returned to her native Ecuador, only to be denied entry. Her ties to Bolívar
and her dead brother's politics made her an enemy of the state. President
Juan José Flores would not have a fiery agitator like her in the county.

Nearly destitute, with only her faithful black servants Jonatás and Nathán
to accompany her, she crossed the border and settled in Paitá, a small Peruvian seaport. There she opened a humble store, framed with a sign reading
"Tobacco. English Spoken. Manuela Sáenz." Two year later, Flores relented
and gave her permission to return to Ecuador. "How kind you are," she
replied curtly. "The worst is that the damage is done; I will not return to my
native soil since you know, my friend, that it is easier to destroy something
than to make it new." Thorne reportedly sent her money that she refused to
accept. After he was murdered in June 1847, she also refused any part of the
inheritance that he provided, English gentleman to the end. Manuela also
outlived her two servants.

A few people who recalled her glory days stopped to visit. Herman Melville
(1819–91) stopped to visit while on a whaling expedition in 1841, a decade
before writing his great epic *Moby Dick*. She sometimes translated the letters of English-speaking seagoing men to their Latin American lovers.
Giuseppe Garibaldi (1807–82), Italian freedom fighter and "Hero of Two
Worlds," talked with her in 1851, describing her as "the most gracious and
charming matron." Famed Peruvian writer Ricardo Palma also visited. "I
never passed by without spending an hour of delightful conversation with

Doña Manuela Sáenz." About a decade before her death, she fell and dislo-
cated her hip, making her more dependent upon others. Unfortunately, her
death would also erase much of the rich, historical record about her. She
died on November 23, 1856, during a diphtheria epidemic in Paitá. To prevent the spread of the disease, officials burned all her belongings, including
precious letters, mostly from her beloved Bolívar.

CHAPTER 16

From Demagogue to Demigod

The rancor against Bolívar gradually cooled in the decade following his death. As Chris Conway has pointed out, a national cult of Bolívar emerged in Venezuela between 1830 and 1842. During this period, termed "the Conservative Oligarchy" (1830–47), civil wars and other brutal political traumas suffered by the nascent republic generated a profound yearning for unity. In 1835, pro-Bolívar Gen. Santiago Mariño led a separatist movement in eastern Venezuela. The coup, known as the Guerra de Reformas, failed, but the government's inflexible treatment of its leaders widened existing schisms between conservative and liberal factions. Calls for political clemency for the defeated "Reformistas" brought the issue of national history to the fore. Many politicians and much of the public concluded that soldiers of the past, regardless of their mistakes, deserved to be honored by the nation. Even from the grave, Bolívar continued to shape political debate and conflict in his homeland.

During this acrimonious and divisive time, the shadow of Bolívar, whose remains had lain in Colombian exile since 1830, took on renewed symbolic importance. On February 9, 1842 (twelve years after Bolívar's death), his onetime adversary José Antonio Páez petitioned Congress to return the Liberator's ashes to his native Caracas, an act that would fulfill Bolívar's deathbed wish. Congress decreed that this should be done with proper decorum and with the participation of the governments of New Granada (Colombia) and Ecuador. Venezuela invited both governments to send representatives to Santa Marta in November to exhume Bolívar's remains.

On Sunday, November 13, 1842, Capt. Jonathan Jones Wheeler of Philadelphia wrote in the logbook of his brig *Caracas:* "Having lain in Laguayra
[La Guaira] 6 Days and having discharged our outward cargo and taken in
a sufficiency of bricks and stone for ballast and having been chartered by
the Venezuelan Government for $1000 per month to proceed to St. Martha
as one of the vessels of the Expedition to Convey to Laguayra the remains
of the Liberator Gen. Bolívar, we got under way at 4 O'Clock P.M. Clear
weather and wind from the Eastward."

On Thursday, December 15, 1842, Captain Wheeler entered his ship's cabin.
He sat down at the table where he customarily wrote. He opened a new
ledger and carefully titled the first page: "Journal of a Voyage in the brig
Caracas, to accompany an expedition from Venezuela to New Granada, for
the remains of Bolívar." As the hours passed, the captain recorded another
episode in Bolívar's life and death.

Captain Wheeler's Journal

For twelve years the ashes of Bolívar lay in peace in the Cathedral of
St. Martha. On his death bed it had been his request that he should be
removed for interment to his native city of Caracas. Time has silenced
the voice of detraction, for even the great and good have made their enemies; and the memory of his virtues and his services was becoming dearer
and dearer to his countrymen. They had pondered them deep in their
hearts, and they were the theme of every tongue.

"And praising what is lost
Make the remembrance dear."

The Congress of Venezuela in March 1842, passed a decree to comply
with his last request, and to ask his remains of the Government of New
Granada, to which they responded in the affirmative. Preliminaries having been settled, preparations were made to put them in execution, and
on the 13th November, 1842, a small fleet took its departure from the port
of Laguayra for that purpose, bearing with it the prayers and wishes of
the inhabitants of Laguayra and Caracas for its safe and speedy return.

The fleet included a Venezuelan government schooner *Constitution,*
(manned by a post captain as chief of the expedition); the French ship
Circe, of thirty-two guns, sent by the French Government in honor of the
occasion; and an American merchant brig, the *Caracas* of Philadelphia,
chartered by the Venezuelan Government.

The *Constitution's* cabin had been enlarged and fitted up in an elegant
manner with black silk drapery and an altar, and she was to bring back

the remains. On board this vessel went none other than the Commodore, his officers and crew, and an officer of engineers for the purpose of taking views [with a daguerreotype].

On board the *Circe,* went by invitation, the Hon. Commissioners for the reception of the body, and also two relatives of the deceased General.

On board the *Caracas* went sixteen cadets, young men of the first families of Caracas, gentlemanly and soldier-like in their deportment. They were under the command of a lieutenant, and were to form a guard of honor at the reception of the body. . . .

In the course of the next day, the 14th, we passed the Island of Curaçao, still holding our course to the northward and westward, to clear the Island of Aruba. During the night having obtained our northing, we steered West, and on the morning of the next day hauled into the south and west for the land, and saw the coast of Guajira. This country lies to the westward of the Gulf of Maracaibo, and the coast is rather dreaded and avoided by navigators for it is inhabited by an unconquered race of Indians with whom the whites have had but little intercourse.

Still running before a brisk gale, in the afternoon we made the coast of New Granada, and toward evening saw its lofty mountains lifting their snowy peaks, glittering with sun beams, into the blue vault of Heaven.

These mountains are a spur of the Andes. At a distance of fifty miles I measured the angle of altitude, and with corrections for dip and curvature of the earth, found their height to be 15864 feet which in that latitude is 1082 feet above the line of perpetual congelation.

On the morning of the 16th, we went into the harbor of St. Martha and anchored. Here we found waiting, to accompany the expedition in its return, H. B. M. sloop *Albatross* of 16 guns, and H. M. K. of the Netherlands sloop *Venus* of 18 guns. . . .

St. Martha is situated on a sandy plain, surrounded by mountains, the streets at right angles, the houses low, principally of one story, with white fronts and large door and windows, as is common to all Spanish built places. It contains about 5000 inhabitants, and is situated 1725 geographical miles near South from Philadelphia. . . .

On the 20th, in the afternoon, the exhumation of Bolívar took place, attended by all the officers civil and military of the place, the officers of the men of war, the Commissioners of New Granada from the Capital Bogota, and the Commissioners from Venezuela. Those from the Equador had not arrived, for even distant Quito had sent a deputation. The difficulty of traveling in this country is very great from the badness of the routes, and although it was known that they had been on their way for more than a month, it was not known where they were at this time.

The full and impressive music and chanting ceased, and there was silence in the Cathedral. The covering of stone was removed from the grave which was immediately under the dome in the center of the church, and the coffin was exposed to view. The lid and head were then taken off and there lay the remains of the great Bolívar. The scull was partly exposed to view as were some of the ribs, which had fallen in, and the rest was covered with the moldering cerements of the grave.

O mighty spirit! dost thou lie so low?
Are all they conquests and they glories
Shrunk to this little measure?

No! the spirit of liberty that he instilled into the hearts of his countrymen shall live for ever. The precepts and the instructions that he bestowed upon them shall be cherished by them to the latest posterity.

After some few relics of the lead and moldering coffin had been distributed to those near the grave, the remains were placed in a rich but neat black coffin and conveyed to the foot of the altar. The service of the dead again commenced, and the Cathedral was visited by great numbers of people until late at night.

The 21st was the day appointed for the delivery of the remains to the Venezuelan Commissioners for the conveyance of them on board.

In the afternoon, a procession was formed consisting of all the before mentioned officers and many citizens and a battalion of infantry, and the coffin born by officers alternately relieved, the foreign officers assisting, was carried to the place of embarkation where it was given in formal charge of the commissioners of Venezuela. It was then placed in the barge of the *Constitution*, which together with the crew, was dressed in mourning, and accompanied by the boats of the men-of-war, was rowed to the schooner. The services at the church had protracted the time, and as the coffin was taken on deck, the glare of the minute guns broke through the gloom of the evening.

The next day, the 22d, was appointed for our departure, and every nautical preparation having been made for a long and arduous beat to windward of five hundred miles, we were busy early in the morning in receiving the baggage of the Commissioners who had honored the *Caracas* with the preference of a passage to Laguayra. Part of the cadets were transferred to the *Constitution*, and at 9 o'clock the Commissioners came on board. Then the *Constitution* and *Caracas* got under way—the *Circe*, *Albatross* and *Venus* having been at sea almost half an hour. . . .

On the 24th there were no vessels in sight, and we continued on for the coast of St. Domingo, expecting there smoother water and a chance for land breezes. We arrived at the Rocas, an Island 70 miles north of Laguayra, a place that had been appointed for our rendezvous on the 7th. Decr., in fifteen days, against a boisterous sea and adverse currents, during which time the wind did not vary more than one point from E. by N., having had of course a dead beat all the distance.

The Hon. Commissioners consisted of Dr. José Vargas, a distinguished scholar and Senator of the Republic; Dr. Manuel Ustáriz, son of the author of the declaration of independence and of the constitution of Venezuela, whose father perished by order of the cruel and bloody General Boves in 1813, a year aptly designated by the Colombians as the year of Death, from the number of cold blooded massacres and executions of the countrymen by the hands of the Spaniards.

José María Carreño, a general of division. In this mild and unostentatious gentleman you see the victor of many battles. He is now covered with wounds and the loss of an arm in the service of his country. It was not his first visit to St. Martha, for there in a hard fought action, he had driven the Spanish army from their last foothold in New Granada. There too, subsequently, he had stood at the death bed of his beloved Commander-in-chief. Father José Cipriano Sánchez, the venerable Prebendary of the Cathedral of Caracas, now over sixty years of age, was acting as grand chaplain for the removal of the body.

When such men as these respond to the call of their government and without fee or reward, leave their comfortable homes to encounter a boisterous voyage by sea, it shows that they had patriotism to support their noble enthusiasm. . . .

On the evening of the 12th, the *Venus* not having made her appearance, the fleet got under way for Laguayra, and at 2 o'clock in the morning, we were within three miles of the port, having run over a wind in eight hours, a distance of seventy-two miles.

We again tacked off the land and did not enter the harbor until 7 o'clock, when we ran in and anchored. Our colors were at half mast, as were those on the walls and batteries on shore. The fleet then laid their yards to a St. Andrew's cross. The body was to remain this day and the next on board the schooner.

I had expected at St. Martha to have found the flag of my country flying from a National vessel, but there were none. I certainly thought to have found one on our arrival at La Guayra. But there too, I was disappointed.

What the policy or wisdom was that dictated this, I know not; for it would have been but a small boon of courtesy to have bestowed upon a sister Republic, and one too, that like ourselves, had struggled through a period of gloom to a bright and glorious Independence.

On going on shore I found that extensive preparations had been made and were still in progress for the reception of the body. The streets had been carefully swept and then strewn with sand. The landing place was festooned with black, and adorned with arches of palm boughs, and the fronts of all the houses along the main street were hung with black, or in the progress of being so.

On the 14th, the body still remained on board, and strangers were thronging in from the country and from the capital.

On Thursday, the 15th, accompanied by all the boats of the vessels in the port, it was carried on shore in the schooner's barge, and when placed on the pier, the Commissioners that had been to St. Martha, gave up their precious charge to another appointment.

The echoes of the minute guns rolled from cliff to valley of the lofty Silla, as the procession to slow and solemn music, passed through the sable drapers of the streets and the remains reached the church, there to lie in state until the morrow, when they will be borne to Caracas, distant twelve miles; again to be met by further honors and a mourning population.

They will then be taken to the Cathedral, their final resting place, and the last request of Simón Bolívar the Liberator will have been complied with.

The polished marble of Italy will rear its column above his ashes, but his memory in the hearts of his countrymen shall outlive the work of the sculptor. (Wheeler's "Journal" originally appeared in the *Morning Courier* and *New York Enquirer* on January 10, 1843.)

FROM DEMAGOGUE TO DEMIGOD

Bolívar still had not completed his final journey. The cathedral would not be his final resting place. In the 1870s, President Antonio Guzmán Blanco (1829–99) disturbed the Liberator once more, but again to honor him. Guzmán Blanco knew well the vagaries and intrigue of Venezuela politics. A magnetic, forceful figure, he helped depose Páez in 1863 and seven years later led a successful revolt against José Ruperto Monagas. Egocentric, not unlike Bolívar, he commissioned countless portraits and statues of himself.

In a message to Congress in 1874, Guzmán Blanco ordered further honors for the Liberator: "It is not enough that Venezuela's heroes be preserved for posterity on the pages of history. Their ashes should be guarded with religious respect, in this manner insuring an everlasting monument of national gratitude." A few days later the president declared the Church of the Santísima Trinidad of Caracas to be the National Pantheon. He instructed that the remains of Venezuela's "Illustrious Heroes of Independence" be preserved there, along with those of other eminent men named by the president and approved by the Senate.

In February 1876 Guzmán Blanco ordered that the transfer of remains begin. He informed Congress that European specialists would move the monument of the Liberator in the cathedral to the central nave of the Pantheon, where it would stand as the apex of national glory. Guzmán Blanco appointed a *junta directiva* (board) to implement his order. The board buried the remains of Páez, Arismendi and his wife, Señora Luisa Cáceres de Arismendi, Urdaneta, and about thirty other heroes. It then prepared an elaborate three-day ceremony for the transfer of Bolívar's remains.

At noon on October 28, 1876, a long procession escorted Bolívar's remains to the Pantheon. Only the president, the junta directiva, important officials, and members of the press entered the temple dedicated to Venezuela's immortals. Doctor Eduardo Calcaño (1831–1904), man of letters and greatest orator of his day, dramatically addressed the assembly from the pulpit:

> Señores:
> Like a trembling skiff on the immensity of the ocean, like a migrating bird face to face with the profundities of infinite space that he is forced to traverse, so is the orator of today before the solemn majesty of this most high occasion, with the undeclinable assignment of ascending to inaccessible summits, to Olympic heights that dominate the world, and with my voice broadcast to all people and all generations the colossal glory which is the patrimony of humanity. . . .
> Titan [Bolívar] leveled the Andes beneath his stride, and made a seat of Chimborazo on which he conversed with Time and Destiny.
> Others dissolved parliaments; he convoked congresses. Others throttled the Republic; he founded republics and gave them as surety his prestige and power. Others beheaded the people; he educated them for liberty. Others divided territories in order to tyrannize and exploit them; he held them together in the powerful unity of democracy and consecrated them,

with the kiss of his genius, to be the custodians of civilization with the cult of human rights, the philosophy of justice, the permanent law of progress, the sovereignty of the people, and the ennoblement of man on the throne of personal dignity.

This is the great continental work of Bolívar, that which has elevated his stature to the heavens and transformed him into an object of stupendous admiration for the Ages.

In order to make myself in some degree worthy of the prestigious solemnity that overwhelmed by smallness with its grandeur, I placed myself between two great orators in order that their light might shine on my countenance, and their eloquence lend its vibration to my words.

Thus, after having before my eyes the prophecy of Zea, the great orator of times past, and the virile accent of Guzmán Blanco, the best orator of our times, I pronounce the new apocalypse of Bolívar's future glory.

All that we here witness is not yet the apotheosis of Bolívar. His apotheosis will have effect when more lustroms have passed and the great destinies of America have been realized. When ten or more powerful and happy nations seated on the skirt of the Andes send from ports of a peaceful Ocean the products needed for the existence of the Old World in exchange for what the Old World has discovered and improved in industry and the arts, for progress and civilization.

When thousands of steamboats plough the immense net of rich rivers from the Orinoco to the Straits of Magellan, and when locomotives cross that vast territory where the sound of labor and the vigor of ideas prevail—then, on top of all this grandeur will be the figure of Bolívar radiating its glory to all horizons of the earth, as the sun radiates its light over the universe.

BOLÍVAR'S LEGEND AND LEGACY

Bolívar continues to cast a huge shadow across Venezuelan and Latin American history and politics. Even during his lifetime, parents named their children in honor of his feats. Aide Daniel O'Leary named his son, the first of nine children, for his comrade. His son would take charge of publishing thirty volumes of his father's memoirs between 1879 and 1888. Simon Bolivar Buckner, born in 1823 in Hart County, Kentucky, went on to become a famous military officer, like his namesake. Buckner graduated from West Point in 1844 and later went into business in Louisville. In 1860, he pushed successfully for the creation of a large Kentucky militia and, as inspector general, took charge of the training. Buckner favored neutrality at the beginning of the Civil War, but when the legislature turned strongly Unionist, he tilted toward the Confederacy in reaction. In September 1861, he received a commission as Confederate brigadier general. He survived the war and died in 1914.

In addition to namesakes, Bolívar is remembered in countless works of literature, both fiction and historical. In 1931, Venezuelan novelist and essayist Arturo Uslar Pietri, born in 1906, published his vivid novelized account of the Liberator's Venezuelan campaign. His historical novel, *Las lanzas coloradas,* stands as a powerful example of Spanish American regionalist literature.

In "Bolívar: Poema" (1955), Guatemalan writer Miguel Angel Asturias, a Nobel Prize winner, recast the Apostle's Creed to honor the Liberator: "I believe in Liberty, Mother of America, creator of sweet seas upon earth, and in Bolívar, her son, Our Lord, who was born in Venezuela, suffered under Spanish power, was fought against, felt death on Mount Chimborazo, and with the rainbow descended in hell, rose again at the voice of Colombia, touched the Eternal with his hands and is standing next to God."

Landmarks honor his memory throughout Latin America. But statues of the Liberator also dot the globe, including ones standing in Ottawa, New York City, Washington, D.C., New Orleans, Cairo, Paris, and in London's Belgrave Square. Occasional criticism has arisen, but Bolívar has for the most part retained his status as a demigod. Plaza Bolívar honors him in Santa Fe de Bogotá, the city that spent more than a million dollars in 1998 restoring the house where he and Manuela spent many blissful hours together. "This house sums up the moments of glory, joy and delight that Bolivar had for his triumphs and also of sadness and deception for the betrayals by his friends," said Elvira Cuervo de Jaramillo, president of Bogotá's historical restoration society, which helped with the project.

Every two years a biennial International Simón Bolívar Prize celebrates his memory. Established by the government of Venezuela and awarded through UNECSO, the prize rewards activities that contribute to the freedom, independence, and dignity of peoples, to the strengthening of solidarity among nations, or activities that have facilitated the quest for a new international, economic, social, and cultural order. The first award was made during the bicentennial of Bolívar's birth. According to British historian Tristam Platt, Bolívar even worked his way into the cosmology of some Andean Indians. Like Jesus Christ, he became linked in Indian religious beliefs to the traditional "sun of justice."

Statue of Simón Bolívar in Washington, D.C. Photograph by Ralph Blessing

Venezuela historian Germán Carrera Damas has decried "the cult of Bolívar" that persists in deforming the nation's historiography. Other historical figures and events go unexamined and forgotten in Venezuela's myopic adulation of Bolívar. To others, however, "the cult of Bolívar is the main reason for unity among Venezuelans." This view, expressed by historian and former President Ramón J. Velasquez, remains strong. "His ideas are still current. They're not just something you go to the library to read about."

Given his significance, it is not surprising that varied political groups have seized upon his memory for their own purposes. In January 1974, members of the M-19 revolutionary group of Colombia stole a saber that had belonged to Bolívar. They hoped that the high-profile theft would generate sympathy for their cause and link them in the public's mind to the Liberator's legacy. The plan backfired miserably, as the Colombian people expressed outrage, not support. M-19 even lost the sword for a couple of years. Seventeen years after the theft, on January 31, 1991, the guerrilla organization returned the long-missing saber. It remains a vital political symbol for the nation.

The sword of Bolívar's counterpart in Argentina, José de San Martín, received similar reverential treatment. The old soldier bequeathed his sword to Juan Manuel de Rosas, dictator of Argentina during the 1840s. In 1880 San Martín's remains were transferred from France to Buenos Aires and buried at the Metropolitan Cathedral. In 1897 the Rosas family formally presented his sword to the Argentine nation. It holds a place of honor in the National Historical Museum. The San Martín Museum in Buenos Aires and a colossal monument at Mendoza to the crossing of the Andes also commemorate his contributions.

Controversy continues to surround the Liberator in death as it did in life. In 1988 Christie's planned to auction some of Bolívar's medals, jewelry, and other artifacts. Outraged nationalists responded by forming the Association for the Recovery of Venezuela's National Patrimony. According to the auction house, the government of Venezuela had ignored prior offers to purchase the collection. Pressured by inflamed nationalism, the Venezuelan government bought the items for $2.9 million before the auction date.

In September 1987 several leftist revolutionary groups in Colombia joined together to form an umbrella organization, the Simón Bolívar Guerrilla Coordination (CGSB, Coordinadora Guerrillera Simón Bolívar). Constituent groups included the Revolutionary Armed Forces of Colombia (FARC, Fuerzas Armadas Revolucionarias de Colombia), the National Liberation Army (ELN, Ejercito de Liberación Nacional), and the M-19. This cooperation somewhat strengthened the insurgent movement in the nation. In August 1999, the CGSB kidnapped Monsignor José de Jesús Quintero Díaz, bishop of the Diocese of Tibú, which lies in the north of Colombia.

In 1989 Colombian Nobel Prize–winner Gabriel García Márquez touched off more protest with *The General in His Labyrinth*. The novel offers a candid, unflattering depiction of Bolívar in his dying days. García Márquez tried to create a realistic, human portrait of the dying Liberator. He has Bolívar suffering from insomnia, delirium, intestinal gas, bad breath, and other all-too-human foibles of a sick, dying man. As one reviewer noted, the novel "stripped Bolívar of the aura of ascetic saintliness." Questioning the Liberator's demigod status angered many patriots in Colombia and Venezuela.

García Márquez also initiated a reconsideration of Manuela Sáenz, long maligned for her adultery and outspokenness. "She really is perhaps the most important woman in Latin American history," notes Venezuelan historian Denzil Romero. "She had more political influence than even Eva Perón," the former first lady of Argentina popularized in the musical *Evita*. She is now portrayed not just as a mistress but also as the liberated, intelligent, forceful woman she was. Venezuelan director Diego Risquez presented a positive interpretation of her in his 1998 film "Manuela Sáenz." Owing to the destruction of her personal documents at her death, historians have largely neglected her. The signal exception is Victor Von Hagen, who tried to reconstruct her life in his 1989 biography *The Four Seasons of Manuela*.

Bolívar's status as a demigod became crystal clear in August 1994 with the appearance of a painting, *The Liberator Simón Bolívar 1994*, by Juan Davila, reproduced in the magazine *La Epoca*. According to a Reuter's news report, the avant-garde painter, born in Santiago, Chile, in 1946, depicted the Liberator as "a smirking transvestite with lace stockings and no pants." Reuter's reporter Roger Atwood described the portrait as showing Bolívar with "a woman's breasts, no pants and giving the finger." The Liberator sits astride a multicolored horse. Because his work had received public funding from Chile's Fondart, the scandal took on added national and international political dimensions.

Furious protesters in Venezuela, Colombia, and Ecuador decried reproductions of the painting issued on postcards and in newspapers. Ambassadors from the three nations issued an official protest to Chile, terming the painting "a smear campaign" against Bolívar and "an affront to the national dignity of the people of Venezuela." Colombia's ambassador to Chile termed the painting "gutter art." The Bolivian government chimed in with its own protest against the "offensive and grotesque" work.

Venezuelan protesters burned the Chilean flag in front of the Chilean embassy in Caracas and gathered in protest at Bolívar's imposing statue near Congress. Many demanded that Davila's painting be burned. Housewife Aurora Pineda screamed, "I'm crying because it hurts me. It's not right that the father of our country be mocked." Litdell Díaz, a student, said, "My dignity is offended. Bolívar is here. He's not dead. He's in each one of his children."

The Chilean foreign minister asserted that "a couple of pea brains or a couple or rowdies, or even 10 of them, do not affect the respect we have for Venezuela." Four days after the protest, the Chilean foreign ministry issued a public apology for the "disrespectful" work. "The ministry has presented the government of Chile's apologies to the governments of Venezuela, Colombia and Ecuador in hopes that this unfortunate incident will not affect our broad and fertile relations." The Liberator's legendary status remains powerful political medicine.

The Liberator received a kinder remembrance at the hands of two playwrights. In 1994, Samuel S. Ullman presented his brief twenty-five-minute look at *The Youth, Bolívar.* In late January 1995, the opera *Simón Bolívar* opened in Norfolk, Virginia. Written by Scottish-born Thea Musgrave and directed by Lillian Garrett-Groag (of Argentina), the opera powerfully evokes the high drama and tragedy of the Liberator's life. Reviewing the premiere performance, Edward Rothstein described the opera as "a tragedy, in which honorable political goals become muddied, and idealism is thwarted by messy human realities"—an apt summation of Bolívar's real life. Onstage, Bolívar sings a song that includes the Liberator's despairing judgment, "Those who serve a revolution plough the sea."

At the same time as recorded gunfire echoed on the opera stage in Virginia, real gunfire resounded along the border between Ecuador and Peru. Just as in Bolívar's time, political conflict again engulfed two of the nations he helped liberate. The neighbors violently renewed a boundary dispute dating back more than half a century. Ecuador lost about half its Amazonian territory to Peru in a war fought in 1941. Ecuador has never reconciled itself to the loss of its eastern lands, possibly rich in oil and other minerals. Periodically, the two sides renew the shooting, usually around the anniversary of the peace treaty signed in January 1942. Regional conflicts today remain as real and violent as in Bolívar's time. The Liberator, to his dismay, would certainly understand.

Bolívar casts a long shadow and remains a potent political symbol in his native land. On October 13, 1997, U.S. President Bill Clinton spoke at the Liberator's tomb in Caracas. He had done his homework. "Mr. President, let me begin by thanking you for your warm introduction and your invitation to speak at this sacred place. I am deeply honored to be the first foreign leader ever to address the people of Venezuela at the tomb of Símon Bolívar. It is especially fitting that we meet here at the *Panteón Nacional* for the Liberator belongs not only to Venezuela and the other nations of the Andes. Bolívar belongs to all the Americas. He stands alongside Washington and San Martín in the pantheon of liberty's heroes. He was the first to imagine a hemisphere of democracies united by shared goals and common values. His example stirred the hearts of men and women throughout our region. Indeed, today, we in the United States can still mark the frontier of our nation in the 1820s by finding our towns, our counties, our villages named Bolivar in the states of Missouri, Ohio, Tennessee and West Virginia."

In December 1998, Venezuelans elected as their president Hugo Chavez, a Populist and unabashed self-proclaimed Bolivarian. For Venezuelans, Chavez said, "God is the supreme commander, followed by Bolivar and then me." He also recommended that the nation establish a new name, "the Bolivarian Republic of Venezuela." In early 1999, he launched a massive public works program called "Bolívar 2000." He also pledged to transform education by creating "Bolivarian schools." His political rallies are marked by large crowd movements that he calls the "Bolivarian wave." Later during the year, on July 24, Bolívar's birthday, Chavez removed the Liberator's bejeweled sword and carried it triumphantly but reverently through the streets of Caracas. In September he presented a replica of the sword to Pope John Paul II during a visit to the Vatican. In April the following year, Brazilian President Fernando Henrique Cardoso received a replica of the sword presented to him by Chavez at the presidential palace. Despite massive economic problems and questions about what he terms his "Bolivarian Revolution," Venezuelans reelected Chavez in July 2000.

In October 2000, Cuba's Fidel Castro visited Caracas and placed flowers at the Liberator's tomb at the National Pantheon. He and President Chavez then examined Bolívar's jewel-encrusted sword before visiting a nearby home used by Cuban independence hero José Martí during a brief stay in Venezuela in 1881. Castro also received the keys to the city.

Bolívar, lately honored by Chavez, unwittingly helped sow the seeds of such subsequent conflict and political division. Without question, he played a heroic, historical role in liberating South America from Spanish rule. Although Sucre's great victories in Peru doubtless wounded his pride, the Liberator succeeded wonderfully in his lifelong quest for glory. Regrettably, however, his political goal of South American unification failed, in part, because of Bolívar's flaws of character and vision.

Fearful of social revolution, Bolívar and many leaders after him repressed demands by the masses for social justice, economic opportunity, and political participation. Intransigent liberals fought reactionary conservatives, but both elite factions agreed on keeping power safely out of the hands of the masses. The constitution he authored granted excessive, almost monarchical powers to the executive. Executive abuse of power has plagued Latin American politics ever since. Throughout the nineteenth century, disruptive, personalistic caudillos often exerted autocratic rule in Spanish America.

Bolívar's one-time chief of staff H. L. V. Ducoudray Holstein offered a harsh but prescient appraisal in 1829: "The worst of Bolivar's acts is the last, where he has impudently thrown off his flimsy mask, and declared that 'bayonets are the best, the only rules of nations.' This pernicious example, it is to be feared, will be followed by other chieftains, in the new Spanish Republics." Writing in 1950, historian Arthur P. Whitaker extended the criticism of Bolívar into the twentieth century. His continued influence "betokens not so much growing gratitude for the hero of independence, the liberator, as an increasing use of his prestige for political purposes: the Bolívar cult is largely an expression of the conservative reaction in Latin America. It is one of the chief obstacles to democracy in those parts in which Bolívar's name carries weight."

We should not condemn Bolívar, however, as uniquely shortsighted or power-hungry. On the contrary, many of his views typified those of the Creole elites of his time. George Washington, Bolívar's North American counterpart, learned from setbacks and matured into a capable, skilled political leader. Had Bolívar been able to learn from his political mistakes as quickly as he did from his military defeats, he might have charted a happier political course for South America. Latin America needed a statesman of Washington's caliber and found none. However, as Lester D. Langley's comparative analysis of *The Americas in the Age of Revolution* (1996) shows, caudillo rule, Centralist-Federalist civil wars, and other divisive conflicts engulfed most of Spanish America after independence, not just those lands once controlled by Bolívar.

Bolívar's political shortcomings tarnish the shining glory of his military victories, but even on the battlefield there was erratic performance, ranging from brilliance to negligence. However, legendary figures generate their own power that is seldom diminished by the historical facts. Bolívar's greatness still inspires patriotism and political idealism more than two centuries after his birth. Many Venezuelan buildings display his words of wisdom, such as "Morality and enlightenment are our first necessities."

In a recent commentary on the Liberator's continuing influence, Larry Rohter (*Montreal Gazette*, August 8, 2000) asked a simple yet complex question, "Which Bolívar?" "There is one Bolívar, for instance, who praised democracy as 'the most sacred source' of power, but there is also another who once proclaimed that 'necessity recognizes no laws.' One Bolívar admired George Washington as the ideal 'citizen-hero' who 'fills my bosom with emulation,' while another famously and bitterly remarked that 'the United States seems destined by providence to plague Latin America with misery in the name of liberty.' [Venezuelan President] Chavez describes himself as a disciple of Bolívar, and some of his more ardent followers have gone so far as to suggest he is the 'reincarnation of the Liberator.' But his vision of Bolívar is one 'very much adapted to his own purposes,' said Jesus Sanoja Hernández, a prominent political commentator here."

Guillermo Morón, a leading Venezuelan historian, pointed up the same contradiction. The Bolívar that Chavez "likes is the one who centralized power," said Morón. "The Bolívar that the opposition likes, in contrast, is the one who respected the law, consulted even his enemies and tried to create an impartial system of justice for all." At different points in his eventful life, Bolívar did indeed act in contradictory, sometimes destructive ways, but he remained ever mindful of his quest for glory.

In 1983 UNESCO published a volume that included "Bolívar's Proclamation to the Soldiers of the United Army of Liberation in Pasco on July 29, 1824." He delivered the speech a few days before the decisive battles of Junín and Ayacucho. Bolívar exhorted his men:

> Soldiers! You are about to complete the greatest task that Heaven has entrusted to men, the task of liberating an entire world from slavery.
>
> Soldiers! The enemies you have to destroy boast of their fourteen years of triumphs; they will, therefore, be well placed to match their weapons against your own, which have excelled in a thousand battles.
>
> Soldiers! Peru and the whole of America place in you their hopes for peace, the daughter of victory. Liberal Europe, too, is watching you, spellbound, since the freedom of the New World is the hope of the Universe. Would you dash such hopes? No, no, no!

Bolívar's words and deeds serve as powerful reminders that one determined individual, even one with serious flaws of character and temperament, can dramatically shape the course of human history.

APPENDIX

Highlights of Simón Bolívar's Life and Times

1750	Francisco de Miranda born in Caracas.
1773	December 1, Simón's father, Juan Vicente de Bolívar y Ponte, marries his mother, Concepción Palacios y Blanco.
1778	José de San Martín born in Argentina.
1783	July 24, Simón José Antonio de la Santísima Trinidad de Bolívar y Palacios born in Caracas, Venezuela.
1786	January 19, Bolívar's father dies.
1789	French Revolution.
1792	July 6, Bolívar's mother dies.
1795	Runs away from his guardian, Don Carlos Palacios. Tutored by Simón Rodríguez.
1797–78	Tutored by Andrés Bello.
1798	July 4, commissioned as a second lieutenant in the cadet corps of the Militia of Aragua.
1799	January 19, departs for Spain to complete his education, learning much from the Marquis de Ustáriz. Writes his first letter from Vera Cruz. George Washington dies.
1802	February, sees and admires Napoleon Bonaparte in Paris. May 26, marries María Teresa Rodríguez del Toro, his cousin; they return to Venezuela.
1803	January 22, María Teresa dies; Bolívar pledges never to marry again.
1804	Returns to Europe; in Paris he enjoys the elite social circle of Fanny Du Villars. Again meets his tutor Simón Rodríguez and travels with him. December 2, witnesses the coronation of Napoleon.
1805	August 15, climbs Monte Sacro (Aventine Hill) in Rome and vows to liberate his homeland. December 27, initiated as a mason of the Scottish rite in Paris.
1806	Miranda's invasions of Venezuela fail.

1807	Returns to Caracas, Venezuela, by way of the United States (Charleston, Washington, Philadelphia, New York, Boston).
1808	February, Napoleon Bonaparte invades Spain; Charles IV abdicates the throne; Napoleon's brother Joseph Bonaparte is crowned king of Spain, deposing Ferdinand VII.
1809	July 28, appointed chief justice of Yare.
1810	April 19, Spanish captain general of Venezuela is ejected from power by criollo elites who swear allegiance to Ferdinand. June 10, Bolívar travels to London as an envoy to seek support for Venezuela's revolt against Bonaparte's authority. Bolívar also meets with Francisco de Miranda and convinces him to return to Venezuela, where they both arrive in December.
1811	July 4, Bolívar addresses the Patriotic Society. July 5, congress declares Venezuelan independence. In the ensuing civil war, Bolívar serves under Miranda. First Republic, or Patria Boba.
1812	March 26, massive earthquakes strike Venezuela, killing perhaps 20,000 people. July 6, loses the important seaport Puerto Cabello to the Royalists. July 24, Miranda surrenders to Monteverde. December 15, writes the Cartagena Manifesto.
1813	May 14, begins "Admirable Campaign" of military victories, which ends with his entry to Caracas on August 6. June 18, declares war to the death against Spaniards and Canary Islanders. August 7, named "Liberator" after victories in Mérida and Caracas. Second Republic established.
1814	Second Venezuelan Republic collapses under attack by Juan Boves. Bolívar flees to New Granada, hoping to rebuild an army to liberate Venezuela.
1815	Napoleon defeated at Waterloo. Ferdinand VII returns to the Spanish throne. Pablo Morillo and Spanish troops reconquer Caracas. September 6, issues the "Jamaica Letter" from exile. December 24, lands in Haiti.
1816	Third Republic. March 31, launches the Los Cayos Expedition from Haiti. Invades at Barcelona, with arms and support from Haiti's President Petión.
1817	Manuel Piar and Bolívar drive Royalists from Angostura. October 16, Piar executed.
1818	January 30, meets for the first time José Antonio Páez, llanos caudillo. Continued fighting. Establishes official organ, *Correo de Orinoco*.

1819   February 15, opens second Congress at Angostura. Crosses the Andes and on August 7 defeats Royalists at Boyacá, liberating Colombia. December 17, creates the Republic of Colombia, with three departments, Cundinamarca, Quito, and Venezuela.

1820   27 November, signs armistice with Royalist Gen. Pablo Morillo.

1821   Renewed fighting after broken armistice; June 24, defeats Royalists at Carabobo, liberating Venezuela. President of the new republic of Gran Colombia.

1822   April 7, defeats Royalists at Bomboná; May 24, Sucre defeats Royalists at Pichincha, securing independence of Ecuador. United States recognizes the Republic of Colombia. June 16, takes Manuela Sáenz as his lover. July 13, incorporates Guayaquil into Colombia. July 27, meets privately with José de San Martín in Guayaquil.

1823   August, sails for Peru to prosecute the southern campaign. December, U.S. President James Monroe issues his doctrine.

1824   Bolívar becomes increasingly ill. August 6, defeats Royalists at Junín. December 9, Sucre defeats Royalists at Ayacucho, ending Spanish resistance in South America.

1825   Attempts to consolidate political and other institutions in Peru and Colombia. Growing conflict with José Antonio Páez over control of Venezuela. Great Britain recognizes newly independent Spanish American republics.

1826   June 22, meeting of representatives to the Congress of Panama, called by Bolívar. Separatist rebellions led by Páez and others challenge Bolívar rule. November 30, proclaimed president-for-life of Peru.

1827   Páez temporarily submits to Bolívar's authority; Bolívar experiences growing conflict with Pablo de Santander in Colombia. July 5, visits then leaves his native city of Caracas for the last time.

1828   Following failure of the Convention of Ocaña, on June 24, assumes dictatorial powers in Colombia. September 25, another failed assassination attempt, foiled by Manuela Sáenz.

1829   Páez separates Venezuela from Gran Colombia.

1830   Continued political conflict and secession movements. May 8, leaves Bogotá, ill and planning exile. June 4, Sucre assassinated. December 1, arrives prostrate in Santa Marta, Colombia. December 10, dictates will and final proclamation. December 17, Bolívar, reviled and rejected, dies in exile, awaiting departure to Europe.

1842   Body repatriated from Colombia to Venezuela's Pantheon of Heroes.

1856   Manuela Sáenz dies in Ecuador.

GLOSSARY OF SPANISH TERMS

afrancesado	Francophile, "Frenchified," admirer of things French, including the Revolution
audiencia	High court and council
balandra	Sloop
cabildo	Town council
canario	Native of the Canary Islands, off Africa
castas	Persons of mixed ancestry, considered lower class by Creoles and Peninsulars
caudillo	Political/military strongman, often backed by a private army
Creole	White person of Spanish ancestry born in the Americas
Cortes	Spanish parliament, congress
encomendero	Colonial-era holder of a grant of Indian labor
extranjero	Stranger, foreigner
flechera	Long, narrow canoe, up to fifty feet long; from *flecha*, arrow
gachupín	Derogatory term for a Spaniard
Granadino	Resident of New Granada (Colombia)
Juanas	"Janes," camp followers
junta	Committee or assembly
Libertador	Liberator
llanos	Tropical plains of interior Colombia and Venezuela
llanero	Cowboy, horseman of the llanos
mata	Forest of dense trees and shrubs on the llanos
matuano	White, elite society of Caracas, Venezuela; from the delicate white shawls upper-class women wore to church
mestizo	Person of mixed ancestry, usually European and Indian

mulatto	Person of mixed white and black ancestry
pardo	Dark-skinned person; in Venezuela usually a synonym for mulatto
pardocracia	Rule by the nonwhite masses, a fear of many Creoles
patria	Homeland, fatherland
patria boba	"Foolish fatherland," Venezuela's short-lived first republic
Peninsular	Spaniard from the Iberian Peninsula
personalismo	Political tendency to blindly follow a charismatic leader
piragua	Small canoe
saya y manto	Typical walking dress of Lima (skirt and cloak)
soroche	Mountain sickness, characterized by dizziness and vomiting
Tierra Firma	Mainland (literally "firm land"), as opposed to Caribbean islands
zambo	Person of mixed black and Indian ancestry

BIBLIOGRAPHY

A GUIDE TO FURTHER READING

Bolívar lived a fascinating, controversial, intensely studied life. We have used a wide mix of sources in writing this biography. Primary sources, written by persons participating in the struggles for independence, bring immediacy, detail, and passion to the narrative. Equally important are secondary sources, penned later by Latin American, European, and North American historians. Archival manuscripts and printed documents and other sources abound (see sources consulted).

Most important of the primary sources are the various letters, speeches, and pronouncements of Bolívar, Santander, Páez, and others. The edited and written works produced by Venezuelan historian Vicente Lecuna are by far the most significant. We quoted many letters from the *Selected Writings of Bolívar,* compiled by Lecuna and translated by Lewis Bertrand. Also important are memoirs written by many of the other principals, including Páez, Urdaneta, Miller, Paz, and O'Leary. Edited documentary collections by Larrazábal, Cortázar, Grases, and Davila added important firsthand information. Spanish and English-language newspapers of the early nineteenth century provided vital facts on ship movements and reports of battles. C. P. Jones (*The Americas*, January, 1984) has summarized impressions of Bolívar taken from ten nineteenth-century British periodicals. See sources consulted for full citations of both primary and secondary sources.

Secondary sources, many unabashedly idolizing the Liberator, abound. For a sampling of pro-Liberator opinion, see the "testimonios" in Jorge Campos, *Bolívar* (1984). For the views of his detractors, see José Sant Roz, *Nos Duele Bolívar* (1988). Lecuna's *Crónica razonada de las guerras de Bolívar* in three volumes is probably our most utilized secondary source. Among English-language books, we commend the following to readers who wish to pursue specific details of Bolívar's life and exploits. *Insurrection or Loyalty* by Dominguez and Lynch's *Spanish-American Revolutions* analyze the causes of independence. Belaúnde's *Bolívar and the Political Thought of the Spanish American Revolution* offers insights into the competing ideologies of the independence era.

Robert Gilmore's *Caudillism and Militarism* surveys the political conflicts and complications in Venezuela during the nineteenth century. David Bushnell offers the standard description of Santander's career. John J. Johnson's *A Hemisphere Apart* analyzes the failure of the young United States to support the Latin American Patriots. William Spence Robertson's *Life of Miranda* remains the classic study of the tragic precursor to independence. Antonio Cussen examines the poetry and career of Andrés Bello, who accompanied Bolívar on his mission to London in 1810.

Readers with access to academic libraries will also enjoy primary sources, including memoirs and studies by Humboldt, Whymper, Vowell, Hippisley, Biggs, Proctor, Robinson, and Semple. The authoritative *Encyclopedia of Latin American History and Culture*, edited by Barbara A. Tennenbaum, offers additional biographical information on most of the major leaders in the wars of independence. John Lynch (*History Today*, July, 1983) and Bryan Hodgson (*National Geographic*, March, 1994) have written short, popular, readable summaries of the Liberator's life. Indeed, anything written by Lynch is well worth reading. The February, 1983, issue of the *Hispanic American Historical Review* carried several essays by prominent scholars commemorating the bicentennial of the Liberator's birth. The volume of essays selected by J. L. Salcedo-Bastardo and published by UNESCO in 1983 also offers insightful commentaries and documents on many aspects of Bolívar's career.

During the late 1990s, several studies of varying quality have placed Spanish America's independence era in broader context. *The Independence of Spanish America*, by Jaime E. Rodríguez O., is critical of Bolívar; indeed, portions of it read like a latter-day version of Madariaga's pro-Spanish apologetics. The book also greatly underestimates the many forces and issues dividing Spain and Spanish America. Rebecca A. Earle's *Spain and the Independence of Colombia, 1810–1825*, marshals strong evidence that counters the Rodríguez theories and well elaborates the many failures of Spanish policy and implementation during this tumultuous era.

Holy Madness by Adam Zamoyski, *The Americas in the Age of Revolution* by Lester Langley, and *Liberators* by Robert Harvey successfully place independence into a wider historical context but add little to our understanding of Bolívar's specific role and actions. Langley is by far the most trustworthy, although his treatment of Bolívar is very brief. Harvey offers the reader a compelling narrative but is given to occasional journalistic hyperbole: "Less than half a century later, Spain's empire vanished without trace" (p. 1). As anyone who has traveled in Spanish America can plainly see, "traces" of the mother country's influences—language, culture, architecture—remain everywhere. Zamoyski is more useful for a flavor or "spirit of the times" than for historical rigor. In his preface he warns, rather ominously, that "there was nothing remotely methodical about my explorations," "I sometimes quote people out of strict context," and "I have not gone in for the same rigorous verification of sources that I would when researching a closely defined subject." Finally, he frames his story within a rather contrived, strained series of Roman Catholic themes and images. Caveat lector.

The General in His Labyrinth, by Colombian novelist Gabriel García Márquez (and Nobel Prize winner), and *Bolívar: Liberator of a Continent*, by Bob Boyd, offer refreshing approaches for readers who prefer historical fiction. The former is compelling and insightful; the latter a much lighter treatment laced with contrived dialogue.

A new biography of Bolívar for a general English-language audience has been sorely needed. Gerhard Masur's treatment, translated from German in the 1940s and last revised in 1969, is generally cited as the most comprehensive English-language treatment. That book, however, is seriously flawed, with its racist tone and preposterous cultural stereotypes. The interpretation exhibits an almost nineteenth-century reliance on racial and environmental determinism.

Masur often attributes actions to stereotypes based on race, climate, or national identity. "The Basque toughness and stamina inherited by Bolivar became more volatile and sensuous through the merging with tropical blood" (p. 21). Masur writes of "the tropical vitality and sensuality of Bolívar" (p. 32). The translation, faithful to German syntax, makes ponderous reading. Factual errors, such as confusing Alexander Cochrane and his nephew Thomas (p. 56) also mar the text. The book includes editorial quirks, such as the odd decision to omit first names. Such incomplete references make it easy for the reader, expert or not, to confuse Cochranes, Wilsons, and other protagonists with the same last name. Finally, the last edition appeared decades ago in hardcover only.

Another major biography by Spanish nationalist Salvador de Madariaga (1952) includes unsubstantiated psychobabble and archaic ethnic and racial stereotyping. "His blood was mixed; and though it was so very slightly, matters of character and spirit can hardly be determined by quantitative laws. Though the drops of Indian and black blood in his veins may have been few, were indeed, few, the tensions which these drops brought to his inner structure were probably high—for he was high-pitched by nature."

Sounding like a latter-day Spanish apologist, Jaime E. Rodríguez O., in *The Independence of Spanish America* (1998), has repeated some of the sharply anti-Bolívar views of Madariaga. For example, "The emancipation of Spanish America did not merely consist of separation from the mother country, as in the case of the United States; it also destroyed a vast and responsive social, political, and economic system that functioned well despite its many imperfections" (p. 244). Responsive? Functioned well? For whom? Rebecca A. Earle's masterful analysis of *Spain and the Independence of Colombia* offers a host of evidence of Spain's ineffectual, counterproductive administration of its colonies.

Rodríguez also contends that "Spanish America was not a colony of Spain but an integral part of the Spanish Monarchy, a heterogeneous confederation." Bolívar and his Creole colleagues certainly did not agree with this view, and neither do we. Rodríguez further argues, against overwhelming evidence, that "although the Bourbon reforms initially harmed some areas and groups even as they benefited others, the Spanish Crown doubtless would have eventually reached acceptable accommodation with all concerned. Events in Europe at the end of the eighteenth century, however, prevented an orderly readjustment" (p. 35). Destructive, contradictory actions by the court of Ferdinand VII, the Spanish Cortes, and Spanish liberals, which Rodríguez seriously underestimates, alone render null this counterfactual speculation. Again, Rebecca Earle makes abundantly clear the manifest shortcomings of Spanish colonial policy.

In many cases, Latin American intellectuals have merely used history to construct partisan arguments. A stark example is the polemical literature about Juan Manuel de Rosas of Argentina that uses the nineteenth-century dictator to support twentieth-century political views, ranging from nationalism to Peronism. Much of the Bolivarian literature is likewise rendered suspect by its shrill partisanship and utter contempt for the canons of professional scholarship. In contrast, we seek to understand Bolívar, a complex and often contradictory man, not to praise or condemn him. A figure as influential and fascinating as Bolívar deserves more than crass racial or partisan stereotyping. He failed in his dream of unifying Latin America into a single, strong, cohesive nation. Despondent just before his death, he wrote despairingly that "treaties are scraps of paper . . . and life a torment." Many of the difficulties that bedeviled him have yet to be resolved in Latin America.

INTERNET SOURCES

Online resources on the Internet also add to our knowledge of the Liberator. Do recall the incredible ephemerality of Web sites. These sites functioned as of mid-2002. If one has disappeared, use the search engine www.google.com , which has a cache feature that can retrieve "disappeared" sites.

1. "Battle of Carabobo." Shockwave animated recreation, www.prodi.com.ve/home/antecedentes1.htm.
2. "Bipolar Disorders," Mental Health.net, mentalhelp.net/disorders/sx20.htm.
3. "Brief biography of Gabriel García Márquez," www.proseworld.com/marquez.html.
4. DDB Stock Photo, "Paintings and statues of Bolívar," www.dbstock.com.
5. Chami, Pablo, "Latin American Independence Leaders," www.pachami.com/English/latinoamericaE.html.
6. Chami, Pablo. "San Martín's Home Page," www.pachami.com/English/ressanmE.htm.
7. "Columbia Electronic Encyclopedia," www.infoplease.com.
8. John V. Lombardi, "History and Our Heroes—The Bolívar Legend," jvlone.com/bolivar2e.html.
9. "Luces de Bolívar en la Red," www.bolivar.ula.ve/.
10. "Online Bibliography on Bolívar," www.bolivar.ula.ve/cgi-bin be_alex.exe? DESCRIPTOR=Bibliograf%Eda&nombrebd=bolivar&recuperar=20.
11. Orange Blossom Special, Issue No. 30, "Simon Bolivar and the Liberation of South America," www.orangeblossom.demon.co.uk/simon-bolivar.html.
12. "Simón Bolívar, El Hombre," wekker.seagull.net/bolivar.html.
13. "Simon Bolivar, the Liberator of South America," About.com Homework Help, history1800s.about.com/homework/history1800s/library/weekly/aa122498.htm.
14. USS Simon Bolivar (SSBN 641), lab-elec.com/sb/sbolivar.htm.
15. "Venezuela Tuya, Biografias de Venezuela," www.venezuelatuya.com/biograWas/index.htm and Virtual American Biographies at www.famousamericans.net.

SOURCES CONSULTED
Archives and Manuscripts

Archivo Nacional de Colombia, Bogotá.
Fundación John Boulton, Caracas, Venezuela.
State of Louisiana. *Survey of Federal Archives in Louisiana. Conspicuous Cases in the United States District Court of Louisiana.* Transcription of the Case Papers and Other Interesting Documents Pertaining to Trials and Indictments, Dating from the Establishment of the Federal Court in 1806. 1st ser. 7 Vols. Baton Rouge, 1939–40.
Trinidad Duplicate Dispatches, 1815 and 1816. Office of T. C. Cambridge, Port of Spain.
Venezuela, Hojas de Servicio, Secretaria de Guerra y Marina, Papeles sin Clasificación, Caracas, Venezuela.

Books and Articles

Acosta Saignes, Miguel. *Introducción a Simón Bolívar.* Mexico City: Siglo Ventiuno Editores, 1983.

Adams, Jerome R. *Latin American Heroes: Liberators and Patriots from 1500 to the Present.* New York: Ballantine Books, 1991.

Aljure Chalela, Simón. "Bibliografía sobre Manuelita Sáenz." *Boletín Cultural y Bibliográfico* 18, no. 2 (1981): 234–53 [Colombia].

———. "Muestras de bibliografía bolivariana." *Boletín Cultural y Bibliográfico* 16, no. 2 (1979): 202–27 [Colombia].

Andrews, George Reid. "Spanish American Independence: A Structural Analysis." *Latin American Perspectives* 12, no. 1 (winter, 1985): 105–32.

Andrien, Kenneth J. *The Kingdom of Quito, 1690–1830: The State and Regional Development.* Cambridge: Cambridge University Press, 1995.

Angell, Hildegarde. *Simón Bolívar: South American Liberator.* New York: W. W. Norton, 1930.

Anna, Timothy E. "Economic Causes of San Martín's Failure in Lima." *Hispanic American Historical Review* 54, no. 4 (November, 1974): 657–68.

———. *The Fall of Royal Government in Peru.* Lincoln: University of Nebraska Press, 1979.

———. *Spain and the Loss of America.* Lincoln: University of Nebraska Press, 1983.

Archivo Histórico Nacional. *Archivo del General José Antonio Páez 1818–1820, Tomo Primero.* Bogotá: Archivo Histórico Nacional, 1939.

Arnade, Charles W. *The Emergence of the Republic of Bolivia.* Gainesville: University of Florida Press, 1957.

Austria, José de. *Bosquejo de la Historia Militar de Venezuela.* 2 vols. Caracas: Academia Nacional de la Historia, 1960.

Ayala Mora, Enrique, ed. *Simón Bolívar: Pensamiento político.* Sucre, Bolivia: Universidad Andina Simón Bolívar, 1997.

Ayure, Wilderson A. "Historia y fábula en el Bolívar de García Márquez." *Huellas* (Colombia) 27 (1989): 46–56.

Baralt, Rafael María, and Ramón Díaz. *Resumen de la Historia de Venezuela desde el año 1797 hasta el 1830.* 2 vols. Paris: Brujas, Paris, Desclee, De Brouwer, 1939.

Barbier, Jacques, and Allan J. Kuethe, eds. *The North American Role in the Spanish Imperial Economy, 1760–1819.* Manchester: Manchester University Press, 1984.

Barroso Alfaro, Manuel, comp. *La espada de Bolívar.* Caracas: Banco Principal, 1991.

Belaúnde, Victor Andrés. *Bolívar and the Political Thought of the Spanish American Revolution.* Baltimore, 1928. Reprint, New York: Octagon Books, 1967.

———. "Factors in the Colonial Period in South America Working toward a New Regime." *Hispanic American Historical Review* 9, no. 2 (May, 1929): 144–53.

Bemis, Samuel Flagg. *John Quincy Adams and the Foundations of American Foreign Policy.* New York: Knopf, 1949.

Bethell, Leslie, ed. *The Independence of Latin America.* Cambridge: Cambridge University Press, 1987.

Bierck, Harold Alfred. *Vida pública de Don Pedro Gual.* Caracas: Ministerio de Educación Nacional, Dirección de Cultura, 1947.

Biggs, James. *The History of Don Francisco de Miranda's Attempt to Effect a Revolution in South America, in a series of letters by that gentleman who was an officer under that general, to his friend in the United States.* Boston: Oliver and Munroe, 1810.

Blanco, José Felix. *Bosquejo de la Revolución de Venezuela.* Caracas: Academia Nacional de la Historia, 1960.

Blanco, José Felix, and Ramón Azpurúa, eds. *Documentos para la historia de la vida pública del Libertador de Colombia, Perú y Bolivia.* 14 vols. Caracas: Imprenta de "La Opinión Nacional," 1875–77.

Blossom, Thomas. *Nariño: Hero of Colombian Independence.* Tucson: University of
   Arizona Press, 1967.
Boletín de Historia y Antigüedades (Colombia) 70 (1983); 84 (1997). Special thematic
   issues on Bolívar.
Bolívar, Simón. *Bolívar y el pensamiento panameño.* Ed. José A. Reyes Geenzier.
   Panama City: Imprenta Edilito, 1983.
———. *Bolívar, ideas de un espíritu visionario: Antología.* Ed. Edgardo Mondo.
   Caracas: Monte Avila Editores, 1990.
———. "Discurso de Angostura: Texto definitivo." *Boletín de la Academia Nacional de
   la Historia* (Venezuela) 63, no. 252 (1980): 913–99.
———. *Escritos fundamentales.* Caracas: Monte Avila Editores, 1982.
———. *"Mi Delirio sobre el Chimborazo" de Bolívar.* Ed. Pedro Grases. Caracas:
   Ediciones de la Sociedad Bolivariana de Venezuela, 1963.
———. *Textos: Una antología general.* Ed. Ignacio Sosa. Mexico City: SEP/UNAM,
   1982.
Borrero Garcés, Luis Enrique. "La batalla de Bomboná: Un desastre para el ejercito
   libertador." *Boletín de Historia y Antigüedades* (Colombia) 74, no. 757 (1987): 395–
   402.
Boulton, Alfredo. *Los Retratos de Bolívar.* Caracas: n.p., 1957.
———. *Miranda, Bolívar, y Sucre: Tres Estudios Iconográficos.* Caracas: Imprenta
   Nacional, 1959.
Bourne, Ruth. *Queen Ann's Navy in the West Indies.* New Haven: Yale University Press,
   1939.
Bowman, Charles H., Jr. "The Activities of Manuel Torres as Purchasing Agent, 1820–
   1821." *Hispanic American Historical Review* 48, no. 2 (May, 1968): 234–46.
Boyd, Bill. *Bolívar: Liberator of a Continent.* New York: S. P. I. Books, 1998.
Brading, David. *The First America: The Spanish Monarchy, Creole Patriots, and the
   Liberal State, 1492–1867.* Cambridge: Cambridge University Press, 1991.
Briceño Perozo, Mario. "Bolívar y Urdaneta." *Boletín de la Academia Nacional de la
   Historia* (Venezuela) 63, no. 252 (1980): 853–67.
———. "¿Como desmitificar a Bolívar?" *Boletín de la Academia Nacional de la
   Historia* (Venezuela) 67, no. 267 (1984): 477–83.
———. "La herencia de Bolívar." *Boletín de la Academia Nacional de la Historia*
   (Venezuela) 71, no. 282 (1988): 301–10.
Briceño-Iragorry, Mario. *Casa León y su tiempo: Adventura de un anti-héroe.* Caracas:
   Typografía Americana, 1947.
Burkholder, Mark A. "From Creole to Peninsular: The Transformation of the
   Audience of Lima." *Hispanic American Historical Review* 52, no. 3 (August, 1972):
   395–415.
Burkholder, Mark A., and David S. Chandler. *From Impotence to Authority: The
   Spanish Crown and the American Audiences, 1687–1808.* Columbia: University of
   Missouri Press, 1977.
Burns, E. Bradford. *Latin America: A Concise, Interpretive History.* 6th ed. Englewood
   Cliffs: Prentice-Hall, 1994.
Bushnell, David. "The Last Dictatorship: Betrayal or Consummation?" *Hispanic
   American Historical Review* 63, no. 1 (February, 1983): 65–105.
———. *The Santander Regime in Gran Colombia.* Newark: University of Delaware
   Press, 1954. Reprint, Westport, Conn.: Greenwood Press, 1970.
———. "Simón Bolívar and the United States: A Study in Ambivalence." *Air Univer-
   sity Review* 37, no. 5 (1986): 106–11.

———, ed. *The Liberator Simón Bolívar: Man and Image.* New York: Knopf, 1970.

Caldera, Rafael. "Simón Bolívar." *Américas* 33, no. 4 (1981): 44–48.

Campbell, Leon G. *The Military and Society in Colonial Peru, 1750–1810.* Philadelphia: American Philosophical Society, 1978.

Campos, Jorge. *Bolívar: Biografía ilustrada.* Barcelona: Ediciones Destino, 1963.

———. *Bolívar.* Valencia, Venezuela: Editorial Notitarde, 1984.

Carrera Damas, Germán. *Bolívar.* Montevideo: Biblioteca de Marcha, 1974.

———. *Boves: Aspectos socio-económicos de la guerra de la independencia.* 3d ed. Caracas: Ediciones de la Biblioteca Universidad Central de Venezuela, 1972.

———. *Coloquio Internacional: Pensamiento, acción y vigencia de Simón Bolívar.* Caracas: Monte Avila Editores, UNESCO, 1990.

———. *El culto a Bolívar: Esbozo para un estudio de la historia de las ideas en Venezuela.* Caracas: Universidad Central de Venezuela, 1969.

———. "Simón Bolívar, El culto heroico y la nación." *Hispanic American Historical Review* 63, no. 1 (February, 1983): 107–45.

Cacau Prada, Antonio. *Francisco de Paula Santander: "El Cucuteño" Fundador de la República.* Villa del Rosario de Cúcuta: Editorial Kelly, 1990.

Carrillo, German D. "La parodia de la historia en El General en su Laberinto." *Inter-American Review of Bibliography*, 41, no. 4 (1991): 601–606.

Codazzi, Agustín. *Atlas físico y político de la República de Venezuela.* Paris: Lith. de Thierry Fres. a Paris, 1841.

Collier, Simon. *Ideas and Politics of Chilean Independence, 1808–1833.* Cambridge: Cambridge University Press, 1967.

———. "Nationality, Nationalism, and Supranationalism in the Writings of Símon Bolívar." *Hispanic American Historical Review* 63, no. 1 (February, 1983): 37–64.

Comisión Nacional del Centenario. *Documentos del Archivo de San Martín.* 12 vols. Buenos Aires: Imprenta de Coni Hermanos, 1910–1911.

Conway, Christopher Brian. "Imagining Bolivar: Mythic Representation and Official Memory in Nineteenth-Century Venezuela." Ph.D. diss., University of California, San Diego, 1997.

Corrales, Manuel Ezekiel, ed. *Documentos para la Historia de la Provincia de Cartagena.* 2 vols. Bogotá: M. Rivas, 1883.

Cortázar, Roberto, ed. *Correspondencia dirigida al General Francisco de Paula Santander.* 14 vols. Bogotá: n.p., 1964–70.

———, comp. *Cartas y Mensajes del General Francisco de Paula Santander.* 8 vols. Bogotá: n.p., 1953–55.

Cortés Vargas, Carlos. "Military Operations of Bolívar in New Granada: A Commentary on Lecuna, *Crónica razonada de las guerras de Bolívar.*" *Hispanic American Historical Review* 32, no. 4 (November, 1952): 615–33.

Costa, Octavio R. *Bolívar: Más allá del tiempo y del espacio.* Miami: Ediciones Universal, 1998.

Costeloe, Michael P. *Response to Revolution: Imperial Spain and the Spanish American Revolutions, 1810–1840.* Cambridge: Cambridge University Press, 1986.

Cuevas Cancino, Francisco. *Bolívar en el Tiempo.* 2d ed. Mexico City: El Colegio de México, 1982.

Cummins, Light Townsend. *Spanish Observers and the American Revolution, 1775–1783.* Baton Rouge: Louisiana State University Press, 1991.

Cushing, Caleb. "Simón Bolívar." *North American Review* 28 (January, 1829): 203–26.

———. "Simón Bolívar and the Bolivian Constitution." *North American Review* 30 (January, 1830): 26–61.

Cussen, Antonio. *Bello and Bolívar: Poetry and Politics in the Spanish American Revolution.* Cambridge: Cambridge University Press, 1992.

Dauxion-Lavaysse, Jean François. *A Statistical, Commercial, and Political Description of Venezuela, Trinidad, Margarita, and Tobago.* London: G. and W. B. Whittaker, 1820.

Davila, Vicente, ed. *Archivo del General Miranda.* 24 vols. Caracas: Editorial Sur-America, 1929–1950.

Davis, Harold Eugene. "Simón Bolívar: Political Idealist or Realist?" *Inter-American Review of Bibliography* 33, no. 2 (1983): 161–70.

Davis, Robert H. *Historical Dictionary of Colombia.* 2d ed. Metuchen, N.J.: Scarecrow Press, 1993.

Davis, Roger. "The Local Dynamics of National Dissent: The Ecuadorian *Pronunciamientos* of 1826. *Historian* 55, no. 2 (winter, 1993): 289–303.

Dealy, Glen. "Prolegomena on the Spanish American Political Tradition." *Hispanic American Historical Review* 48, no. 1 (February, 1968): 37–58.

De Grummond, Jane Lucas. *Envoy to Caracas: The Story of John G. A. Williamson, Nineteenth-Century Diplomat.* Baton Rouge: Louisiana State University Press, 1951.

———. *Renato Beluche: Smuggler, Privateer, and Patriot, 1780–1860.* Baton Rouge: Louisiana State University Press, 1983.

———, ed. *Caracas Diary, 1835–1840: The Journal of John G. A. Williamson, First Diplomatic Representative of the United States to Venezuela.* Baton Rouge: Louisiana State University Press, 1954.

del Río, Daniel A. *Simón Bolívar: A Sketch of His Life.* Clinton, Mass.: Colonial Press, Bolivarian Society of the United States, 1965.

Díaz, José Domingo. *Recuerdos sobre la Rebelión de Caracas.* Madrid: Imprenta de L. Amarita, 1829.

Díaz González, Joaquín. "El juramento de Simón Bolívar en el Monte Sacro." *Boletín de la Academia Nacional de la Historia* (Venezuela) 67, no. 266 (1984): 291–301.

Díaz-Trechuelo Spínola, María Lourdes. *Bolívar, Miranda, O'Higgins, San Martín: Cuatro vidas cruzadas.* Madrid: Encuentro Ediciones, 1999.

Dominguez, Jorge I. *Insurrection or Loyalty: The Breakdown of the Spanish-American Empire.* Cambridge: Harvard University Press, 1980.

Ducoudray Holstein, H. L. V. *Memoirs of Simón Bolívar, President of the Republic of Colombia; and of His Principal General.* Boston: S. G. Goodrich, 1829.

Dupouy, Walter, ed. *Sir Robert Ker Porter's Caracas Diary, 1825–1842.* Caracas: Dupouy, 1966.

Duque Escobar, Iván. *Simón Bolívar, una visión dispersa.* Santa Fe de Bogotá, Colombia: n. p., 2000.

Dyer, George B., and Charlotte L. Dyer. "The Beginnings of a United States Strategic Intelligence System in Latin America, 1809–1826." *Military Affairs* 14, no. 2 (summer, 1950): 65–83.

Earle, Rebecca A. "'A Grave for Europeans?': Disease, Death, and the Spanish-American Revolutions." *War in History* 3, no. 4 (1996): 371–83.

———. *Spain and the Independence of Colombia, 1810–1825.* Exeter: University of Exeter Press, 2000.

Espriella, Ramiro de la. *Las ideas políticas de Bolívar.* Santa Fé de Bogotá, Colombia: Editorial Grijalbo, 1999.

Faye, Stanley. "Commodore Aury." *Louisiana Historical Quarterly* 24 (1941).

Fisher, John R. "Royalism, Regionalism and Rebellion in Colonial Peru, 1808–1815." *Hispanic American Historical Review* 59, no. 2 (May, 1979): 232–57.

Fisher, John R., Allan J. Kuethe, and Anthony McFarlane, eds. *Reform and Insurrection in Bourbon New Granada and Peru.* Baton Rouge: Louisiana State University Press, 1990.

Flinter, George Dawson. *A History of the Revolution of Caracas; comprising an impartial narrative of the atrocities committed by the contending parties, illustrating the real state of the contest ... together with a descriptive of the Llaneros.* London: T. and J. Allman, 1819.

Forester, C. S. *The Age of Fighting Sail.* New York: Doubleday, 1956.

Frank, Waldo. *Birth of a World: Bolívar in Terms of His People.* Boston: Houghton Mifflin, 1951.

Fundación John Boulton. *Cartas del Libertador, Tomo XII, 1803–1830.* Caracas: Fundación John Boulton, 1959.

Gaitan de Parms, Blanca. *La Mujer en la vida del Libertador.* Bogotá: Cooperativa Nacional de Artes Gráficas, 1980.

Galdames, Luis. *A History of Chile.* Trans. and ed. Isaac Joslin Cox. Chapel Hill: University of North Carolina Press, 1941.

García Camba, Andrés. *Memoirs del General García Camba para la historia de las Armas Españolas en el Perú, 1809–1825.* 2 vols. Madrid: Editorial América, 1916.

García Márquez, Gabriel. *The General in His Labyrinth.* Trans. Edith Grossman. New York: Knopf, 1990.

———. "The General's Departure." Trans. Edith Grossman. *New Yorker* 66, no. 22 (July 16, 1990): 30–42.

Gerbi, Antonello. *The Dispute of the New World: The History of a Polemic, 1750–1900.* Rev. ed. Pittsburgh: University of Pittsburgh Press, 1972.

Gil Fortoul, José. *Historia constitucional de Venezuela.* 3 vols. 3d rev. ed. Caracas: Editorial "Las Novedades," 1942.

Gil-Montero, Martha. "The Liberator's Noble March." *Américas* 45, no. 3 (May, 1993): 6–17.

———. "Manuela and Simón." *Américas* 42, no. 2 (March, 1990): 6–15.

Gil-Montero, Martha, and Judy Bustamante. "The Marchioness and the Marshal." *Américas* 46, no. 2 (March, 1994): 6–14.

Gilmore, Robert L. *Caudillism and Militarism in Venezuela, 1810–1910.* Athens: University of Ohio Press, 1964.

———. "The Imperial Crisis, Rebellion, and the Viceroy: New Grenada in 1809." *Hispanic American Historical Review* 40, no. 1 (February, 1960): 1–24.

Glick, Thomas F. "Science and Independence in Latin America (with Special Reference to New Granada)." *Hispanic American Historical Review* 71, no. 2 (May, 1991): 307–34.

González, Godofredo. "Bolívar y el Congreso." *Revista de la Sociedad Bolivariana de Venezuela* 37, no. 125 (1980): 7–17.

Graham, Gerald S., and R. A. Humphreys, ed. *The Navy and South America, 1807–1823: Correspondence of the Commanders-in-Chief on the South American Station.* London: Navy Records Society, 1962.

Graham, Maria Dundas. *Journal of a Residence in Chile, during the Year 1822.* Reprint New York: Frederick A. Praeger, 1969.

Graham, Richard. *Independence in Latin America: A Comparative Approach.* 2d ed. New York: McGraw-Hill, 1994.

Graham, Robert Bontine Cunninghame. *José Antonio Páez.* London, Heinemann, 1929.

———. *Rodeo: A Collection of Tales and Sketches.* Ed. A. F. Tschiffely. Garden City: Doubleday, Doran and Co., 1936.

————. *The South American Tales and Sketches of Robert B. Cunninghame Graham.*
    Ed. John Walker. Norman: University of Oklahoma Press, 1978.
Greene, Carol. *Símon Bolívar: South American Liberator.* Chicago: Children's Press, 1989.
Greene, Jack P. "The American Revolution." *American Historical Review* 105, no. 1
    (February, 2000): 93–102.
Griffin, Charles. *The United States and the Disruption of the Spanish Empire, 1810–1822.*
    London: P. S. King and Sons, 1937.
Grisanti, Angel. *El Precursor Miranda y su Familia.* Madrid: Ministerio de Educación
    Nacional, Dirección de Cultura, 1950.
Guerra, Francois-Xavier. "The Spanish-American Tradition of Representation and Its
    European Roots." *Journal of Latin American* Studies 26, no. 1 (1994): 1–35.
Hamer, Janice. "Liberator: Simón Bolívar Is Thea Musgrave's Newest Opera." *Opera
    News* 59, no. 8 (January 7, 1995): 20.
Hamill, Hugh M., ed. *Caudillos: Dictators in Spanish America.* Norman: University of
    Oklahoma Press, 1992.
Hamnett, Brian. "The Counter-Revolution of Morillo and the Insurgent Clerics of
    New Granada, 1815–1820." *Americas* 32, no. 4 (April, 1976): 597–617.
Hanke, Lewis. "Baptis Irvine's Reports on Simón Bolívar." *Hispanic American
    Historical Review* 16, no. 3 (August, 1936): 360–73.
————. "Simón Bolívar and Neutral Rights." *Hispanic American Historical Review* 21,
    no. 2 (May, 1941): 258–91.
Hartog, H. *Aruba: A Short History.* Aruba: Ediciones Van Dorp, 1973.
————. *Curaçao: A Short History.* Aruba: De Wit Stores, 1973.
————. *A Short History of Bonaire.* Aruba: De Wit Stores, 1978.
Harvey, Robert. *Liberators: Latin America's Struggle for Independence, 1810–1830.*
    London: John Murray, 2000; New York: Overlook Press, 2000
Hasbrouck, Alfred. *Foreign Legionaries in the Liberation of Spanish South America.*
    1928. Reprint. New York: Octagon Books, 1969.
Heredia, José Francisco. *Memorias sobre las revoluciones de Venezuela.* Paris: Garnier
    Hermanos, 1895.
Hippisley, Col. Gustavo. *Narrative of the Expedition to the Rivers Orinoco and Apuré in
    South America, which sailed from England in November 1817, and joined the patriotic
    forces in Venezuela and Caracas.* London: J. Murray, 1819.
Hodgson, Bryan. "El Libertador Simón Bolívar." *National Geographic* 185, no. 3
    (March, 1994): 36–65.
Holden, Robert H., and Eric Zolov, eds. *Latin America and the United States: A
    Documentary History.* New York: Oxford University Press, 2000.
Hood, Miriam, ed. *In Honour of Daniel O'Leary, Edecan, and Historian of Simón
    Bolívar the Liberator.* London: Venezuelan Embassy, 1978.
Hoover, John P. *Admirable Warrior: Fighter for South American Independence.* Detroit:
    B. Ethridge Books, 1977.
————. *Sucre, Soldado y Revolucionario.* Trans. Francisco Rivera. Cumaná: Editorial
    de la Universidad de Oriente, 1975.
Huck, Eugene R. "Bibliography on Simón Bolívar in West Georgia College Library."
    South Eastern Latin Americanist 36, no. 3 (winter, 1993): 31–42.
Humboldt, Alexander von. *Personal Narrative of Travels to the Equinoctial Regions of
    the New Continent during the Years 1777–1804.* Trans. Helen María Williams. 7 vols.
    London: Longman, Hurst, Rees, Orme, and Brown, 1814–1829.
————. *Political Essay on the Kingdom of New Spain.* Trans. John Black. 4 vols. New
    York: I. Riley, 1811.

Humphreys, R. A. "The Historiography of the Spanish American Revolution."
   Hispanic American Historical Review 36, no. 1 (February, 1956): 81–93.

"Inventing Bolívar." *Economist,* July 22, 1989.

Izard, Miguel. *El miedo a la revolución: La lucha por la libertad en Venezuela (1777–1830).* Madrid: Editorial Tecnos, 1979.

Johnson, John J. *A Hemisphere Apart: The Foundations of United States Policy Toward Latin America.* Baltimore: Johns Hopkins University Press, 1990.

Johnson, John J., and Doris Ladd. *Simón Bolívar and Spanish American Independence, 1783–1830.* Princeton: Van Nostrand, 1968.

Johnson, Willis Fletcher. *The History of Cuba.* 5 vols. New York: B. F. Buck, 1920.

Johnston, Henry P. *The Yorktown Campaign and the Surrender of Cornwallis, 1781.* New York: Harper & Brothers, 1881.

Jones, C. P. "The Images of Simón Bolívar as Reflected in Ten Leading British Periodicals, 1816–1830." *Americas* 40 (January, 1984): 377–97.

Kamen-Kaye, Dorothy. *Speaking of Venezuela.* Caracas: Caracas Journal, 1947.

Karsen, Sonja. "Alexander von Humboldt in South America: From the Orinoco to the Amazon." *Studies in Eighteenth-Century Culture* 16 (1986): 295–302.

Kimberly, Nick. "Musgrave and Simón Bolívar." *Opera* 46, no. 1 (January 1, 1995): 24.

King, James F. "The Colored Castes and the American Representation in the Cortes of Cádiz." *Hispanic American Historical Review* 33 (February, 1953): 33–64.

———. "A Royalist View of the Colored Castes in the Venezuelan War of Independence." *Hispanic American Historical Review* 33 (November, 1953): 526–37.

Kinsbruner, Jay. *Independence in Spanish America: Civil Wars, Revolutions, and Underdevelopment.* Rev. ed. Albuquerque: University of New Mexico Press, 2000.

Knapton, Ernest John. *Empress Josephine.* Cambridge: Harvard University Press, 1963.

Knight, Franklin W. "The Haitian Revolution." *American Historical Review* 105, no. 1 (February, 2000): 103–15.

Kuethe, Allan J. *Military Reform and Society in New Granada, 1773–1808.* Gainesville: University of Florida Press, 1978.

Langley, Lester D. *The Americas in the Age of Revolution: 1750–1850.* New Haven: Yale University Press, 1996.

Laplance, J., and J.-B. Pontalis. *The Language of Psycho-analysis.* Trans. Donald Nicholson-Smith. New York: W. W. Norton, 1973.

Larrazábal, Felipe. *La vida y correspondencia general del Libertador Simón Bolívar.* 2 vols. Caracas: Imprenta del Espejo, 1878.

Lawrence, E. "Bolivar, Liberator of South America." *Harper's Magazine* 40 (1869–70): 594–603.

Lecuna, Vicente. "Bolívar and San Martín at Guayaquil." *Hispanic American Historical Review* 31, no. 3 (August, 1951): 369–93.

———. *Catálogo de errores y calumnias en la historia de Bolívar.* 3 vols. New York: Colonial Press, 1956–58.

———. *Crónica razonada de las guerras de Bolívar.* 3 vols. New York: Colonial Press, 1950.

———, ed. *Cartas del Libertador.* 12 vols. Caracas: Comercio, 1929–59.

———, ed. *Papeles de Bolívar.* Caracas: Comercio, 1917.

———, ed. *Proclamas y Discursos del Libertador.* Caracas: Comercio, 1939.

Lecuna, Vicente, comp.; Harold A. Bierck, Jr., ed.; Lewis Bertrand, trans. *Selected Writings of Bolívar.* 2 vols. New York: Colonial Press, 1951.

Lemley, Henry Rowan. *Bolívar: Liberator of Colombia, Ecuador, Peru, and Bolivia.* Boston: Statford, 1923.

Lockey, Joseph Byrnes. *Pan Americanism: Its Beginnings.* New York: Macmillan, 1920.

Lofstrom, William L. *The Promise of and the Problem of Reform: Attempted Economic and Social Changes in the First Years of Bolivarian Independence.* Ithaca: Cornell University Press, 1972.

Lombardi, John V. *Venezuela: The Search for Order, the Dream of Progress.* New York: Oxford University Press, 1982.

López, Manuel Antonio. *Recuerdos Históricos del Colonel Manuel Antonio López, Ayudante del Estado Mayor General Libertador, Colombia i Perú, 1819–1826.* Bogotá: J. B. Gaitan, 1878.

López Contreras, Eleazar. *El pensamiento de Bolívar Libertador.* Havana: Editorial Lex, 1950.

Lovera De-Sola, R. J. "La carta apocrifa de Bolívar a Fanny du Villars." *Boletín de la Academia Nacional de la Historia* (Venezuela) 78, no. 312 (1995): 195–206.

Lozano y Lozano, Fabio. *Anzoátegui, visiones de la guerra de Independencia.* Bogotá: Academia Colombia de Historia, 1963.

Ludwig, Emil. *Bolívar: The Life of an Idealist.* New York: Alliance Book Corp., 1942.

Lynch, John. "Bolívar and the Caudillos." *Hispanic American Historical Review* 63, no. 1 (February, 1983): 3–35.

———. "Simón Bolívar and the Spanish-American Revolutions." *History Today* 33 (July, 1983): 5–10.

———. *The Spanish-American Revolutions, 1808–1826.* New York: W. W. Norton, 1973.

———, ed. *Latin American Revolutions, 1808–1826: Old and New World Origins.* 1965. Rev. ed., Norman: University of Oklahoma Press, 1994.

McFarlane, Anthony. *Colombia before Independence: Economy, Society, and Politics under Bourbon Rule.* Cambridge: Cambridge University Press, 1993.

McGann, Thomas F. "The Assassination of Sucre and Its Significance in Colombian History, 1828–1848." *Hispanic American Historical Review* 30, no. 3 (August, 1950): 269–89.

McNerny, Robert F. "Daniel Florence O'Leary: Soldier, Diplomat, and Historian." *Americas* 22, no. 3 (January, 1966): 292–312.

Madariaga, Salvador de. *Bolívar.* 1952. Reprint, New York: Schoecken Books, 1969.

Manning, William R., ed. *Diplomatic Correspondence of the United States Concerning the Independence of the Latin American Nations.* 3 vols. New York: Oxford University Press, 1925.

Marichal, Juan. "Bolívar and the Age of Constitutions." *Harvard Library Bulletin* 32, no. 2 (1984): 176–87.

Martin, Percy Alvin. *Simón Bolívar, the Liberator.* Stanford: Stanford University Press, 1931.

Martínez G., Miguel A. *Aspectos económicos de la época de Bolívar.* 2 vols. Caracas: Academia Nacional de la Historia, 1988.

Masur, Gerhard. "The Conference of Guayaquil." *Hispanic American Historical Review* 31, no. 2 (May, 1951): 189–229.

———. *Simón Bolívar.* 1948. Reprint, Albuquerque: University of New Mexico Press, 1969.

Metford, J. C. J. *San Martín, the Liberator.* 1950. Reprint, New York: Philosophical Library, 1971.

Mijares, Augusto. *El Liberator Simón Bolívar.* Caracas: Academia Nacional de la Historia de Venezuela, 1994.

Miller, Gary M. "Status and Loyalty of Regular Army Officers in Late Colonial

Venezuela." *Hispanic American Historical Review* 66, no. 4 (November, 1986): 667–96.

Miller, John. *Memorias del General William Miller.* 2 vols. Madrid: Editorial América, 1918.

Minguet, Charles. *Bolívar y el mundo de los libertadores.* México: Universidad Nacional Autónoma de México, Coordinación de Humanidades, Centro Coordinador y Difusor de Estudios Latinoamericanos, 1993.

Mitre, Bartolomé. *Historia de San Martín y de la emancipación sudamericana.* 6 vols. Buenos Aires: L. J. Rosso, 1938.

Moreno, Edilberto. "Bolivarian Ideals Reawakened." *Américas* 40, no. 5 (September, 1988): 53–54.

Moreno de Rojo, Raquel. "Reflexiones: Los siete documentos principales del Libertador." *Boletín de la Academia Nacional de la Historia* (Venezuela) 65, no. 259 (1982): 731–55.

Morillo y Morillo, Pablo. *Mémoires du Général Morillo, comte de Carthagene, Marquis de la Puerta, relatifs aux principaux événemes de ses campagnes en Amérique de 1815 a 1821.* Paris: P. Dufart, 1826.

Morón, Guillermo. *A History of Venezuela.* London: George Allen and Unwin, 1964.

Mosquera, Tomás Cipriano de. *Memoria sobre la vida del General Simón Bolívar, Libertador de Colombia, Perú y Bolivia.* Bogotá: Imprenta Nacional, 1954.

Navarro, Monseñor Nicolas E. *Diario de Bucaramanga: Estudio Crítica y Reproducción Literalísma del Manuscrito Original de L. Peru de Lacroix.* Caracas: Tipografía Americana, 1935.

Nicholson, Irene. *The Liberators: A Study of Independence Movements in Spanish America.* London: Faber, 1969.

O'Connor, Francisco Burdett. *Un irlandes con Bolívar: Recuerdos de la independencia.* Madrid: Sociedad Española de Librería, 1915.

———. *Recuerdos de Francisco Burdett O'Connor.* La Paz: González y Medina, 1915.

O'Leary, Daniel F. *Bolívar y la emancipación de Sur América.* Madrid: Sociedad Española de Librería, 1915.

———. *Bolívar and the War of Independence: Memorias del General Daniel Florencio O'Leary.* Trans. and ed. Robert F. McNerney, Jr. Austin: University of Texas Press, 1970.

———. *The "Detached Recollections" of General D. F. O'Leary.* Ed. Robin A. Humphrey. London: Athalone, 1969.

———. *Historia de la Independencia: La Emancipación del Perú según la correspondencia del General Heres con el Libertador, 1821–1830.* Madrid: Editorial América, 1919.

———. *Memorias del General Daniel Florencio O'Leary, Narración.* Ed. Pedro Grases. 3 vols. Caracas: Sales, 1964.

———. *Ultimos años de la vida pública de Bolívar: Memorias del General O'Leary. Tomo apendice (1826–1829).* Madrid: Editorial América, 1916.

O'Leary, Simon B., ed. *Memorias del General O'Leary.* 32 vols. Caracas: Imprenta de la "Gazeta Oficial," 1878–1883.

Ortega Ricaurte, Enrique. *Luis Brión de la orden de Libertadores, Primer Almirante de la República de Colombia y General en Jefe de sus Ejercitos, 1782–1821.* Bogotá: Editorial Minerva, 1953.

Otero D'Costa, Enrique. *Vida del Almirante José Padilla, 1778–1828.* Bogotá: Fuerzas Militares, 1973.

Páez, José Antonio. *Autobiografía del General José Antonio Páez.* 2 vols. 1869. Reprint, New York: H. R. Elliot, 1946.

Páez, Ramón. *Wild Scenes in South America, or Life in the Llanos of Venezuela.* New York: Charles Scribner, 1862.

Paine, Lauran. *Bolivar the Liberator.* New York: Roy, 1970.

Parra Pérez, Caracciolo. "Bolívar y sus amigos del extranjero." *Revista de la Sociedad Bolivariana de Venezuela* 36, no. 122 (1979): 61–71.

———. *Historia de la Primera República de Venezuela.* 2 vols. Caracas: Biblioteca Ayacucho, 1992.

———. *Mariño y la Independencia de Venezuela.* 5 vols. Madrid: Ediciones Cultural Hispanica, 1954– .

Paz, José María. *Memorias Póstumas del General José María Paz.* 3 vols. Madrid: Editorial América, 1917.

Peloso, Vincent C., and Barbara A. Tenenbaum. *Liberals, Politics, and Power: State Formation in Nineteenth-Century Latin America.* Athens: University of Georgia Press, 1996.

Pereyra, Carlos. *Bolívar y Washington: Un paralelo imposible.* Madrid: Editorial América, 1915.

———. *La Juventud Legendaria de Bolívar.* Madrid: M. Aguilar, 1932.

Pérez Sosa, Elías. *El espíritu democrático del Libertador.* 4th ed. Caracas: Litografía del Comercio, 1939.

Pérez Tenreiro, Tomás. "La pérdida de Puerto Cabello—año 1812." *Boletín de la Academia Nacional de la Historia* (Venezuela) 64, no. 254 (1981): 289–302.

Pérez Vila, Manuel. *Para acercarnos a Bolívar: Vida, bibliografía, escritos.* Caracas: Equinoccio, 1980.

———. *Simón Bolívar, His Basic Thoughts: Biographical Sketch and Selection of Documents.* Caracas: Academia Nacional de la Historia, 1980.

Petre, F. Loraine. *Simón Bolívar.* London: J. Lane, 1910.

Phelan, John L. *The People and the King: The Comunero Revolution in Colombia, 1781.* Madison: University of Wisconsin, 1978.

Platt, Tristan. "Simón Bolívar, the Sum of Justice and the Amerindian Virgin: Andean Conceptions of the Patria in Nineteenth-Century Potosí." *Journal of Latin American Studies* 25, no. 1 (February, 1993): 159–85.

Poudenx, H., and F. Mayer. *Mémoire pour servir a l'historie de la révolution de Caracas.* Paris: Impr. de Crapalet, 1815.

Prieto, Luis B. *Simón Bolívar: Educator.* Garden City, N.Y.: Doubleday, 1970.

Proctor, Robert. *Narrative of a Journey Across the Cordillera of the Andes, and of a Residence in Lima and Other Parts of Peru, in the Years 1823 and 1824.* London: Hurst, Robinson, and Co., 1825.

Rappaport, Armin, ed. *The Monroe Doctrine.* New York: Holt, Rinehart, and Winston, 1964.

Rausch, Jane M. "The Santander Historical Collection: A Brief Report about a New and Important Documentary Resource." *Inter-American Review of Bibliography* 43, no. 3 (1993): 451–54.

Restrepo, José Manuel. *Diario político y militar, 1819–1858.* 5 vols. Bogotá: Imprenta Nacional, 1954.

———. *Historia de la revolución de la República de Colombia en la América meridional, 1827.* 6 vols. Medellín: Bolsilibros Bebout, 1969–70.

Riaño, Camilo. *La Campaña Libertadora de 1819.* Bogotá: n.p., 1969.

Rippy, J. Fred. "Bolívar as Viewed by Contemporary Diplomats of the United States." *Hispanic American Historical Review* 15, no. 3 (August, 1935): 287–98.

Rivas Vicuña, Francisco. *Las guerras de Bolívar.* 2 vols. Caracas: Editorial Victoria, 1920–21.

Robertson, William Spence. "The First Legations of the United States in Latin America." *Mississippi Valley Historical Review* 2, no. 2 (September, 1915): 183–212.

———. *The Life of Miranda.* 2 vols. Chapel Hill: University of North Carolina Press, 1929. Reprint, New York: Cooper Square, 1969.

———. "The So-Called Apochryphal Letters of Colombres Mármol on the Interview of Guayaquil." *Hispanic American Historical Review* 23, no. 1 (February, 1943): 154–58.

Robinson, J. H. *Journal of an Expedition 1400 Miles up the Orinoco and 300 up the Arauco.* London: Black, Young and Young, 1822.

Rodríguez, Mario. *"William Burke" and Francisco de Miranda: The Word and the Deed in Spanish America's Emancipation.* Lanham, Md.: University Press of America, 1994.

Rodríguez O., Jaime E. "The Emancipation of America." *American Historical Review* 105, no. 1 (February, 2000): 131–52.

———. *The Independence of Spanish America.* Cambridge: Cambridge University Press, 1998.

Rodríguez Villa, Antonio. *El Teniente General Don Pablo Morillo, Primer Conde de Cartagena, Marqués de la Puerta 1778–1837.* 2 vols. Madrid: Editorial América, 1920.

Rojas, Reinaldo. *Historiografía y política sobre el tema bolivariano.* Barquisimeto, Venezuela: Fondo Editorial Buría, 1986.

Rojas, Ricardo. *San Martín: Knight of the Andes.* Trans. Herschel Brickell and Carlos Videla. New York: Doubleday, Doran and Co., 1945.

———. *El Santo de la Espada.* Buenos Aires: Librerías Anaconda, 1933.

Rothstein, Edward. "Bolívar as an Idealist Whose Dreams Are Thwarted by Messy Reality." *New York Times,* January 27, 1995.

Rourke, Thomas. *Man of Glory: Simón Bolívar.* New York: William Morrow, 1939.

Rudolph, Donna Keyse and G. A. Rudolph. *Historical Dictionary of Venezuela.* 2d ed. Latham, Md.: Scarecrow Press, 1996.

Ruschenberger, William Samuel Waithman. *Three Years in the Pacific; Including Notices of Brazil, Chile, Bolivia, and Peru.* Philadelphia: Carey, Lea and Blanchard, 1834.

Salcedo-Bastardo, José Luis. *Bolívar: A Continent and Its Destiny.* Ed. and trans. Annella McDermott. Richmond, England: Richmond Publishing Co., 1977.

———. *Bolívar: El nacer constante.* Caracas: Editorial Ariel, 1985.

———, ed. *Simón Bolívar: The Hope of the Universe.* Paris: UNESCO, 1983.

Sant Roz, José. *Nos Duele Bolívar.* 2d ed. Mérida, Venezuela: Damocles Editores, 1988.

Scott, J. M. *The White Poppy: A History of Opium.* New York: Heinemann, 1969.

Semple, Robert. *Sketch of the Present State of Caracas; Including a Journey from Caracas through La Victoria and Valencia to Puerto Cabello.* London: R. Baldwin, 1812.

Shafer, Robert J. *The Economic Societies in the Spanish World, 1763–1821.* Syracuse: Syracuse University Press, 1958.

Shepherd, William R. "Bolívar and the United States." *Hispanic American Historical Review* 1, no. 3 (August, 1918): 270–98.

Sheridan, Philip John. *Francisco de Miranda: Forerunner of Spanish-American Independence.* San Antonio: Naylor, 1960.

Sherwell, Guillermo Antonio. *Simón Bolívar: Patriot, Warrior, Statesman, Father of Five*

Nations: A Sketch of His Life and Work. 1921. Reprint, Clinton, Mass.: Colonial Press, Bolivarian Society of Venezuela, 1951.

Siso Martínez, J. M. *Historia de Venezuela.* 6th ed. Mexico: Editorial Yocima, 1962.

Slatta, Richard W. *Comparing Cowboys and Frontiers: New Perspectives on the History of the Americas.* Norman: University of Oklahoma Press, 2001.

———. *Cowboys of the Americas.* New Haven: Yale University Press, 1994.

———, ed. *Bandidos: The Varieties of Latin American Banditry.* Westport, Conn.: Greenwood Press, 1987.

Sociedad Bolivariana de Venezuela. *Escritos del Libertador.* Caracas: Sociedad Bolivariana de Venezuela, 1963.

Stearns, Peter N., ed. *Encyclopedia of Social History.* New York: Garland, 1994.

Stevenson, William B. *A Historical and Descriptive Narrative of Twenty Years' Residence in South America.* 3 vols. London: Hurst, Robinson and Co., 1825.

———. *On the Disturbances in South America.* London: J. Ridgeway, 1830.

Stoan, Stephen K. *Pablo Morillo and Venezuela, 1815–1820.* Columbus: Ohio State University Press, 1974.

Stoetzer, O. Carlos. *The Scholastic Roots of the Spanish American Revolution.* New York: Fordham University Press, 1979.

Tennant, Anne W. "The Glorious Renunciation." *Américas* 49 (July, 1997): 44–50.

Tenenbaum, Barbara A., ed. *Encyclopedia of Latin American History and Culture.* 5 vols. New York: Charles Scribner's Sons, 1996.

Thorning, Joseph F. *Miranda: World Citizen.* Gainesville: University of Florida Press, 1952.

Torrente, Mariano. *Historia de la Revolución Hispano-Americana.* 3 vols. Madrid: Imprenta de L. Amarita, 1929–30.

Trend, John Brande. *Bolívar and the Independence of Spanish America.* Reprint, Clinton, Mass.: Colonial Press, Bolivarian Society of Venezuela, 1951.

Ullman, Samuel S. "The Youth, Bolívar." *Plays* 53, no. 7 (May, 1994): 9–17.

Urdaneta, Amendaro and Naphtali. *Memorias del General Rafael Urdaneta adicionadas con notas ilustrativas y algunos apuntamientos relativas a su vida pública.* Caracas: Gobierno Nacional, 1888.

Urdaneta, Rafael. *Memorias del General Rafael Urdaneta.* Madrid: Editorial Americana, 1916.

Uribe Uran, Victor Manuel. "'Kill All the Lawyers!': Lawyers and the Independence Movement in New Granada, 1809–1820." *Americas* 52, no. 2 (October, 1995): 175–210.

Uslar Pietri, Antonio. "Bolívar the Liberator (1783–1830)." *UNESCO Courier* 36 (February, 1983): 4–7.

———. *Historia de la Rebelión popular de 1814.* Caracas and Madrid: Edime, 1962

Valero Martínez, Arturo, ed. *En defensa de Manuela Sáenz: La libertadora del Libertador.* Guayaquil, Ecuador: Editorial del Pacífico, 1988.

Vallenilla Lanz, Laureano. *Cesarismo democrático y otros textos.* Caracas: Biblioteca Ayacucho, 1991.

Van Loon, Hendrik Willem. *Jefferson and Bolívar: New World Fighters for Freedom.* London: Harrap, 1966.

Vargas, Francisco Alejandro. *Nuestros Próceres Navales.* Caracas: Imprenta Nacional, 1964.

Vaucaire, Michel. *Bolívar, the Liberator.* Trans. Margaret Reed. Boston: Houghton Mifflin, 1929.

Verna, Paul. *Pétion y Bolívar: Cuarenta Años de Relaciones Haitiano-Venezolano.* Caracas: n.p., 1969.

————. *Robert Sutherland: Un amigo de Bolívar en Haiti.* Caracas: Fundación John Boulton, 1966.

Villacrés Moscoso, Jorge W. "La entrevista de Bolívar y San Martín en Guayaquil, precursora de las actuales conferencias cumbres internacionales." *Boletín de la Academia Nacional de la Historia* (Venezuela) 68, no. 270 (1985): 411–16.

Von Hagen, Victor Wolfgang. *The Four Seasons of Manuela: The Love Story of Manuela Sáenz and Simón Bolívar.* New York: Duell, Sloan and Pearce, 1952.

Vowell, Richard L. *Campaigns and Cruises in Venezuela and New Granada, and in the Pacific Ocean from 1817 to 1830.* 3 vols. London: Longman and Co., 1831.

Webster, Charles K., ed. *Britain and the Independence of Latin America, 1812–1830: Select Documents from the Foreign Office Archives.* 2 vols. 1938. Reprint, New York: Octagon Books, 1970.

Whitaker, Arthur P. "Pathology of Democracy in Latin America: A Historian's Point of View." *American Political Science Review* 44, no. 1 (March, 1950): 101–18.

————. *The United States and the Independence of Latin America, 1800–1830.* 1941. Reprint, New York: W. W. Norton, 1964.

Whymper, Edward. *Travels amongst the Great Andes of the Equator.* London: J. Murray, 1892.

Woodward, Margaret L. "The Spanish Army and the Loss of America, 1810–1824." *Hispanic American Historical Review* 48, no. 4 (November, 1968): 586–607.

Worcester, Donald E. *Bolívar.* Boston: Little, Brown, 1977.

Yanes, Francisco Javier. *Relación documentada de los principales sucesos ocurridos en Venezuela desde que se declaró estado independiente hasta el año de 1821.* 1840. 2 vols. Reprint, Caracas: Editorial Elite, 1943.

Yarce Maya, William Fernando. "Los caballos en la vida del Libertador." *Boletín del Archivo General de la Nación* (Venezuela) 70, nos. 238–39 (1980): 95–101.

Ybarra, T. R. *Bolívar, the Passionate Warrior.* New York: Ives and Washburn, 1929.

Zamoyski, Adam. *Holy Madness: Romantics, Patriots and Revolutionaries, 1776–1871.* New York: Viking, 1999.

Zimmermann, Arthur F. "Spain and Its Colonies, 1808–1820." *Hispanic American Historical Review* 11 (November, 1931): 439–63.

Newspapers

(Boston) Recorder, 1816–19.

Correo del Orinoco (Angostura; today Ciudad Bolívar), 1818–21.

Gazeta de Caracas, October 24, 1808, to December 25, 1810 (Sesquicentennial of Independence facsimile reproduction, Caracas, 1960).

Kingston Chronicle (Jamaica), 1831.

Morning Courier and New York Enquirer, January 10, 1843.

(New Orleans) Louisiana Gazette, 1816–31.

(Philadelphia) National Gazette and Literary Register, 1822–31.

Royal Gazette (Kingston, Jamaica), 1811–30.

Trinidad Gazette (Port of Spain), 1820–21.

INDEX